2004

THE BEDFORDSHIRE HISTORICAL RECORD SOCIETY

Officers

President: Samuel Whitbread

Vice-President: Martin Lawrence

Treasurer: Barbara Doyle
196 Castle Road, Bedford MK40 3TY

Secretary: Richard Smart
48 St. Augustine's Road, Bedford MK40 2NO

General Editor: Gordon Vowles
5 Beauchamp Place, Willington, Bedford MK44 3QA

THE PUBLICATIONS OF THE BEDFORDSHIRE
HISTORICAL RECORD SOCIETY
VOLUME 83

THE SHINY SEVENTH

THE 7th (SERVICE) BATTALION BEDFORDSHIRE REGIMENT AT WAR 1915–1918

M. G. Deacon

THE BEDFORDSHIRE HISTORICAL RECORD SOCIETY

THE BOYDELL PRESS

© Bedfordshire Historical Record Society, M.G. Deacon and Mike J. Adams 2004

All Rights Reserved. Except as permitted under current legislation
no part of this work may be photocopied, stored in a retrieval system,
published, performed in public, adapted, broadcast,
transmitted, recorded or reproduced in any form or by any means,
without the prior permission of the copyright owners

First published 2004

A publication of
Bedfordshire Historical Record Society
published by The Boydell Press
an imprint of Boydell & Brewer Ltd
PO Box 9, Woodbridge, Suffolk IP12 3DF, UK
and of Boydell & Brewer Inc.
PO Box 41026, Rochester, NY 14604–4126, USA
website: www.boydellandbrewer.com

ISBN 0 85155 069 X

ISSN 0067–4826

Details of previous volumes are available from
Boydell & Brewer Ltd

A CIP catalogue record for this book is available
from the British Library

This publication is printed on acid-free paper

Printed in Great Britain by
Antony Rowe Ltd., Chippenham, Wiltshire

Contents

	Page
List of Illustrations	vii
Acknowledgements	x
Introduction	xi
Abbreviations	xv
Glossary	xviii

Part One

The War Diary	1
1915	2
1916	29
1917	63
1918	92

Part Two

The Personal Diary of Second Lieutenant Henry J. Cartwright	107

Appendix A: Battalion Moves	128
1. Table of Moves and Locations	128
2. Selected Operational Orders	133

Appendix B: Battles	
1. Battle Operational Orders	164
2. Battle Reports	178
3. Congratulatory Telegrams	192
4. Battlefield Walks	196

Appendix C: Casualties	
1. Casualty Lists	224
2. Places of Birth of Other Ranks Who Died	237
3. Comparative Battle Casualties – Other Ranks Only	238

Index of Names	241
Index of Place Names	252
Organisation Names Index	259

Illustrations

Plates   Page
1. Thomas Edwin Adlam VC — xx
2. Lance Corporal Arthur Edward Atkins — xxi
3. The headstone of Private William Charles Billington — xxii
4. Captain Oliver Kingdon MC — xxiii
5. Captain Thomas Reginald Jack Mulligan — xxiv
6. Second Lieutenant David Arnold Roeber — xxv
7. Captain Sidney Tabor, Adjutant of the battalion in the latter half of 1917. — xxvi
8. Second Lieutenant Theodore Percival (also known as Thomas Percy) Wilson — xxvii
9. Second Lieutenant Henry J. Cartwright, author of the Personal Diary — 106
10. Attack on the Pommiers Redoubt: a view from the 7th Bedfords' trenches towards the German lines attacked on 1 July 1916 — 205
11. A view from the front trench of the Pommiers Redoubt towards the 7th Bedfords' starting positions — 206
12. Attack on the Pommiers Redoubt: view from the bank above the Mametz-Montauban road towards the furthest point reached by 7th Bedfords on 1 July 1916, White Trench — 207
13. Capture of Thiepval, 27 September 1916: the view from the crossroads of the D73 and D151 — 210
14. Attack on the Schwaben Redoubt, 28 September 1916: the view from the road towards La Grande Ferme, looking towards the Schwaben Redoubt — 213
15. Attack on the Schwaben Redoubt, 28 September 1916: the view of the axis of advance by the right flank of the 7th Bedfords' attack — 214
16. Attack on the Schwaben Redoubt, 28 September 1916: the view from the rough location of "Cartwright's Post", the furthest extent of the 7th Bedfords' advance — 215
17. Attack on Achiet le Grand, 13–17 March 1917: the view from the top of the sunken lane looking towards Achiet le Grand — 217
18. Attack on Chérisy, 3 May 1917: view from the top of the slope of the area attacked by A Company — 220
19. Attack on Glencorse Wood, 10 August 1917: the view from the 7th Bedfords' front line towards what is left of Glencorse Wood, near Ypres — 223

Figures   Page
1. Attack on the Pommiers Redoubt, 1 July 1916: the ground as it was then — 203
2. Attack on the Pommiers Redoubt, 1 July 1916: the ground today — 204
3. Capture of Thiepval, 27 September 1916: the ground as it was then — 208
4. Capture of Thiepval, 27 September 1916: the ground today — 209

5.	Attack on the Schwaben Redoubt, 28 September 1916: the ground as it was then	211
6.	Attack on the Schwaben Redoubt, 28 September 1916: the ground today	212
7.	Attack on Achiet le Grand, 13–17 March 1917	216
8.	Attack on Chérisy, 3 May 1917: the ground as it was then	218
9.	Attack on Chérisy, 3 May 1917: the ground today	219
10.	Attack on Glencorse Wood, 10 August 1917: the ground as it was then	221
11.	Attack on Glencorse Wood, 10 August 1917: the ground today	222

Dedicated to some of those, now departed, to whom I owe much:

Sergeant George Deacon MM
7th (S) Battalion Bedfordshire Regiment
a gallant soldier who was my first point of contact with the Battalion
and, through it, the Great War in general

Robin and Jean Deacon
my parents
who always fostered my love of history and
encouraged me to believe in myself

Calvin Miller
former Sergeant, USAF, and my father-in-law
who was looking forward to reading the book on its publication

Acknowledgements

This has been a labour of love. I originally completed the transcription in my lunch hours at work in Bedfordshire & Luton Archives & Records Service. Of course, a lot of work has been put in since, most in my own time but, inevitably, some during work hours. I would like to thank County Archivist Kevin Ward for his understanding in allowing me to do this.

I would also like to thank my fellow Operations Manager at Bedfordshire & Luton Archives & Records Service, Nigel Lutt, for his help in pointing out illustrations I could use "from stock".

I would particularly like to thank Mike J. Adams of Letchworth for contributing the Diary of his great uncle Henry Cartwright which provides a wonderful splash of colour after the black and white of the War Diary itself. Mike rang me up out of the blue, as he had heard I was interested in the 7th Battalion and offered to e-mail me a copy of the diary. Subsequently he was kind enough to agree to the diary's publication here, together with the photograph of his great uncle.

I would also like particularly to thank Gordon Vowles for all his encouragement to me, initially in putting the Diary forward as a possible publication and latterly for his help in his role of General Editor (the last time he performed in this heroic, but largely thankless, role).

Finally, I would like to thank my wife Gretchen for living with this project for so long, encouraging me in my labours and taking a sympathetic interest in my love of study of the Great War as a whole, even to the extent of allowing herself to be dragged around muddy fields in France and Belgium.

Photographs

The photographs in this volume are property of the author, with the following exceptions:

    Plate 1, Thomas Adlam: Royal Anglian Regiment, held by Bedfordshire & Luton Archives & Records Service, ref. X550/8/4

    Plate 2, Arthur Atkins: privately deposited with Bedfordshire & Luton Archives & Records Service, ref. X550/8/uncat

    Plates 4, 5, 6, 7 and 8, Oliver Kingdon, Thomas Mulligan, David Roeber, Sidney Tabor and Theodore Wilson: Royal Anglian Regiment, deposited with Bedfordshire & Luton Archives & Records Service, ref. X550/1/82

    Plate 9, Henry Cartwright: Mike J.Adams

Introduction

This volume consists of three main parts: firstly the War Diary of the 7th Battalion, Bedfordshire Regiment; secondly, a private diary kept by one of its officers, Second Lieutenant Henry J. Cartwright, during his time in France, and, thirdly, appendices detailing some facts and figures about the battalion, a selection of Operational Orders it received and descriptions of battles in which it was involved.

A War Diary was kept by each unit of battalion size and larger (including such formations as brigades and divisions) while on active service during the First World War. The diary was intended to be a record of the unit's doings, and was written by the Adjutant. The diaries were completed in a number of identical copies, of which one was kept by the unit itself and one sent to the War Office. Bedfordshire & Luton Archives & Records Service (BLARS) has the battalion copy; The National Archives has the War Office copy. This transcription is of the BLARS copy.

The Bedfordshire Regiment became the Bedfordshire & Hertfordshire Regiment in 1919 and in 1958 was amalgamated with the Essex Regiment to form the 3rd Battalion, Royal Anglian Regiment. The Regiment had used Kempston Barracks as a training facility and depot base. When it gave the building up BLARS cleared the building and the records taken formed the Bedfordshire & Hertfordshire Regiment Collection under the reference number X550. Included in these records were the War Diaries of each battalion and that of the 7th Battalion which was allotted the reference number X550/8/1.

The BLARS copy of the diary contains a large number of Operational Orders. These were received from Brigade, Division, Corps or Army Headquarters and dealt with such matters as moving from one area to another, training to be carried out and, of course, attacks to be made on the enemy. Selections of these appear in the Appendices together with reports on battles in which the battalion took part, written by the Commanding Officer of the time. The Appendices also contain statistics on such matters as where the battalion was at any one time and numbers of men killed in selected actions.

War Diaries vary a lot from unit to unit and depend on the nature of the man writing them. For example, the entries by Captain Meautys at the beginning of the battalion's tour of duty are very full indeed whereas those completed later by others (including Howard Seys-Phillips, a local man who was a relation of the Howard family of Clapham Park) are much less detailed. Culture of the battalion also seems to have played a part. By and large the 7th Battalion Diary is quite punctilious about recording events of importance and is informative about the battalion's state and conduct. The diaries held by BLARS for the 4th and 6th Battalions, Bedfordshire Regiment, by contrast, are very summary and make much less interesting reading: even descriptions of battles are treated very summarily.

The War Diary is the official account of the part the battalion played in the war. The editor was fortunate in being offered a contrast to this in the personal diary kept by Henry Cartwright. This was offered for publication by the officer's great nephew,

Mike Adams, and forms a fascinating counterpoint to the War Diary. Compare the death by drowning of Private Groves, the suicide of Private Griffin (on 21 May and 18 June 1916 respectively) and the descriptions of the Battle of Chérisy (3 May 1917), for example.

I have tried to render the layout, punctuation and spelling of the War Diary (as well as that of 2nd Lieutenant Cartwright) as faithfully as I can. This means that punctuation, spelling and grammar vary widely but help to catch the flavour of the Adjutant scribbling in a damp dugout with a pencil stub as shells exploded in the distance, or of typing up entries in Battalion Headquarters in a cottage, tent or stable behind the lines. The only substantial change I have made is to delete the frequent references to appendices that have not survived in the copy of the War Diary held by BLARS: injunctions to "see appendix" would have been confusing given that this volume has appendices of its own.

By the time this volume is published there will be less than a platoon strength of British First World War veterans left alive and their struggle will pass, in the next few years, entirely from the category of living memory into that of recorded history. In spite of this, or perhaps because of it, interest in the Great War to End All Wars is greater than ever.

We think we know so much about the war from all the accounts that have been left of it, yet still a great deal remains either misunderstood or disputed. There are a number of stereotypes of the Western Front, in particular, that do not really ring true when one begins to read the record in depth. Two examples will suffice. Troops did not spend all their time shivering or sweating in front line trenches; by far the majority of time was spent away from the front line resting, on fatigues or training. Not all the generals were remote figures in comfortable châteaux miles away from the action; over seventy British officers of General rank were killed in the war.

One area of considerable dispute concerns the ability, or lack of it, of the British senior commanders. The popular view, perhaps begun by David Lloyd George in his memoirs and fostered by memories of the dreadful slaughter of the war, was that the British generals were incompetent, lazy and callous. They had no idea of how to fight a modern war, they never visited their troops in the front line and did not care how many died. This view has been championed by Australian historians, in particular, fuelled by a spirit of nationalism which wants to see Britain's commanders as "butchers and bunglers", comparing unfavourably with Australian commanders such as General Monash. In recent years this accepted view of things has been challenged. It is argued that the British generals in 1914 probably did not have much of an idea of what a modern all-out war would involve, but there again, nor did anyone else.

Throughout the war the performance of the British High Command varied, in part due to the strengths and weaknesses of individual commanders thrust into the limelight. However, the general performance (if I may so term it) improved at the end of the war as new tactics, such as the use of tanks, aerial reconnaissance, creeping barrages, sound ranging of enemy artillery and others, were all put to use. The terrible casualty levels of the intervening years owed much to the essential struggles between offensive and defensive tactics in which each side tried to gain the upper hand, trumping the other's previous practices. The British Army of the Hundred

Days of August–November 1918 was employed very differently to the Army of the First Day of the Somme in July 1916 or the slog towards Passchendaele in July–November 1917.

As far as callousness is concerned, the British generals were certainly no worse than those of the other protagonists. If casualty figures are any guide, the German and French generals were a good deal more callous than those of Britain. This is backed-up by the record of men like Falkenhayn who wished to "bleed the French Army white" or French General Mangin who earned the soubriquet "Butcher" from his troops.

Another area of dispute involves, once again, Australian historians' view of the war and touches quite closely on the 7th Bedfords. The Australian contention, supported by contemporary attitudes of Australian soldiers and accepted by many British historians, is that the Australian troops were of much better quality than the British. They are portrayed as rugged individualists who fearlessly attacked the enemy after or while British attacks failed due to lack of the proper offensive spirit. Such nationalism is not surprising but, modern research shows, is probably flawed. The Australians, along with the New Zealanders, Canadians and South Africans, were extremely fine troops and their Divisions were amongst the best the British Army had. However, there was at least an equal number of British Divisions whose record matches, or in some cases, surpasses that of the Australians. One of these British Divisions is the 18th (Eastern), one of whose battalions was the 7th Bedfords. It is clear that the great success 18th Division had on 1 July 1916 gave it a reputation as a "fighting division" and its later deployment bears this out. It had one serious reversal, at Chérisy in 1917, but its other actions invariably had some success attaching to them. Even during the great retreat of March/April 1918, for example, the 7th Bedfords launched a successful counter-attack (at Baboeuf), and helped to stem the German advance by the gallant action at Cachy in April, carried out in conjunction with the Australians.

The Bedfordshire Regiment was not restricted, of course, to Bedfordshire men. It was War Office policy to ensure that battalions did not contain too many men from one area, to avoid the crippling impact on local communities if a battalion was wiped out. The Bedfordshire Regiment included a large number of men from Hertfordshire, as the Hertfordshire Regiment only had one front line battalion whilst the Bedfordshire Regiment had seven. This was recognised after the war by the amalgamation of the two regiments into the Bedfordshire & Hertfordshire Regiment. A glance at the 7th Bedfords' dead will show that the majority were Hertfordshire men, with Bedfordshire men coming second. Substantial numbers were from the neighbouring counties of Huntingdonshire and Northamptonshire, and from London. There was also a large number of men from Staffordshire, which seems to be due to former North Staffordshire and South Staffordshire Regiment men who were wounded being returned to duty in the 7th Bedfords – presumably as an effort to water-down the local nature of the units involved to prevent the effect of casualties on each locale. Numbers of men also came from Kent and Sussex, the Diary itself noting that reinforcements reaching the battalion on 26 December 1917 were from "the Sussex district".

I hope that this transcription of the 7th Bedfords' War Diary will be of some use, in the most minor way, in the greater arguments regarding the Great War, and in dispelling a few myths. I hope, too, that it will serve to refocus, very slightly, popular study of the war. It is noticeable that the majority of popular books studying individual battalions taking part in the Great War are about the famous Pals battalions from the north of England. This is also reflected in the numerous television documentaries on the war or battles within it. Never a television programme about the Battle of the Somme goes by without some reference to or study of the Accrington Pals. This is, presumably, because these battalions have a mystique and a pathos about them, being drawn from close-knit communities and suffering terrible numbers of casualties which devastated those communities – for the Pals battalions were a real anomaly, having been raised by local towns and boroughs in the first flush of patriotism after the declaration of war. By contrast, the less glamorous, run-of-the-mill county regiments have been a little overlooked. It is hoped that this transcript of the War Diary of one of those county battalions will go some way towards addressing this situation.

Abbreviations

The exact presentation of many of these abbreviations varies throughout the book. This is because editorial policy has been to transcribe the diaries as faithfully as possible. Thus, for instance, points are sometimes used and sometimes not, use of capital letters is not consistent, and some abbreviations sometimes appear in italics.

2/Lt	Second Lieutenant	BLARS	Bedfordshire & Luton Archives & Records Service
&c.	and so on		
A/	Acting		
A&S High	Argyll & Sutherland Highlanders	Bn	Battalion
		Bns	Battalions
AA	Anti-Aircraft	BO	Battalion Order
Actg	Acting	Br	Brigade
Adj	Adjutant	Br.Gen	Brigadier General
Adjt	Adjutant	Brig	Brigade
Adjut	Adjutant	BSM	Battalion Sergeant Major
AG	Adjutant General		
Amb	Ambulance	Buffs	East Kent Regiment
Ammn	Ammunition	Cap	Captain
AP	Appendix	Capt	Captain
Appdx	Appendix	CC	Company Commander
Appx	Appendix	Cheshires	Cheshire Regiment
Arty	Artillery	CO	Commanding Officer
ASC	Army Service Corps	Co	Company
ATN	18th Division [the letters 'atn' when spoken quickly sounding like '18', the Division's badge incorporated these letters]	C.of E.	Church of England
		Col	Colonel
		Comdr	Commander
		Commdg	Commanding
		Comp	Company
		Coy	Company
Attd	Attached	Coy Qr Mr	Company Quartermaster
Ave	Avenue		
Batt	Battalion	Coy.S.M.	Company Sergeant Major
Battln	Battalion		
Battn	Battalion	Cp	Corporal
Batty	Battery	Cpl	Corporal
Bay	Bayonet	CQMS	Company Quartermaster Sergeant
Bde	Brigade		
Bdles	Bundles	CSM	Company Sergeant Major
Bedf	Bedfordshire Regiment		
Bedfords	Bedfordshire Regiment	DCM	Distinguished Conduct Medal
Beds	Bedfordshire Regiment		
BF	Bayonet Fighting	Div	Division
Bgde	Brigade	Divl	Divisional
BHQ	Battalion Headquarters	Divn	Division

DSO	Distinguished Service Order	Lt	Lieutenant
E	East	Lt.Col	Lieutenant Colonel
ENE	East North East	Maj.Gen.	Major General
ESE	East South East	Manchesters	Manchester Regiment
ET	Evening Tactical	MC	Military Cross
ETR	Evening Tactical Report	MG	Machine Gun
FA	Field Ambulance	M.Guns	Machine Guns
Feby	February	MGC	Machine Gun Corps – a unit of the British Army
F.G.C.M.	Field General Court Martial	Middlesex	Middlesex Regiment
F'ing	Fighting	Middx	Middlesex Regiment
FOO	Forward Observation Officer	Mins	Minutes
		MM	Military Medal
FP	Field Punishment	MN	Midnight
Fus	Fusiliers [usually 11th Battalion Royal Fusiliers]	MO	Medical Officer
		MP	Military Police
		M/S	Message
Fusrs	Fusiliers	MTR	Morning Tactical Report
Gen	General		
Genl	General	M'x	Middlesex Regiment
GOC	General Officer Commanding	N	North
		NCO	Non-Commissioned Officer
GS	General Service [Wagons]	NE	North East
HA	Heavy Artillery	N.Hants	Northamptonshire Regiment
Hd.Qrs	Headquarters		
Hdqrs	Headquarters	NNE	North-North-East
HE	High Explosive	NNW	North-North-West
H.Explosive	High Explosive	Norfolks	Norfolk Regiment
Ho	House	Northants	Northamptonshire Regiment
Hows	Howitzers		
HQ	Headquarters	Nthants	Northamptonshire Regiment
Hqrs	Headquarters		
HQts	Headquarters	NW	North West
Hy	Heavy	OC	Officer Commanding
i/c	in charge	Off.	Officer[s]
In	Inches	Offr	Officer
Inf	Infantry	OR	Other Ranks
Infy	Infantry	OR	Orderly Room
Inst	Instant	Oxford & Bucks	Oxfordshire & Buckinghamshire Light Infantry
IT	Infantry Training		
K.Liverpool	King's (Liverpool Regiment)		
		Para	Paragraph
L	Left	Pd	Paid
L/C	Lance Corporal	Pdrs	Pounders
L/Cpl.	Lance Corporal	Plat	Platoon
L.Gun	Lewis Gun	Pn	Platoon
LI	Light Infantry	Pt	Point
Lieut	Lieutenant	PT	Physical Training
L/Sgt.	Lance Sergeant	Pte	Private

Q.M.	Quartermaster	RWK	Royal West Kent Regiment
QMG	Quartermaster General	S	South
Qr.Mr	Quartermaster	(S)	Service (as in 7th (S) Battalion)
Qrs.Mr	Quartermaster		
Queens	Royal West Surrey Regiment	SAA	Small Arms Ammunition
R	Right [can also mean Regiment]	SE	South East
		Sec	Section
RAMC	Royal Army Medical Corps	Sect	Section
		Sergt	Sergeant
R.Berks	Royal Berkshire Regiment	Sgd	Signed
		Sgt	Sergeant
R.Fusiliers	Royal Fusiliers	Sigs	Signals
Rd	Road	S.P.	Strong Point
Rds	Rounds	Sq	Square
RE	Royal Engineers	SSE	South-South-East
Ref.	Reference	SSW	South-South-West
Regt	Regiment	S.Staffords	South Staffordshire Regiment
Regtl	Regimental		
Revd	Reverend	Stn	Station
RF	Royal Fusiliers	Str	Strong
RFA	Royal Field Artillery	SW	South-West
RFC	Royal Flying Corps	Sub.Sec.	Sub Sector
R.Fus	Royal Fusiliers	Suffolks	Suffolk Regiment
Rgt	Regiment	TM	Trench Mortar
RQMS	Regimental Quartermaster Sergeant	TMB	Trench Mortar Battery
		T.Mortars	Trench Mortars
Royal Fus	Royal Fusiliers	TO	Transport Officer
Royal Warwicks	Royal Warwickshire Regiment	Tr	Trench
		Trng	Training
RSM	Regimental Sergeant Major	UP	Unpaid
		VC	Victoria Cross
R S.Major	Regimental Sergeant Major	W	West
		Wilts	Wiltshire Regiment
R.Sussex	Royal Sussex Regiment	WNW	West North West
Rt	Right	WP	Waterproof
RTO	Regimental Transport Officer	WSW	West South West
		Yds	Yards
R.Warwicks	Royal Warwickshire Regiment		

Glossary

Adjutant   An officer who undertook the battalion's administration, including, for example, writing up the War Diary and issuing Operational Orders.

Battalion   A body of men, notionally comprising 37 officers and 977 other ranks. In practice, strength was around 700–800 or many less if no reinforcements had been received for some time. A regiment contained a number of battalions, anywhere from 1 to 20 or more. A battalion contained a headquarters and four companies.

Battery   A body of artillery, being 6 guns with their crews and train in the British Army.

Boche/Bosche   A French term for Germans, used consistently in the Diary and particularly by Col. G.D. Price.

Brigade   A number of battalions, almost always 4 until 1918, when the number fell to 3.

Company   A body of men notionally comprising 6 officers and 221 other ranks except for the Headquarters Company, which consisted of 6 officers and 93 other ranks. Headquarters and 4 companies made a battalion. A Company contained 4 platoons. Notionally commanded by a Captain.

Corps   A number of divisions between 2 and 6.

DCM   Distinguished Conduct Medal: the highest medal, below the Victoria Cross, for other ranks.

Division   A number of brigades, usually 3, plus an attached battalion of pioneers.

DSO   Distinguished Service Order: the highest decoration, below the Victoria Cross, for officers.

Field Ambulance   Not an ambulance in the modern sense, but an area close behind the lines where wounds were treated.

Footballs   Projectiles fired by British Trench Mortars.

Howitzers   Artillery pieces firing shells with a much higher trajectory, and consequently shorter range, than cannons.

Lyddite   High explosive chiefly made from picric acid, used in British shells and named after Lydd in Kent, where it was developed.

MC   Military Cross: the lowest decoration for bravery for officers.

MM   Military Medal: the lowest decoration for bravery for other ranks.

Pioneers   Troops used mainly for duties such as digging, laying barbed wire etc., although they were also trained to fight.

Pip Squeaks   Small gas shells.

Platoon   A body of around 30–40 men, commanded by a Lieutenant or Second Lieutenant; 4 platoons formed a Company (except for Headquarters Companies). A platoon comprised 4 sections.

Sausages   Nick-name for a type of German shell.

Section   A group of men commanded by a non-commissioned officer and between 5 and 9 other ranks. 4 sections comprised a platoon.

VC Victoria Cross: the highest decoration for bravery, open to all soldiers, officers and other ranks.

Whizz Bangs German shells of 5.9-inch calibre, so called due to the noise they made in flight.

Plate 1. Thomas Edwin Adlam VC, here shown during the Second World War. He had been a teacher between the wars but was recalled in 1939 and served in the Royal Engineers as Embarkation Commandant at Tilbury and, later, at Glasgow. He ended the Second World War as a Lieutenant Colonel.

Plate 2. Lance Corporal Arthur Edward Atkins of D Company, from Watford. He was killed aged 21 at the capture of Thiepval on 27 September 1916 and is buried in Connaught Military Cemetery, Thiepval.

Plate 3. The headstone of Private William Charles Billington, from Mount Pleasant, Aspley Guise. He was killed at the capture of Thiepval and buried in Connaught Military Cemetery, Thiepval. This is an example of the standard layout of Commonwealth War Graves Commission headstones.

xxiii

Plate 4. Captain Oliver Kingdon MC, from New Southgate, London. He joined as a Second Lieutenant and was killed on 24 April 1918 at the Battle of Cachy when a Captain in command of C Company. His body was never recovered and he is commemorated on the Pozieres Memorial to the Missing.

Plate 5. Captain Thomas Reginald Jack Mulligan, Company Commander of D Company. He joined the battalion on 19 July 1916 and left it after being wounded at the capture of Thiepval on 27 September 1916.

Plate 6. Second Lieutenant David Arnold Roeber from Forest Hill, London. He joined the battalion on 19 July 1916 and was killed on 15 August the same year during a dummy raid, along with three other ranks. He is buried at Ration Farm Military Cemetery, La Chapelle D'Armentieres.

Plate 7. Captain Sidney Tabor, Adjutant of the battalion in the latter half of 1917.

Plate 8. Second Lieutenant Theodore Percival (also known as Thomas Percy) Wilson. He joined the battalion on 18 July 1916 and was killed at Thiepval on 28 September 1916. He is buried in Mill Road Cemetery, Thiepval.

PART ONE

The War Diary of the 7th (Service) Battalion, Bedfordshire Regiment

1914

When Britain went to war on 4 August 1914 it had a small professional army which, by the standards of France and Germany, was tiny. It was realised that this army would not be able to sustain a long war without massive growth and, while some people thought it would be "all over by Christmas", Lord Kitchener, for example, predicted, with uncanny accuracy, a war of four years' duration. On the outbreak of war the Bedfordshire Regiment (traditionally the 16th Regiment of Foot) contained three battalions, two of them active service battalions (the 1st and 2nd) and the other a depot battalion to train new recruits and post them to the two active service battalions as needed. The 1st Battalion was at Mullingar in Ireland, the 2nd Battalion at Roberts Heights, Pretoria, South Africa. The 3rd Battalion, as might be expected, was at Kempston Barracks. A further battalion, the 4th (Extra Reserve) Battalion existed as a secondary depot battalion, and this later saw active service in France as part of 63rd (Royal Naval) Division. The 3rd Battalion remained a depot battalion throughout the war and saw no active service.

The most obvious source of additional manpower was the Territorial Army, which then, as now, consisted of part-time soldiers, often referred to as Saturday Afternoon Soldiers. The Bedfordshire Regiment fielded one such battalion, the 1/5th Battalion which would serve at Gallipolli and later in Egypt and Palestine. Two other Territorial battalions were formed as the 2/5th and 3/5th in September 1914 and June 1915, but these did not serve overseas.

The Territorials alone, however, could not provide Britain with the additional troops that the country needed and so a large number of New Army Battalions were formed. These were also commonly known as Kitchener Battalions, after the Secretary of State for War. Lord Kitchener wanted an army of 70 divisions for the long war he envisaged and set about recruiting with alacrity. In some ways the recruiting was, to begin with, hardly needed: so great was the desire to "do one's bit" that over 100,000 men signed up in the first few days. The new battalions created for these men were designed to serve for the duration of the conflict and were known as Service Battalions. There were five categories of New Army battalions labelled K1 to K4 (K standing for Kitchener, of course), depending on which New Army they joined (there were three, later four of these new armies, 2nd–5th). The fifth category were battalions raised by localities which subsequently clothed, housed and fed them until the War Office took over that responsibility in 1915; these included the famous Pals Battalions (see Introduction).

The Bedfordshire Regiment had three of these New Army battalions (some regiments had many more: the Royal Fusiliers, for example had seventeen, the Northumberland Fusiliers nineteen). The 6th Battalion served with the 37th Division until disbanded in May 1918 and the 8th Battalion served with the 24th Division, later the 6th Division, until disbanded in February 1918.

The 7th (Service) Battalion was intended to form part of the new Third Army and was thus a K2 battalion. It was formed in Bedford in September 1914 and was attached, at first, to the 15th Division at Aldershot. On 25 February 1915 it was transferred to the 54th Infantry Brigade, part of the newly formed 18th (Eastern) Division, where it would remain until it was reduced to a training cadre on 25 May 1918. The 18th Division was based at Colchester, moving to Salisbury Plain in May 1915 for final training before leaving for France in July that year, when the War Diary begins.

The Army suffered a great number of casualties (wounded as well as killed) in the retreat from Mons, the battles at Mons and Le Cateau and the near-run First Battle of Ypres, as well as the great allied victory on the Marne that halted the German advance. The Territorial and later New Army battalions were urgently needed to fill the gaps. The lack of numbers limited the British involvement in France and Belgium to a holding action until well into 1915.

1915

This was a year when the British Army learned many things, mostly from disasters in the various offensives that it launched. On the Western Front most offensives ended up as disastrous failures, and the British Army was not alone in this, the French and Germans suffering in just the same way. The main reason was that defensive technology – trenches, barbed wire, machine guns, high calibre shells and quick fire breach loading artillery all favoured the defensive and an army well dug-in and equipped could usually withstand any attack. The problem was further exacerbated by communications. Even when an attack was successful it was often many hours before the situation was known at headquarters and reinforcements got up, by which time the successes were quite likely to have been reversed by enemy counter-attacks, leaving the reinforcements conducting fruitless attacks against a line as strong as, if not stronger than, at the start of the battle.

The reasons for the poor communications were threefold. Firstly, the headquarters were often some way back. The reason given for this in popular mythology is that the generals were too cowardly or too devoted to a life of luxury to get too close to the front. In reality this is not just inaccurate, but unfair. Britain lost over seventy generals to enemy action during the course of the war, usually those who not only got too close to the front but crossed into No Man's Land to conduct a personal reconnaissance. Secondly, although field telephones were extensively used, the wires were very easily cut by shell fire. This meant that runners, or the famous carrier pigeons, had to be used. Thirdly, the runners or pigeons used when telephone lines were cut took time to reach their destination and might be killed or lost on the way.

The major actions on the Western Front involving British troops in this year are outlined below.

Neuve Chapelle, 10–12 March 1915 This attack by the British IV Corps and the Indian Corps was an outstanding success on the first day, largely due to the weight of the artillery barrage. The second day saw a series of largely fruitless and extremely costly attacks against newly consolidated German positions. The Germans counter-attacked on 12 March but gained little ground. Haig then called off any further British attacks.

Second Battle of Ypres, 22 April – 25 May 1915 This battle saw the first successful use of poison gas in warfare when the Germans overran positions north of Langemarck held by French Algerian troops but were fought off by the 1st Canadian Division on their flank. Over the next few weeks the Germans gained much ground, despite costly British counter-attacks, but could not take Ypres itself. Among villages taken were Langemarck, Pilckem, St Julien, Gravenstafel, Broodeseinde, Zonnebeke, Frezenberg, Verlorenhoek and Westhoek. Hill 60 (captured by the British on 17 April) was also retaken. Overall casualties included nearly 60,000 British, 10,000 French and 35,000 Germans.

Festubert, 9–26 May 1915 This battle was an attack which ended in large numbers of casualties and failure. It caused the famous "Shell Scandal" due to British guns having insufficient shells to use in bombardment, which was seen as the sole reason for the failure. As an outcome, David Lloyd George was appointed to head a Munitions Committee, which played an important role in his later elevation to Prime Minister.

Loos, 25 September 1915 – 8 October 1915 This attack by British troops using poison gas for the first time made some progress in the quarries and slag heaps near Hulluch, but ultimately the battle was another costly failure. Large French attacks were also made around Vimy and in Champagne. At the end of the offensive Britain had lost another 60,000, France around 250,000 and Germany around 140,000 men, dead and wounded. Sir John French, the British Expeditionary Force's Commander-in-Chief, was blamed for this failure and was replaced by Sir Douglas Haig on 19 December 1915.

Codford		
25-7-15	9am	Transport of regiment left CODFORD for service abroad 106 men and 3 officers
26-7-15	1.45pm	7th Bedfords left Codford for service abroad. Marching out strength 820 and 31 officers arrived Folkestone at 8.30 and embarked with 54th Bde HQ on S.S.Onward. On arrival at Boulogne sur Mer the battalion marched to Ostronove Rest Camp
27-7-15	7.5pm	Battalion left rest camp for Gare Centrale, Boulogne.

4   THE SHINY SEVENTH

		Entrained at 8pm and arrived at FLESSELLES at 2.15am 28-7-15
Talmas		
28-7-15		Marched from FLESSELLES to TALMAS where the battalion was billeted. Brigade Conference at 5.30pm
29-7-15		Battalion spent the day cleaning billets. Company parades
30-7-15		Battalion route march NAOURS-LA VICOGNE-TALMAS. Trench digging in afternoon
31-7-15		Parades under company arrangements. Water supply in village becoming low Battalion probably moving back to NAOURS
1-8-15		<u>Sunday.</u> Church parade for Battalion in the morning. Officers sketching class under Adjutant in afternoon. Weather hot and sultry slight rain towards evening
2-8-15		Battalion marches to VAL DES MAISONS with Brigade to be inspected by GOC 3rd Army at 2.30pm. Heavy rain on the way there and back. GOC expressed his entire satisfaction at the Brigade's turn out
3-8-15		Battalion route march TALMAS-VILLERS [BOCAGE]-TALMAS. Conference at HQ of Batt at 6pm. Weather wet
4-8-15		Musketry "rapid fire and loading" by companies in valley SW of TALMAS. Bombing practice for all bombers. Machine Guns inspected at Bde HQ NAOURS at 2.30pm
5-8-15		Bombing Parade and Coy parades in the morning demonstration in smoke helmets and respiration men made to pass through room full of chlorine gas. Weather wet and showery
6-8-15		Weather too wet for battalion route march. Conference of officers at 9.30am. Company route marches in the afternoon. Brigade conference at Middlesex HQ in the afternoon
7-8-15		Very wet day. Battalion at musketry in the morning
LA NEUVILLE		
8-8-15	4pm	Battalion marched with Brigade to LA NEUVILLE. Passed starting point at 4.15. Arrived LA NEUVILLE at 10pm where Battalion billeted. Weather very hot and the march very trying. B Coy detached from Batt at MOLLIENS-AU-BOIS to act as rearguard. This coy arrived at midnight
9-8-15	9am	Orderly Room 9am. Morning spent in cleaning and settling into billets
10-8-15		Parade for NCOs under Adjutant at 7am. Route march for Battalion 9.30am WERRIEUX [QUERRIEU?]-DAOURS-LA NEUVILLE weather hot and sultry. Lecture to officers and NCOs by Bombay[lacuna]
11-8-15		Musketry for all coys. Parade for Rt ½ batt at [lacuna] conference at 6pm

12-8-15	9am	Route march LA NEUVILLE-LA HOUSSOYE-LA NEUVILLE [lacuna] NCOs at 7am under Sgt Major. Lecture [lacuna] for all trained bomb throwers
13-8-15		Headquarters visited Amiens to visit French [lacuna] GOC Brig and Div and Gen.Morland [lacuna] methods of French confluage [camouflage?]
14-8-15	9.30am	Route march R ½ batt. 5½ miles forced march time taken 1hr 16 mins
	2.10am	Route march L ½ batt 5½ miles forced march time taken 1hr 12 mins packs behind. The left half batt perhaps started too soon after dinner and consequently lost 13 men
15-8-15		Church parade at 10.30am in the Middlesex area cancelled owing to rain. Holy Communion at 7am
16-8-15		Rapid marching to LA HOUSSOYE by companies in morning. Musketry under Company arrangements in the afternoon. 50 reinforcements arrived from Base Camp at Étaples
17-8-15		Parades under company arrangements
18-8-15		Musketry in morning. Route march in afternoon DAOURS-PONT NOYELLES
19-8-15		Digging in morning. Musketry in afternoon. Weather showers
20-8-15		Rapid marching in morning. Bombing. Bayonet fighting. Lecture to all Subalterns by Adjutant in evening. Conference for all officers at 5pm. Weather fine
21-8-15		Parades under company arrangements
22-8-15		Batt moves to RIBEMONT by route vide attached table of march [not attached]
23-8-15	9am	Col, Adj and officers of A & B Coys proceeded to trenches under guidance of Bde Major 154th Bde for preliminary view of trenches
	6pm	A & B Coys, Col and Adj proceed to trenches for instruction. A Coy attached to 8 A&S High, "B" to 5th Seaforths. Vide attached scheme [not provided]
24-8-15	9am	Training carried out under Company arrangements
	3pm	Control Post furnished by Battalion at cross roads near SUCRERIE
25-8-15	9am	Training carried out under Company arrangements. D Coy route march. Owing to absence of Adjutant in trenches the following entries were not made until his return
	10am	All last night enemy shelled our trenches but inflicted little damage. Sap at 475 was [overwritten on original and impossible to decipher]
26-8-15		Organised [overwritten on original and impossible to decipher] in order to try and dislodge [unclear] of the enemy who was damaging our line. Last night quieter than the 25th
	6pm	C & D Coys left for trenches to undergo instruction. C Coy relieved A Coy and D Coy relieved B Coy. The Col and Adjutant were relieved by Major Mills the 2nd in command.

27-8-15	8pm	The Col & Adjutant visited 8 East Surrey Regiment during day to arrange movements for relief of that batt by the 7th Beds one slight casualty in the morning in A Coy Reliefs completed only one casualty in B Coy
	12MN	Last night reported quiet by C Coy following report was sent to HQ by C Coy attached. A & B Coys spent today in cleaning up kit etc.
28-8-15		Parade for A & B at 7am in arms drill, Draft of 20 men posted to Battalion on arrival
29-8-15		Situation unchanged. Church parade in morning
30-8-15		A & B Companies proceeded to trenches to undergo company instruction as such. They relieved C & D companies without casualties arriving at RIBEMONT at 4am on 31st
31-8-15		Day spent in cleaning up. A & B companies returned to RIBEMONT at 11.30pm. Showery
1-9-15		Conference for all mounted officers at 10.30am HQ 54th Brigade. Parades under Coy arrangements. Weather variable
2-9-15		A & B Coys digging E of LAVIÉVILLE, cancelled owing to rain. O.C.Companies proceed to trenches to take over
3-9-15		Batt relieves 8th East Surreys in accordance with scheme attached [not attached]

BÉCORDEL Trenches

5-9-15	10pm	3 men of A Coy while returning from patrol were wounded. Two evacuated to FA one returned to duty otherwise night passed quietly except for usual sniping
6-9-15		Day passed quietly at 4.45 our guns shelled working party in BOIS FRANCAIS at 5.40 Germans exploded a mine on left of us in MIDDLESEX line at 6.30 this was followed by bush fire on both sides from rifles and machine guns. Our guns also firing some rounds. Remainder of night peaceful
7-9-15	10.50am	Germans fired two rounds of HE which fell to the S of BONTÉ REDOUBT. Our guns replied with three rounds of shell. Weather fine and warm. Casualties 3 wounded
	10pm	Royal Fusiliers blew up a mine. This was followed by rapid fire and machine gun fire. R.Fusiliers occupied lip of crater. Our casualties one killed one wounded
8-9-15	8am	Work with every available man on SOUTH AVENUE communicating trench
	4.15am	4pm–7pm our guns fired two shells on BOIS FRANCAIS. Germans replied with about 40 shells which caused no visible damage. Wire reported weak in front 91 & 92 steps are being taken to repair this; our patrols reported enemy's snipers in trench 486. These caused some trouble until our guns fired 5 rds which silenced sniping from this direction.
9-9-15	11pm	Organised machine gun fire; at 8.30 our guns shelled crater in Fusiliers' lines. Parapet blown down & 10 casualties reported. At 11pm Germans exploded mine opposite R.Fusiliers

	4.30pm	Intermittent shelling all day. Enemy searched for our M.Guns behind trenches 93 & 94.
10-9-15	4.15am	Heavy transport heard on MAMETZ-FRICOURT road. This shelled by our M.Guns. RONDALL AVENUE and ground in rear of trenches 93-94 shelled by enemy. German spy reported to be in trenches masquerading as an Artillery Officer. Train heard in direction of Fricourt. German flares are not now igniting. Red & green flares from behind FRICOURT are being used for enemy artillery guidance.
	10am	22 Mortar Batty shells fired at trenches 87-88. One man of C Coy wounded
	10.45	Trench mortar fire ceases.
	4.30pm	Sounds of work heard in No.3 listening post right of sector D2. Mining Expert sent to confirm this. M.Guns detected in long white house extreme edge of FRICOURT. Working party reported in German first line trench just S of FRICOURT. Trench Mortar fired 22 shots into centre section one man killed. Mortar believed to be situated due N 9 in 493 as ground is freshly broken here and a flash was seen at the same spot last night. Intermittent shelling
11-9-15	4am	Morning Tactical Report. Intermittent shelling by Artillery between 5pm and 7pm. Working party reported at pt.491 not heard after 1am. A Dud shell fired by our guns at 10pm. Enemy observed in long grass opposite 93 trench. Fired at. Line reported held more strongly owing to considerable number more rifle flashes. Enemy's M.Guns located at corner of sq. trench due E of 3 in 493. Tunnel reported being dug from left to right of Aeroplane Trench not yet confirmed No.2 & 3 listening report sounds of mining at 2am. Train heard crossing a viaduct at 7.55 it then stopped. Trench 87 reports sound of dull thumps at regular intervals. German casualty whistle heard at 2.25 and 2.50am. Our officer Commdg D Coy reports great coolness of signallers who mended their wire in three places while under shell fire
12-9-15	4.15am	Morning Tactical Report Sound of heavy transport on CONTALMAISON-FRICOURT Road at 9.45. Our guns were informed. Sound of train heard as usual at 9.45pm behind FRICOURT. Patrols sent out in front of trenches and on our right & left; return having nothing to report. Wire mended in front of trenches 91-92 & 93. Patrol at 6.45 reports new posts of enemy in junction of roads in front of trench 90. This was successfully bombed with rifle grenades much to the annoyance of the enemy who opened a hot fire without doing any damage. On our right enemy considerably quieter. This change suggests new regiment. Large explosion heard some distance on our right front between 3 & 3.30pm. Several rounds by big guns fired in same direction.

	4.15pm	Evening Tactical Report New German communication trench observed N of church at FRICOURT. Aeroplane activity considerable. Intermittent Artillery firing. Time fuzes used by Mortar Battery the day before yesterday are being forwarded for your inspection. Situation unchanged.
13-9-15	4am	Morning Tactical Report Mine exploded on right of Northants. Rapid fire opened on both sides. This was followed by Artillery fire from the enemy which was as usual preceded by green lights. Situation now quiet. One Coy of King's Own in trenches for instruction by platoons. Casualties 2 wounded.
	4.15pm	Evening Tactical Report Enemy trench mortar located in Willow Bed at 6 of 486 from listening post in trench 88 digging was heard surmised that they are continuing towards trench 487. Aeroplane reconnaissance by our aircraft. Situation otherwise unchanged.
14-9-15	4.15pm	A shell exploded in rear of trench 88 this evening. A strong smell of pepper and snuff was experienced for about 25 mins. A German working party was shelled by our guns at 9.15pm. Three white flags have been observed in German second line between BAZENTIN-LE-PETIT & BAZENTIN-LE-GRAND no apparent reason for these. Bombs thrown from Willow Bed at 6 of 486 after pointing out spot personally to Artillery C.O. C Coy reported no further action from the spot. German Gun reported in trees W. of 2nd line trenches FRICOURT
	3.25pm	Situation calm. Intermittent Artillery Fire at 6.10am. A man was observed at pt 495 in the open passing between two German trenches. He appeared to be dressed in civilian clothes, without rifle or equipment. An N.C.O. firing front 92 trench hit a sniper at pt 486. casualty whistle blown and commotion caused. A man was observed firing near a cart 50 metres N of 486. Looked like a boy of 16 dressed in khaki.
15-9-15	3.20am	Morning Tactical Report Trenches 87, 88, 93 & 94 heavily shelled by aerial torpedoes at 7.30pm 40 yds of communication trench & 30 yds of fire trench levelled by bombardment. Our patrol from 93 trench got right up to enemy's trip wire. Voices heard. Patrol reported rifles fired at regular intervals, are of an opinion that all rifles are fixed at regular intervals down the trench and are fixed [fired?] by anyone passing. Trenches & parapet repaired during the night. Other patrols sent out during the night passed along enemy's front at about 60 yds away & report nothing heard. They are of opinion that line is very lightly held. they bear out opinion of first patrol re rotation & measure of enemy's rifle fire. Two shells fired during the bombardment gave out a very

		pungent smoke like phosphorus but had no evil effect as men passed through the fumes.
	3.50pm	<u>Evening Tactical Report</u> Artillery exchanged shots at 12.30 noon some grenades were fired at 6th Northants at about 12.30 noon. Situation otherwise unchanged.
	4.30pm	Ref D701 E.T.Report. Supplementary information herewith. During the last half hour a noise like the beat of an engine heard very plainly by numbers of men. The engine has half second beats & can be heard quite plainly even back at C Coy's Hd.Qrs. believe opposite to trench 89 & 88.
16-9-15	3.55am	<u>Morning Tactical Report</u> Enemy fired two shells into BONTÉ REDOUBT at 7.30pm. These shells were amalgamated with phosphorous & a sample was forwarded to you last night. A Red rocket was sent up from FRICOURT at 9.15pm a cart was seen over FRICOURT at 9.30pm to be ablaze in front of trench 92 this was probably due to a flare. At 7.30pm enemy shelled our fire trenches with Whiz Bangs. No damage was done. At 10.45pm a 2nd Red light was seen over FRICOURT. At 10.30pm a mine was exploded, this was followed by a little rapid fire from the enemy. Our guns replied to the above with a salvo of shrapnel & H.Explosive a patrol returned at 1.30 reported they had got right up to the German lines & heard voices & sound of rifles being loaded. Are of opinion trench in front of FRICOURT strongly held. Saw no enemy trip wire or patrols. Report German M.Gun in trench 92. Patrol reports flares are sent up from trenches behind a front trench. My right Coy report unusual quietness of enemy & report line very held [very lightly held?]. No sniping from this part of line & only occasional M.G. Fire. Patrols still out further information will be obtained later.
	3pm	Evening Tactical Report Situation very quiet. Desultory artillery fire on both sides 3 out of 5 of our H.Explosive shells fired at 12 noon to-day were "DUDS". Patrol which went out early this morning got within 30 yards of Aeroplane Sap but heard nothing.
17-9-15	3.15am	A Coy King's Own left trenches at about 10.30pm. My O.C. right sector reports enemy shelled communication trenches in rear of D1 at 6.45. He is of an opinion that enemy heard relief taking place. Our artillery replied with shrapnel 3 of which failed to explode. Red lights were seen at 7.17pm & 7.25pm. Apparently one Red light means clear the fire trench & a double Red light a signal for artillery to commence fire. Patrols from 86 trench got within 30 yds of German trench report very little sound from enemy's trench. Further reported that they thought that sap opposite trench 84 & 85 was unoccupied and had not been increased

	3pm	**Evening Tactical Report** Situation very quiet. Sniper located by Observer in white house in FRICOURT. 3 men observed working in new German trench N of FRICOURT. Patrols report only one or two men in German line in front of 9-291 trenches
18-9-15	2.55am	**Morning Tactical Report** Explosion of German Mine at 9pm opposite TAMBOUR. More activity than usual from German trenches. Very few flares. Pumping heard from direction of FRICOURT at 5.15pm. Our guns fired on FRICOURT. A man was seen to run into a house. Transport heard behind German lines at 10.0pm. A sniper was located about 100yds from German lines shortly afterwards a shout was heard followed by a whistle probably casualty whistle. More firing from enemy trenches than usual. Reports from patrols will follow when they return.
	3.0pm	**Evening Tactical Report** Considerable aeroplane activity. Intermittent artillery fire from both sides. German working party seen in 2nd line opposite trench 88. Dispersed by our fire. Situation unchanged.
19-9-15	2.50am	**Morning Tactical Report** Usual desultory artillery fire from 5.45pm. Rapid fire opened on TAMBOUR at 6.45pm at about same time enemy fired four small rifle grenades from trench in front of FRICOURT on to trench 91. Damage nil we replied by rifle fire. Enemy work in two reliefs one of which snipe more & are more active than the other. Bomb officer reports great visibility of Brock lighter situation otherwise unchanged. A Red flash away on the left at 12.15am. Cause not known.
	2.40pm	**Evening Tactical Report** Enemy exploded a small mine opposite 91 trench at 3.45am. No sequel. Enemy searched for our Machine Guns with artillery & although dropping a shell right on to one emplacement did no damage as the gun had been previously changed to another. We continue to harass them with this gun in WILLOW AVENUE. Aeroplane trench shelled by our Artillery this morning. Situation otherwise quiet.
20-9-15	3.30am	**Morning Tactical Report** German seen in trench N of point 486 young about 19 wearing grey forage cap & uniform at 6.45 enemy fired 4 bombs at 91 trench. Our guns replied. 8pm sound of transport heard on our left. Also humming noise like a Zeppelin. Enemy bombed our trenches with rifle grenades at 10.25pm. We replied with bombs from catapult. Situation unchanged. Mr.Hine wounded slightly while out on patrol duty. Probably only be away two or three days
	3.0pm	**Evening Tactical Report** Allied aeroplane shelled by enemy over FRICOURT at

21-9-15	3am	8.0am this morning. Four rifle grenades were fired into a house behind 87 trench. Situation otherwise quiet. Night quiet on the whole. Successful bombardment of AEROPLANE trench yesterday evening by our guns. Germans replied with 8 whiz bangs which did no damage. A German in a white coat was seen moving about in FRICOURT. Careful watch has been kept on point where railway cutting joins road passing through 87/88 trenches. At 8pm flames were seen at this point. Fire was opened & a M.Gun replied. Rapid [fire] was then given by us & this spot has been searched also by mine bombs. No further flashes have been seen from this point but a large bomb exploded about 50 yards from the centre of trench 88. Patrol from 93 trench report firing only from two places on a front of 200 yards. Patrol reached enemy trip wire. Firing reported to be done from holes level with ground and not from over the parapet or through loopholes. A direct hit was scored on enemy's trench by our mortar from 91 trench at 6pm. Alertness & co-operation of our Artillery specially mentioned by firing line. The M.Gun which is thought to fire when the enemy is standing to is now considered to be someone hitting on a box, but this is still uncertain

Méaulte

21-9-15	6.34pm	Regt relieved by Middlesex & returns to MEAULTE and is billeted there total casualties up to date OR 10 killed, 7 wounded, 1 Officer wounded. Regt congratulated by G.O.C. 54th Bde whose A.P.8 remarks are attached [not included]. 1 Coy (B) at BÉCORDEL. 1 Coy. (C) at Pt.107.
22-9-15		Day spent in cleaning up of billets.
23-9-15		Attack Practice in the evening towards MORLANCOURT.
24-9-15		C Coy returned from Pt.107. Weather wet, advanced guard scheme in the evening towards Morlancourt.
25-9-15		A Coy relieved N.Hants at 107. Field manoeuvres in the evening. Weather wet.
26-9-15	10am	Church parade
	12pm	Conference at noon for all officers
27-9-15		Weather very wet
28-9-15		Weather very wet, route march & parade under Company Arrangements.
29-9-15		Whole Battn marched by Coys to VILLE SUR ANCRE for hot baths.
30-9-15		Manoeuvre parade on Morlancourt Rd, attack scheme. Weather cold[?] and indifferent
1-10-15		Weather fine Parades under Coy arrangements
2-10-15		Weather fine. Instruction in wire entanglements by coys in the morning.
3-10-15		Church parade. Weather fine.
4-10-15		Weather dull and showery, cold. Conference of 18th Div. at 4pm.

D2 Trenches
5-10-15 Battalion relieved 12th Middlesex in Sector D2 trenches. Relief orders and sketch map attached herewith marked [not included]
5-10-15 3.0pm Evening Tactical Report
Situation unchanged
6-10-15 2.45am Morning Tactical Report
Enemy shelled trenches 85 with whiz bangs at 5.15pm. Our guns replied on FRICOURT trenches. At 4pm evening fired 5 large trench mortars which filled part of Trench 88. Our guns replied with shrapnel and HE At 4.45pm enemy commenced bombardment with aerial torpedoes 40 of which were fired on trenches 87-90. Considerable damage and havoc was done. This is now being cleared. Our guns fired and scored hits on spot where these shells were thought to come i.e. just N of E in CIMRE at pt.06. At 11.15pm the enemy sent a shell in direction of MÉAULTE. Wind light E to NE. Night very foggy.
2.45pm Enemy fired four shells on SOUTH AVENUE as Oxford & Bucks were relieving. The shells which fell on C Coy last night are reported to be 6in shells. Two of these were sent over at 2pm. They were fired from the direction of LA BOISSELLE. Arrangements are now being made to shell these guns from Sector D3 as shrapnel is no use against them
7-10-15 2.15am Morning Tactical Report
Wind NE. Centre section of D2 heavily bombarded with aerial torpedoes. Bombardment started at about 3.0pm and continued at irregular intervals until 6pm. Some delay was caused in getting into communication with the heavy artillery owing to the wire to the Howitzer Batty being broken. At about 6pm our guns fired eight heavy shells and after a short interval several more. This stopped the bombardment. Nearly all shells fell in rear of 88 trench near well. One shell fell on 92 trench at 6.15pm. Considerable damage has been done in rear of trenches 87-88. Patrols report centre sap of aeroplane trench occupied and covered with wire. The road with the centre in front of this sap does not contain snipers holes in the bank as supposed. Left sap unoccupied. Red lights observed over FRICOURT at 6.50pm and 7.50pm and green light at 8.35pm. Capt.King arrived at 8.30pm and is now superintending evacuation of buried men. Estimated casualties Oxford & Bucks 6 killed, 20 wounded, Bedfords 7 wounded. Mortar located pt.73 and at pt.50 NE of 73 in an angle of trench. Oxford & Bucks attached for instruction as per attached schedule AP10 [not attached]
2.45pm <u>Evening Tactical Report</u>
Several High Explosive shells from enemy fell to left of Estaminets. Two aerial torpedoes exploded at 2.25pm near left sector Hdqrs immediate counterstraffe by our Heavy

Batty. It would appear that enemy's object is to raise [raze] all buildings. Staff Captain of 18th Div is now down in the trenches. Wind NW.

8-10-15   2.15am   <u>Morning Tactical Report</u>
Enemy again threw aerial torpedoes on our centre sector starting at 2.25pm. Heavy Batty at once replied and firing ceased at 10pm. A working party on pt.43 was twice caught by our guns. It is thought that our Heavy batty did serious damage at this point. As the enemy were persistent with their working parties [they] were silenced by our howitzers. Wind ESE

2.20pm   <u>Evening Tactical Report</u>
Twenty rifle grenades fired into BOIS FRANCAIS at 11am from heap of sandbags at top end of middle sap in Aeroplane Trench. This was at once counterstraffed by our guns. Enemy working party reported at point where our heavy shells exploded last night. They were seen to be carrying away felled wood to their trenches. These were fired on by our shrapnel. This party was dispersed three times by D82. Wind E. Patrol this morning in front of centre sector proceeded down Railway Cutting as far as road F9A68 and reported no sign of enemy.

9-10-15   2.15am   <u>Morning Tactical Report</u>
At 7.30pm German working party reported at point 73 our shrapnel & HE Guns opened fire noise of tools being hastily dropped was then heard. Transport heard E of FRICOURT 8.15pm. German sniper was shot opposite sector right yesterday while endeavouring to signal the direction of our shots. Patrols sent out report no hostile patrols encountered. Mine exploded at 6.30pm in BOIS ALLEMAND followed by short burst of rapid fire and grenades our guns fired a section salvo as counter strafe to this – wind dead calm now. Occasional easterly gusts.

2.15pm   <u>Evening Tactical Report</u>
Observatory report Germans seen carrying timber in aeroplane trench. A bright light was shewn on road N of FRICOURT at 8pm last night at the same time German transport was heard. A German in blue uniform was seen in aeroplane trench at 11.30am. Wind North East.

10-10-15   2.15am   <u>Morning Tactical Report</u>
Considerable improvement noticed in enemy's shooting. At 9.50 enemy fired on ALBERT we at once counter strafed on FRICOURT. Observers and sentries reported two masked snipers east of aeroplane trench. These kept putting up dummies and firing from behind and between them. The dummies and snipers were dressed the same and could be easily seen through glasses. After 3 hours we scored a hit and the enemy ceased. Red flare sent up from FRICOURT at 9pm in an easterly direction. Enemy flares appeared to have increased in range. Wind NE increasing in strength.

	2.30pm	<u>Evening Tactical Report</u> Patrols report enemy wire opposite FRICOURT in hollow damaged in places. Working party noticed in trench 73. This was continually fired at by our Machine Guns. Dummies are being used to draw fire in enemy's line. Sounds of heavy hammering heard in FRICOURT. Column of smoke went up from behind Hill (S) of Aeroplane Trench at 7am. Wind SE.
11-10-15	2.15am	<u>Morning Tactical Report</u> Two rifle grenades fell behind well in centre of sector last night. These are reported to have been fired from pt.73 from the same spot as from where the aerial torpedoes came from. Large mound of earth reported in the trees at F3C93. A mine exploded in TAMBOUR at about 6.15pm. This was followed by a short burst of rapid fire from the enemy. Sound of orders shouted and movement of transport was heard in FRICOURT last night. Sound of music believed to be a band was also heard.
	2.30pm	<u>Evening Tactical Report</u> Patrols recovered flag put out by 12th Middx. Another patrol was hit in front of trench 88 apparently in [sic] from a MG about pt.75. Two Machine Guns located at F9B71 and F9B53. Two trench mortars were fired into D1 at 12.20 from trees at SW corner of FRICOURT not absolutely certain about it being at pt.73. A large column of smoke was seen in German trench at F9C54 at 6.45am. Wind ENE
12-10-15	2.15am	<u>Morning Tactical Report</u> The trench mortar used against the Fusiliers yesterday afternoon was reported on as follows. It was firing from a range of about 700. The shells could be distinctly seen in the air. The shells were exploded by the time fuse as two burst in mid air while others buried themselves some time before exploding. Position located is F9B17. After the guns had searched this spot no more firing was experienced from the enemy's mortar. At 3.15 several rifle grenades were thrown on to the well in the rear of trench 87-88 and also several whiz bangs one of which fell very near Coy hdqrs. Our guns retaliated. Between 6 and 8pm two large search lights were seen. These were thought to be operated on from behind the BOIS DE MAMETZ. At 8.55pm a rocket was sent up from LA BOISSELLE which burst into many Very lights. This was followed by flares on both sides. Patrols sent by left sector report that they got quite close to the German lines. Fire reported to be only coming from 3 positions in a front of 300yds. Wind East. Yesterday there was a conference a Bde Hqrs Major Jones appointed CO BÉCORDEL garrison on the 9th October. Lt.Bull took over command of B Coy
	2.30pm	<u>Evening Tactical Report</u> Fresh earth has been thrown up 200yds east of communication trench behind AEROPLANE TRENCH.

Spot is being watched. A German has been seen running along their parapet for last three mornings for about 50yds. A white flag was seen at German trench at 7pm. Wind SSE SSW

13-10-15   2.15am   Morning Tactical Report
Enemy fired 20 heavy trench howitzers at 2.30pm which fell around railway station and estaminet in left section of D2. Our guns replied with Lyddite and shrapnel. At 4.30pm the bombardment started again over 16 shells falling in the same place. Communication trenches round the estaminet were knocked in otherwise no damage was done. Parapet intact. Two trench howitzers fired into their position, is positively reported to be F3C8½7. At 4pm German sniper was shot at F9B62 he was wearing a kind of brown canvas helmet with eye holes. Very heavy bombardment has been heard since 2pm on our left. Patrols reported all quiet and encountered no enemy patrols. We fired a bomb into German lines from trench 94 with some success. Wind very slight NNE.

2.15pm   Evening Tactical Report
Further inspection shows that the spots from which the trench mortars were fired are as stated in my report of yesterday. The emplacement appears to be covered by grass screens. Red glow seen in the sky last night thought to be a burning village about 15 miles north. 4 small HE shells were sent over the estaminet at 10am. Wind SSE.

14-10-15   2.15am   Morning Tactical Report
A few rifle grenades were sent over trench 88 at 4.20pm and fell away [in] the ruins. At 5pm enemy again started bombardment with trench torpedoes. A portion of the parapet was destroyed and communication trenches blocked in sections 91. These have now been repaired. We successfully bombed German trenches S of the TAMBOUR with catapults. Our guns replied to the torpedo bombardment. One shell appeared to hit direct on emplacements to prevent [fire?] but ricocheted this also happened in the case of two others which apparently hit the same spot. Can it be that the Germans dig a lot of loose earth round their emplacements to prevent shells from bursting? The emplacements were three reported yesterday viz F3C87, F3C8½7. This information is positive. Smoke caused by the discharge of torpedoes was clearly seen from Btn.HQ and again located to these spots. A large German working party was reported at SW corner house of FRICOURT at 9.[0]8pm and again at 10.15pm and 1am. On each occasion our artillery fired a salvo of shrapnel and a great commotion and sounds of tools being dropped was heard. Up to this time the party have not returned. A French bullet was fired into our lines today from the enemy. A mine exploded in BOIS FRANCAIS at 5.20pm. No damage reported

Méaulte
15-10-15	Battn relieved by 12 Middx in accordance with AP [not attached] rest of day spent in cleaning up of billets
16-10-15	Parades on this day were, Bomb Drill and throwing, running & physical exercises. Afternoon spent in carrying out a practice alarm. Weather moderate.
17-10-15	Church parade. Weather raw. Major Jones left for England.
18-10-15	Running parade at 6.30am. A Bomb attack was carried out by A & B Coys in the morning. Afternoon parades as on work programme. Weather fine.
19-10-15	Battalion was bathed in the morning. Bombing Drill was carried out at other times. In the afternoon a bomb attack was carried out. Weather fine.
20-10-15	Running drill at 6.30am. Bombing Drill was carried on during the day. Lt.Lacey appointed Bde M.G.Officer until further orders.
21-10-15	Parades as usual today. Weather still fine.
22-10-15	Running drill & physical exercise at 6.30am. Rest of day spent in Bomb Drill & Bomb Throwing. Weather fine warmer than usual.
23-10-15	Usual programme of work for this day, with Bombing chief parades. Weather fine.
24-10-15	Church Parade. Weather moderate. Pte.Waterton left on leave for England.
25-10-15	Battalion relieved 12th Middx in D2. Relief completed 10am. Weather Very Wet. 2/Lt.Baden and Sgt.Drummer left on leave to England.

Trenches D2

25-10-15	2.15pm	Hammering heard at F3D11. Observation is being kept on this point. Wind strong SE.
26-10-15	2.15am	8 Smoke Rockets fired from direction of FRICOURT fell near SOUTH AVENUE at 3.30pm. These were believed to be an Artillery Test as Guns fired directly afterwards. Other reports state these rockets came from our lines. Working party opposite trench S of pt.73 dispersed by Grenade & M.G.fire. Our 6″ Batty fired 12 shots between 5 & 6pm into enemy's trenches behind BOIS ALLEMAND. Cat & dog seen by sentry in trench 85 going towards BOIS FRANCAIS, coming from German lines. Wind easterly.
	2.0pm	Considerable artillery activity on both sides this morning. Working party shelled in cemetery street we retaliated on German trenches. Notice boards have been put out by the enemy opposite 88 trenches. Two sections of enemy left trench at F4G03 they were dressed in grey and dirty drill. Wagon and cyclist seen on FRICOURT-MAMETZ road. Fired on by our Guns. Smoke observed from trench at F30C515. Flash and smoke from heavy Gun was noticed coming from a ravine near large tree in open ground 1000yds NW of MAMETZ. Reported to F.O.O.

27-10-15	2am	During afternoon of 26th considerable artillery activity. At 5.40pm two heavy trench mortars were fired in direction of D1. At 12.15 midnight enemy sent over a shell in direction of MÉAULTE we replied with two heavy shells. These burst at F3C82 with good effect. Trench mortars located at F9D88 but not absolutely certain. Enemy Machine Guns rather more active than usual. Very little rifle fire. Lt. & Qrs.Mr.F.Corner & Lt.Lloyd left for leave.
	3pm	Wind NNW. Artillery activity on both sides between 10.20am and 12 noon. Situation otherwise unchanged.
28-10-15	2.15am	At 3.20pm small trench mortar bombs from F3C6552 fell on D2A and C our guns replied on FRICOURT. Between 3 & 4pm our Guns were busy registering an enemy's batty at X29A several shots were also fired at communication trench X27. At 4.25pm our guns successfully caught a party of enemy at F4b30. Enemy's snipers not nearly so active. There is a peculiar absence of rifle fire. In spite of repeated shelling and fire from our Guns there appears to be still considerable activity in the wood SE of FRICOURT. Wind NNW.
28-10-15	2.15pm	Evening Tactical Report Artillery activity between 10.30am and 12.30 noon and enemy fired small trench mortar bombs at 11am on trench 84 F9D57 and several at F9D46. Our artillery retaliated. Wind SW.
29-10-15	2am	Morning Tactical Report At 8pm enemy fired rifle grenades and trench mortars at F9D6570. Our Guns retaliated. Frequent flares sent up from Aeroplane trench and trench 65 traversed by Machine Gun from FRICOURT. At 9pm our guns fired 6 rounds into BOIS ALLEMAND. Sentry reports sound of gong from enemy trenches directly this ceased. Rifle fire from F3C68513 is directed straight to the front and not to the flanks as was the former case. Different troops less highly trained are believed to be in front as the rifle fire is exceedingly scarce, the enemy only firing with mortars and rifle grenades.
	2.35pm	Evening Tactical Report Mine exploded at F3C37 at 6.30am. Enemy sent over Grenades and mortars into the left of our sector at 8.30am. Our Guns retaliated with H.E. on F3C7545 and the enemy ceased offensive action. Working parties of enemy at F4b30 and X21d44 fired on by our artillery. Trench mortars were fired from F3C7575 and F3b19. Wind SW
30-10-15	2am	Morning Tactical Report German working parties were heard at F9B16 and F3C83, F9B1568 and at F9B55. These were fired on by our guns it is believed with some effect. Rather more rifle fire tonight. Enemy fired rifle grenades and shrapnel over left of trench 88F9A56. Our Guns retaliated on FRICOURT and German trenches opposite this spot. There was considerable artillery

		activity on both sides during yesterday afternoon. Working party caught by our rapid fire at 7pm at point F3C70. Wind SE.
	2.45pm	Evening Tactical Report
		Artillery activity on both sides 8am to 9am. Trench Mortars & Rifle Grenades were fired on Trench 91. Our artillery at once retaliated and enemy ceased hostilities. 9.50am working party reported F9a9508. Wind SW slight. Our artillery fired on working party.
31-10-15	2am	Morning Tactical Report
		Between 1pm & 4.30pm considerable artillery activity on both sides. Our snipers report they shot a man at F3C83. Rifle grenades were fired from F3C8005 & F9H by enemy. Working Parties fired on at F9B52 & F2C80.
	2pm	Evening Tactical Report
		3 aircraft passed over our lines at 8am going East. They were fired at by Enemy Machine Gun from pt.80. Enemy are making an emplacement at F3C7530. Enemy Machine Gun fired last night from pt.80.
1-11-15	2.15am	Morning Tactical Report
		Working party mending wire was reported between F9B18 and F9A9598 at 8pm. This was dispersed by our Guns. At 2pm bomb fell near railway bridge and did some damage. Our Guns replied. Much activity at pt.F3C73 this is probably used for observing in day and sniping. Occasional bombing and artillery fire (Lts.W.H.Bull, L.H.Keep & F.W.Smith and 2/Lt.Benson left for leave.
	2.55pm	10.18am a mine was exploded in the BOIS FRANCAIS and another in the TAMBOUR at 3.25am. Artillery activity on the part of the enemy. Shells falling from F9C74. Enemy Machine Gun located at F3C5058 almost complete absence of rifle and Machine Gun fire. Wind SSE.
2-11-15	2.15am	Morning Tactical Report
		At 5.30pm enemy fired heavy trench mortars from F3C7575 on to the left of our sector. We retaliated by blowing down their parapet with 6″ shells & 18 pounders. At 7.30pm and 9.30pm enemy again sent over trench mortars but we replied in the same way with heavy artillery and they have now ceased. A M.Gun has been laid on the Gap in their parapet. Enemy M.Gun fired from F3C81 traversing the front of our sector. Earth has been thrown up at F9B3287. Sentry reports hearing whistle directly after our heavy guns had fired tonight (2/Lt.Baden & Sgt.Drummer returned from leave).
	2.35pm	Artillery Tested last night, time taken 3 mins. Short burst of enemy M.Gun fire believed to come from F9B71. Wind NNW. Situation otherwise quiet.
3-11-15	1.30am	Our Guns registered with new ammunition yesterday at 3pm and enemy replied with some shrapnel on Railway Avenue. Sentry reports sound of mining at F9A84 but this has not yet been confirmed. Wind NW.

	2.35pm	<u>Evening Tactical Report</u> Artillery activity on both sides, otherwise situation quite quiet. Wind NW.
4-11-15	2.15am	<u>Morning Tactical Report</u> Enemy transport heard at 8.45pm behind FRICOURT on CONTALMAISON Road. Our own transport distinctly heard at 7.15pm. This was very loud. 10pm sound of train E of FRICOURT. Enemy's transport appeared normal. Rather more rifle fire last night. Hitherto there has been a marked absence of the same. At 11.45 enemy sent three large shells into MÉAULTE. Working party reported at F3C5055. This was fired on by our Machine Guns. A party of 30 was seen to pass the Gap at F4B30 this afternoon. Lt.& Qr.Mr.F.Corner & Lt.Lloyd returned from leave.
	2.30pm	<u>Evening Tactical Report</u> Working party was heard at pt.73 at 9am this was shelled by our Howitzers and field guns. Trench Mortar reported to be firing from F3I73 at 12 noon our guns retaliated. Grenades were fired at the same time from F3C8602 just east of FRICOURT-CONTALMAISON Rd. Wind NE.
5-11-15	2am	<u>Morning Tactical Report</u> At 6.55pm a red rocket which burst into 4 stars was sent up by enemy. This was immediately answered by a big German Gun from near BOIS ALLEMAND. Machine Gun active fired several times on BONTÉ REDOUBT. Sentries report hearing enemy transport at 7.50pm and 7.00pm and our own transport at midnight. Grenades reported to be fired from F3C8602 are now said to be fired from F3C81. Lt.Prior of Mining Coy investigated sounds heard at F9A84 he listened from two points and attributes noises heard to rats or to relief of sentries he intends to make doubly certain tomorrow when he will listen again.
	2.40pm	<u>Evening Tactical Report</u> Motor lorry heard behind enemy's lines going East from FRICOURT at 4.35pm [am?]. Artillery test on trench 91 2.30am took 7 mins. Enemy's artillery fired 3 shells in rear of 86 trench at 11.50am. Our artillery retaliated on pt.73 and F3C94. 12-18 noon our artillery retaliated on enemy's trenches opposite TAMBOUR where they had been firing whizbangs. WIND E.
6-11-15	2am	<u>Morning Tactical Report</u> Enemies' transport heard in FRICOURT and sounds of movement in front trenches of enemy at 7.15pm. A heap of earth has been thrown up at F4C56 and a rectangular hole has been observed in the road bank at F3C7725. At 3.35pm enemy fired 4 rifle grenades from F3C81 on to F9A67. A train was heard near Mametz at 6–5pm and another in FRICOURT at 8pm. Wind NE

Méaulte
| 6-11-15 | 6.10am | Battn was relieved by 12th Middx Regt in D2. Relief |

		complete 10am. Rest of day spent in cleaning up of billets etc. Weather fine, crisp.
7-11-15		Church Parade. Weather fine.
8-11-15		The Battn was bathed today. Afterwards bombing practices were carried out. Weather fine.
9-11-15		Usual fatigues were carried out today. All other available men bombing parades. Running drill 7–7.30am. Weather moderate.
10-11-15		Fatigues and parades as usual today. Weather wet. Capt.W.H.Bull, Lts.E.W.Benson & L.H.Keep & 2/Lt.F.W.Smith returned from leave on the evening of the 9th.
11-11-15		Parades and fatigues as usual. Weather fine. Capt.& Adj.P.R.Meautys, Capt.E.Clegg & Capt.H.Ramsbotham left for leave
12-11-15		Battn with Transport was inspected by GOC 54th Inf Bde at DERNANCOURT 10.30am today. Weather wet but rain stopped in time for the inspection. In the afternoon bombing drill was carried out.
13-11-15		Usual fatigues & parades today. Weather fair.

Trenches D2

14-11-15		Btn relieved by 12 Middx in Sector D2. Relief complete 10am.
	2.45pm	**Evening Tactical Report** Front line trenches shelled at intervals by whiz-bangs & light HE. Four of the former were fired during relief at trench 87, no damage done. Trenches 84 & 86 were shelled at 11.30am, the former apparently from a Batty behind FRICOURT & the latter from a Batty N of FRICOURT. Our Artillery retaliated. Wind WNW light. We relieved 12th Middx at 10am.
15-11-15	1.50am	At 8.30pm last night two coloured lights one red and one green were observed behind German trenches & fired in a backward direction. Night exceptionally quiet. Patrols sent out, but nothing to report.
	3.15pm	**Evening Tactical Report** During night patrols were out but had nothing to report. Intermittent M Gun fire from direction of TAMBOUR over trench 87. Enemy working party reported at 2.30am at F3B45. Our artillery fired four shrapnel with good effect. At 2.25am one red flare was sent up by enemy opposite 87 trench nothing happened however. M Gun observed firing from F3C7827
16-11-15		**Morning Tactical Report** Afternoon of 15th quiet except for intermittent firing by our Artillery over TAMBOUR and BOIS FRANCAIS. At 8.20pm a trench mortar was active firing from about F9B9005. A true bearing of 90 degrees from the top of 85 Street. The direction could be ascertained accurately as the mortar assembled [sic – resembled?] a rocket in its flight

and left a trace of light behind it but the distance from which it was sent up was hard to gauge. At 8.35pm our 18pdrs replied with two salvos 21 rounds being fired in all. the shells fell 100 to 150 yds too far. Two blind mortars were sent up by the enemy. Considerable amount of enemy M.G. & rifle fire during early part of night. This quietened down & has remained quiet since. Weather dead calm cold and frosty. Standing patrols sent out at 10pm

| | 3.5pm | Evening Tactical Report |

The early hours of the morning were very quiet with very little rifle fire. An enemy working party was seen at F9B6015, which was shelled with two rounds bursting about F9B6530. No earth was thrown up however after this. At 9am enemy fired 8 whiz-bangs on RAILWAY AVENUE. A considerable amount of long range firing by our heavies took place during the morning. Wind N during early morning, now dead calm

| 17-11-15 | 2.15am | Morning Tactical Report |

At 4pm a thick mist came up obscuring enemy lines. The night has been exceptionally calm. At 8.10pm a Verbal message from Northants to "Stand to" was passed down the line. At 8.30pm "Stand down" was ordered. Advantage was taken of the mist to thoroughly examine our wire which is none too good and requires some attention. Wind dead calm.

| | 2.45pm | Evening Tactical Report |

Enemy were very quiet during the night & early hours of the morning except for isolated rifle shots directed at certain fixed spots, which were probably fired from fixed rifles. During the morning there has been practically no firing at all. Patrols had been arranged for midnight onwards but owing to the exceeding Bright Night these were cancelled except opposite 84 trench which went out at 3am & returned at 4am with a Nil report. Wind light westerly breeze

| 18-11-15 | 2.5am | Morning Tactical Report |

At 3.30pm yesterday afternoon 3 heavy trench mortars fell over trench 84 two bursting high in the air. This mortar was firing from the same spot as previously reported 90 degrees true bearing from top of 85 Street. At 5.30pm our 6 inch howitzers sent over 4 well directed shots after which mortar was quiet. At 6pm an enemy mine was blown up opposite 83 trench followed by a few rifle grenades & rifle shots. A working party seen at F3C8005 was fired at by our M.G. at 12.45 am. The night has been very quiet, there being no rifle fire, which seems to indicate a relief having taken place. Owing to exceeding bright night no patrols sent out. Wind dead calm.

| | 2.25pm | Evening Tactical Report |

Enemy working party reported at F3C7327 at 5.30am we fired two belts from M.Gun. Enemy sent over two pip-squeaks at 2am. Night & morning particularly quiet

19-11-15		probably due to heavy mist. Motor M.Gun has taken up position & is carrying on intermittent fire. Wind dead calm
		Morning Tactical Report
		Enemy have been remarkably quiet during night hardly a rifle shot being fired and no flares being sent up. Standing patrols are out as this inactivity may mean the enemy have patrols out. There is a certain amount of rifle fire to the N of Fricourt but none to the south which seems to indicate that these two parts are held by different Bns. At 6.15pm our M.G. from left of 86 trench traversed enemy lines drawing fire from a German M.G. about F9B5526. Motor M.G. has been active at intervals. Enemy fired a whiz-bang at it about 11pm. Patrols so far have nothing to report except that ground in front of trench 91 is full of shell holes affording possible cover for patrols. Wind light east breeze.
	2.45pm	Evening Tactical Report
		Night very quiet until about 4am, when a few flares were sent up. Two whiz bangs were fired from enemy battery SE of FRICOURT on our left. At 8.30am a working party at F9B5828 was seen and fired at by snipers and MG. About 11am our light guns shelled the aeroplane trench several shells falling right into it. This brought a reply from the enemy who put 10 shells over 83 & 84 trenches but little damage was done. These appeared to come from two batteries one near MAMETZ and one near BOIS RONDE. Wind ENE. Capt & Adj.P.R.Meautys, Capt.E.Clegg, Capt.H.Ramsbotham returned from leave
20-11-15	2.15am	Morning Tactical Report
		Enemy fired light HE at our trenches 83 & 84 yesterday about 4.30pm, but did little damage. This was in retaliation for our artillery practice. During the night there has been very little rifle fire by the enemy but a considerable amount of M.G. activity firing from F9B5028 with another from the TAMBOUR region. Wind light easterly breeze
	2.35pm	Artillery test last night on 93 trench took 7 minutes. At 10.45am enemy sent 2 rifle grenades over trench 94. Much artillery activity this morning on both sides. Our artillery shelled FRICOURT and F4A51. Two enemy machine guns were seen firing from F9B5820 and F3C3022 last night. Wind SSE
21-11-15	2.30am	Morning Tactical Report
		Between 4pm & 4.30pm enemy sent over some heavy trench mortar shells in trench 83. Our guns replied at once. At 6.30pm enemy sent over 4 shells two of which fell short and the other falling at F9C68. Transport heard in Fricourt at 5.35pm. Wind light NE
	2.30pm	Considerable artillery activity on both sides this morning. Our guns fired on FRICOURT F3C73 and F9b6015. the enemy replied with several whiz-bangs. A German sniper was observed to run from F3C7548. Arrangements are now being made to fire on this with artillery and machine guns

Méaulte
22-11-15	6.30–7.30am	Running Drill. Weather misty
	7am	N.C.O.s parade under Regimental Sergt.Major
	12 noon	Inspection of comforts & kit by General Officer Commanding Division with Colonel G.D.Price & Major Mills – also O.C. 10th Corps, Gen.Morland
23-11-15	9.30am–1pm	Bomb Throwing Drill carried out with live & dummy bombs. All men available paraded Afternoon – 2 Platoons B Coy. practised Bomb Attack on Morlancourt Rd. 2 Platoons Musketry.
24-11-15	6.30–7.30am	Running Drill – Weather Fair
	7am	N.C.O.s parade under Regt.Sergt.Major
	9.30am–1pm	Bombing carried out as on 23.11.15 Afternoon 2 Platoons C Company practised Bomb attack on Morlancourt Rd 2 Platoons – Musketry
25-11-15	6.30–7.30am	Running Drill. Weather Fine & Dry
	7am	N.C.Os parade under R.S.Major
	9.30am–1pm	Bombing as yesterday
	2–4pm	2 Platoons B Coy. carried out Bomb attack on Morlancourt Rd.
26-11-15		Day Quiet. Nothing to report. Parades as usual
27-11-15		Day Quiet. Nothing to report. Parades as usual
28-11-15		Day Quiet. Nothing to report. Weather turned suddenly cold.
29-11-15		Day Quiet. Nothing to report. Weather Rained all day
30-11-15		Relieved 6th Northants in D/1 via 107 as Maidstone Ave & South Avenue fallen in. Relief took all day

Trenches D1
1-12-15		Nothing to report. Night extremely quiet. Wind SW.
2-12-15		We exploded a mine at C2 at 3.15 effect not yet known. At 8pm enemy exploded a mine in C/2 27 Norfolks reported buried in a sap. Between 7 and 9.45 enemy fired whiz-bangs which fell in the rear of Rue Albert. Our guns replied. Artillery test on Trench 82 took 1 minute and very little rifle fire. A Bomb exploded in front of 77 trench F – at 8.45pm. Our Artillery retaliated on enemies' lines. The mine at 8pm was followed by Trench Mortars to which our guns replied. Wind SE
	2.15pm	E.T.R. Enemy fired 6 Rifle grenades from F.10.C3565. We replied with rifle grenades. At 12 noon enemy shelled Rue Albert with whiz-bangs, we retaliated with 2 rounds of Battery fire after which active hostilities ceased. Water seen thrown out of trenches at F10.C55 and fresh chalk thrown up at F10C3066. Signalling in Morse was reported from direction of Bray and answered from high ground E of Fricourt. Weather Wet.

3-12-15	2am	M.T.R. Between 7 & 9pm enemy sent over several whiz-bangs which fell behind H.Q. our guns retaliated on Bois Allemand each time. A machine gun was observed to fire from F9D8570. It is noticed that enemy's flares are almost all sent up from 2nd line. Motor heard at work opposite 76 trench possibly a pump. Night very wet and trenches falling in. Every effort is being made to clean them. Wind S-SW. Mine expected to go off opposite 82 trench.
	1.30pm	E.T.R. Enemy working party dispersed with bombs from catapults opposite trench 82 early this morning. We accounted for one of the enemy at F9D85.75 he was shot by our sentry. This was confirmed by other sentries. Artillery test on trench 82 took 1 minute. Enemy bombed trench 77 at 2.15pm. We replied with artillery fire and trench mortars.
	12.1pm	General Maxse inspected D/1 Sector with Adjutant. favourable report on appearance of men.
4-12-15	2am	M.T.R. Enemy fired several rifle grenades into trench 78 during afternoon causing 4 casualties. Artillery 18 pounders retaliated. About 3.30pm enemy working party reported opposite trench 82 who were immediately bombed with catapults. Whistles were heard which would indicate casualties on their side. About 5pm enemy fired a small camouflet opposite trench 80 F9D75.70 doing no damage to our trenches. No enemy activity during night. Wind Fresh NW. Weather misty & wet.
3-12-15	6.30 to 6.40pm	Enemy played along parapets with machine gun
	6.30–9pm	Enemy sent over on R.3 some 10 to 12 whiz-bangs at least 8 of which failed to explode
4-12-15	2.20pm	E.T.R. Increased activity in enemy's snipers. 1 man of ours killed at 8.30am. Enemy sniper located at F9D75.72. We bombed this spot & enemy retaliated with whiz-bangs. A mine exploded at 12 noon apparently on our right. Wind S.W. Weather Wet & changeable.
5-12-15	2am	M.T.R. Afternoon & night very quiet with exception of desultory whiz-bangs fired most of which failed to explode. Our artillery retaliated on each occasion. Particularly no rifle fire. Wind SW. Dull & Wet. E.T.R. Enemy sent over several rifle grenades this morning. We retaliated with trench mortars, catapults and artillery. Quiet since 12.30 noon. Wind slight S.W.
6-12-15	2am	M.T.R. At 3pm artillery was tested with rockets at the same time the forward trench joined in the aggression & sent over 12 bombs from the West Gun and 6 rifle grenades. A direct hit was scored with the West Gun on an enemy sniper post at F10C06. Result not known. Between 7 & 9pm enemy sent over a few whiz-bangs which were all duds & fell behind our trenches. We retaliated shot for shot. Enemy machine gun twice traversed our trenches tonight.

	2pm	Enemy rifle fire rather more active. An attack was organized on the enemies' sap where smoke was seen yesterday, this attack is now in progress and a detailed report will be sent later. Wind S.W. Weather Rough & Wet. E.T.R. At 11am enemy bombed 78 trench. Our artillery replied. Otherwise quiet
7-12-15	2.5am	M.T.R. At 3.30pm we bombed the enemy's lines at F10C73 with trench mortars. Officer reported seeing two wheels fly into air. At 4pm our guns fired on enemy machine gun emplacement at same spot. Enemy gun has not fired from there tonight. A patrol tonight carried out a long reconnaissance of ground at F10 C55-45. Detailed account to follow. Sample of enemy wire brought in. Enemy reported to be using a fixed rifle at F10C46. Otherwise quiet. Wind W, fair to wet. E.T.R. Nothing to report – Line quiet. Wind S.W. One casualty through man meddling with detonator
8-12-15	2am	M.T.R. Between 2.30 & 3pm yesterday the Trench Mortar Battery fired 5 rounds at enemy trenches about F10D19. The mortars were well placed & threw up a lot of black earth. At the same time we fired 2 new converted Mills Rifle Grenades one of which failed to explode. the other fell among enemy wire about F10C76. There has been practically no rifle or M.G. fire though earlier in the evening a machine gun from the Tambour fired a little, the bullets passing well above our heads to next Sector. Our 6 inch guns retaliated with 6 shells which fell just behind F10C25.65. Between 9.30 & 10pm about 15 whiz-bangs were sent over by the enemy apparently from opposite 81.82 trenches. No damage was done. Wind strong WSW. Dull & wet.
	2.30pm	German M.G. fired from F10C60.52 at 4.30am. Enemy shelled Rue Albert at 10.30am. We retaliated with trench mortars. Wind N.W. Fair to dull. Mine (ours) to go up at 4.45pm.
	3.30pm	Relieved by 12th Middlesex

Méaulte
9-12-15	Companies bathed. Weather Wet. Nothing to report
10-12-15	Conference for Staff Capts & Adjutants at Bde Recreation Room. Weather Dull. Nothing to report
11-12-15	Nothing to report. Wind E. Day fair. Parades as per Programme of Work. General Hinckey C.O. 54th Bde. wounded with shrapnel in the leg
12-12-15	Nothing to report. Wind S.E. Day Dry & Cold. Parades as per Programme of Work
13-12-15	Nothing to report. Wind N.E. Day Dry & Cold. Parades as per Programme of Work
14-12-15	Nothing to report. Wind N.E. to E. Day Frosty & Cold. Parades as per Programme of Work. Lt.Col.Shoubridge took command of 54th Bde.

15-12-15	Morning	Brigade scheme carried out on Morlancourt Road. Weather Fair
	Afternoon	Bombing parades etc. as per Programme of work.

Trenches D/1

16-12-15	3pm	Relieved 12th Middlesex. Nothing to report. Weather fair.
17-12-15	2am	M.T.R. Enemy active with rifle grenades against 77 & 78 trenches at 8pm. They were silenced by our guns. Line otherwise very quiet. Occasional enemy flares sent up from their 2nd line. Enemy machine gun from F9B71 fired on 83 trench at 10.30pm. Wind S.E.
		E.T.R. Enemy very active all day along the sector. The enemy carried out a bombardment of considerable intensity using canisters, trench mortars, sausages & whizbangs. We retaliated with West Guns, trench mortars, howitzers, field batteries & siege guns. The enemy were silenced at 1pm after several casualties to us. The enemy fired a considerable number of rifle grenades to which we replied with 15 bombs from the West Gun. Wind S.S.E. Weather fair to wet. 1st Cheshires on Right Flank, 11th R.Fusiliers on Left Flank, 12th Middx in reserve at Méaulte
18-12-15	2am	M.T.R. At 7.35 pm enemy again started bombarding us with sausages but were silenced by the heavy battery and howitzers. Enemy keep sending over rifle grenades to which we reply with West Guns. Machine Guns have been laid over gaps in the enemy's parapets caused by our shells. Wind S. Weather – Fair
	2pm	E.T.R. Enemy very quiet all this morning. We sent over a few rifle grenades but they were not replied to. A machine gun was in position all last night to cover the gaps in the enemy's parapets which had been made by our guns yesterday. Wind S.
19-12-15	2am	M.T.R. Between 3 & 4 o'clock the enemy started sending over rifle grenades, sausages, bombs & whiz-bangs. Five rifle grenades fell in rear of 78 trench and failed to explode. We retaliated with bombs from West Gun firing at enemy front line trench about F10C65 one or two trench mortars and a few shells when all was quiet again. Sausages fell in rear of Rue Albert behind trench 83 knocking in entrance to L/3 mine shaft, killing one man and wounding another. Position from which sausages were fired approx F9B1065. The siege battery traversed this trench effectively and silenced the enemy trench mortar. At 6.10pm sounds of hammering were heard as proceeding from about F10C75. A salvo from our artillery was fired and appeared to take effect. Simultaneously one M.G. fired and work ceased until 8.15pm when our M.G. again silenced them. At 8pm sentry reported wire being thrown out in front of enemy trench F9D89. Our artillery sent over two salvos of shrapnel & work was stopped. Several whiz-bangs were fired from the enemy lines up to about 10pm but no

	1.30pm	damage done. Wind fresh N.E. – Fair 1st Norfolks relieved 1st Cheshires in Sector C/11 on our right flank during night. E.T.R. Enemy sent over about 20 small mortars at intervals along our line this morning. This was probably in retaliation to wire-cutting which our guns were carrying out opposite trench 94. At 1pm enemy sent over about 12 small whiz-bangs. We replied with rifle grenades and West Guns. Enemy now quiet. Wind N.E.
20-12-15	2am	M.T.R. Enemy fired 15 to 20 rifle grenades at our West Gun position. We replied with 18 bombs from West Gun and catapult. Sentry in 76 trench reported screams heard after one of our shots at F10C36. Several small trench mortars fired by enemy in pairs from close behind their first line. Night very quiet and no artillery activity. Wind fresh N.E. till 9pm since when calm. Weather – fair & dry E.T.R. At 7am we bombed enemy's trench with West Guns. They replied with rifle grenades. German working party heard in trench at F10C26 were bombed by us. They retaliated with small mortars. Our artillery were active on Bois Allemand during the morning. Wind N.N.W. General Jackson, 55th Bde. visited D/1 and vicinity this morning
21-12-15		M.T.R. About 4.30pm enemy fired 12 rifle grenades. We retaliated with artillery. No damage done. At 7pm working party seen at F10C4560. M.G. fired one drum at them and then again at intervals but party did not appear again. Everything very quiet with little rifle fire. Wind light N.N.E. E.T.R. Enemy very quiet. Two mines exploded believed away on our right at 8.10am and 8.30am. At a practice alarm 12 minutes was taken for all support bombs etc. to be got in position. This included the platoons coming from R/3. Wind S.E. Weather wet & misty.
22-12-15		M.T.R. Night very quiet on the whole. Very little rifle fire. At 9.50pm enemy dropped 2 heavy shells on our trenches our guns retaliated. Enemy machine gun traversed our lines at 10pm position not yet located. Enemy shelled C/2 at 11.30 to which our guns retaliated. Wind N-W.
	2pm	E.T.R. Enemy quiet in D/1. Nothing to report in that Sector. A lively artillery duel has been taking place all morning. D/2 was shelled heavily. W: W.S.W. Fair to rain. 2 2/Lts joined from Base. H.Cathcart-Nicholls & F.E.Dealler
23-12-15	2am	M.T.R. At 2.15pm the enemy commenced a lively bombardment of our left sub-sector. They sent over several sausages and altogether about 60 shells of different calibre. We retaliated with our guns sending over 80 rounds including several heavy shells and some from our howitzers where upon the enemy ceased all offensive. No damage was done by the enemy. Mine explosions were felt at 6.10 & 9.30pm. Vicinity of these not yet located. At 8.30pm

		German heavy battery from Mametz fired 2 rounds. Wind W.
	2pm	E.T.R. Artillery activity on both sides during the morning. Our Machine guns fired at F10C50.45 and F10.C46 during the night. Germans have pushed over a lot more wire from their parapets at F10.C50.45. Morning otherwise quiet. Fair to Fine. 16th Royal Warwicks relieved 1st Norfolks on our right flank Sector C/2. Conference of C.O.s & Adjutants at Bde.H.Q. 3.30pm.
24-12-15		M.T.R. During yesterday afternoon we shot two men at approx F9D99 this making five men shot at that point. The work being carried on there appears to be important. At 2.15pm we fired 3 of the new Ball Bombs from West Gun to which enemy replied with rifle grenades. German heavy Arty Battery from S.E. of MAMETZ fired seven rounds about 2pm falling behind C.2. Our 18pdrs & 119th Hy Batty both registered during afternoon. Night very quiet. Wind strong S.W.
	2pm	E.T.R. A certain amount of artillery activity otherwise morning quite quiet. 8 Germans seen at 1.30pm crossing the gap in front of quarry in full marching order. It might mean a relief is taking place

Méaulte

	3.30pm	Relieved by 12th Middlesex Regt.
25-12-15		Football Tournament
	4.30pm	Christmas Dinner
26-12-15		Battalion bathing. Weather Fair
27-12-15		Early Morning: Running Parade. Morning: Musketry. Afternoon: Bombing
28-12-15		New Draft joins 7th Bedfords
29-12-15	5.0pm	Heavy bombardment of D2. Coys stood to.
30-12-15		Attack scheme at MORLANCOURT. Weather Fair
31-12-15		E.T.R. Relief still in progress. All quiet, nothing to report. Wind S.E.
	2pm	Relieved by 12th Middlesex

1916

This year saw the first blooding of Kitchener's Army on the Somme. This terrible battle lasted from 1 July to 18 November and was a result of the equally terrible Battle of Verdun. Verdun was a massive attack by the Germans and a blatant attempt by the German Commander-in-Chief, Erich von Falkenhayn, to "bleed France white". It began on 21 February and lasted until 16 December and eventual casualties amounted to about 400,000 French and 340,000 Germans. It was thus almost as much of a disaster for Germany as for France, leading to Falkenhayn's dismissal

The British offensive on the Somme was designed to take the pressure off the embattled French armies and came about largely due to the pleading of the French Commander-in-Chief, General Joseph Joffre. It is often forgotten that the French played a major part in the Somme offensive too, suffering some 200,000 casualties.

The thing that is chiefly remembered about the Somme is, of course, the dreadful First Day, 1 July, when the British army lost more casualties than ever before, or since, in a single 24-hour period. Some 57,470 men became casualties on that beautiful summer's day, of whom 19,240 were killed or later died of their wounds. It is interesting to note that the 18th Division, of which the 7th Bedfords formed a part, and the 30th Division on its right, were the two most successful British Divisions on that day, taking all their objectives. Many Divisions made absolutely no advance at all, being forced back to their starting points by overwhelming German artillery fire and counter-attacks.

Why was the 18th Division so successful compared to its fellows? There are probably four reasons.

1. They and the 30th Division both benefited from French artillery fire on their right which was more effective in suppressing the German artillery than was its British counterpart.
2. The 18th Division had been superbly trained. Its Commanding Officer, Sir Ivor Maxse, was a rigorous and innovative trainer, a fact recognised when he was sent back to England to devise and preside over new training methods for new recruits. The training carried out by the 7th Bedfords near Picquigny is highlighted by Colonel Price, in his report after the battle, as an important contribution to their success. The training ground had been chosen as it closely resembled the terrain over which the attack of 1 July would take place and, as Lieutenant Cartwright notes in his diary, had been laid out with representations of all British and German trenches.
3. Hand in hand with good training went the sensible tactics employed by the 18th Division. It is well known that on the First Day of the Somme, the British infantry got up out of their trenches, when the bombardment ended, and advanced at a slow walk, encumbered by 60lb packs, in many waves which were mown down by German machine guns. This was so in some areas, but not in the case of the 18th Division. Reading the War Diary and Colonel Price's report makes this clear. The Bedfords were already out of their trenches as the bombardment was coming to an end, so that they could get across No Man's Land

(comparatively wide at this point) more quickly. B Company left the trenches two minutes before the bombardment ceased and C Company must also have left their trench early as they are noted as crossing their wire as the bombardment ended. Colonel Price's report also notes that B Company, at least, doubled down the slope, that is, they moved much more quickly than at a slow walk. The Operation Orders for the coming battle also make it clear that the 7th Bedfords, at least, were not weighed down by the 60lb packs, as the following section, the list of things to be carried by each man, makes very clear: "Rifle and equipment *less pack*; 1 Bandolier in addition to his equipment ammunition (170 rounds in all); 1 days ration and 1 iron ration; 1 waterproof sheet; 2 sandbags [these would be empty]; 1 yellow patch on haversack on his back; 2 Smoke Helmets".

4. The ground was somewhat easier in this sector than in some others, which included, for instance, the steep slopes up to Thiepval, or being surrounded by the enemy on three sides, as in the attack on Ovillers-La Boiselle. The Division was also attacking to its front rather than at an oblique angle as parts of the 7th Division were in their attack on Fricourt, for example, which laid that division open to enfilading machine gun fire.

In many ways the Battle of the Somme should be regarded as a campaign with numbers of smaller battles within it. It is true that there was fighting on most days but there were certain days on which major pushes occurred. The 7th Bedfords took part in two of these pushes, the First Day, and the attack on Thiepval and the Schwaben Redoubt on 26–29 September. It is worth noting the other main phases of the Battle of the Somme:

- 7–11 July: attacks on Mametz Wood;
- 8–14 July: attacks on Trones Wood, eventually captured by the 18th Division, specifically the 12th Middlesex, the 6th Northants and the 7th Royal West Kents;
- 14–17 July: the Battle of the Bazentin Ridge;
- 15 July – 3 September: the attacks on Delville;
- 20–30 July: attacks on High Wood;
- 23 July – 3 September: the Battle of Pozieres Ridge;
- 6 August – 3 September: fighting for Mouquet Farm;
- 3–6 September: the Battle of Guillemont;
- 9 September: the Battle of Ginchy;
- 15–22 September: the Battle of Flers-Courcelette, on the first day of which tanks were first used and helped in the capture of Flers;
- 25–28 September: the Battle of Morval;
- 25–29 September: the Battle of Thiepval Ridge;
- 1–18 October: the Battle of Transloy Ridge;
- 1 October – 11 November: the Battle of Ancre Heights;
- 7 October – 5 November: attacks on the Butte de Warlencourt, which marked the limit of the advance, the Butte itself (an ancient burial mound) not being taken.

By the end of the Battle (or battles) of the Somme, Britain and its Dominions of Canada, Australia, New Zealand and South Africa had suffered 419,654 casualties. German casualties are estimated at anything between 437,000 and 680,000. This makes the important point that there were no real winners of the Battle of the Somme, the Germans losing about as many men as the British and French combined. In a very real sense all the nations taking part were losers, losers of vast numbers of lives thrown away for a small corner of France about twenty miles wide and six miles deep.

Trenches D1

1-1-16	2.0am	M.T.R. Patrols have been out all night between the gaps on our front but nothing unusual is reported. A German working party at F10C7555 appeared but being fired on at once by our machine guns dispersed immediately. A bombing party has been all night at the far end of sap in 83 trench. This sap is being deepened, already 16 yds have been accomplished. Six reels of barbed wire have been put out opposite 83 trench. Enemy quiet in our sector but at 11.30 and onwards during the last ½ hour of the old year, kept up Machine Gun and Artillery fire on Sector D2. Our guns retaliated. Enemy are being kept under very close supervision by patrols.
1-1-16	2.0pm	E.T.R. Very quiet day. Our artillery fired a few registering shots. Enemy working party seen at F1D55, Artillery informed & point registered, if see again will be fired at. Wind S.S.W.
2-1-16	2.0am	M.T.R. Night very quiet. Advanced standing patrols, report work being carried on in enemy's lines at about F9D7880 and the German trench running from AEROPLANE trench to WHITE crater was held by about one man every 4 or 5 yards. About 5 yards of sap in 83 has been completed. 42 feet of wire has been put up in MATTERHORN gap. A continuous line of wire has now been erected opposite 83 trench but this will be still further strengthened. Wind W-W.S.W. Battalion on our left 11th Bn Royal Fus.
	2.0pm	A working party was shelled in CANTERBURY AVENUE at 11.30 A.M. Our guns retaliated and enemy ceased fire. Morning very quiet. Trenches very wet again after rain. Wind W.
3-1-16	2.0am	M.T.R. Enemy sent up flares on left subsector and rifle fire in this quarter more frequent. A patrol went out to investigate Sunken Rd. A specimen of wire opposite German trenches in front of 83 trench is sent for inspection. This patrol was one of numerous ones sent out and was led by an officer 2/Lt Rawes in order to give men confidence. Its object was to examine enemies' wire and to instruct and train new patrol leaders. Night otherwise very quiet. Wind S.W. Work has been continued on sap in 83 trench and 30ft of wire has been put up opposite 79 trench. Our patrols again active in crater gaps, battalion on our right 1st Cheshires

	2.0pm	E.T.R. Our guns registered sap head at F10D0506 on C2. Four grenades were sent over 77 trench we replied with West Guns and T.Mortars. Enemy fired a few small shells into 83 trench at 11.45 A.M. Our howitzers replied on the Aeroplane trench. Wind W. strong
4-1-16	2.0am	M.T.R. This afternoon enemy shelled RUE ALBERT with small H.E. and a T.M. fell behind 75 trench. This was in retaliation to our guns which fired on F10C96 and Mametz. At 8 P.M. we sent over 4 T.M. shells and several bombs from West guns in reply to some bombs which enemy put into 78 trench. Our T.M. is now out of action having destroyed its own firing platform. Patrols have been continually sent out but report nothing up to present. Work has been carried on in sap at 83 trench. Communication with Batt on our left has been improved by digging a path parallel to existing impassable trench. 12 yds of wire completed opposite 83.
	2.0pm	E.T.R. Enemies' trench mortar emplacement located F3A7850. Enemy working party located opposite to Matterhorn and dispersed by our guns. Occasional Rifle grenades on Front trenches. Situation otherwise quiet. Wind S.W.
	12 noon	G.O.C. 18th Div. inspected section D/1.
5-1-16	2am	M.T.R. Patrol was sent out last night to investigate German sap by white crater. Specimen of wire and report of patrol following. Between 3 and 4pm enemy fired several whiz-bangs & rifle grenades. We replied with 10 rifle grenades and 12 T.M.Bombs on F10C6970 where wood was seen to fly in the air. All enemy activity then ceased. Enemy machine guns regulated by red and green rockets very active on our working parties. Wind S.S.W. strong.
	9-11am	Bombardment going on somewhere left of our lines – ALBERT way. Weather Fair to dry
	2pm	E.T.R. Much aeroplane activity this morning. Our guns registered on enemy trenches in front of 77 trench. Enemy noted signalling with flash lamps in trenches in front of Quarry F10C76. Enemy snipers more active firing at periscopes. Wind W.
6-1-16	2am	M.T.R. Enemy sent over 2 rifle grenades near Watling Street at 6.30pm and at midnight we replied with 4. Considerable more rifle fire than usual. Enemy busy trying to smash our periscopes. Enemy heavy howitzers search for our guns at 9.30pm. Night otherwise quiet. Wind W.
	2.15pm	E.T.R. At 8.15am enemy sent over numerous rifle grenades and trench mortars apparently aimed at L/18. Their grenades outnumbered ours so we retaliated with trench mortars. These did exceedingly good work. Timber was blown into the air from enemy lines opposite to the Fort. We must have inflicted serious damage on enemy. All active hostilities ceased on their part after our mortars had fired. Wind W. Weather Fair

7-1-16	1.45am	M.T.R. At 4.30pm enemy fired 8 H.E. shells in rear of the Bn HQrs but did no damage. Rifle fire more frequent especially opposite trench 83 where enemy very persistently hitting our parapet. At 10.30pm enemy started to send over bombs and rifle grenades but upon our replying with 2 trench mortars they at once ceased. Every endeavour is being made to reclaim Matterhorn trench. Wind W. 16th R.Warwicks on our right flank C/2 Sector.
	2.30pm	E.T.R. Enemy fired a few shells at our working parties in Rue Albert and one or two rifle grenades but morning otherwise very quiet. Wind W. weather Fair to rain & mist
8-1-16		Morning Tactical Report. At 7.30am in response to our rifle grenades enemy shelled Bn H.Q. and Watling Street quite heavily for about 10 minutes. They were silenced by our Guns and trench Mortars. Several of enemy's shells fell also either side of Old Kent Road and between Maple Redoubt and 71 South. More flares were sent up by enemy last night but less firing. Wind L[ight?] N.W.
		Evening Tactical. German working party observed at F10C2062 about 10am. dispersed by our Guns. German working at F.10.C.45-61 fired at by one of our patrols and was sent [seen?] to fall. Corroborated by 2 N.C.O.'s who were observing at the time. Wind – W.N.W. Relieved by 12th Middx midday. Good weather 16th Warwicks on Right, 11th R.FUS. on Left.

Méaulte

9-1-16		Nothing to report. Good weather
10-1-16		Nothing to report. Weather Fair. Some Sun.
11-1-16		The Commander-in-Chief was in neighbourhood but did not pay us a visit
12-1-16		Nothing to report. Weather dull
13-1-16		8 shells fell in fields behind Hd.Qrs. near a bombing party & a football match. No damage.
14-1-16		Nothing to report. Instruction in Wire erecting by R.E.
15-1-16		Nothing to report. Instruction in Wire erecting by R.E.
16-1-16		Relief of 12th Middx in D/1. Good weather. Enemy shelled the hill after all our men were over. Wind S.S.E. 16th Warwicks on right flank, 6th Northants on left

D/1 Trenches

17-1-16	2am	<u>Morning Tactical Report</u> From 3.30pm–4.30pm enemy fired several whiz bangs on to our left subsectors. At 6.15pm our machine guns dispersed enemy working party opposite to the Fort. At 9pm enemy sent over sausages and canisters all of which hit the roof of a dug out and severely bruised six men. We retaliated with trench mortars and enemy are now quiet
	2pm	<u>Evening Tactical Report</u> Smoke seen issuing from dugouts opposite Matterhorn Gap. Morning quiet. Our Artillery Registering. Wind

		S.E.–E. Some excitement prevails in well-informed circles on account of a sham attack and heavy straffing which we intend administering tonight. Reports will appear later
18-1-16	2am	M.T.R. Detailed reports on mine operations were despatched to you at 9.30pm. Night quiet except for occasional trench mortar from enemy. After mine explosion enemy traversed our line with trench mortars doing a good deal of damage in places. This is being repaired. Wind S.E.
	2pm	E.T.R. Work is being carried out on sap round edge of new crater. Situation quiet. Wind S.
19-1-16	2am	M.T.R. Full report of mine explosion forwarded at 6.15pm. The explosion appears to have been a double one. Enemy kept up persistent bombardment with trench mortars and rifle grenades until 11pm when they were silenced by our trench mortars and guns. Total casualty from Gas 13, 2 of whom have died. Gas casualties were greatly reduced by coolness of Cpl.Blanshard & Cpl.Ivory who entered mine shaft & removed all gassed men. Work is being carried on cleaning damaged trenches. Wind S.S.W.
	2pm	E.T.R. Morning quiet until 12 noon when our 4.5 guns commenced firing on German trench mortar positions about F10.C65.60 and enemy replied with trench mortars on 79 trench. Work is being continued on clearing front trench round Matterhorn. Wind S.S.W. slight
20-1-16	2.25am	M.T.R. At 2.45pm this afternoon Germans sent over whiz-bangs in rear of trench 84 which was followed by 10 more. No damage done. Mine felt about 9pm apparently in Tambour. Germans also fired 8 salvos from light field pieces at R.Sussex Pioneers working in Rue Albert some of which fell near Park Lane. Our 18 pounders replied and the enemy ceased fire. Enemy trench mortar fairly active between hours of 5pm and 11pm. Our trench mortars replied in every case. Saps are being pushed out in new crater and wire put out in front. Wind S.W.
	4.5pm	E.T.R. Situation abnormally quiet until 9.30am when Germans sent over some rifle grenades into right sector. During the morning mud was observed being thrown out of trench 81 the snipers were informed and were able to stop the enemy working. In right sector a German working party was observed throwing up earth at F10C42.6 at about 8.30am. The F.O.O. turned the 18 pounders on and work ceased. At 11am several Germans were seen looking over their trench at F10C45.60. None of them wore hats and they continued to observe for some time. The T.M.Officer was informed and two footballs were sent over which fell near the spot. Our machine gun fired 500 rounds into the German wire which had been put out round new crater in Fort gap. The wire was considerably damaged and the enemy were not able to continue their wiring. Wind S.W.
21-1-16	4.15am	M.T.R. Enemy very quiet up to 10.30pm when several rifle

THE WAR DIARY 1916   35

		grenades were fired into 84 trench from the Aeroplane all falling short. We replied with our Ribemont grenades from battery. At 8.40pm a sentry reported 3 Germans at about F10.C65.50. Bombs were thrown at them and they disappeared. Movements were observed on further edge of crater opposite 82. We fired 2 Mills rifle grenades which had the desired effect. Canister fired from F10C70.65 at 10.35 which landed behind Fort – a dead Wind S.W.
	4.15pm	E.T.R. Enemy very quiet except for a few rifle grenades over 79 & 82 trenches this morning. We retaliated with our Ribemont batteries & the enemy ceased. Wind S.S.W.
22-1-16	4.10am	M.T.R. Between 5 & 7pm enemy fairly active with their trench mortars, one landing in a small dug out in 77 trench containing 4 persons. 1 N.C.O. & 1 Man killed. Mine blown by us at 10pm. A special report has been sent in. Enemy very quiet in left subsector subsequently evidently mending his own parapet. At 12.35am a patrol of 3 Germans was seen in lip of new German crater. Three shots were fired and one of them was hit. Wind S.S.W.
	4.15pm	E.T.R. There was some artillery activity during the morning our 18 pounders shelling Aeroplane trench & fire trench east of it. The Germans replied vigorously on Rue Albert, 83 communication trenches and Canterbury Avenue. they were also shelling a few men who were wiring in front of gun positions. Possibly they suspected a relief. Wind W.
23-1-16	4.15am	M.T.R. Enemy very quiet up to 5pm yesterday afternoon the time we exploded the mine. It was entirely successful and filled in greater part of Quarry Gap the new crater extending to within 5 yards of Round Pond on right and about 5 yds of Fort crater on left being about 30yds from our front line at nearest point. This information was brought in by 2nd Lt.G.H.A.Hughes with patrol. This patrol and also a party sent out from Quarry were fired on from further side of Round Pond. Two saps are being dug to new crater one from left of Quarry and the other from right of Fort.
	4.15pm	E.T.R. Morning very quiet until 9.30am when enemy sent over a few rifle grenades in the Rue Albert. Our rifle grenade battery silenced enemy. One German was shot by a sentry post opposite Fort. Heavy bombardment heard this morning further south. Wind S.S.W.
24-1-16	4.15am	M.T.R. Enemy very quiet up to 5.15pm at about which time the T.M. in C/2 sent over 4 or 5 footballs. This brought retaliation on our sector behind 77 trench one falling right in fire trench & blocking it. Our T.M. then joined in and after sending a few more trench mortars and rifle grenades enemy sent over two 5.9" shrapnel shells aimed at our T.M. position. This finished the strafe and except for one more T.M. at 12.45 the rest of night has been quiet. Two bearings taken on German T.M. position shows it to be about

		F10.C90.65. They apparently have two machines, one laid on C/2 and the other on 77 trench. Examination of new crater in Quarry Gap shows it to be very deep with steep sides. Wind slight W. breeze.
	E.T.R.	Enemy very quiet and no activity on either side
	3pm	Relieved by 12th Middlesex
Méaulte		
25-1-16		Bathing carried out
26-1-16	10.30am	Enemy sent over one round battery fire at men playing football North Rd end. No damage done.
	3pm	Enemy sent two rounds battery fire over MÉAULTE one round of which were duds, otherwise day quiet. Parades carried out.
27-1-16	10.30am	Enemy sent over 6 shells which landed North Rd end of Village. No material damage.
	8pm	Notification received that 48th Division were being gassed. Stood-to with helmets ready. All clear by 8.33pm. Enemy sent another round battery fire at same place at about 10pm. Parades carried out.
28-1-16		Day quiet nothing to report. Bombardment heard on our right. Germans gain ground from French.
29-1-16		Day quiet until 2.30pm when Germans sent over 6 high explosives shrapnel which landed behind No.101 High St. injuring two Ptes in R.E. They repeated this again at 4.15pm since when all has been quiet, except for increased bombardment heard on our right
30-1-16		Day quiet. Nothing unusual to report. Weather misty
31-1-16		Day quiet until 5 pm when enemy gassed D/2 sector. Battalion move off, battle order, to sandpits on Le Carcaillot-Bray Road. After an exchange of artillery & machine gun fire during which period several enemy shells passed over Méaulte, everything quietened down and Battalion returned to billets at 7.15pm
1-2-16		Nothing to report. Day quiet
2-2-16		Nothing to report. Day quiet
3-2-16	11.30am	Enemy sent over 3 dud shells one of which slightly damaged a house near church
	2pm	March to La Houssoye according to attached table of moves [attached moves, section missing] ... soon as relief has been reported complete. After this 6th Northants and 1 Company 7th Bedfords at Bécordel will come under G.O.C. 20th Bde. The Coy 7th Bedfords at Bécordel will remain as Garrison until relieved by a Coy of 20th Bde. On 5th Feby, after which it will join its Bn at La Houssoye. O.C.Garrison will report when he has handed over and will not move until permission is obtained from 20th Bde HQrs. 1 Btn 20th Bde will be relieving the 7th Queens in D/3 on 5th Feby. This Btn will move by the Willow Ravine its transport by the Albert-Bellevue Farm Road. Completion of relief will be reported by both Btns to 54th Bde HQrs

	Méaulte. 54th Bde HQrs will close at Méaulte on completion of relief on 4th Feby. It will open for routine correspondence at the Shooting Lodge at 12 noon 4th.
6pm	Arrived La Houssoye

La Houssoye

4-2-16	Nothing to report. Day quiet
5-2-16	Nothing to report. Day quiet. Conference at Bde H.Qrs.
6-2-16	Nothing to report. Day quiet
7-2-16	Nothing to report. Day quiet
8-2-16	Nothing to report. Day quiet
9-2-16	Nothing to report. Day quiet
10-2-16	Nothing to report. Day quiet. Major Mills on leave. Capt.Meautys C.O.
11-2-16	Nothing to report. Day quiet
12-2-16	Nothing to report. Day quiet
13-2-16	Nothing to report. Day quiet. 2/Lts B.C.Foster & Ross Taylor arrived
14-2-16	Nothing to report. Day quiet
15-2-16	Information from Bde. That a German captured by the French stated that the Germans were attacking over D Sector on early morning of 15th but nothing happened
16-2-16	Nothing to Report. Very rough weather
17-2-16	Nothing to Report. Played Middlesex Rugger – Won
18-2-16	Nothing to Report. Lieut.E.W.Benson rejoined from Hospital
19-2-16	Rained all day. Zeppelin over Amiens with a bomb. Brigade visited Orderly Room
20-2-16	Fine Day. Played 12th Middlesex Soccer – Won
21-2-16	Rained all day. Conference for C.O.s & Adjutants at Bde.Hqrs
22-2-16	Nothing to Report. First night of Bde. Boxing Competition – New Bde Major arrived (Capt.R.Davidson)
23-2-16	New Staff Captain (Lt.Stutfield) arrived & Visited Orderly Room
24-2-16	Snowed very heavy. Accident at Bde. Bombing School Lt.Smith & 2nd Lt.I.H.M.Ross-Taylor injured
25-2-16	Snowed all day. Nothing to report
26-2-16	Beat Middlesex Soccer. Brigade Boxing Final
27-2-16	Nothing to Report
28-2-16	Nothing to Report
29-2-16	Move to Corbie ordered for 1.3.16. Vide 54th Brigade Operation Order attached. 18th Division transferred to 13th Corps.

Corbie

1-3-16	Arrival at Corbie. Conference for C.O. & Adjt. At 8pm at Bde.H.Q.
2-3-16	C.O. Adjt. & Coy Commanders visited trench which it is proposed we are taking over – A Sector
3-3-16	C.O. & Adjt. Conf. At Bde. 11am

4-3-16	9am	Fitting Clothing and Route Marches under company arrangements. Weather very cold and windy – frequent sleet & snow.
5-3-16	3.30pm	Marched from Corbie to BRAY-SUR-SOMME. G.O.C. 54th Brigade and G.O.C. 18th Div. Both inspected the battalion while on the march and expressed their approval of march discipline and general appearance of troops. March orders attached herewith [not attached].

Carnoy Trenches

6-3-16	2pm	Relieved 2nd Yorkshire Regt. in Sector A.2. Relief Completed 9.30pm. Relief Orders attached herewith [see Appendix A2.1]. 12th Middx on right 22nd Manchesters on left.
7-3-16		Night very quiet. Sharp Frost which made trenches very sticky. Work commenced on Dug out at H.Qrs. and cleaning of communication trenches. General Maxse visited the sector.
8-3-16	3.30am	<u>Morning Tactical Report</u> At 5.20pm enemy sent over some heavy shells towards BRAY and fired several rifle grenades, most of which fell short near 50 trench. Situation otherwise calm. Wind N.N.E. Br.Gen.Shoubridge visited sector 10am.
	3.15pm	<u>Evening Tactical Report</u> Enemy sent over one or two rifle grenades which fell short of 48 trench. We dispersed a working party by our Artillery Fire at A2D8152. At 2pm enemy whizzbanged Centre Coy. and Montauban Road but were silenced by our guns. Enemy aircraft was driven back over its own lines by one of our aeroplanes. Wind E.N.E. Situation quiet.
9-3-16		Day fine but dull and cold. C Coy. relieved B Coy. in centre subsector. 11th R.Fus. relieved 12th Middx on our right and 22nd Manchesters relieved 21st Manchesters on our left last night. G.O.C. 54th Brigade inspected our trenches with O.C. R.E. Enemy very quiet except for an occasional rifle Grenade into centre subsector
10-3-16		Day fine but dull. Considerable fall of snow which made trenches very muddy. Battn. conference over Defence scheme at H.Qrs. 2 pm. Enemy very quiet all day and night. Heavy bombardment has been going on tonight N. of Albert.
11-3-16		Day fine. Fus. relieved by 12 Middx in A.1. We relieved by 6 N.hants. Relief complete 10.45 pm. Operation Orders attached herewith [not attached].

Bray

12-3-16		Nothing to report. Fine Day.
13-3-16		Nothing to report. Fine day.
14-3-16		Day fine. Adjutant and Brigadier Visited trenches together. A Bosch aeroplane dropped 2 bombs at the end of Bray 9pm. 53rd Brigade moved into 30th Div.

15-3-16	Relieved 6th Northants in A2. Relief completed 10.40pm. Operation Orders attached [see Appendix A2.2]. Part of 53rd Brigade moves as per March Table.

Trenches A2

16-3-16	Sniping fairly vigorous on part of enemy. 1 Cpl. Sniped in B Coy (in Saps) otherwise enemy quiet. Fine, but dull day, slight rain about 4 pm. 55th Brigade move to Corbie. Vide March table.
17-3-16	Day fine. More than usual aerial and artillery activity.
18-3-16	Day fine & quiet. Nothing to report.
19-3-16	Bedfords relieved by 6th Northants. 12th Middx vacated Bronfay for A.1. & 7th Beds took over Bronfay. Relief complete at 10.5 pm.
23-3-16	Nothing to Report. G.O.C. Div. & Corps visited Bronfay & A2 Sector. Morning Wet.
24-3-16	Nothing to report.

A2 Sector

25-3-16	Relieved 6th Northants in A2 – relief completed 9.15 pm. 11th Fusiliers on right.
26-3-16	Quiet Day. Cold. No movement at all.
27-3-16	Relieved 6th Northants & went to Bray. Fusiliers relieved by 12th Middx.

Bray

28-3-16	Very quiet day. Much Finer. Fatigues & training carried on.
29-3-16	Attempted to Snow in morning, afternoon quiet. Nothing to report.
30-3-16	Nothing to report. Day Quiet
31-3-16	Nothing to report. Day Quiet & Fine.
1-4-16	Fine Day. Nothing to report.
2-4-16	Fine Day. Relieved 6th Northants in Sector A.2. Relief completed at 10.5p.m.

A.2.

3-4-16	Fine Day. Enemy quiet. 11th R.Fus. relieved last night from Bronfay & now in A.1.
4-4-16	Fine Day. Enemy quiet. Nothing to report.
5-4-16	Considerable enemy activity with Artillery during morning. Several rifle grenades landed right into our trenches.
6-4-16	Situation calm. Nothing to report.
7-4-16	Concerted Straff on craters with 2″ T.M., Stokes Gun, 18 pdrs & Hows. Considerable damage done. Enemy reply very feeble.
8-4-16	Relieved by 6th Northants. Went to Bronfay Farm. Relief complete 9.30 p.m.

Bronfay

9-4-16	Nothing to report. Whole Battalion on fatigues.
10-4-16	Nothing to report. A German captured by the French gave

		particulars of an impending attack on "A" Sector but nothing so far happened.
11-4-16		Intermittent shelling of Bronfay & district. One shell hit extreme corner of barn but no damage.
12-4-16		An uneventful day.
13-4-16	2am	Severe hostile bombardment of Bronfay & district with 10cm & 15cm shells. Battn. "Stood To" and "Stood Down" again at 4am. Germans raided A2 subsector (6th Northants holding the line). Several casualties. One man of ours on morning fatigue & in front line at the time – missing. Several dead Bosches lying out between the lines at 6am. 1 Captured & sent to Brigade.
14-4-16		Sorting out & burying Germans occupied our attention & no unusual movements of us or the Germans.

A2

15-4-16	Relieved 6th Northants in A2 yesterday. 12th Middx relieved by 11th R.Fus. Nothing to report.
16-4-16	Captured a Bosche prisoner of 6th Entrenching Bn who took part in raid with 62nd Regiment on 13/14 night.
17-4-16	Situation calm. Weather cold wet & windy.
18-4-16	Enemy very quiet. Nothing to report. Fine weather.
19-4-16	An uneventful day.
20-4-16	Relieved by 6th Northants. Nothing to report.

Bray

21-4-16	Nothing to report.
22-4-16	Day Quiet. Nothing to report.
23-4-16	Day Quiet. Nothing to report.
24-4-16	Day Quiet. Nothing to report.
25-4-16	Day Quiet. Nothing to report.

A2

26-4-16	Relieved 6th Northants in A2 Sector early morning. Relief complete 12.40pm. Hostile aeroplane dropped bombs just by Bray Church. A Hole in road and windows etc. broken was the only damage. No casualties. We raided German trenches night of 26/27th. No killed but 2/Lieut.H.Driver wounded & 13 others.
27-4-16	Quiet day. Nothing to report.
28-4-16	Quiet day. Nothing to report.
29-4-16	Enemy shelled Carnoy for about 2½ hours. No damage nor casualties.
30-4-16	Quiet day up till evening. Enemy shelled support line & Hd.Qrs. for about 1½hrs. rather heavily – Communication trenches to front line damaged. 8 casualties.
1-5-16	Nothing happened of any importance in A2 Sector. 12th Middx. were relieved by 11th R.Fus. in A1. 30.4.16. 19th Manchesters on our left. General Officer Commanding 54th Brigade requested the C.O. to publish in battn. Orders the communiqué appearing in the Times of 29th April

THE WAR DIARY 1916   41

		respecting the raid carried out on night of 26/27th April by D Company. Complimentary Order attached [see Appendix B3.1].
2-5-16		General MacAndrew visited trenches in morning. Fine Day. Enemy very quiet day & night. 2/Lieut.H.J.Cartwright joined for duty. Capt.L.H.Keep & Capt.W.H.[Bull] sat as members of a F.G.C.M. in A1 Sector Headquarters at 10.30 a.m. Revd.G.Jarvis Smith (Wesleyan Chaplain) posted to the Battn. by 54th Brigade.
3-5-16		2nd Wiltshire Regiment relieved 11th Royal Fusiliers on our right. Day and night was fine & enemy quiet except for an occasional shell towards Bronfay.

A/2/BRAY

4-5-16		Day quiet. relieved by 18th King's Liverpool Regt. 21st Brigade. Relief completed at 9.15 pm with no casualties. two companies proceeded to Froissy (A & B) & two companies (C & D) took over billets in BRAY. Battalion Headquarters in No.4 Rue Gambetta BRAY. Arrived in billets early morning of 5th

BRAY

5-5-16	2–3am	A very heavy Artillery duel on our right in the direction of FROISSY. Fine day & warm. General cleaning up & resting prior to proceeding on fatigue tomorrow.
6-5-16		Fatigue taken over from 30th Division. D Company at BRONFAY working on tramway line from BRONFAY FARM to BILLON WOOD. A Company sent 50 men to Ecluse Mericourt for permanent fatigue of unloading barges. Brigade School of Instruction for Specialists commenced at Oissy. Sent 5 Officers & 70 Other ranks.
7-5-16		Fatigues & training carried on. Physical Training in early morning. Adjutant's parade for All N.C.O's & men available at 10 a.m. Weather Fine & dry.
8-5-16		Fatigues & training carried on as per programme. Weather cold rained most of the day. Nothing exciting occurred in BRAY. Everything very quiet.
9-5-16		Fatigues & training carried on as per programme. The Defence Post allotted to this Battn. by 30th Division is the area NE of BRAY with an Office representing the Battalion at road junction L 9 d 92. Musketry range opened at field just off Cappy Road. Brig.Genl.H.Shoubridge proceeded on leave Lt.Colonel G.D.Price in command of 54th Brigade. Weather Fine & dry.
10-5-16		Training & fatigues carried on as per programme. 2 Officers & 13 Other ranks proceeded on leave (12th to 21st) day quiet. Weather Fine & Dry. C.O. called a conference of Company Commanders at 10 a.m. Musketry carried out on the range. All employed men & details fired. Weather Fine & Dry.
11-5-16		Training & fatigues carried on as per programme. Nearly

	all men employed on fatigue. Those not on fatigue paraded at 10 a.m. under the Adjutant. Day cold & squally.
12-5-16	Training & fatigue carried on as per programme. Day very quiet; nothing of importance occurred. At night a few shells dropped near the La Neuville end of BRAY. Day wet & dull.
13-5-16	Early hours of morning a severe bombardment went on between the Germans & the French. A few shells fell near FROISSY & BRAY. A few bugles sounded the "Standfast" in BRAY but the excitement died down about 2.30 a.m. Fatigues carried on but parades cancelled on account of rain.
14-5-16	Fatigues & training carried on. Weather changeable with rain. Lieut.Colonel G.D.Price appointed Commandant of 18th Divisional School vice Colonel Fiennes to date from 20th May. Col.Price proceeded to 18th Div. Headquarters.
15-5-16	Fatigues & training carried out as usual. Captain E.Clegg assumed command of the Battn. until Major G.P.Mills returns from leave. A Company & B Company vacated billets at Froissy & joined the other two companies at Bray. French troops arrived at Froissy & took over our vacated billets.
16-5-16	Fatigues & training carried out as usual, most of the Battn. being on fatigues. 2/Lieuts.H.H.Pizey & W.H.Bennett joined for duty & posted to D Company. Fine weather & warm. Enemy aeroplane over Bray during morning about 8 a.m.
17-5-16	Major G.P.Mills returned from leave and assumes command of the Battn. from 18th inst. inclusive. Very fine weather. Training and fatigues carried out as usual. Nothing of importance occurred.
18-5-16	Fine day, very warm. Received notification that following decorations had been awarded by Commander-in-Chief. D.S.O. – 2/Lieut.H.Driver; D.C.M. – L/Sgt.Mills Cox; Military Medal – Cpl.A.H.S.Joyce and L/Cpl.Lancaster. Most of the Battn. on fatigue. Those who were left carried out Bombing & Bayonet Exercises under the Adjutant.
19-5-16	Very Fine day – warm. Training and fatigues as usual. Nothing of importance happened in Bray. A few shells of large calibre dropped in the vicinity of Bray at about 7 p.m.
20-5-16	Night quiet. From 8 a.m. till about 9.30 a.m. the BRAY-CORBIE Road was steadily shelled by large calibre shells. No damage to our billets but a few casualties & a slight damage was sustained by the S.Staffords. Day very fine.
21-5-16	Divine Service, Voluntary. Fine & quiet day. No 15635 Pte.F.E.[J]Groves accidentally drowned while bathing near the Bridge on the BRAY-FROISSY Road. Court of Enquiry proceedings held & forwarded to A.G. & 54th Brigade.
22-5-16	Fine Day & quiet. A German aeroplane over BRAY during early hours but was dispersed by our A.A. Guns.
23-5-16	Day dull & Showery. Nothing of importance occurred.

24-5-16	Fine Day & quiet. Brigadier General Visited BRAY & called into our Hdqrs. Fatigues & Training carried on as usual. Nothing to report.
25-5-16	Fine day. 4 Officers arrived: 2/Lieut.R.B.Rednall, 2/Lieut.A.H.C.Gibson, 2/Lieut.G.J.Luscombe. 2/Lieut.J.Cunningham. Fatigues as before. Bn.Hq.Qrs. moved from Rue Gambetta to Rue Phillipe Auguste. Not such good billets as those we vacated but after being cleaned up they looked more respectable.
26-5-16	Bronfay tram line fatigue discontinued & carried on by 53rd Brigade. We took over fatigues of 7th Buffs, cable burying for XIII Corps Artillery. Draft of 7 N.C.O's & 70 men arrived from Base (5th Entrenching Battn.). Fine day & quiet.
27-5-16	Fine day. captain J.H.Bridcutt proceeded on leave & 2/Lieut.F.E.Dealler took over the duties of Adjutant. 2/Lieuts J.D.Hopper & G.B.Hasler joined for duty.
28-5-16	Divine Service – Voluntary. Capt.L.H.Keep & Sergt.Cornell proceeded on course at 4th Army School. Brigadier General Shoubridge visited Hdqrs 10–11 a.m. Fine day, another lot of N.C.O.'s & men proceeded to 54th Brigade Schools of Instruction in place of those returned 27-5-16.
29-5-16	Fine day. fatigues carried on as usual. Town Major BRAY inspected the billets & congratulated on [sic] all ranks on the improvements effected.
30-5-16	Fatigues carried on as before but had to commence at 4.15 a.m. to enable men to get back to bathe during morning. Fine day. 7th Bn. Bedfordshire Regiment mentioned in Sir Douglas Haig's first despatch published in London Gazette Supplement 29-5-16.
31-5-16	G.O.C. 54th Brigade visited BRAY, called into our Headquarters to discuss matter of fatigues. Division require 600 men. Difficult to find them. Fine Day.
1-6-16	Quiet Day & Fine. 70 men of B Company employed on Barge Fatigue; remainder and all available N.C.O.s and men of A & D Companies employed on burying cable for 13th Corp[s] Heavy Artillery. Battn. H.Qrs. in Rue Phillippe Auguste. A Company next door B Company Rue Faidherbe, C Company Rue Phillippe August[e], D Company Rue Faidherbe.
2-6-16	Fine Day. Usual Fatigues during the morning. Similar fatigues at night commencing at about 10 pm so that men could get a holiday on Saturday & Sunday. During fatigue, heavy strafe of our guns began on German lines. (Manchesters said). We had 1 killed and 2 wounded by M.G. fire.
3-6-16	No fatigues except B Company on Barge fatigue. Day fine. Instructions received that cable burying fatigue for Corps would cease from Sunday inclusive, and that we should be employed on cable burying fatigue for 18th Div. Sigs.

4-6-16	Day Quiet night of 3/4th saw some heavy Artillery duels, but nothing of importance occurred. B & D Companies marched to Corbie to take over fatigues of 1 Coy. 6th Northants and 1 platoon 12th Middx. Operation Orders attached [see Appendix A2.4–5]. General Maxse visited Hd.Qrs. to discuss fatigues and arranged that we should furnish 70 men for barges and the remainder on cable burying fatigue for Sigs. 18th Division.
5-6-16	Day Quiet. Unsettled weather. Nothing unusual to report. 2/Lieut.J.H.R.Rawes assumes command of D Company pending the return of Capt.T.E.Lloyd from leave. Leave allotment reduced from 13 places to 9 places. the following honours appeared in the King's Birthday Honours List. D.C.M. – 3/7753 L/Cpl.A.Jones. Military Medal: 3/7669 L/Cpl.A.Lancaster; 22101 Cpl.A.H.S.Joyce; 17514 Private W.[sic C.] Wilsher. fatigues as usual. Furnished guard for 53rd Bde. H.Qrs.
6-6-16	Day quiet; wet weather. Draft of 7 N.C.O.s and 38 men arrived from No.2 Entrenching Battn. Fatigues as usual. Captain E.Clegg returned from leave after being a spectator of the great naval battle on H.M.S. "Revenge".
7-6-16	Wet day with occasional bursts of sun. News of the tragic death of Lord Kitchener reached Bray about 4 pm and caused great consternation and general depression. Fatigues as usual.
8-6-16	Wet day; very miserable weather. Captain J.H.Bridcutt returned from leave night of 7th inst and resumed duties of Adjutant morning of 8th inst. 2/Lieut.F.E.Dealler acting adjutant returns to his company at Corbie.
9-6-16	Day Quiet with showers of rain. C Company and part of A on cable fatigue, remainder of A on barge fatigues & other small guards etc. Leave allotment reduced to 4 places per Battalion. Amiens placed out of bounds to all British troops except those on very special urgent business.
10-6-16	Orders for move received. Handed over fatigues to 10th Essex Regt. (18th Div) B & D Companies moved by train from Corbie to Picquigny. Indifferent weather.
Bray/Picquigny 11-6-16	A & C Companies and Bn Hd.Qrs. moved from Bray to Picquigny to commence Brigade Training. Operation Orders attached [see Appendix A2.6]. Arrived Picquigny 10.20 am. Brigadier General T.H.Shoubridge met the Battn at the Station and watched it march to billets. Headquarters in the main Amiens road.
[Picquigny] 12-6-16	Men were given a clear day. Brigadier, C.O. and all officers visited the practice trenches in the morning and the N.C.O.s proceeded to the same place at 12.30 pm. Weather dull and

	rainy. Draft of 49 arrived during night and early morning of 13th inst.
13-6-16	Wet morning. Draft paraded and sorted out. First real day of Brigade Training. All the Bn. out at practice trenches. Returned about 6 pm.
14-6-16	Fine Day. Brigade Training carried out according to programme. At 11 pm the time is advanced one hour, 11 pm becoming 12 midnight. Lieut.H.C.Browning relinquishes post of T.O. and returns to duty with B Coy.
15-6-16	Fine Day. Brigade Training carried out practice attack on trenches. Bn on duty for Brigade. Furnished Bde H.Q. Guard and Picquigny Sanitary fatigue.
16-6-16	Fine Day. Brigade carried out practise [sic] attack on trench. Battn. returned to billets at 6.30 pm. 2/Lieut.H.Cathcart-Nicholls proceeded to Hd.Qrs R.F.C. on probation as an observer.
17-6-16	Good weather. Bn. proceeded to practise trenches for Brigade Training and returned to billets at 6 pm.
18-6-16	Orders received for Bn to move to Grovetown Camp and be attached to 53rd Bde. but were cancelled about noon. Bn out on the training are practising the attack. No 23738 Pte.Griffin J C.Coy shot himself – died in Field Amb.
19-6-16	Fine Day. Btn. on duty for Brigade. Furnished H.Qrs Guard & Town Major's Sanitary Fatigue.
20-6-16	Fine day. Companies training under company arrangements. Leave allotment reduced to 3 places every 10 days. 2/Lieut.F.E.Tilton proceeded to R.E. Dump Bray to relieve 2/Lieut.Covell sick. Brigade Open Air Concert.
21-6-16	Companies training under company arrangements. Captain E.Clegg sat as member of F.G.C.M. at Town hall Picquigny.
22-6-16	Quiet Day. Men given a rest to prepare for move tomorrow.

[Picquigny/ Grovetown Camp]

23-6-16	Battn moved from Picquigny to Grovetown Camp in accordance with attached Operation Orders No.19. Arrived Grovetown Camp about 3 pm. Changeable weather. Very hot and much rain.

[Grovetown Camp]

24-6-16	Battn. at Grovetown till 11.30 pm. Moved to A.2. Sector Trenches and took over 54th Brigade Battle Front.

[Carnoy Trenches]

25-6-16	Holding the line. Area rather crowded and casualties a few above normal. Artillery bombardment going on all day and all night. Germans made feeble reply by day but seemed to wake up at night.
26-6-16	Artillery bombardment as yesterday. Heavy retaliation and many casualties. One shell fell in C Coy. Off. Mess. 2/Lts Baden & Hasler killed. Capt.Clegg, 2/Lts Doake & Johnson wounded.

27-6-16	Bombardment carrying on. 11th R.Fusiliers arrived at Carnoy and went into support line. Orderly Room and officers dugouts shared on account of limited space.
28-6-16	Fine Day. 12th Middlesex took over front line of 54th Brigade from 7 Bedfords. 7 Bedfords proceeded to Bray arriving at 1 am 29.6.16.
29-6-16	Fine Day. Btn. resting and cleaning up.
30-6-16	Fine Day. Battalion proceeded to trenches Carnoy. 54 Brigade concentrated in trenches of 54 Brigade Battle Front. 11th R.Fusiliers & 7 Bedfords in attacking line 6th Northants in support 12 Middx in Reserve. Operation orders in War Diary of July.

Carnoy Trenches

1-7-16	At about midnight on night of June 30th/July 1st 1916 the whole of the 54th I.Brigade was concentrated on its Battle Front ready for the assault on morning of 1st July. Assaulting Battalions were 7th Bedfords & 11th R.Fusiliers, in support: 6th Northants and in reserve 12th Middlesex. An artillery bombardment waged heavily all night and increased in intensity up till 7.30 am, Zero Hour, when the assaulting Battalions stormed the German first line trenches. Operation Orders appended [see Appendix B1.1]. A special account of the events is being compiled by the Commanding Officer and will be appended hereto also [see Appendix B2.1].

Pommiers Redoubt

2-7-16	At about 2 am, after consolidating as much of Pommiers Redoubt & Beetle Alley & New Trench as was possible in the time, the Battalion returned to Carnoy from the enemy's captured trenches & rested. At about 7 pm. the Battn. moved forward again as a reserve Battn to Emden & Austrian Trenches (German). Battn.Hd.Qrs. at Piccadilly.
3-7-16	Battn. remained in these Trenches all day till about 6 p.m. and then returned to Carnoy in Caftet Wood. 2 coys remaining in German first line trenches. Battn.Hd.Qrs. at Suicide Corner on the Montauban Road.
4-7-16	Battn. resting in Carnoy Wood positions as on 3rd inst. general attack progressing favourably. Much traffic, guns and convoys, in Carnoy.

Carnoy

5-7-16	Battalion remained all day in Carnoy & Caftet Wood. Weather changeable with intermittent rain.

Carnoy, The Loop

6-7-16	Battalion in Carnoy & Caftet Wood till about 6 pm when it moved forward to Pommiers Trench & Caterpillar Trench. Battalion headquarters at the Loop. Soon after arrival enemy shelled Battn.Hdqrs. with Lachrymatory shells. No material damage but slight discomfort was caused.

The Loop
7-7-16   Battalion still holding Caterpillar Trench & Pommiers Trench which the enemy subjected to much Artillery Fire. Weather wet and accommodation in German trench dugouts somewhat limited.
8-7-16   Battalion still holding Caterpillar Trench & Pommiers Trench. Rather more artillery activity than usual. A machine Gun emplacement was hit by a shell & 4 of the team were killed. Dull & wet weather.
9-7-16   Weather fine. Battalion relieved at 5.30 pm by 14th Bn.Kings Liverpool Regt. and returned to dugouts in the vicinity of Bronfay Farm. A complimentary letter received from 54th Brigade regarding "Good Patrol Work" which has been recognised by the Corps Commander.

Bronfay/Bois des Tailles
10-7-16   Battalion moved from Bronfay Farm district to BOIS des TAILLES leaving dugouts at 11 am and arriving at Camp at about 3 p.m. the entire Brigade & Bde.Hd.Qrs. billeted here. Qr.Mr.Stores remained at Grovetown. Fine weather.

Bois des Tailles
11-7-16   Battalion resting & cleaning up. Bathing by companies during the morning and afternoon. A draft of 50 which had arrived on 7th were brought up from Grovetown Camp & posted to Companies.
12-7-16   Fine weather. Battalion remained at Bois des Tailles. Nothing of special importance to the Battalion occurred during the day – received orders for move to Trigger Wood.

Bois des Tailles/Trigger Wood
13-7-16   Battalion marched from Bois des Tailles to Trigger Wood (South of Bronfay) via Grovetown Camp & Bray-Bronfay Road. Arrived about 12 noon and remained till about 1 am next morning. Fine weather. Enemy shelling Suzanne during the night.

Trigger Wood/Maricourt
14-7-16   Received sudden orders just after midnight of 13th inst. to proceed to Maricourt. A very heavy Artillery Battle raged during the entire night and did not cease till after dawn of 14th inst. The Brigade was wound up with orders to retake Trones Wood which had been lost by the 55th Brigade. The 12th Middlesex & 6th Northants Regt. were the assaulting Battns, 11th Royal Fusiliers held the advanced trenches, 7th Bedfords were in Reserve in Trenches at Maricourt. On night of 13/14th July the German 2nd line trenches were taken from Bazentin-le-Petit to Longueval including the woods at these villages.

Maricourt
15-7-16	Battalion at Maricourt. Head Quarters in dugouts about 500 yards from Maricourt Wood on the Montauban Road. First portion of enemy's third line penetrated at Bois de Fourneau.
16-7-16	Battn. remained in same position. Orders were received to hold ourselves in readiness to attack in conjunction with 11th Royal Fusiliers the village of Guillemont. As the leading Companies were moving off at about 2 pm to get into their battle positions the time was postponed and eventually the orders for the assault for that day were cancelled.
17-7-16	Fresh orders were received regarding the assault on Guillemont. 53rd Brigade were to co-operate in the attack, their objective being the north eastern half of the village. At the same time a Battalion of Bantams from the 53rd [sic 35th] Division were to attack Ginchy from the edge of Delville Wood. These orders were again cancelled but Battn. remained under orders to move at a moment's notice to battle positions previous to assaulting Guillemont. Middlesex & Northampton Regts relieved by 2 Battns. of Bantams from 35th Division.
18-7-16	At about 3 pm it was rumoured that the 54th Brigade would not be called on to attack Guillemont owing to the heavy casualties it incurred on July 1st and in the re-taking of Trones Wood. Enemy's artillery very active throughout the day. 4 pm the Battn. cookhouse was shelled and some casualties sustained. Left Maricourt very suddenly at about 9 pm and proceeded to Bois des Tailles (North) taking over same camp as before.

Bois des Tailles
19-7-16	Fine day. Men given a rest to clean up after somewhat rough time in trenches. Nothing of importance occurred. Following Officers who joined the Battn. while in Maricourt were posted to Coys as stated: Lieut.W.G.Lacey A Coy. 2/Lieut.H.F.Trewman B Coy. 2/Lt.T.E.Adlam C Coy. 2/Lieut.I.H.M.Ross Taylor A Coy. 2/Lieut.C.B.Kydd B Coy. 2/Lieut.R.E.Moyse C Coy. 2/Lieut.E.G.Pernet A Coy. 2/Lieut.D.S.Roeber C Coy. Capt.T.R.J.Mulligan D Coy. 2/Lieut.T.P.Wilson B Coy. 2Lieut.H.F.Graves C Coy. 2/Lt.J.H.Kay D Coy.
20-7-16	Day Fine & quiet. Expecting orders to move today but first Line Transport only moved, and proceeded to destination unknown, bivouacing one night near Querrieux. Following officers arrived and posted to Coys: – 2/Lt.R.D.Hunston (A), 2/Lt.H.Potts (D), 2/Lt.W.Rankin (B). Capt.E.E.Bull (B Coy.) Employed as supernumerary Transport Officer.

Bois des Tailles/Citerne
21-7-16	Battn. moved from Bois des Tailles and marched to

Edgehill Station (between Buire & Dernancourt) arriving there at 11 am. Owing to heavy traffic it did not entrain till 3 p.m. and eventually arrived at Longpré at 9 pm. After a long delay it was entrained to Wiry arriving there at 11 pm. From Wiry the Battn. marched to Citerne where it was billeted – hour of arrival about 12.30 am 22-7-16.

Citerne
22-7-16
The Battn. hoped that it would remain at Citerne but at 5 pm orders were suddenly received for the whole Brigade to move on morning of 23rd. The Battn. in consequence paraded at 2 am. 23rd proceeding by route march to Longpré (distance 9 miles) and there entrained for St.Omer. The whole of the 1st & 2nd Line Transport went with the Battn.

Wallon Cappel
23-7-16
The Battn. arrived at Arques at about 2.30 pm after resting two hours it proceeded to the village of Wallon Cappel distant about 9 miles arriving there at 8 pm. Between 2 am and 8 pm the Battn. in addition to a very tiring train journey marched 18 miles and was under arms 18 hours.

24-7-16
Day fine. Nothing of importance occurred. Battn. Rested after yesterday's strenuous journey.

25-7-16
Battn. Parades under Adjutant 7 am till 11 pm. Afternoon – Recreation.

26-7-16
General Maxse inspected the Battn. Formed up in mass in a field opposite Battn. Orderly Room. The Battn. Paraded as strong as possible in dull order. 29 officers & about 650 O.R. being present. The Battn was highly complimented for turning so clean [,] well clothed & shod after its recent heavy fighting. On completion of the inspection the Div. Comdr. Called all officers together and spoke in very high terms of praise of both officers, N.C.O's & men who had taken part in the recent fighting. He particularly mentioned the splendid fighting spirit of the Battn. and thanked the C.O. (Lt.Col.G.D.Price) & all concerned for the very efficient manner in which the attack on the Pommiers Redoubt was carried out on the 1st July. This being the anniversary of the Battn's landing in France the surviving Officers (12 in number) assembled for dinner at the Battn.Hdqrs. Mess. A very enjoyable evening being spent.

27-7-16
Route marching carried out by Companies. Orders received to move further forward tomorrow.

Steam Mill Bailleul
28-7-16
The Battn. left Wallon Cappell at 9 a.m. & proceeded by Brigade route march to the Steam Mill W of Bailleul via Hazebrouck, Borre, Pradelles, Stazeele & Moolenaeker. A very hot day which tired the men severely. Arrived at Steam Mill about 2 pm. Draft of 4 N.C.O.s arrived.

29-7-16	Fine hot day short route march carried out under Company arrangements. Inspection of recent draft by C.O. Lewis Gunners trained by Lewis Gun Officer.
30-7-16	Fine hot day. Company training carried out. Bombers, snipers, Lewis gunners & Signallers trained under Specialist Officers.
31-7-16	Fine hot day. Platoons trained under Company arrangements. Bombers, snipers, Lewis gunners & Signallers continued their training. C.O. & 2nd in Command interviewed at 54th Brigade Hqrs by General Plumer commanding 2nd Army.
1-8-16	Musketry training on small range. Many new rifles found to be too stiff for "rapid". These are being altered by Armourer Sergt. All specialists training under specialist officers. Weather fine & hot.
2-8-16	Platoon training under Company Officers, Specialists training under specialist officers. Weather hot & fine. Demonstration at 2nd Army Bomb School (destruction of trenches by 2″ mortars, consolidation of destroyed position & provision of shelters in same).
3-8-16	Company training. Weather hot & fine. C.O., 2nd in Command, Adjutant, 4 Company Commanders, Lewis Gun Officer & Sniping Officer proceeded by bus to Armentieres & made at [sic] tour of trenches to be shortly taken over by this battalion, on the Armentieres-Lille road.
4-8-16	Fine & hot. Lecture by Gas Expert & examination of Anti-Gas Appliances. Orders received to move tomorrow to Erquinghem.

Erquinghem

5-8-16	Proceeded at 5.30 a.m. by route march to ERQUINGHEM via BAILLEUL arriving at 9.0 a.m. Battalion billeted at ERQUINGHEM. Fine cool day.

Left Sub Sector B Sector

6-8-16	Took over trenches in Left Sub Sector of B Sector astride the ARMENTIERES-LILLE road, from the 1st Batt. Wellington Regiment, 1st New Zealand Brigade. Relief started at 9.30 p.m. & was completed by midnight.

B.2. Sector

7-8-16	Fine day, with very light N.W. breeze. Enemy very quiet. Work done on front line parapets & wire in front of support line.
8-8-16	Fine day, light N.W. wind. Enemy very nervous during hours of darkness as though he expected a raid. Day quiet.
9-8-16	Fine day, very slight S.E. wind. Enemy active during night with bombs. Two men very slightly wounded. About 50 heavy shells fired into ARMENTIERES during day. German of 156th Regt. surrendered at 1 p.m. after he was missed by a sentry.

10-8-16		Dummy raid carried out by Artillery on next sector to the North. Enemy replied with machine guns & artillery, the latter was feeble. Two hostile working parties dispersed by Lewis gun fire. Our artillery registered.
	2.30p.m.	Rifle grenades on Leith Walk. Fine, hot day. One casualty in wiring party.
11-8-16		Enemy very quiet all day. Wind light from S.W. Weather fine. Somewhat foggy at night. Enemy stood to in fog & appeared jumpy.
12-8-16		Machine guns fired at intervals during night, causing one casualty in our wiring parties. Quiet day on our front.
13-8-16		Quiet day. In the evening at 9.20 p.m. we fired 50 rounds from Stokes Mortars at enemy's machine gun position, silencing the gun for the night. Enemy's retaliation did no harm to us. Enemy's wiring party dispersed during night.
14-8-16		Very quiet day. Our artillery cut two gaps in enemy's front wire in preparation for a dummy raid. Lewis guns fired on gaps during night.
15-8-16		Day quiet. At 10 p.m. a dummy raid was carried out. Our artillery & mortars bombarded a section of enemy's trenches for 30 minutes & then simulated a lift, at the same time we showed pole targets above our parapets & sent over smoke. Enemy manned his parapet & opened fire with machine guns & rifles. A very heavy fire was then opened by our 18 pounders & Stokes mortars & it is thought that enemy suffered severe losses. His artillery reply was feeble. Our losses were 2nd Lieut.Roeber & 3 O.R. killed & 2 O.R. wounded.
16-8-16		Very quiet day. Relieved at 10.45 p.m. by 6th Northants. battalion took over billets vacated by 6th Northants in RUE MARLE.

RUE MARLE
17-8-16		Quiet day. Companies bathing & preparing for move to BOIS de NIEPPE

La Motte
18-8-16	5.15am	First platoon left RUE MARLE followed at 5 minutes intervals by remaining platoons & marched to ERQUINGHEM. The battalion then proceeded by motor lorries & buses to LA MOTTE in the BOIS DE NIEPPE
	10am	arriving at 10 a.m. We took over the camp vacated by the East Surreys about 1 mile S. of LA MOTTE. Officers & N.C.O.s instructed in keeping direction in a wood in the afternoon & later the companies practised the attack through the BOIS DES VACHES. Fine day, rained heavily during night.
19-8-16	9am	Companies practised in the attack through BOIS DES VACHES, returning to camp at 2 p.m. Companies practised in the attack at night through BOIS DES VACHES returning at midnight. Fine day.
	2pm	

At 8 p.m. on the night of the 19th August, 1916, the Officer Commanding 7th Bedfordshire Regt. received the following orders: –

"On the night of 20/21st August, 1916, the 7th Bedfords will relieve the Battalion holding the BOIS DES VACHES wood on a line running North almost central of the wood and through the second S. in BOIS DES VACHES.

Map Reference – France, 1/20,000

Completion of relief will be reported to Bde. Headquarters. At dawn on the 21st inst. 7th Bedfords will attack and endeavour to make good the north-western portion of the BOIS DES VACHES from a line running North almost central of the wood and through the second S. in BOIS DES VACHES, as far as the canal.

On arrival at the canal the line should be consolidated and strong points put in to strengthen the position"

20-8-16	9am	Battalion practised the attack through BOIS DES VACHES up to central drive making strong points along this. G.O.C. 54th Brigade was present & criticised the operations at the close. Fine day.
21-8-16	2am	Battalion practised in an attack in a wood at dawn also relief of another Battalion already in position see orders
	5am	attached. Battalion moved in motor buses & lorries to

RUE MARLE

	5.30pm	ERQUINGHEM & from there marched to billets in RUE MARLE. Conference of Officers & N.C.O.s held at 5.30 p.m. on lessons learned during previous 3 days training in wood fighting. Fine Day.
22-8-16		Battalion remained in billets. Fine quiet day. N.C.O.s & new officers paraded under Adjutant.

ERQUINGHEM

23-8-16	10am	Battalion marched to ERQUINGHEM by platoons at 5 minutes interval. N.C.O.s & officers paraded under adjutant. Fine day, rain at night.
24-8-16	10am 6.30pm	Battalion drill under C.O. battalion left ERQUINGHEM at 6.30 p.m. & marched, accompanied by transport to BAILLEUL station. After a hot meal the battalion entrained for St.POL.

LA THIEULOYE

25-8-16	5.30am	The battalion detrained at St.POL & after breakfast in station yard marched to LA THIEULOYE where it went into billets. Fine hot day.
26-8-16		Companies trained in advanced & rear guards. Very heavy rain interfered with training. Heavy rain, dry intervals.
27-8-16		Company training in forenoon. At 2 p.m. battalion practised forming up for an attack from trenches & carried out an attack from trenches in A2 area. Heavy showers at times.
28-8-16	8am	Battalion marched to BOIS des HEROMBUS & was

	exercised in forming up for attack in a wood & attacking through a wood, clearing parties, carrying parties & runners being used. Heavy showers at times. After a midday meal the battalion returned to billets at 5 p.m. In the evening the 18th Divisional Brass Band played for 1½ hours in the village.
29-8-16	Company training in billets during morning & battalion training on A1 area in afternoon. Forming up at night for attack at dawn practised. Heavy thunderstorm, men got very wet on the way home.
30-8-16	Wet day. Company training lectures etc. in billets.
31-8-16	Brigade training in an attack at dawn on two lines of German trenches. Fine day. Corps commander & Divisional commander present. On 26/8/16 a reinforcement of 23 O.R. arrived & on 30/8/16 a further reinforcement of 5 O.R.
1-9-16	Training carried out according to Brigade and Battn Programme. Battn visited C2 Area, left billets 1 p.m. arrived back 6.30 p.m. Fine morning wet afternoon and night. 2/Lieut.A.W.Brawn appointed Adjutant's understudy. Night operations carried out. Bn left billets 8.30 p.m. arrived back about 12.30 p.m.
2-9-16	Weather fine; companies proceeded to D Training Area for Wood fighting, left billets 1.30 pm arrived back 6 p.m. Draft of 2 Lance Corporals and 28 men arrived from 9th Battn. and posted to companies as per Battn. orders. Adjutant proceeded on leave to England.
3-9-16	Church Parade Service held at 10 am in field just behind LA THIEULOYE Church. Fine Day but wet evening. No training parades. Major G.P.Mills and Capt.Percival proceeded on leave to England.
4-9-16	Battn. received orders to proceed with the Brigade to a new Training Area of reserve (5th) Army in accordance with operation Orders attached. Wet and changeable weather.
5-9-16	About 5 a.m. orders were issued cancelling the move. Battn. did not therefore proceed but carried out training on Brigade Training Area A1. Wet weather. 4 men trained in the rapid construction of tunnelled dugouts in Northern part of Wood in U.10.a. under Capt.Chase, R.E.
6-9-16	Battalion remained in billets in morning; proceeded to Wood in U.10.a for practice of intensive digging. C.O., Adjutant and Coy Commanders attended a demonstration in "Rapid construction of Shelters". Corps & Divisional Commanders and officers from other divisions also were present. 1 Lewis Gun Detachment (D Coy.) carried out an experiment of a Lewis Gun Detachment sheltering in a dugout during a bombardment and rapidly emerging the moment a hostile barrage lifts. Experiments carried out in the morning and afternoon. Fine weather.
7-9-16	Morning spent in training under Company Commanders in the vicinity of billets. Battn. proceeded to B area and

	practised "Rapid construction of tunnelled dugouts" and "Following up a barrage" Returned to billets at 6 p.m. Fine weather.
8-9-16	Fine weather. Morning spent in vicinity of billets under company Commanders. In afternoon Battn. proceeded to "C" Area and continued practising Intensive Digging and Following up a barrage. Returned to billets about 7 p.m.
Ternas 9-9-16	54th Brigade marched as a column to MONCHÉAUX Area in accordance with Operation orders attached. destination of 7th Bedfords: – TERNAS at which place the Bn. arrived at 11.30 am, leaving LA THIEULOYE at 8.15 am and proceeding via ORLENCOURT and MARQUAY.
IVERGNY 10-9-16	Battn. continued its march with 54th Brigade and proceeded to IVERGNY at which place it arrived at 1.40 pm, leaving TERNAS 10 am and proceeding via HOUVIN-HOUVINGEUL – ESTRÉE WAMIN – BEAUDRICOURT. Operation Orders attached. Fine weather. On midnight 10/11 Sept. 18th Division is transferred to the Reserve Army.
RAINCHEVAL 11-9-16	Battn. proceeded to RAINCHEVAL "O" Area Reserve Army in accordance with operation Orders No.31 attached. Left IVERGNY at 8 am by bus, and proceeded to HALLOY. Debussed at HALLOY and proceeded by march route to destination via THIEVRES & MARIEUX. Arrived RAINCHEVAL 2.15 p.m. Battn. Hq.Qrs. at École des Garcons General Maxse inspected the march discipline of the Brigade during the three days of the march, and expressed his general satisfaction.
12-9-16	Training carried out under company commanders; early morning running parades; parades at 9 am for instruction in Bombing, Bayonet Fighting and Musketry. Commanding Officer visited Observation post in vicinity of THIEPVAL. Day Quiet and dull; Some Rain.
13-9-16	Training carried out in the following subjects: – Following up a barrage, bayonet Fighting, Physical Training, Bombing etc. Companies paraded at 3 pm and went for a short march, Outposts etc. practised.
14-9-16	Fine Day. Captain Percival returned from leave and resumed command of "A" Coy. from 13th inst. Major G.P.Mills & Capt & Adjt J.H.Bridcutt also returned from leave on 13th inst. battn. was out practising bayonet Fighting, Bombing, Barrage etc. as previously. Two men who were casualties 1st July joined from Hospital.
15-9-16	Fine Day. Companies out training in the morning under Company Commanders. Afternoon – Battn paraded at 3pm

	and practised outposts duties. Battn. received notification to be ready to move at 6 hours notice. Captain A.E.Percival visited trenches in the vicinity of Thiepval.
16-9-16	Fine day. Training by companies in bayonet Fighting, Bombing, Physical Training, Barrage, Digging etc. carried out as usual, no orders to move being received.
17-9-16	Sunday. Fine Day. bathing all day by companies. F.G.C.M. in battn. Orderly Room in morning. C & D Companies attended Church Parade at 11 am. Major G.P.Mills visited trenches in the vicinity of Thiepval. At 4 pm G.O.C. Brigade held a conference of Bn. Commanders, Coy. Commanders etc. in Orderly Room. Stokes Mortar Demonstration by 54th T.M.Battery at 3pm on ground just North of Raincheval. 2/Lieuts H.A.Reaney, H.G.Merchant and S.C.Tremeer joined Bn. for duty from 9th Battn.
18-9-16	Captain Mulligan visited trenches in the vicinity of THIEPVAL. Wet morning. Commanding Officer lectured all Officers & N.C.O's. in Battn. Orderly Room 9.30am. Brigadier General Shoubridge visited Bn.H.Qrs. and conferred with C.O. 2/Lieut.E.F.Piercy joined Battn. for duty.
19-9-16	Changeable weather. Companies practised training as before. Capt.L.H.Keep proceeded to trenches in vicinity of Thiepval. Information received of following awards for gallantry. Captain A.E.Percival – Military Cross. 18257 Pte.H.W.Fish, "C" Coy now 1st Bn.Bedford R. – D.C.M.
20-9-16	Fine Day. Battn. proceeded to training area and practised the attack.
21-9-16	Companies proceeded independently to the Training Area and practised Bombing, Bayonet Fighting etc. Information received of the award of the Medal of St.George (Third Class) to 18257 Pte.H.W.Fish, late 7th Bedfords, now 1st Beds. 2/Lieut.H.B.Stewart appointed Bn.Lewis Gun Officer. 2/Lieut.H.C.Cannell joined.
22-9-16	Fine Day. Companies training independently in the morning – practiced short route marching in afternoon. Received orders to move on 23rd inst. time uncertain.

VARENNES

23-9-16	Battn. proceeded by Route March from Raincheval to VARENNES via ARQUEVES – LÉALVILLERS – ACHEUX, leaving Raincheval at 9am and arriving at VARENNES at 12 noon. Fine Day. C.O. attended Brigade Conference at Bde H.Qrs, HEDAUVILLE. Major G.P.Mills inspected reserve trenches in THIEPVAL WOOD.
24-9-16	Fine Day. Church parade in the morning.

N.BLUFF AUTHUILLE

25-9-16	Battalion proceeded by Route March via HEDAUVILLE – BOUZINCOURT – MARTINSART & BLACK HORSE

		BRIDGE to AUTHUILLE (NORTH BLUFF) arriving 2.30 p.m. – Major Mills & four Company Commanders reconnoitered front line & forming up trenches, south of THIEPVAL Hdqrs & A & B Companies at N.BLUFF – C & D Companies in PAISLEY AVENUE in THIEPVAL WOOD. Orders issued for 54th Bgde to attack THIEPVAL & SCHWABEN REDOUBT. 7th Bedfords in Reserve. Heavy Bombardment. Enemy shelled N.BLUFF heavily. Fine Day.
26-9-16	12.30pm	Fine Day. Zero hour for intense bombardment fixed for 12.30 p.m. Assaulting battalions to leave their trenches at 12.30 p.m. Received news that the 1st objective (road running E. & W. through THIEPVAL) had been taken & assault progressing well. C.O. & Adjutant summoned to 54th Bgde. H.Qrs. owing to situation requiring consideration, 2nd objective not having been taken.
	11p.m.	Orders received for Battalion to move forward to dugouts in the vicinity of THIEPVAL & to be in position at 1 a.m. for the purpose of clearing up & consolidating the 2nd objective (North face of THIEPVAL).

THIEPVAL

27-9-16	2 a.m.	The Comdg Officer (Lt.Col.G.D.Price) & Adjutant (Capt.J.H.Bridcutt) arrived at the Chateau in THIEPVAL after conferring with Lt.Col.Maxwell 12th Middx. commanding the scattered portions of the three Battalions i.e. 12th Middx, 11th Royal Fusrs, 6th Northants the C.O. (Lt.Col.Price) decided to attack the untaken portion of THIEPVAL i.e. the N.Western part of village. Dispositions for the attack were as follows C & D Coys Commanded by Capts.Keep & Mulligan respectively were detailed for the assault which was to be carried out in two Lines (Waves) with C Co. on the Right, D Co. on the Left. A & B Coys. were sheltered close at hand in German Dug-outs. ZERO was fixed for 5.30 A.M. The morning was extremely dark & the assaulting Coys had great difficulty in forming up for the attack on the correct alignment. At about 5.45 AM all was ready & a few minutes later the two Lines advanced sweeping across the untaken portion of Ground & trenches. Two M.Guns & a good deal of Rifle fire opened from the enemy's lines but our troops (7th Bn Bedfords C & D Coys.) continued to advance & in a short time were in possession of the German trenches on the North-Western face of THIEPVAL. Capt.Mulligan, 2/L Potts fell badly wounded during this action 36 prisoners were taken & about 100 Germans killed by Rifle fire & Bayonets. This action tho. apparently small was of the utmost importance as without the whole of the Village of THIEPVAL & the trenches surrounding it being captured the whole Line of Attack was held up. So to the 7th Bn.Bedfords (especially C & D Coys) belongs the honour & Glory of the final

		destruction of one of the Germans strongest positions & one which they had boasted could never be taken (i.e. THE VILLAGE OF THIEPVAL & its defences) Our casualties were 2 officers above mentioned & about 110 O.R. in the above action. The other three Battns of the 54th Bde. who made a former attack on THIEPVAL had been withdrawn to cover in our Support Area. The Bn. held the line it had gained until 1 P.M. the following day at which hour it continued the attack as stated hereafter.
28-9-16		From early morning until 12 Noon every one was going at high pressure preparing for another attack on the ground which included a very high ridge & a Redoubt called the "SCHWABEN REDOUBT" to the North of THIEPVAL. At 12 Noon the Battalion was ready for this attack and disposed as follows A & B assaulting Coys, D Coy. Dug-out Clearing, C Coy. Bn. Reserve a full description of the battle that followed is attached to this diary [see Appendix B2.2].
29-9-16	5 a.m.	About this hour the 1st/5th Yorkshire Regt. who had moved up during the night relieved the Battn. in the front trenches & they (7th Bedfords) were withdrawn to THIEPVAL and placed in Reserve. The Bn. sheltered in dug-outs during the day shell fire being particularly fierce
30-9-16	4 a.m.	In the early hours of the morning the Battn. was relieved by the 7th Bn. West Kent Regt. & returned to billets in Mailly-Maillet Wood (List of Honours & Awards recommended attached) During the period mentioned in this diary the Battn. (7th Bedfords) went into action on two occasions. The Moral of the Battn. was extremely high. The men fought with determination & skill, gained all their allotted objectives, & received the highest praise from their Brigadier, Divisional Commander, Corps Commander, Army Commander & especially congratulated by the G.O.C., Sir D. Haig

MAILLET WOOD

1-10-16	After being relieved from the Captured THIEPVAL Position the battalion rested in huts for the day in Mailly-Maillet Wood – G.O.C. 54th Bde. visited the battalion and Addressed them in very high terms of congratulation on their Moral, & Stubborn fighting. he said "The 7th Bn. Bedfordshires were one of the best fighting battalions it was possible to find & he was very proud to have such a battalion under his command" he particularly referred to the severe fighting & the daring manner they had snatched from the Bosch a position they boasted of being "impregnable & impossible for the English to take".
2-10-16	Battn. left the above place marched to ACHEUX Station & travelled in trucks (40 in each) to CANDAS, from this Station the battalion moved into billets, A & B Coy. &

Battn.H.Qts. at VACQUERIE C & D Coys. at GORGES reaching billets about 10 p.m.
½ Bn. billeted VACQUERIE.
½ Bn. GORGES

VACQUERIE/GORGES

3-10-16　Time devoted to cleaning up, checking all kits & making up deficiencies lost in action.
Bn.H.Q. VACQUERIE

4-10-16　Classes of officers & N.C.Os. formed for Special Instruction in bayonet fighting – Battn. exercised in Close order drill.

5-10-16　Classes of officers & N.C.Os. formed for Special Instruction in bayonet fighting – Battn. exercised in Close order drill.

6-10-16　Training in all its details commenced; Bombing, Sniping, Lewis Gun, Signalling Message Runners (going across Country) put into real going order.

7-10-16　The above training rapidly pushed forward. Corps Commander expected but he did not turn up.

8-10-16　Training programme continued. The following Officer [sic] joined as Reinforcements and were posted as under 2nd Lt.H.M.Woodyer A Co. 2/Lt.R.J.Clarke A Coy. 2 Lt.J.J.Murray A Coy. 2.Lt.A.H.Waddy D Coy. These were a good stamp of recruit officers.
BILLETS AS ABOVE

9-10-16　Training programme Continued.

10-10-16　Training pushed forward rapidly, battalion to be ready by 16th to move forward for further fighting.

11-10-16　Training. Draft of 158 Other Ranks arrived from England all of which were well equipped, of good Physique, and a marked improvement on previous drafts (except they had no marching powers).
C.I.C. Genl.Sir Douglas Haig visited the Billets, Saw the above draft chatted with many officers N.C.Os & men as he passed from one place to the other. No inspection was arranged as he wished to pay a visit to unit carrying on in the ordinary way. Lt.Col.G.D.Price who had taken Command of the 53rd Infantry Brigade on the 6th inst. till the 10th inst. took over Command of the 54th Infantry Brigade, Protem, on the 11st inst. the vacancy in both cases being caused by the Brigadier being granted Special Leave to England. Major G.P.Mills commanded the Battn. during the absence of Lt.Col.Price as above.

12-10-16　Training continued. The undermentioned officers arrived as reinforcements on the night of the 11/12 & were posted on the 12th to Coys as under.
2 Lt.T.H.Elderton B Co. 2 Lt.L.G.Angas A Co. 2 Lt.F.A.Walker A Co. fine stamp of young officers knowing something of what was required of them as a Platoon Leader.

13-10-16		Training.
14-10-16		Training. Orders received from Brigade (54th Infantry) to the effect that the 18th Divn. had opened advance Divisional Hd.Quarters at Albert, the 53rd Brigade had moved up in readiness for attack on Regina Trench – The 54th Brigade would move to Beauville – All necessary arrangements made for the Bn to move (to-morrow morning) Advance billeting parties detailed to proceed ahead at 2 pm to-day – but, this was cancelled just before time to march off.
15-10-16	Morning	A & B Coy. left Vacquerie C & D Coys. GORGES & marched to Beauval.

BEAUVAL

16-10-16	Morning	Continued the above march from BEAUVAL to VADENCOURT WOOD (Marched in Brigade).

VADENCOURT WOOD

17-10-16	Morning	Continued the above march from VADENCOURT WOOD to BOUZINCOURT.

BOUZINCOURT

18-10-16	Morning	Inspection of all personal kits, C.O. Adjt. & all Coy.Comdrs. proceeded by Bus to Visit Front Line 54th Bde Sector North of COURCELETTE.
19-10-16	Morning	Battn Marched from BOUZINCOURT to ALBERT & billeted.

ALBERT

20-10-16	Morning	Battn Training in ATTACK practice in fields near Albert.
21-10-16	Morning	Battn Training in ATTACK practice in fields near Albert.
22-10-16		Voluntary Church Service. Afternoon ATTACK PRACTICE.
23-10-16		Holding front Line trenches – Regina.
24-10-16		Holding front Line trenches – Regina.
25-10-16		Holding front Line trenches – Regina.
26-10-16		Relieved from above trenches to Billets in ALBERT.
27-10-16		Held up by weather from carrying out prepared attack, Copy of orders attached – battn Billet in Albert & its vicinity
28-10-16		Held up by weather from carrying out prepared attack, Copy of orders attached – battn Billet in Albert & its vicinity
29-10-16		Held up by weather from carrying out prepared attack, Copy of orders attached – battn Billet in Albert & its vicinity
30-10-16		Held up by weather from carrying out prepared attack, Copy of orders attached – battn Billet in Albert & its vicinity
31-10-16		Held up by weather from carrying out prepared attack, Copy of orders attached – battn Billet in Albert & its vicinity
1-11-16		In billets. Coy. & Battn. training carried on in the vicinity of Albert.
2-11-16		In billets. Coy. & Battn. training carried on in the vicinity of Albert.

3-11-16	4.30pm	Relieved the 8th Battn.Suffolk Regt. in REGINA TRENCH. Copy of Orders attd.

REGINA TRENCH

4-11-16	In Trenches Bn.Hd.Quarters at R.29 Central (Map Ref Miraumont – 1/20000). 2/Lt.A.W.Brawn took over the Regimental transport – vice Lt.H.C.Browning who took up comd. of A Coy. Lts.D.S.Keep & H.C.Browning appointed acting Captains whilst Comdg A Coy – Copy of order attd. [not attached].
5-11-16	In trenches as above.
6-11-16	Relieved from Trenches & move to Bivouacs in TARA Hill near Albert.

TARA Hill

7-11-16	Training of Coys. carried out in vicinity of Bivouac. List of Awards for Gallantry attd.

Albert

8-11-16	Training by Coys. Lt.W.Mason joined the battalion for duty as Transport Officer but a Transport Officer Lt.Brawn was serving in charge of the Transport & doing well Lt.Mason was attd to the 54th Brigade.
9-11-16	Training from Billets in & around Albert.
10-11-16	Training from Billets in & around Albert.
11-11-16	Training from Billets in & around Albert.
12-11-16 3.30pm	Bn. detailed to relieve 8th Bn.Suffolk Regt. in
13-11-16	TRENCHES – (REGINA) 12/13 Copy of orders attd.
14-11-16	remained in Trenches until night of 15/16 when
15-11-16	they were relieved by the 11th Canadian Brigade. The Battn. moved back to Huts in OVILLERS (X.13.b.29) Albert Map. During this tour in trenches all preparations were made for Attack on MIRAUMONT but the weather was very wet & it was not carried out before the Bn. was due for relief.

OVILLERS

16-11-16	Bn. employed in improving the Communication Trench in 54th Brigade Sector.
17-11-16	Bn. employed in improving the Communication Trench in 54th Brigade Sector.
18-11-16	Bn. employed in improving the Communication Trench in 54th Brigade Sector.
19-11-16	Bn. employed in improving the Communication Trench in 54th Brigade Sector.

St.RIQUIER

20-11-16	Until the 25th the Bn. marched back to rest billets in the St.RIQUIER district: to enjoy a well earned rest, the
25-11-16	march close on sixty (60) miles was performed by easy stages Not one man fell out.

AGENVILLERS	
26-11-16	Battn. Billeted for the night at AGENVILLERS.
MILLENCOURT	
27-11-16	Bn. moved into its final billets at MILLENCOURT.
28-11-16	The battalion in rest billets. Training carried on daily.
29-11-16	Refitting & overhauling all Kits, Clothing, Transport etc.
30-11-16	
1-12-16	Battalion in rest billets Re-organising, Re-fitting & making up all deficiencies.
2-12-16	As above. Party of one officer & 14 N.C.Os & men allowed to proceed to England on Ten days Leave. Congratulatory message from Corps Commander received. Copy attached [see Appendix B3.13].
3-12-16	Training in the Attack. Trench digging. Improving billets etc.
4-12-16	Training in the Attack. Trench digging. Improving billets etc.
5-12-16	Training for Attack, Advance Guards etc. Lt D.S.H.Keep appointed acting Captain from 28 October 1916. Lt.H.C.Browning from 29th Oct 1916.
6-12-16	Training for the attack in Brigade.
7-12-16	Training for the attack in Brigade. Two officers & 10 O.R. proceeded to England on leave for Ten days.
8-12-16	Brigade Training. Draft of 194 N.C.Os. & men joined the battalion a very good lot of men on the whole but their drill was not all that could be desired & their knowledge of Training limited.
9-12-16	Training of all Specialists, Sectionised, each unit made up to its full strength such as Bombers, Snipers, Signallers, Runners, Lewis Gunners & so on.
10-12-16	Training of all Specialists pushed forward. the following appointments were made, 2/Lt.G.J.Luscombe Sniping Officer, 2/Lt.H.M.Woodyer Reserve Bombing Officer, 2/Lt.Waddy A.H. Reserve Lewis Gun Officer, 2/Lt.W.P.Cannell Town Major, Domvast.
11-12-16	Specialist & Coy. Training in all its detail pushed forward with all speed. No.14622 Pte.Gough, G.E. 12702 Cpl.Mulrien, B., 15213 Thompson, A. 14135 Corpl.Dean, W. were awarded "The Military Medal" for Gallantry.
12-12-16	Coy. and Battalion preparing for change of Billets.
13-12-16	Coy. and Battalion preparing for change of Billets.
Domvast	
14-12-16	Battalion changed billets from Millencourt by March Route.
15-12-16 to 24-12-16	Battn. Training, Coy. Training, all Specialists, Brigade Schools of Instruction opened up for Special Instructions.
25-12-16	Christmas Day, this was spent by the battalion in real Christmas form. Presents of Pudding, Fruit, Nuts,

	Cigarettes etc. had been received from Sir Frederick Price, lady Price, Col & Mrs.Hudson, Mrs.Heneker, wife of the late Brigadier, 54th Brigade. The men were supplied with a good Christmas dinner, quart of beer per man & so on which was followed by Entertainment. The officers dined together in one billet. Each Coy. had their dinner Separate. A most enjoyable day was spent by every one in the battalion, the C.O. (Lt.Col.G.P.Mills) visited each mess & the health of all was toasted.
26-12-16	Clearing up after the Christmas repast.
27-12-16	The Bn. was specially selected to carry out the attack as per Somme battles & give demonstration before many Generals and high officials. The attack was from trenches & carried out with such precision & steadiness that they were very highly Complimented by all concerned. The organisation of the Coys. was checked & illustrated in full detail all unit Commanders understudies & specialists showed the most complete knowledge of their Military business & duties & were held up as a pattern to other regiments to which the Crowd of Spectators with many of the Staff belonged. The staff of the 5th Army & Corps were present.
28-12-16	Specialists Training, Coy. Training continued, Concert held in a Large Barn used as recreation room.
29-12-16	Training during the morning, Paper Chase & Boxing Competition afternoon & evening. During the absence on Leave of the Brigadier, Lt.Col.G.P.Mills took over Command of the 54th Brigade.
30-12-16	Training Continued of all Specialists; Bn. & Coys.
31-12-16	Training pushed forward with all speed so as to obtain a high Standard of efficiency during the Spell of rest.
<u>Note</u>	During the period of the month the battalion has been in rest billets enjoying a much need [sic] rest after the Somme battle. Organisation, refitting, Training Specialists; Training Drafts; Special Instruction given to young officers, N.C.Os. indifferent shots & all specialists such as Bombers, Snipers, Lewis Gunners, Runners, Signallers etc. etc. being particularly dealt with.
	The General Routine has been to work extremely hard from 9 A.M. to 1 P.M. daily, Games in the afternoon, lectures, Concerts, Boxing Entertainments & other forms of enjoyment being indulged in every evening, which has resulted in the battalion appearing very Smart, Merry & Bright & very fit for fighting.

1917

1917 was a year of great changes in some areas and the same old depressing features in others. The Asquith administration had fallen at the end of 1916 and David Lloyd George now led a coalition government. General Joffre had been kicked upstairs as military adviser to the French government in December 1916 and his replacement was Robert Nivelle. On 6 April the United States of America entered the war as a result of American casualties from the new unrestricted submarine warfare by Germany and the interception of the Zimmermann note suggesting that Germany would support a Mexican invasion of the southern USA. If the Allies gained a new power during the course of the year they lost an old one when the Russian government and monarchy fell in November and peace was signed with Germany on the 15th of that month. Overall the loss of Russia, with its primitive armies led by incompetent generals, was more than made up for by the imminent promise of the arrival of millions of Americans, unblooded but keen to play their part. They would not enter combat until 1918 but this promise of their arrival would help to shape German strategy by the year's end. A further change in 1917 was that, during March and April, Germany actually gave up ground in France, largely as a result of the hammer blows received on the Somme. The German Army retired on a front from Arras to Soissons to the defences of the Hindenburg Line. It was as part of the follow up operations that the 7th Bedfords attacked and captured Achiet le Grand in March.

During 1917 Britain would come close to defeat as the German U-Boats strangled its supply lines across the Atlantic. This led to the panic measure of ploughing up large areas of ancient meadow and pasture, turning it into arable fields. However, the crisis was averted, not on the farm, but in the Admiralty when the convoy system, long advocated by some, was introduced and the number of sinkings of British shipping decreased markedly.

Another crisis struck France when wholesale mutiny ran through the army as a result of bloody and unsuccessful attacks and dreadful living conditions in and out of the line. This problem was eventually stemmed but forced Great Britain and her Dominions into a protracted slog in Flanders to take the pressure off its crumbling ally further south. It is salutary to note that France, with a total population of 40 million, suffered 1.3 million dead (3.25% of her population) during the war. Great Britain with a population of 45 million suffered 888,000 (around 2%).

It was on the battlefield of the Western Front that things remained much the same with large "pushes" resulting in even larger numbers of casualties. General Nivelle planned a large offensive in the spring which was designed to be halted if no progress was made. However, attacks had a momentum of their own which, once unleashed, proved impossible to stop so quickly. This spring offensive was a combined Anglo-French operation. The French attacked in Champagne and along the River Aisne but made little progress, losing 118,000 men in the first four days. Then the mutinies began and effectively ruled France out of further aggressive operations for the rest of the year.

Britain was involved in three major offensives in 1917. First came the Battle of

Arras, lasting from 9 April to 27 May. It began well with the great Canadian victory at Vimy Ridge, but quickly developed into the traditional head-butting against a brick wall of German defences. The Australians lost severely at Bullecourt, for example, and the 7th Bedfords were handed their first severe check on a battlefield at Chérisy. These attacks cost Britain and her Empire around 150,000 casualties for a maximum advance of three miles between Liévin and Héninel. Next came that battle which, above all, perhaps, has come to symbolise the futility of First World War battles in the minds of the English-speaking world, the Third Battle of Ypres – commonly called, from the name of the last village to be captured, the Battle of Passchendaele, of which more below. Finally, late in the year, on 20 November, the British Third Army assaulted Cambrai with a massed tank attack. As with Arras and Third Ypres, the first day was very successful, but the usual problems of communications and vigorous German response meant that by 3 December most of the gains of the first day had been lost and some territory that the British had held at the start of the battle was also lost.

The Third Battle of Ypres lasted nearly as long as the Somme the previous year, beginning on 31 July and ending on 10 November, one year and one day before the end of the war itself. In many ways the battle can have been said to have started on 7 June when General Plumer's Second Army seized the Messines Ridge in a brilliant coup involving the explosion of a series of huge mines (some failed to go off and still lie somewhere under the wet Flemish fields). Subsequent fighting was less successful and the attack was called off after a week. There was then a vital delay of over a month whilst Field Marshal Haig switched the attack from the Second Army to the Fifth Army and its direction from the careful, meticulous Plumer (one of the best, if not the best, of British generals in the war) to General Gough who was thought to be more enterprising and dashing but might better be described as rash.

It was Gough's relentless aggression, often flying in the face of military reality on the ground, the clever German defences and the wettest summer for many years that eventually caused the British attack to stall and the casualty tally to mount. The ground became waterlogged and many wounded men died in a quagmire of mud. This was the typical First World War battlefield of legend, covered with oozing mud, shell holes and thousands of rotting corpses. In mid-August the level of casualties and the lack of gains on the ground brought the army's morale to an all-time low and Gough was relieved. Plumer, once more, took over the task of slogging on through the mud towards the Passchendaele Ridge, which was finally taken by the Canadians in November. The battle had cost some 320,000 British and Dominion casualties for a gain of five miles. The Germans lost around 200,000 which, for them, was nearly as great a disaster. As with the Somme the previous year, there were only losers in this battle.

The major stages of the battle were as follows:

31 July – 2 August: the Battle of Pilckem Ridge;
16–18 August: the Battle of Langemarck;
20–25 September: the Battle of the Menin Road;
26 September – 3 October: the Battle of Polygon Wood;
4 October: the Battle of Broodseinde;

9 October: the Battle of Poelcapelle;
12 October: first Battle of Passchendaele;
26 October – 10 November: second Battle of Passchendaele.

Domvast
1-1-17	Training carried on in vicinity of billets and Training Area.
2-1-17	Training carried on in vicinity of billets and Training Area. Boxing Tournament was held in the evening in a Barn used as a Recreation Room. The preliminaries had previously been contested, these being the finals some good Boxing was witnessed.
3-1-17	Training programme continued, most of the Corps were employed [in] intensive digging.
4-1-17	Training as above. Bn.Hd.Quarter Coy. was formed of all details and specialists. Major J.H.Bridcutt was appointed O.C. all Specialist Officers being i/charge of their respective detachments such as Signallers, Lewis Gunners, Snippers [sic], Scouts etc. etc. This organisation was started to keep under proper control men who were always away from their own Coys. Coys. continued to pay these men but all other administration was carried on independent of their Coys.
5-1-17	Training continued. Every man having been recently supplied with the new Box Respirators was passed thro. a "GASS" [sic] Chamber. The Chamber was improvised by the fitting up of a little out building of a French Cottage in the village of DOMVAST.
6-1-17	Coy. Training & Specialists Training pushed forward. 2/Lts Trewman & Kydd, Corpl.Mears, L/Cpl.Morris, L.Cpl.Hersted qualified as Bombing Instructors at 54th Bde.Bombing School.
7-1-17	Divine Service held in a field near billets.
8-1-17	Training continued.
9-1-17	Training continued. A draft of 10 men re-joined the Bn. after being away a short time suffering from slight wounds etc. they were re-posted to their former Coys.
10-1-17	Making all arrangements for moving forward to-morrow.

Line of March
11-1-17	Bn. left Domvast & march to PROUVILLE.

Line of March
12-1-17	Bn. marched from PROUVILLE to CANDAS.

Line of March
13-1-17	Bn. rested in Billets at Candas.

Line of March
14-1-17	Bn. marched to Rubempré Area. Advance parties sent forward to visit Trenches.

Trenches
15-1-17	Bn. relieved the 2/6th Royal Warwick Regt. in the

to 19-1-17	trenches Copy of Operation Orders attached [see Appendix A2.10].
20-1-17	Bn. quartered in Warwick Huts with detachments at THIEPVAL (in Support) the whole Bn. were employed on R.E. duties in the 54th Br. Sector.
21-1-17	Cleaning up during the day, trench digging at night.
22-1-17 to 23-1-17	Bn. was billeted in Warwick Huts with a detachment (C Coy.) at THIEPVAL, the Bn. was in Support & carried out R.E. fatigues every night.
24-1-17 to 27-1-17	Relieved 12th Middx. in Trenches where the Bn. remained until night of 27th. Copy of orders attd.

Martinsart Wood

28-1-17 to 31-1-17	Bn. quartered in Huts in MARTINSART Wood, furnishing working parties for R.E. work, with one Coy. digging Communication Trenches near front Line, this Coy. is billeted in Support Line (Sleeping in Tents) working during the night, in spite of the intense Cold, frost & Snow the men appear very fit and are changed over (i.e. relieved by another Coy. every 3rd day). Every opportunity is taken to improve backward men. Classes for Drill, Musketry, Snipping [sic], Scouting, Signalling, also for N.C.Os & young Officers who require extra tuition are kept going daily except when the Bn. is actually in trenches. Casualty List for the month attached.
1-2-17 to 8-2-17	Battn. billeted in huts in Martinsart Wood finding working parties to improve & dig new Trenches in 54th Bde Sector. Classes for Young Officers, N.C.O.s & backward men in progress. Training for all Specialists rapidly pushed forward i.e. Lewis Gun, Signalling, Bombing, Snipping [sic], Scouting Classes going daily from 10 A.M. to 1 P.M. Musketry for indifferent shots.
9-2-17	One Bn of the 54th Brigade (i.e. 11th Royal Fusiliers) moved into the line in relief of 8th Norfolk Regt. the rest of the Brigade including 7th Bedfords remained in Huts in Martinsart Wood every available N.C.O. & man being employed on fatigues in the trenches. Later in the day one Coy. (C Coy.) was ordered forward (in Support of 12th BN. Middx) the Coy. was billeted in STUFF REDOUBT and was employed on defence work under the orders of O.C. 12th Bn. Middx.
10-2-17	The Bn. (less C Coy. who remained in Stuff Redoubt) moved forward into Dug outs at THIEPVAL, with Bn. H.Qrs. in the Wonder Work, they, the Bn. were employed on night fatigues in vicinity of front line.
11-2-17	Arrangements for relief by 55th Infy.Bde. at night.

THIEPVAL

12-2-17	On the night 11/12 Feby. the Bde was relieved by the 55th Infy. Bde. the 7th Bedfords being ordered to remain in their present position (Dug-outs in THIEPVAL).

Warwick Huts

13-2-17 — Bn. moved into Warwick Huts every one employed in fatigue near front line making preparations for attack which was booked for 16/17 Feby.

14-2-17 — Fatigue in front Line Sector, the whole Battn.

15-2-17 — Checking all fighting Kit, ready for moving forwards for Operations each Coy. was paraded & inspected & everything checked. Extra S.A.A., Bombs, Very lights etc. etc. drawn & issued to individuals.

16-2-17 — Bn. moved to its position in Support & was distributed as follows 2 Coys A & B in Dug-outs in FARBACK Trench 2 Coys C & D in Moucquet FARM, Bn H.Qrs in No.8 Dug-out in ZOLLERN Trench the above was in accordance with G.O.C.s instruction, 54th Bde.

17-2-17 — This was termed Z Day (day of battle) all arrangements were complete for the attack by 4 A.M. a report to that effect being sent to H.Qrs 54th Brigade. The attack to be carried out was planned on the usual System for attacking from trenches the final objective being the South MIRAUMONT TRENCH which defends the Southern portion of Petit Miraumont Village. At 5.45 A.M. our Barrage opened (The attacking troops being formed up ready before this hour during this forming up they were heavily shelled by the Bosche who had apparently detected or gained information that something was taking place. Many casualties were suffered by this shell fire adding to the difficulties of making a good start) according to schedule time the assaulting troops 11th Royal Fusiliers & 6th Northants (& 12 Middx Dug-out clearing) advanced. 7th Bedfords being in Brigade Reserve were not allowed to move & so remained in their night positions. The battle progressed in the usual way until the 2nd objective was reached (a spot called the Boom ravine) about 500 yds short of the final objective (South Miraumont Trench) here it was found almost impossible to advance further as most of the officers had become wounded also many N.C.O.s & men. As soon as this fact had been established orders were issued by the G.O.C. 54th Bde for the assaulting troops to entrench & make dispositions for holding the ground they had gained, this was done & by nightfall the work of consolidation was well advanced. A Counter Attack was to be expected & in view of this the G.O.C. 54th Bde ordered Two Coys 7th Bedfords to be moved forward into Close Support. One Coy (A Co) moved to a spot about 500 yds behind the front line known as the GULLEY & B Co to REGINA Trench, the former Coy. assisted in consolidation work, Patrolling, Carrying etc. during the night. The front gained in the Battle by the 54th Bde. was reconnoitred by all Coy. Commanders ready in case of necessity to carry out the relief of the attacking Bns this however was found to be unnecessary & all troops remained in their present positions for the night and the obscurity of the position was quickly cleared up and a strong front line established with the remnants of the 6th Bn Northants, 12th BN Middlesex. The 11th Royal Fusiliers was after nightfall withdrawn to Moucquet Farm & placed in Reserve. the day following (18th Feby)

In the field
18-2-17
The whole Brigade was relieved by the 55th Infy. Brigade the 54th being withdrawn to Huts in the Martinsart Area. 7th Bedfords being in GLOUCESTER huts & employed on R.E. fatigues. During this period the 4 Coys of the Bn were commanded by the following: captain H.C.Browning A Coy, 2nd Lt.H.Driver B Coy, Captain L.Keep C Coy., Capt.D.Keep D Coy. Casualties for the fight are said to be (1000) one thousand N.C.O.s and men & 35 Officers. the 11th Royal Fusiliers & 6th Northants suffered the heaviest.

19-2-17
to 28-2-17
The Battn billeted in GLOUCESTER huts & employed on R.E. fatigues making wire etc.

St.Pierre Divion
1-3-17
to 4-3-17
Preparation & move from Gloucester Huts to tents and Dug-outs in St.Pierre Divion (A Coy Warwick Huts). The whole of the Bn employed on fatigue, road making, between Grandcourt and Miraumont. As many officers and N.C.Os. being sent to reconnoitre front line daily

5-3-17
The Battalion continues to be employed on road making area being worked on East Miraumont Road Petit Miraumont end.

6-3-17
Only two companies required for road making. A Coy at Warwick huts employed on tramway Third Company at Mill road camp training its specialists.

7-3-17
Battalion employed on road making area East Miraumont Road.

8-3-17
Road making continued.

9-3-17
Road making continued.

10-3-17
Battalion employed on mending East Miraumont Road. Warning received to prepare for a move into action.

11-3-17
All fatigues stopped. Battalion to make itself fit for action. A Company to remain at Warwick huts.

12-3-17
Operation orders received to the effect that the 54th Brigade will relieve the 53 Brigade in the line on the night 12/13 March. The 7th S Battalion Bedfordshire Regiment will be situated as follows on complete [sic] of relief.

D Coy: Platoon in SP No 4 G 26 c 7.5.
         Platoon in SP No 4 G 26 c 4.2.
         Platoon in SP No 4 G 26 C 3.6.
         Platoon in SP No 4 G 25 d 6.c.

[All above] now occupied by 6th Royal Berkshire Regiment
MAP Sheet 57 d SE
C Coy will occupy Resurrection Trench now occupied by 8th Suffolk Regiment

B Coy will occupy South Miraumont Trench now occupied by 8th Suffolk Regiment
A Coy will occupy Quarry L 35 d 1.6.
Battalion Head Quarters will be at L 35 d 3.6.

LINE facing LOUPART LINE

12-3-17   8 AM   Orders received from Brigade to occupy Loupart Line and push forward beyond, making final objective the sunken road on the face of Hill 130 and to consolidate the hill. Operation orders issued to companies. D Company will push forward in four waves and occupy the Loupart Line. C Company will follow in close support and pass over D Company in the Loupart Line and occupy the sunken road on Hill 130. D Company will act as close support to C Company pushing forward as soon as C Company has passed over them. A Company will occupy Loupart Line on the right of the Bihucourt road and B Company the Loupart Line on the left of the Bihucourt road acting as Battalion reserve when C & D Companies have pushed forward. Blankets will be dumped at present positions. Battalion H.Q. will be at Quarry b26.6

St.PIERRE DIVION

12-3-17   10 AM   Brigade conference at Paisley dump on attack against Loupart Line. Operation orders were issued, but are of no consequence as the attack was undertaken prematurely and vital orders received.
8.40 PM   D Company left St.Pierre Divion to relieve 6th Royal Berks as for operation.
9.15 PM   C Company left St.Pierre Divion to relieve 8th Suffolks.
9.30 PM   B Company left St.Pierre Divion to relieve 8th Suffolks.
8 PM   A Company left Warwick huts to relieve 8th Suffolks.
9.40 PM   Colonel Mills Cap Colley adjutant 2nd Lts Rednall and Stewart left St.Pierre Divion for L 35 d 3.6.

Trenches in front of LOUPART LINE

13-3-17   2 AM   Relief reported complete.
3 AM   Brigade order to send patrol along Loupart Line as message received from Australians East of Loupart Wood to the effect that the enemy were retiring. D Company were unable to send patrol by darkness but organised daylight patrol which reported Loupart Line evacuated.
11 AM   D Moved to Loupart Line. C Company followed in support. The companies moved in four open waves each. Although under shell fire and considerably troubled with machine gun fire from ACHIET le PETIT the formations were splendid and the men were wonderfully steady.
12.15PM   C Company passed through D Company and continued in four waves with scouts about 200 yards in advance until held up by heavy machine gun fire about the ACHIET LINE.

70 THE SHINY SEVENTH

	1 PM	D Company moved close up behind C company and A & B companies occupied the LOUPART line.
	2 PM	D Company sent two platoons to hold the left flank while C Company consolidated Hill 130 after considerable resistance.
	4 PM	Finally the position held was the star roads on Hill 130 with the line falling back on the left following the 130 contour and joining up with the 11th Royal Fusiliers about b 26 B 5.9. with the 6th NORTHAMPTON regiment on the right.
Hill 130		
13-3-17	5 PM – 8 PM	Spent in consolidating line G 22 C 9.1. G 21 D 2.5 G 26 B 5.9.
	8 PM	C Company ordered to occupy sunken road from star cross roads to Railway and connect with 62nd on left. A and B companies ordered to move up in close support.
	10 PM	Operations commenced.
14-3-17	1 AM	Sunken road occupied by C Company under very able leadership of Lt.Steel. D Company also in the line on right of C Company A and B Companies in close support, shelling very heavy and intense machine gun fire.
	7 AM – 7 PM	Position held shelling and machine gun fire very heavy all day.
	8 PM	D Company took over whole front line. C Company in support. A & B in reserve.
15-3-17	8 AM – 12 Noon	C Company ordered to attack the Bihucourt line. A Company to act as immediate support. C Company attacked the Bihucourt line, on opening of the attack a very heavy machine gun fire developed from ACHIET le PETIT and the BIHUCOURT trench heavy shelling also took place. The advance under such conditions became impossible and C company dug in about 200 yards down the hill. A company did not advance.
	1 PM – 5 PM	The position was held without change.
	6 PM	Under cover of darkness C Company was withdrawn. A Company held the original line on the sunken road. B Company were in support. D & C companies in reserve
	12 midnight	This order was maintained throughout the day.
16-3-17	6 PM – 12 MIDNIGHT	B Company took over the front line from A Company.
17-3-17	5 AM	All companies were warned to be prepared to advance at dawn. Active patrolling took place.
	8 AM	C Company was ordered to advance in four open waves their objectives being the BIHUCOURT line and finally ACHIET le GRAND and the high ridge beyond. D Company was ordered to support C Company. B Company was ordered to make a flank along the railway line as far as ACHIET le GRAND. A Company was to be in reserve. The operation was carried out with the greatest skill and

		urgency some machine gun fire was experienced at the commencement. Heavy artillery fire was experienced in entering ACHIET le GRAND from which we suffered casualties.
	10 AM	BIHUCOURT line was occupied.
	2 PM	ACHIET le GRAND was occupied.
	3 PM	We had occupied positions round the northern and eastern sides of ACHIET le GRAND and held a strong flank position along the railway on the western side. Positions were consolidated.
	6 PM	Rations were delivered to companies. Battalion H.Q. were established on southern edge of Achiet le Grand.
Achiet le Grand		
18-3-17	3 AM	Brigade ordered posts to be put out 1000 yards in advance to cover the forming up of an advance guard.
	5 AM	Posts complete.
	9 AM	Advance guard of Yorkshire dragoons 6th Northamptonshire Regt and one battery of field guns passed through BIHUCOURT.
	10 AM	Battalion remained in Achiet le Grand.
ERVILLERS		
19-3-17	1 AM	Moved up to ERVILLERS.
	6 PM	B Company found out posts on roads round Ervillers.
	8 PM	D Company sent covering party of two platoons with artillery about two miles out towards St.LÉGER.
20-3-17	3 AM	A B and D Companies made up two complete companies under Cap D.S.H.Keep to support 6th Northants in an attack on Croisilles.
	3 PM	The 54 Brigade was relieved by the 7th Division.
	4 PM	The Battalion having been relieved by the 7th Division moved back to the LOUPART LINE.
Marlboro' Huts		
21-3-17	10 AM	The Battalion moved back to MARLBORO' Huts.
22-3-17	9 AM	The Battalion moved back to Contay marched past the Corps Commander at SENLIS.
Bertangles		
23-3-17		The Battalion moved to BERTANGLES.
Bovelles		
24-3-17		The Battalion moved to BOVELLES.
25-3-17		The Battalion rested at BOVELLES.
Salieux		
26-3-17	3 AM	The Battalion went to SALIEUX to entrain – waited 13 hours.
	11.30PM	Entraining completed.
Steenbecque		
27-3-17	5.30 AM	The Battalion arrived at STEENBECQUE station and billeted at STEENBECQUE le BAS.
28-3-17		Cleaning up and refilling and arranging billets.
29-3-17		Organising companies.
30-3-17		Programme of work as follows,
	9.30 AM	Ceremonial Guards with band. Company Drill.

	11 AM	Break
	11.15AM	Specialists classes
	2.30 PM	Football. Games
31-3-17	9.30 AM	Ceremonial Guards. Company Drill.
	11 AM	Company Battle out posts
		A in the open
		B in defence of village
	12–1PM	March discipline and provision of march routine. Rifle inspection by Armourer
	2.30 PM	Football. Games
1-4-17		Church Parade. Inspection of Billets Commanding Officer.
2-4-17	7 am	Physical Training.
	9.30 am	Battalion Route March. Observers used. March discipline. Correct distance & use of water and correct method of carrying pack.
	2.30 pm	Foot Inspection.
	3.30 pm	Conference.
	6 pm	Concert.
3-4-17	7 am	Physical Training.
	9.30 am	Ceremonial Guards with Band.
	10.30	Company extending to Artillery formation from column of route, subsequently to form waves. The method of scouting ground immediately in front.
	12 pm	Specialist classes. Lewis Gunners, Bombers, Scouts.
	2.30 pm	Games, Football. Every man taking part.
	6 pm	Battalion Conference. Capt.W.H.BULL rejoined Battalion for duty. Draft of 7 N.C.Os. & 31 men joined.
4-4-17	7 am	Physical Training. Remainder of day devoted to Battalion Bathing. Draft of 1 man joined Battn.
5-4-17	7 am	Physical Training.
	9.30 am	Battalion Parade. List of Co Organisation
	10.30	Competition in ceremonial Guard mounting. Winners C Company.
	2.30	Football & Physical Games. Draft of 1 man joined Battn.
6-4-17	7 am	Physical Training.
	9.30 am	Ceremonial Guards with Band. Company Drill.
	10.30	Specialists Training. Lewis Gunners, Scouts, Bombers.
	12 pm	Extended Order drill.
	2.30 pm	Football. Games. Draft of 2 men joined Battn.
7-4-17	7 am	Physical Training.
	9.30 am	Ceremonial Guards with Band. Co. Drill.
	10.30	Companies advancing in open formation with scouts in front carried out in form of a drill.
	12 pm	Specialists training. Lewis Gunners, Scouts, Bombers.
	2.30	Inter Co. Football.
	5.30 pm	Battalion Conference.
8-4-17	10.30am	Inspection of Billets by Commanding Officer.
	11.30am	Church Parade.
	2.30 pm	Brigade Transport Competition. The Battn awarded 1st in Pack Ponies class & 2nd in Limbers, Cookers & Water Cart. 3rd Medical Officers Cart.

THE WAR DIARY 1917   73

9-4-17	7 am	Physical training.
	9.30 am	Company Drill.
	10.30	Musketry.
	11.30	Specialists Training.
	3 pm	Games. Capt.G.L.M.Nutwyche reported for duty. Divisional Transport Competition. 2nd prize in G.S. Limber, Wagons.
10-4-17	7 am	Physical Training.
	9.30 am	Platoon Company Organisation.
	2.30	Divisional 5 mile cross country race, C/SM Duffin finished 5th out of field of 50.
11-4-17	7 am	Physical Training.
	9.30	Musketry. Inter Co Lewis Gun Competition in general Turn Out, Changing Points, Tactical Handling & Companies were placed as follows D, C, B, A.
	3 pm	Football, Games etc.
	6 pm	Conference. Draft of 2 N.C.Os. & 4 other ranks joined.
12-4-17	7 am	Physical Training.
	9.30 am	Companies were paraded for inspection by Brigadier, owing to bad weather postponed till following day & company training continued.
	2 pm	Conference Co. Commanders.
	3 pm	Football etc. The Battn won the final in Brigade Competition beating 80th Field Co. R.E. by 6 to nil.
13-4-17	7 am	Physical Training.
	9.30 am	The Commanding officer inspected each Co. paying particular attention to Platoon organisation.
	2.30	Inspection of Battn by Brigadier & he congratulated the C.O. in the good smart appearance of the men.
	6 pm	Company Conference.
14-4-17	7 am	Physical Training.
	9.30 am	Extended Order drill.
	10.30	Platoon Drill.
	11.15	Company Outpost Scheme. Major A.E.Percival rejoined Battn for duty.
15-4-17		Church parade. Inspection of Billets by Major Percival. Major E.Clegg rejoined Battn for duty.
16-4-17	7 am	Company Training. Wet day.
	2.30 pm	Rugby match. Rt half Batt v. left half Batt. Result Left half 2 tries (6 pts) Right half Nil.
	3.30 pm	Soccer match. Battn v. 54th M.G.Coy. Result 54th M.G.Coy. 2 goals, Beds 1 goal (Ball burst 10 minutes before time).
17-4-17		Brigade Training postponed on account of weather. Company training.
	6 pm	Captain C.C.Stewart arrived from 55th F.Ambulance to take over M.O. vice Capt.J.W.Turner.
18-4-17		Company training. Wet day.
	2.30 pm	Capt.J.W.Turner left for England.
19-4-17	9 am	Route March. Inspection of Transport by Col. Commdg 18th Div. Train & Brig. 54th Inf. Bd.

| 20-4-17 | 8.30 am – 2 pm | Batt. under Bde orders formed a line of Outposts N.W. of STEENBECQUE. |
| 21-4-17 | 9 am | Batt. left STEENBECQUE & marched to LA PIERRIERE (Map. ref. P19A centre sheet 36a) where it billeted at 12 noon). |

LA PIERRIERE

22-4-17	10 am	Church parade.
23-4-17	9 am to 6.45 pm	Brigade Training. Outpost scheme.
24-4-17		Company Training.
25-4-17		Company Training.
26-4-17	12.45pm	Left LA PIERRIERE, marched to BAILLEUL les PERNES arrived 6.30 pm & billeted there for night.

BAILLEUL les PERNES

| 27-4-17 | 8.30 am | Marched out by Road & entrained at BOURS at 2.30 pm for ARRAS (The Batt. should have entrained at Pernes but the train was de railed thus making the march 7 miles longer). |
| | 10.30pm | Arrived ARRAS & marched to billets. |

NEUVILLE

| 28-4-17 | 1.30 am | Arrived at NEUVILLE VITASSE (S.E. ARRAS 5 miles) billeted in Hun Trenches (N.20 A 99 map 51 B, S.W. France) |
| | 8.45 pm | Took over Trenches front line (N.W. CHÉRISY Map ref. O 25 D. Sheet 51 B. S.W) from 17th and 20th King's Liverpool Regt. |

TRENCHES

| 29-4-17 | 8.45 pm | Relieved in trenches by 7th (Queens) W.Surreys returned to NEUVILLE VITASSE. |

NEUVILLE

| 30-4-17 | | Billets in village. |
| 1-5-17 | 8.45 | Relieved 6th Northants in R. sub sector Front trenches W. CHÉRISY |

Trenches

| 2-5-17 | | Trenches. |
| 3-5-17 | 3.45 am | The 18th Div. attacked CHÉRISY. The 54th Bd on R. 55th on L. 53rd Reserve. The attack was supposed to take place at dawn Zero being 3.45 am. As a matter of fact it was not light enough to attack until 4.15 am. The barrage commenced badly, being irregular. The Batt. left their trenches before Zero & formed up splendidly, the advance started at Zero, they soon slightly lost direction the men being extended at about 12 paces could scarcely see each other. The Regt. on the left also lost direction & crowded to the Right, thus confusing our attack & causing a further |

loss of direction. Four Tanks were to be used to attack FONTAINE village. One was unable to start, another went but a short distance another one made its way down Wood Trench & then turned & came through our advancing lines, this added to the confusion & some groups retired to the first line again. They were reformed at once by their Officers & again advanced, the Barrage had however gone on & the Batt. was held up at FONTAINE Trench was [sic] was strongly defended, also the wire was thick and undamaged. They came under heavy M.G. fire from VIS en ARTOIS – CHÉRISY – FONTAINE TR. and WOOD TRENCH. Small detachments pushed forward to angle formed by FONTAINE Tr. and WOOD Tr. At this time the majority of the 55th Bd. had reached their first objective on the Left. The position of the Batt. about 10 am was in front of FONTAINE Tr. with their R. thrown back facing WOOD Trench. At this time the Leicesters on the Right had not made good WOOD Trench except a small portion at the Western end. Some groups of the 55th Bd. reached a portion of their second objective. About 11.30 the 14th Div. further to the Left commenced retiring, followed by the 55th Bd. & the Middlesex & some groups of the Bedfords, but about 1 company still remained in Shell holes in front of FONTAINE & WOOD Trenches when at mid day the troops on our left had all got back to the starting Trenches.

	7.15 pm	A new Barrage started, & 2 Coys NORTHANTS attacked on our frontage in which elements of the Batt. joined & which was covered by rapid fire from our advanced Troops, this however was not successful as the enemy put up an intense barrage & the wire in front could not be forced. The whole lot fell back to original front line & held that during the night being relieved early in the morning by the NORTHANTS taking over.
4-5-17	2.30 am	Bedfords relieved in front Trenches by NORTHANTS & fell back to Trenches at N.30.D.
	2.30 pm	The 54th Bd. relieved by 53rd Bd. The batt. marched back in small parties to Trenches at N.14 D 50. E of NEUVILLE VITASSE.

NEUVILLE
5-5-17		Batt. rested & bathed in NEUVILLE
6-5-17 to		Batt. rested
7-5-17		
8-5-17	10 pm	Batt reported at 10 pm in HÉNINEL for R.E. work in communication Trenches. Guides were confused & 2 companies returned not having guides. A Coy. had 1 man killed & 4 wounded.
9-5-17		Batt. resting.
10-5-17	10 pm	Batt. reported to Sussex Pioneers for fatigue on front line Trenches.
11-5-17		Batt. resting.

12-5-17	10 pm	Batt. reported to Sussex Pioneers for fatigue on front line Trenches.
13-5-17	3 pm	Batt. moved out of Trenches at N.14 D 50 to new area at N.32 A.

N.32.a

14-5-17	10 pm	Batt. digging front line Trenches.
15-5-17		Company drill.
16-5-17 to 24-5-17		Batt. resting at N.32.A & providing working parties every second night.
24-5-17 to 27-5-17		Batt. still at N 32 a and finding working parties.

BOVELLES

27-5-17	4.30 pm	Batt. left camp at N 32 a & moved into camp near BOVELLES at S 23 a, changing with the 8th Suffolks.
27-5-17 to 31-5-17		Battn. in camp at S 23 a for Training purposes; latter consisted chiefly of Close Order Drill, bayonet Fighting & Specialist Training with a Brigade Tactical Scheme on the 30th May.
1-6-17		Getting ready for move to trenches. Two Football matches & one cricket match played while here, all of which were won.

Trenches

2-6-17	2.30 pm	Battn moved up into support trenches opposite FONTAINE relieving 7th Queens (55th Bde.) Battn H.Q.s & "D" Coy. in HINDENBERG SUPPORT (SHAFT TRENCH), "C" Coy in CONCRETE TR., "A" & "B" Coys in the ROOKERY.
2-6-17 to 9-6-17		Battn in support in above & finding working parties by night
9-6-17		Relieved 6th Northants in Front Line Trenches (Left Sector), "A" Coy (right) & "B" Coy (left) in front line, "C" & "D" Coys in support. One man wounded in "A" Coy. One German shot by "A" Coy's No.3 Post.
10-6-17		Fairly quiet except for some shelling of the HORSESHOE POST "A" Coy had one casualty.
11-6-17		100 yds. of wire put out by "D" Coy. Patrol sent out by "B" Coy. reported German Bomb Block in CABLE TRENCH held.
12-6-17		D Coy. relieved "B" Coy in Left Sector. 100 yds of wire put out by "C" Coy.
13-6-17		Two Germans shot by "D" Coy's HORSESHOE POST at 2.20 a.m. Identification 459th Regt. Heavy shelling & Trench Mortaring on left Coy's sector during the evening & following night. Lt.F.N.Sherwell was badly wounded by a shell & died at 8.45 p.m. "D" Coy. also had 1 man killed & 5 wounded.
14-6-17		378 Gas Projectors discharged from WOOD TR. at 2.46 a.m. Reported that 200 Germans were seen being

		carried away on stretchers. Heavy shelling of CURTAIN TR. at 2.15 a.m. & 11 a.m. Day otherwise quiet.
15-6-17	3 a.m.	Heavy Barrage on our trenches. This was followed by heavy shelling of CURTAIN TR, throughout the day & during the night there was much shelling & Trench Mortaring. 1 man in "A" Coy. killed.
16-6-17		Some shelling during the day, but on the whole rather quieter.
17-6-17		3 men wounded in "B" Coy. at 8 am; otherwise a quiet day. Battn. relieved in evening by 5th DURHAM L.I. (50th Div.) and marched back to camp at S.17

MONCHY-AU-BOIS

18-6-17	6.30 pm	Left camp at S 17 & marched to MONCHY-AU-BOIS, where Battn. bivouacked for night 18th/19th. Lt.Col.Mills went on leave and Major A.E.Percival took over command of the Battn. during his absence.
	11 pm	Capt.R.O.Clark joined the Battn. & was posted to "A" Coy.

HÉNU

19-6-17	5.30 am	Battn left bivouacs & marched to billets at HÉNU. Draft of 198 O.R. arrived.
19-20-6-17		Bathing, clothing & refitting.
22-6-17		Training.
23-6-17		Musketry on range at COIGNEUX.
24-6-17		C.of E. Service at 10 a.m.
25-6-17		Musketry & Wiring.
26-6-17		Divisional Cross-Country Race. Battn. finished 6th.
27-6-17		Musketry. Battn. Transport Competition.
28-6-17		Wiring & Digging. Battn. Sports.
29-6-17		Training, Attack Formations etc.
30-6-17		Wiring & Attack Formation. Divisional Sports.
1-7-17	10 am	Church Parade.
	2 pm	2nd Lt.Conyers joined the Battn. & was posted to "D" Coy. Draft of 18 O.R. arrived.
2-7-17		Company training.
3-7-17	2.30 pm	The Battn. (less "D" Coy.) marched to DOULLENS and entrained there at 10.15 p.m. Major J.H.Bridcutt D.S.O. rejoined the Battn. from Senior Officers' School, Aldershot.

GODEWAERSVELDE

4-7-17	6 am	Battn. detrained at GODEWAERSVELDE and after taking breakfast marched to billets, arriving about 9.30 a.m. Billets were in scattered farms about 1½ miles N.W. of ABEELE. "D" Coy. followed later in the day & arrived about 7 p.m. Major J.H.Bridcutt D.S.O. took over command of the Battn. Major A.E.Percival becoming 2nd-in-command.
5-7-17	3 p.m.	All officers of the Bn. interviewed by Gen.Jacob G.O.C. 2nd Corps.

OUDERDOM

6-7-17	7.30 pm	Bn. marched into camp near OUDERDOM – (Palace Camp). Draft of 37 O.R. joined the Bn.
8-7-17		700 men sent up for burying cable S. of ZILLEBEKE LAKE – a good deal of shelling, but no casualties.
9-7-17		Camp shelled at intervals during the day – one man killed. Companies were moved to more scattered positions.
10-7-17		Company Training.
11-7-17		700 men engaged in carrying gas shells & T.M.Bombs up to the front line. Heavy shelling all night. Casualties – 3 Killed, 19 wounded.
12-7-17		Company Training.
13-7-17		Company Training.
14-7-17		Working Parties of about 650 found for burying cable. Heavy shelling with Gas Shells prevented any work being done. This shelling lasted for over two hours, during the whole of which time the men wore their Respirators.
15-7-17	2 am	Capt.D.S.H.Keep was killed by a shell on W. edge of ZILLEBEKE LAKE. Other casualties: – 3 wounded, 4 gassed.
16-7-17	6.30pm	Capt.Keep was buried in RENINGHELST CEMETERY with full military honours.
17-7-17	9.30 pm	Shell burst in our lines demolishing one of "B" Coy's Tents, but causing no casualties. 550 men sent up on working parties, Burying cable, carrying etc. casualties in "A" Coy – 4 Killed, 5 wounded.
18-7-17		"A" & "B" Coys. bathed in afternoon at RENINGHELST.
19-7-17		Attack formation practice in morning.
20-7-17	8 am	Lt.Col.G.P.Mills returned from leave & resumed command of the Battn. Major J.H.Bridcutt becoming 2nd-in-command. C & D Coys. bathed. About 450 men sent up on working parties in evening to ZILLEBEKE Area carrying T.M. ammunition etc. casualties 11.
21-7-17		Intermittent shelling of PALACE CAMP during evening & following night; no damage.

WIPPENHOEK

22-7-17	9 am	Battn. marched into camp at WIPPENHOEK (CONNAUGHT CAMP) arriving about 11.30 a.m.
23-7-17		Practice in attack formation.

STEENVOORDE

24-7-17	7 am	Left camp at about 7 a.m. & marched to billets about 2 miles N.W. of STEENVOORDE.
25-7-17		Practice in attack formations.
26-7-17		Practice in attack formations. Second anniversary of Bn's arrival in France.
27-7-17		Practice in attack formations.
	8 pm	2nd Anniversary of Bn's arrival in France was celebrated by a dinner in STEENVOORDE, at which the following, who landed with the Bn. in 1915 were present:

		Brig.Gen.G.D.Price, Lt.Col.G.P.Mills, Major J.H.Bridcutt (guest), Major A.E.Percival, Capt.W.W.Colley, Capt.H.Driver, Capt.O.Kingdon, Capt.H.Ramsbotham, Lt.S.R.Chapman, Lt. & Q.M.F.Corner. Draft of 6 O.R. joined the Bn.
28-7-17		Practice in attack formations.

Wippenhoek
29-7-17	6 am	Left billets & marched to camp at WIPPENHOEK (CONNAUGHT CAMP).
	10 pm	Left WIPPENHOEK & marched to PALACE CAMP, OUDERDOM, arriving early in the morning of the 30th.

Palace Camp
30-7-17		Resting at PALACE CAMP.

New Canal Reserve Camp
31-7-17	2 am	Moved to NEW CANAL RESERVE CAMP, in readiness for the 3rd Btt. of YPRES, which started at 3.50 a.m.
	9.15 am	Commenced to move forward by platoons from NEW CANAL RESERVE CAMP, but on arrival at CH.SEGARD the Bn. was stopped & ordered to return to NEW CANAL RESERVE CAMP, where they spent the rest of the day.
1-8-17		The Battalion in accordance with Brigade Orders moved to Chateau Segard Area No.4.

CHATEAU SEGARD
2-8-17	Spent at Chateau Segard. The men were rested as much as possible and only scouts and runners were sent forward to reconnoitre the route up for pending operations.
3-8-17	A general inspection of kit took place in the morning. In the evening at 7 PM the Battalion moved up by companies to "Railway dugouts" at Shrapnel Corner arriving about 9 PM.

RAILWAY DUGOUTS
4-8-17	Each company spent the day in cleaning out their dugouts and improving the path at the foot of the embankment. The battalion was in support during its occupation of these dug outs.
5-8-17	The companies continued to improve the path at the foot of the embankment and built an esplanade along the triangle pond. Eight scouts and two runners per company and Headquarters reconnoitred the route up to the HOOGE TUNNEL dug outs at the elbow in the HOOGE MENIN Road where our Headquarters were to be for the pending operations. MAJOR BRIDCUTT DSO and the Adjutant attended a conference at Brigade H.Q. at DORMY HOUSE end of RITZ trenches at 6 PM to discuss the general principles of the intended attack.

6-8-17 — Scouts again reconnoitred the route up to the wire. Officers also went up to insure that no mistake should take place when the battalion moved up to the line either to counter attack or relieve the garrison. A practice standing to was ordered at 5.30 PM. B Company reported ready to move off at 5.40 PM and was duly congratulated upon this fine performance.

7-8-17 — Warning orders having been received the Battalion prepared for a move up to the line during the day. Orders were received in the afternoon to relieve the 12 MIDDLESEX in the line in the evening and to carry out the intended attack during the ensuing forty eight hours. All companies had dumped their packs issued their iron rations and water by 6.30 PM. D Company moved off at 7 PM followed by A Company at 7.30 PM, B and C Company moved at 8 PM and 8.30 PM. D Company relieved two platoons of the 12th Middlesex Regiment in the front line from SURBITON VILLAS to the road in J7D (app 1) A company relieved a company of the same regiment in the HOOGE TUNNEL at the elbow in the HOOGE MENIN Road marked with a cross in App I. This company was detailed as counter attack company. B and C companies were situated in the RITZ trenches as Brigade reserve. Battalion headquarters relieved the 12th MIDDLESEX H.Q. in the HOOGE TUNNEL at the elbow in the MENIN road. The relief was completed by about midnight. The night was fairly active, A and D companies encountered considerable hostile shell fire in moving up through SANCTUARY WOOD. Cap H.DRIVER DSO and Cap O.KINGDON put out wire forming up lines about 100 yards in advance of our trenches during the night to facilitate the laying of the forming up tape for pending operations. Lt.STEWART also put down a white tape to make a convenient route from Bn HQ to the firing line in SURBITON VILLAS.

HOOGE TUNNEL
8-8-17 — The battalion held the line. Officers and NCOs were carefully instructed in the ground to be attacked and peculiar features and land marks were pointed out to them, they were subsequently examined to ascertain whether they had thoroughly grasped the situation. Enemy strong points and wired areas were pointed out and noted. About 7 PM a heavy storm blew up and intense rain fell, the ground became exceedingly heavy and very muddy. The attack arranged for the 9th was postponed 24 hours.

9-8-17 — The day proved fine with a good breeze blowing which helped to dry the ground. Officers and NCOs continued to examine the features of the landscape to be attacked over on the following day. In the evening the weather again appeared threatening but blew up fine during the night. Cap

H.DRIVER and Cap O.KINGDON put out the forming up tapes about 10 PM. At 11 PM the leading platoons of B and C companies began to arrive as described in App II [see Appendix B2.3]. After receiving tea and rum the platoons were passed forward with guides to their forming up positions.

GLENCORSE WOOD
10-8-17

At 3.30 AM all companies were formed up for the attack timed for 4.35 AM. C company on the right B Company on the left A Company in close support and D Company in reserve under Caps O.KINGDON, H.DRIVER DSO, R.O.CLARK, J.C.M.FERGUSON. The forming up was carried out in an exceedingly steady manner under considerable enemy artillery and M/G fire and great credit is due to the company commanders for the cool and deliberate manner in which they handled their companies. At zero hour 4.35 an intense British barrage opened and the battalion moved forward close under its protection. A full account of the glorious manner in which all ranks carried out their duties appears in APP.II [see Appendix B2.3]. The battalion famous for its fighting spirit in the past eclipsed all former deeds of gallantry, when heavy wire held up the foremost men, those behind stood on lumps of earth and rubbish and fired over the heads of those cutting the wire, seldom have any troops shown such brilliant dash and utter contempt for the Bosch. By 5.13 AM NONNE BOSSCHEN Wood was reached and at the same time all other objectives occupied. Within an hour SAA Lewis gun drums etc had been dispatched to the advanced positions and much consolidation had been carried out. Very early in the operations the 11th Royal Fusiliers operating on our right and the Queens operating on their right became adversely involved with a Bosch strong point at the N.W. Corner of INVERNESS COPSE and the whole attack on our right became confused and fell back. The Fusiliers fell back from their advanced posts on to a line running along the ridge from the SW Corner of GLENCOURSE WOOD to CLAPHAM JUNCTION. This change in the situation exposed our right flank and necessitated the partial expenditure of D Company to make a defensive flank which was carried out by Cap Ferguson in a quick and clever manner. Very severe fighting resulted later in the day through the unsatisfactory position in which our troops were placed. About 5.30 PM the Bosch showed considerable movement and it became evident that a heavy counter attack was imminent: by 6 PM the attack developed and by 7 PM the situation was severe, the Bosch attacking in mass and our own guns shooting desperately short. This condition lasted till 9 PM by which time although we had lost connection with our advanced posts the main position was still firmly in our hands and the enemy casualties were extremely heavy. About 8.30 PM the 6th Royal Berks were sent up to relieve our companies and one company of Norfolks took over the strong point at the SW Corner of GLENCOURSE WOOD from which the Fusiliers had previously been relieved by us. By 2 AM the Regiment had been completely relieved by the Royal Berks and moved back to CHATEAU SEGARD Area No.4.

Roll of officers in action APP III [see Appendix C1.6]
Casualties APP IV [see Appendix C1.6]
Operation Orders APP V [see Appendix B1.4]
Aeroplane Photo APP VI [not included]

CHATEAU SEGARD [and] DIKKEBUS NEW CAMP

11-8-17		The morning was spent in rest.
	2 PM	The Battalion moved to DIKKEBUS NEW CAMP. The afternoon was spent in clothing and fitting.
12-8-17	4 AM	the Battalion received orders that the 54 Brigade less 7th Bedfordshire Regt would move back to rest billets. The 7th Bedfordshire Regt would be attached to the 53 Brigade. The Battalion was reorganised into four companies of two platoons each, each platoon had one rifle section one rifle grenadier section one bombing section one L/G section. Total Battalion strength about 300.
	11 AM	Orders were received from Division to move into a field close to Div.H.Q. and rest there until the evening.
	2 PM	After dinners the Battalion moved to the field mentioned where the Div.General (General Lee) address [sic] a few words to the men and thanked them for their gallant behaviour in the action of August 10th. He also said that he had given instructions to [sic] we were not to be used unless absolutely necessary.

18 DIV H.Q.

	6.30 PM	The afternoon having been spent in receiving SAA rations etc the companies moved off at 6.30 PM A and D companies to CRAB CRAWL C and B and HQ to RAILWAY DUGOUTS.
	11 PM	The Battalion was in support to 53 Brigade.
13-8-17		The companies prepared for action if necessary, guides etc reconnoitred the routes. During the night HQ and B & C Companies were heavily shelled with gas shells.
14-8-17		Early in the morning we received orders to relieve the 10th Essex Regiment at STIRLING CASTLE. Guides were at once sent up to arrange the relief. Orders were received for us to make an attack on INVERNESS COPSE on the 16th inst. we were surprised after what the general had said only two days before, but all were cheery and ready to do all they could. Major Bridcutt and the Adjutant went up to STIRLING CASTLE to arrange the relief of the 10th ESSEX. MAJOR BRIDCUTT remained up and the Adjutant returned to RAILWAY DUGOUTS to see the companies off.

THE WAR DIARY 1917   83

	7.30 PM	The companies set out for the relief.
	12 MID-NIGHT	Relief complete. Battle Order A and D companies in front line with one platoon C Company attached to each. B Company in reserve.

STIRLING CASTLE

15-8-17		The night having passed off quietly with only the usual amount of shelling the Battalion continued to hold the line. The 6th Royal Berks were on our left and a Battalion of North Staffs on our right. Heavy shelling of our positions took place during the day. B Company was detailed to carry out the attack on the Bosch strong point at J14 c 4.4 NW Corner of INVERNESS COPSE, on the 16th inst. 2Lt.CRAIG being in command examined the ground and explained the situation to his company.
16-8-17		B Company having formed up on the tapes put out by 2nd Lt.CRAIG during the night attacked the enemy strong point at J14 c.4.4. (APP I) This attack was carried out in conjunction with a large offensive by the Division on our left; a heavy shrapnel barrage opened at ZERO hour (4.45 AM) and 4.5 howitzers shot on strong points. Owing to some mistake a battery of 4.5 howitzers detailed to shoot on the enemy's strong point at J 14 c.4.4 fired short and on to our B Company about to move forward to the attack, knocking 50% of their effectives out. Cap Ferguson at once supported with a platoon of D Company but owing to the heavy enemy M/G fire little could be done and the attempt to capture the strong point was abandoned.
	7 AM	the day was chiefly spent in artillery duels no further infantry activity taking place on our sector.
17-8-17		The Battalion continued to hold the line, the 6th Royal Berkshire were relieved by the 12 MIDDLESEX also lent to 53 Brigade by 54 Brigade. This relief took place during night of 16/17. During the night 17/18th the Battalion was relieved by the Rifle Brigade and moved back to DIKKEBUS RAILHEAD.

DIKKEBUS RAILHEAD

18-8-17	11.30AM	The Battalion entrained from DIKKEBUS RAILHEAD and moved to ARNEKE arriving at 4 PM and marching to billets at BUYSSCHEURE arriving at 8 PM. BUSSES were supplied for kits and men who could not march.

BUYSSCHEURE

19-8-17		The Battalion rested.
20-8-17		The Battalion refitted and Bathed.
21-8-17		A draft of 70 having arrived companies commenced reorganising into four platoons.
22-8-17		Training Platoon and Company Drill.
23-8-17	6.30 AM 7.30 PM	The Battalion went to the sea side by bus for a holiday, the scene of these festivities was near DUNKIRK.

24-8-17		The V Army musketry range was allotted to the Battalion. The men were taken there by lorries starting at 9 AM. The rifle shooting of the men was good each man fired 15 rounds at a figure target, and L/Gs had plate firing.
25-8-17		Platoon training.
26-8-17	11 AM	Church parade.
27-8-17		Company training.
28-8-17		Brigade rifle range was allotted to us but owing wet weather we could not use it. A Route March took place.
29-8-17		Companies had a [sic] advantage of training under a special Bayonet fighting instruction.
30-8-17		Company training and specialists training.
31-8-17		Company training.
1-9-17		Battn carried out practice attack. Blank ammunition was used & the new form of attack was adopted.
	5 pm	Divisional Cross Country Race. The Bn. obtained 4th place in the 5 mile contest. Conditions: Teams of 8, first 6 to count. First 5 of Bn team were well up but the 6th man dropped a lot of points.
2-9-17		Bathing.

ARNEKE

3-9-17	12.30	Moved by Route March from BUYSSCHEURE to ARNEKE. Here the Bn was billeted in farms, being very scattered.
4-9-17		Musketry on 5th Army Range EPERLECQUES. Bn was conveyed in lorries and each man fired 3 practice.
5-9-17	7 am	Parade. The abolition of the entry parade had not proved a success, as it led to much slackness.
	9 am	Coy Training – Guard Mounting, Specialists, Coys in attack, Platoon Drill.
6-9-17		Specialist Training followed by Battn in attack.
7-9-17	7 am	Early morning parade.
	9 am	Specialist Training, followed by Platoon Drill.
8-9-17	7 am	Early morning parade.
	11 am	Demonstration of Gas Cloud, whole Battn attended.
9-9-17	11.30am	Voluntary Church Parade. 2nd Lt.R.W.Curtice joined the Battn & was posted to "B" Coy. 2nd Lt.T.N.Donovan joined the Battn & was posted to "A" Coy.
10-9-17	7 am	Parade.
	8 am – 5 pm	Bathing.
11-9-17		Bn. carried out a practice attack with 12th M'x as Moppers Up.
12-9-17	7 am	Parade.
	9 am	Specialist Training & Coy. Drill.
13-9-17		"C" & "D" Coys "Moppers Up" to 11th Royal Fusiliers in attack scheme "A" & "B" Coys. acted as enemy.
14-9-17	7 am	Early Parade.
	9 am	Specialist Training & Platoon Drill.
	3 pm	Cricket match.

15-9-17		Bn. carried out a very successful attack scheme with "Moppers Up" & Enemy, found by 11th Royal Fusiliers. "C" & "D" Coys were attacking "B" Coy Support, "A" Coy Reserve.
16-9-17		5 officers & about 300 O.R. proceeded to the seaside near MARDYCK for the day. Weather good & all ranks much enjoyed themselves.
17-9-17		5 officers & 200 O.R. proceeded to seaside. Remainder carried out Specialist Training. Tactical scheme for officers in evening. Bn. received 1 Bar to M.M. & 29 M.M. for good work on 9th/16th Aug.
18-9-17		Early Parade & Specialist Training. Work stopped by rain. Draft of 16 O.R. M.C. awarded to Lt. & Qr.F.Corner & Capt.J.A.Vlasto, R.A.M.C. and a Bar to M.C. to Capt.W.W.Colley.
19-9-17		Whole Bn. bathed. "C" & "D" Coys acted as "Moppers Up" to 11th Royal Fusiliers in tactical Scheme.
	3 pm	All officers & Platoon Sgts attended demonstration of wiring by 80th Field Coy. R.E. at LEDRINGHEM.
20-9-17		Coy. Training; platoons in attack scheme. Draft of 16 O.R. having joined the Battn. on the 19th were posted on this date.
21-9-17	9 am	Platoons in attack scheme.
	10.45am	"D" Coy's Drill Competition won by No.15 Platoon.
	12.30pm	Presentation of M.C.'s, D.C.M.'s & M.M.'s to 1 officer & 29 O.R. by Brig.-Gen.C.Cunliffe Owen C.B. 2nd Lt.G.H.D.Adams & 20 O.R. joined the Bn. on this date.

SINT-JAN-TER-BIEZEN

22-9-17		Bn. moved by train from ARNEKE to HUPOUTRE and marched from there to TUNNELLING CAMP, near SINT-JAN-TER-BIEZEN, just W. of POPERINGHE.
23-9-17		CHURCH PARADE at 10 a.m.
24-9-17		Platoon training; 8 officers proceeded to 18th Coys School at VOLKERINGHOVE for 4 day course.
25-9-17		Platoon in attack. 5 officers went to 18th Coys School for the day.
26-9-17		Platoon in attack. 5 officers went to 18th Coys School for the day. Draft of 12 O.R. arrived.
27-9-17		Specialist Training & Musketry. 5 officers to 18th Coys School. Draft of 6 O.R.
28-9-17		Specialist Training, wiring etc. 2nd Lts W.N.Brawn, R.C.S.Ransom, F.H.Fox & H.W.Haward joined the Bn. on this date. Bn. dinner to celebrate anniversary of THIEPVAL & SCHWABEN REDOUBT victory.
29-9-17		Coy.Training. Aeroplane Raid at night.
30-9-17		CHURCH PARADE.
1-10-17	9 am	Demonstration of new form of attack to all officers & N.C.O's. Bn. Route March. 2nd Lt.T.H.FLAVELL joined Bn. & posted to "C" Coy.
2-10-17		Coys. in attack schemes. In consequence of several Bombing Raids, 2 Coys were moved into a camp in the wood.

3-10-17		Specialist Training.
4-10-17		Bn. practiced attack over spit-locked trenches etc.
5-10-17		Coy. Training. Draft of 9 O.R. arrived.
6-10-17		Bn. again practised attack.
	8.30 pm	Night operations. Forming up etc.
7-10-17		Church Parade. Very wet day. 2nd Lt.MAW reported for duty.
8-10-17		Coy. Training. Night operations.
9-10-17		Battn. in attack in conjunction with 12th Middlesex Regt.
10-10-17		Coy. Training.
11-10-17		Battn. in attack.
12-10-17		Night operations.
13-10-17		Coy. Training and Route Marches. During the whole of the week ending on this day the weather was very wet, and seriously interfered with training.
14-10-17		Church Parade. Great improvement in the weather.
15-10-17		Rifle Practice on the Range. Every man firing 10 Rounds.

TUNNELLING CAMP

16-10-17	10 am	The Battalion embussed for Canal Bank, arriving there about 12.30 pm. The rest of the day was spent in preparing companies to go up the line.

CANAL BANK

17-10-17		Officers and Scouts reconnoitred the line held by the Royal Fusiliers in order to relieve them the following day. Two days rations were issued to the men in the evening in order to avoid carrying rations up to the line when the Battalion went in.
18-10-17	2 p.m.	The Battalion moved off up the line to relieve the Royal Fusiliers. A halt was made at Hurst Park to rest the men, and allow the day light to give way to dark. The relief was completed soon after 8 pm.

In the Line

19-10-17	The Battalion held the line without any undue incident other than a severe shelling by Gas Shells. The mud was very bad and duck-boards few. The men suffered considerably from cold & wet. The line held consisted of shell holes filled with water.
20-10-17	The line was held by the Battalion until the evening, when it was relieved by the Queens. The Battalion moved back to Irish Farm where it entrained for Tunnelling Camp, arriving there about 7 am in the morning. A certain amount of difficulty was experienced in carrying out the relief owing to bad communications. "D" Coy whose relief was somewhat delayed decided to wait until daylight when shelling would not be so bad. They consequently did not reach Tunnelling Camp until mid-day.

Tunnelling Camp

21-10-17	The afternoon was spent in refitting, bathing the men and attending to feet & boots.

22-10-17		The men were rested and refitted in anticipation of proceeding up the line again.
23-10-17		Some drill exercises were carried out, S.A.A., Lewis Guns etc completed and final arrangements for proceeding to the line for another tour.
24-10-17	9 a.m.	The Battalion embussed for Canal Bank, from whence it marched to Cane Trench. Dinners were served at Cane Trench and rations, water etc. served out to the men for a 48 hours tour in the trenches. In the evening the Battalion relieved the Royal Fusiliers in the line. The relief was completed in the early morning.

In the line

25-10-17	The Battalion held the line successfully. There was a great deal of shelling and incidentally our own guns fired very short.
26-10-17	The Battalion held the line and was relieved in the Evening by the 2/Londons. This relief was about the worst on record, the relieving troops losing their way up and becoming thoroughly disorganised. The relief was not complete until about 10 a.m. next morning, when the Battalion embussed at Canal Bank for Dirty Bucks Camp.

Dirty Bucks Camp

27-10-17		The men spent the day resting.
28-10-17		Refitting and cleaning. Preparing to move on the following day.
29-10-17	9.45 am	The Battalion set out by Route March via International Corner to Putney Camp, arriving there for dinners at 2 p.m.

Putney Camp

30-10-17	Re-organisation of companies & platoons and a little parade drill.
31-10-17	Training commenced in earnest. The usual programmes were prepared and the men carried out Physical Exercises before breakfast and Company and Platoon Drill in the morning.
1-11-17	Training as per programme [see Appendix A2.12].
2-11-17	Training as per programme [see Appendix A2.12].
3-11-17	Training as per programme [see Appendix A2.12].
4-11-17	The Battalion moved to Ondank – Box Camp, entraining at 1 p.m. at PROVEN.

Box Camp

5-11-17	Spent in organising camp, clearing drains, putting up Bomb protection round huts and tents etc.
6-11-17	Training as per programme [see Appendix A2.12].
7-11-17	Training as per programme [see Appendix A2.12].
8-11-17	Training as per programme [see Appendix A2.12].
9-11-17	Training as per programme [see Appendix A2.12].
10-11-17	The Battalion relieved the 6th Royal Berks Regt. in Baboon

Camp, BOEZINGE, and took over the duties of support Battn to the 11th Royal Fusiliers who were in the line.

Baboon Camp
11-11-17 –
13-11-17
Working Parties were found by day and night for carrying up R.E. material to the Front Line. On the evening of the 13th the Battalion relieved the 11th Royal Fusiliers in the Front Line – Houthulst Forest, the boundaries being SANCTUARY ROAD on the right and FAIDHERBE ROAD on the left, in conjunction with the 43rd French Regiment.

Front Line
14-11-17   No particular incident.
15-11-17   At 4.45 pm the Bosche delivered an attack on the junction of the French and British Armies but was repulsed with heavy losses. Colonel Carot commanding the 43rd Regiment personally congratulated the 54th Brigade and in particular the Bedfordshire Regiment on their keenness and dashing manner in repelling the German attack.
16-11-17   No particular incident occurred.
    Midnight   The Battn was relieved by the 6th Royal Berks. Throughout the relief the enemy indulged in severe Gas shelling, which somewhat hindered the relief but on the morning of the 17th at 2 am the relief was complete.

Box Camp
17-11-17   The Battn moved down from the Line by train from BOEZINGE, detraining at Ondank Siding, and moved into Box Camp, and spent the remainder of the day resting.
18-11-17   The Battn refitted and sick were attended to and Coys reorganised for training.
19-11-17   Training as per programme.
20-11-17   Training as per programme.
21-11-17   Training as per programme.
22-11-17   The Battn relieved the 6th Royal Berks in Canal Bank Camp, Boezinge entraining at Ondank Siding at 1 pm and detraining at Boezinge at 1.45 pm. In the evening working parties were found.

Canal Bank
23-11-17   The usual Working Parties were found and a systematic programme of improving the camp was carried out.
24-11-17   Working parties were found for the line and camp improvement programme was continued
25-11-17   Work on camp was continued.
26-11-17   On the evening and early morning of 25/26 the Battn relieved the Royal Fusiliers in the line as per Operation Orders No.182. The relief was complete at 12.30 am. No particular incident occurring.

Front Line
    No particular incident to report during the day.

27-11-17	The Battn held the Front Line without incident.
28-11-17	The Battn held the Front Line without incident.
29-11-17	During the night of 28/29 the Battn was relieved by the 6th Royal Berks. The relief was complete at 12.30 am and the Battn entrained at BOEZINGE, detraining at International Corner and proceeded to "J" Camp, spending the remainder of the day resting (see Operation Order No.183).

"J" Camp

30-11-17	The Battn spent the day refitting.
1-12-17	Refitting and re-organisation of Companies. Special training of Stretcher Bearers.
2-12-17	Church Parades and Bathing at 17th Divisional Baths.
3-12-17	Training as per programme.
4-12-17	The Battalion relieved the 6th Bn. Royal Berks at BABOON CAMP in accordance with Order No.184.

Baboon Camp

5-12-17	The Battalion provided Working Parties from Baboon Camp carrying up to the 11th Royal Fusiliers who hold the line.
6-12-17	The Battalion remained in support in Baboon Camp and again supplied carrying parties for the 11th Royal Fusiliers in the Front Line.
7-12-17	The Battalion still remained in Reserve to the 11th Royal Fusiliers and again supplied Working Parties.
8-12-17	The Battalion relieved the 11th Royal Fusiliers in the Left sub-sector of the line in front of HOUTHULST FOREST on the night of 7th and 8th. The relief was duly completed without incident. Operation Orders attached N.170 [not included]. For photographs of the line see Appendix 3.

in the Line

9-12-17	The Battalion held the Left Sub-sector in the Front Line without incident.
10-12-17	The Battalion again held the line in the front of HOUTHULST FOREST without incident and carried out a certain amount of Wiring.

"J" Camp

11-12-17	The Battalion was relieved by the 7th Royal West Kent Regiment on the night of 10th/11th and entrained at BOEZINGE for "J" Camp, arriving about 7 a.m. The remainder of the day was spent in resting. Operation Orders attached.
12-12-17	Refitting and Inventory taken of damage to equipment etc.
13-12-17	Re-organisation of Companies and inspection of the same by major A.E.Percival, M.C., Commanding the Battalion.
14-12-17	Lieut.Col.G.P.Mills D.S.O. returned to the Battalion from Commanding the Brigade, and duly took over Command

90   THE SHINY SEVENTH

	from Major A.E.Percival, M.C. Company Training was carried out.
15-12-17	Promotions and Appointments were made to complete establishment and Training was carried out as per attached programme [not included].
16-12-17	The Battalion moved from "J" Camp to CLAUDE CHAPPE CAMP, [ROESBRUGGE] HARINGE AREA for Rest period. General Sadleir Jackson took the March – Past and was pleased with the general turn-out of the Battalion. The Battalion arrived in new area in time for dinner; each company being billeted in a separate hut, and one detached Company in Northampton Lines. There was also a Cinema Hall in the Centre of the Camp, which subsequently provided the troops with excellent charcoal.

CLAUDE CHAPPE CAMP

17-12-17	Capt.H.C.Browning took over duties with the Battalion again having been attached to Brigade. A course of five weeks' Training was commenced, as per programme. Major Percival proceeded on short leave to England.
18-12-17	The cinema Hall was burnt down at 10.30 p.m. Fire picquets turned out and the Divisional Fire Brigade attended, but the Hall was completely demolished. A certain amount of danger existed through proximity of other huts and the Horse Transport Lines, which were kept doused with water and fortunately escaped damage.
19-12-17	Training as per programme.
20-12-17	Training as per programme and Inter Platoon Football Matches.
21-12-17	Lieut.Col.G.P.Mills, D.S.O. proceeded on leave to England. Training was carried out as per programme. Lecture by Captain Long, R.E., on "Interception of Wireless Messages and Telephonic Messages" at 2.30 pm. Captain W.J.W.Colley, M.C. took over command of the Battn.
22-12-17	Training as per programme. A Brigade Rifle range was commenced and one Company was employed daily in its construction.
23-12-17	Church Parade and Football occupied the day.
24-12-17 25-12-17 26-12-17	Christmas Holidays. No Parades were held. Christmas Dinners were held by Companies separately from 12 noon to 4 p.m. each man received a Quart of English Beer and Turkeys were obtained from PARIS. There were also Hams, nuts and sweets provided; dinners generally considered a great success. Gen.Sadleir Jackson went round the Brigade to see the Battalions at the Christmas Dinners, and met with a great reception in this Battalion. The Officers held a Dinner at 7 pm in ROESBRUGGE [HARINGE] which, with the efforts of Mr.Davies, the Battalion Mess President, was a great success. A draft of 75 O.Rs. arrived at 11.45 am on 25th and were greatly surprised at having Xmas Dinner provided for them. They

THE WAR DIARY 1917   91

	were chiefly men from 19-25 years of age, and largely from the Sussex district.
27-12-17	Training was carried out as per training programme [see Appendix A2.13]. Football in the afternoon. Capt.S.Tabor, Act. Adjutant proceeded to England on leave & handed over his duties to Capt.H.C.Browning.
28-12-17	Training was carried out as per Training Programme [see Appendix A2.13]. The draft was inspected and definitely allotted to Companies. The Battalion had the use of the Divisional Baths in ROESBRUGGE and clean clothing.
29-12-17	Training as per programme [see Appendix A2.13]. Football in the afternoon. General Sadleir Jackson inspected the Battn and Transport at 8 a.m. and witnessed a Tactical Scheme carried out by the Battn. during the morning. Two Companies of the Royal Fusiliers and a detachment of Vickers Guns supplied an enemy for this scheme. At the Conference afterwards the General pointed out the excellent manner in which the N.C.O's and Section Commanders handled their Commands, and the intelligent manner in which all ranks carried out their duties. In the tactical Scheme it was generally considered to be very much above the average.
30-12-17	Church Parades (Voluntary) Football in the Afternoon.
31-12-17	Training as per programme [see Appendix A2.13] and games in the Afternoon.

1918

For a year which ended in victory, 1918 did not begin very well for the Allies. On 1 January they were stuck in trench lines which had not moved very much, in a strategic sense, in three years. Every great push designed to bring a breakthrough had ended in a welter of blood and disillusion. True, the Germans had suffered as badly, but they were still there and, despite the promised arrival of large numbers of Americans, the Allies knew that large numbers of Germans, from the now defunct Eastern Front, would be arriving soon, flushed with victory over Russia.

Things got much worse on 21 March when the Germans launched their great push and this, unlike its Allied counterparts, seemed to have a real chance of ending the war. A huge hammer blow fell on General Gough's Fifth Army which was pushed aside with ease and sent tumbling back towards distant Amiens. Why did this happen? In part it was the wish of David Lloyd George to prevent the generals killing more men in their own, failed, offensives. He deliberately withheld reinforcements from the armies in the field, which resulted in the strength of each Division being reduced by a quarter, from twelve battalions to nine, each brigade now comprising just three battalions (the 54th Brigade lost the 12th Middlesex, who were disbanded). Nevertheless, they were still expected to hold the same amount of front line as previously. In fact the Fifth Army had had to take over more ground from the French on their right, which left them dangerously stretched. The second reason was that the attack came in an area in which barely more than a scraped front-line trench and a bit of wire existed. To absorb a determined attack at least three lines of trenches were needed, spread over a depth of three miles or more, but these were lacking; they were being built, but only really existed in the minds of the planners. The Germans also used new tactics, using infiltration by storm troopers and the element of surprise; there were no week-long bombardments which signalled, inevitably, that an assault was near.

This combination of factors meant that the attack quickly gained a good deal of ground. Not just the Fifth Army, but the Third as well, was sent rearwards, as were French armies further south. Things looked grim for the Allies. Fortunately the attacks eventually petered out as the Germans quickly outran their lines of supply. Their soldiers were used to privations on account of the blockade by the Royal Navy, which was strangling Germany and preventing much in the way of food and little luxuries reaching the front. When the Germans found chocolate, beer and wine in Allied dugouts, they not unnaturally helped themselves. This, too, slowed their advance, allowing a short breathing space for the Allies to recover. In this breathing space the Allies appointed a Supreme Commander, French General Ferdinand Foch, to co-ordinate an integrated response and this, too, helped them to stem the advance.

The 7th Bedfords were in the thick of things during the retreat and played a small but important part in stopping the German advance. This was the counter-attack at Cachy on 24 April, made in conjunction with other elements of the 18th Division and the Australians. This finally halted the German advance just east of Amiens. Amiens was a strategically vital city which, if lost, might have cut the link between the British and French armies and meant a retreat to the Channel ports and a version of Dunkirk twenty-two years before it actually happened.

That was the 7th Bedfords' last hurrah. It was absorbed into the 2nd Battalion on 31 May because the 2nd Battalion had been greatly reduced in numbers through German attacks around Ypres, which were also part of the great Spring Offensive. With no other reinforcements available, one battalion had to be disbanded and it made sense to keep the Regular 2nd and lose the Service 7th. The 2nd Battalion was transferred to the 18th Division and its Commanding Officer was Arthur Percival of the 7th Bedfords (the same man who, as a General, surrendered Singapore to the Japanese in 1942). Indeed, in many ways the 2nd Battalion was the 7th Battalion by another name as the majority of its officers and other ranks were ex-7ths.

The German armies were themselves sent tumbling backwards on 8 August 1918 in a huge Allied offensive in front of Arras. From there on, in one hundred days the Allies advanced steadily until the Armistice on 11 November 1918, which, by a strange coincidence, saw the British front-line at Mons, where it had had its first battle of the war in 1914. The 18th Division and the 2nd Bedfords played their part in this advance, recapturing Albert, for example, that hub of the Battle of the Somme which had fallen in the Spring Offensive. The advance was not a picnic, however, and the number of casualties was still high – as high, at times, as they had been during certain parts of the Battle of the Somme or at Passchendaele. The difference now was that real territorial gains were seen in return for these casualties – gains measured in miles rather than yards. Because of this and because of the final victory, the casualties of 1918 are not viewed in the public mind with the same horror as those of 1915, 1916 and 1917.

In the three years it had been in France and Belgium the 7th Battalion Bedfordshire Regiment had made a name for itself. It was part of a Division considered to be one of Britain's best during the war. It had captured the Pommiers Redoubt and Thiepval, it had stormed into a hail of fire at Glencorse Wood and helped check the great German advance. Altogether it had lost 804 officers and men on active service, including some who died of wounds after the battalion ceased to exist.

CLAUDE CHAPPE CAMP
1-1-18	Battn Training.
2-1-18	Battn Training. Major A.E.Percival M.C. returned from leave & took over command of the Battn.
3-1-18	Coy. Training, Brigade Cross Country Race in which Bn finished third.

J Camp International Corner
4-1-18	Moved by Route March to J Camp arriving about 12.30 p.m. Roads very slippery owing to frost
5-1-18	Cleaning of Equipment & Short Route March.
6-1-18	Coy. Training, Lt.C.A.Lawrence awarded the Military Cross
7-1-18	Exchange of Equipment, A & D Coys being fitted out in leather & B & C Coys in webbing.
8-1-18	Coy. Training in Strong Point Attack. Draft of 28 O.R. arrived.

9-1-18		Coy. Training. Platoon in attack.
10-1-18		54th Brigade moved into the line again in the HOUTHULST FOREST Sector in relief of 55th Inf. Bde.

BABOON CAMP

	1 pm	7th Bedfords relieved 7th Buffs in BABOON CAMP.
11-1-18		C Coy. practised wiring. Weather very cold.
	5 pm	B & D Coys. employed in carrying wiring material from KOKUIT DUMP to ADEN HOUSE – casualties 1 Killed. 2nd Lt.E.J.Scott joined the Bn. & posted to B Coy.
12-1-18	9 am	C Coy. practised wiring. On night 12/13th inst an extensive wiring scheme was carried out on the Brigade front. 80 O.R. of "C" Coy. were detailed to wire the left sub-sector, A Coy. finding the covering party. The work was successfully carried out with only 3 men wounded.
13-1-18		Bn rested at BABOON CAMP & carried out Pedicuric treatment (i.e. washing & Rubbing of feet).
14-1-18		Final preparations for taking over the line.
15-1-18		Bn relieved 11th Royal Fusiliers in the early morning the in left subsector, relief being complete about 5 am. Night cold & frosty & relief carried out without incident.

Trenches HOUTHULST FOREST SECTOR

15-1-18		Heavy rain all day & shell hole positions became very wet. Night very dark with high wind; fairly quiet day & night. A & B Coys. in front line, D in support & C in reserve.
16-1-18		Fine & bright, considerable enemy artillery activity. Carried out some wiring of front line posts by night. Inter Coy. relief commencing at midnight carried out without incident, C & D Coys front line A support B reserve.
17-1-18		Cold with snow showers. Much water again in front line posts which had to be constantly baled out. A considerable number of duck boards were carried up & put into these posts.
18-1-18		Fine & bright, considerable hostile shelling all day. D Coys H.Q.s received a direct hit, 3 men being wounded.
18-1-18	8 pm	Relieved by 7th Buffs & proceeded by train from

J Camp INTERNATIONAL CORNER

19-1-18		BOEZINGE to INTERNATIONAL CORNER, the Bn being accommodated again in J Camp. Total casualties while in the line 2 killed, 8 wounded. About 200 men were left behind at DUBLIN CAMP & underwent a special course of training. A draft of 12 O.R. had arrived while the Bn was in the line & a second draft of 11 O.R. arrived on 17th inst. Capt.Kingdon also rejoined on this date. Lt.Col.Mills D.S.O., having received an appointment under the Ministry of Munitions, is struck off the strength.
20-1-18		Bathing.
21-1-18		Kit inspection, clothing & cleaning up.
22-1-18		Short Route march & Foot Rubbing Drill.

| 23-1-18 | | Preparing to go into line. (Training Programme 20th/24th Jan attached) [not included]. |
| 24-1-18 | 12 noon | Bn proceeded by train from J Camp to LOWER BABOON CAMP, entraining at BOEZINGE. A carrying party of 60 O.R. was provided. |

LOWER BABOON CAMP
| 25-1-18 | | Laid duck boards & attended to drainage of camp. |

Trenches HOUTHULST FOREST SECTOR
26-1-18	6 pm	Relieved 11th Royal Fusiliers in left sub-sector, relief being completed without incident about 10 p.m.
27-1-18		Very misty all day, which prevented observation. Quiet. Carried out inter Coy. relief commencing at 8 p.m. "A" Coy relieving "D" in left sub-sector & "B" relieving "C" in right sub-sector.
28-1-18		Bright with good observation. Considerable artillery activity all day.
	6 pm	Relieved by 16th Lancashire Fusiliers (32nd Division) & proceeded to LARRY CAMP (near Elverdinge). Casualties during time in line – 1 wounded on carrying party. Map showing HOUTHULST FOREST SECTOR. Map showing Posts.

LARRY CAMP
| 29-1-18 | | Bathing & Cleaning up. |

HEADQUARTERS CAMP, KROMBEKE
| 30-1-18 | | Proceeded by Route March to HEADQUARTERS CAMP, near KROMBEKE, arriving about 1 p.m. |
| 31-1-18 | | Kit Inspection & refitting. |

KROMBEKE
| 1-2-18 to 8-2-18 | | Major A.E.Percival M.C. in Command Training [see Appendix A2.21]. |

Krombeke-Salency
| 9-2-18 to 10-2-18 | | Move to PROVEN by route march; to NOYON by train and to SALENCY by route march [see Appendix A2.22]. |

SALENCY
11-2-18		Arrival of draft of 7 officers and 174 other ranks from 8th Bn. Bedfordshire Regt. which had been disbanded. Hostile Bombing raid. One bomb demolished a billet occupied by "C" Company. Casualties: – Killed; 9 other ranks. Died of Wounds; 1 officer & 2 other ranks. Wounded; 6 other ranks
12-2-18		Training. Lieut. Colonel A.E.Percival, M.C. in Command.
13-2-18		Training. Honours & Awards. Belgian "Decoration Militaire" – 14827 Sergt.Rugman, C.G. "Croix de Guerre" – 12489 Corp.Baker, G.R. and 18416 L/Cpl.Stringer, G.
14-2-18		Move to CAILLOUEL

CAILLOUEL

15-2-18	Move to REMIGNY

REMIGNY

16-2-18	Training. Working parties of 430 at night.
17-2-18	Training. Working parties of 430 at night and 24 by day, Capt.H.Seys-Phillips in Command vice Lieut.Col.A.E.Percival, M.C. attending a training conference.
18-2-18	Training. Working parties as for 17th
19-2-18	Training. Working parties as for 17th.
20-2-18	Training. Working parties as for 17th.
21-2-18	Training. Working parties of 140 by day and 330 by night. Lieut.Col.A.E.Percival, M.C. assumed Command vice Capt.H.Seys-Phillips.
22-2-18	Training. Working parties as for 21st.
23-2-18	Training. Working parties as for 21st.
24-2-18	Training. Working parties of 90 by day and 300 by night.
25-2-18	Training. Working parties as for 24th.
26-2-18	Move to BÉTHANCOURT.

BÉTHANCOURT

27-2-18	Training.
28-2-18	Move to ROUEZ, Capt.O.Kingdon in Command vice Lieut.Col.A.E.Percival M.C. acting Brigade Commander.

ROUEZ CAMP

1-3-18	H.Q.s, A B & D Coys at ROUEZ CAMP; C Coy at NOUREUIL. Capt.O.Kingdon in temporary command of Bn. during absence of Lt.Col.A.E.Percival M.C. commanding 54th Inf. Bde. Officers & N.C.O's reconnoitred assembly position in case of enemy attack. Draft of 5 O.R. arrived [see Appendix A2.23].
2-3-18	2nd Lt.R.W.Coutts R.F.C. joined Bn. for one month's tour of duty.
3-3-18	Orders issued showing action of Bn. in case of enemy attack.
4-3-18	Working Party of 6 officers & 400 O.R. employed in burying cable. Reconaissance of line carried out daily on this & following days. Capt.H.C.Browning, having returned from leave, took over duties of Adjutant.
5-3-18	Working Party of 4 officers & 400 O.R. burying cable. Draft of 12 O.R. arrived.
6-3-18	Working Party as for 5th. 2nd Lt.W.Kerr joined the Bn. from the Tank Corps.
7-3-18	Working Party as usual. Lt.Col.A.E.Percival resumes command of the Bn.
8-3-18	Working Party as usual. Capt.W.J.W.Colley rejoined the Bn & took over duties of 2nd-in-command. Voluntary Rifle Shooting on Range commenced.

9-3-18		Working Party as usual.
10-3-18		Church Service 10 a.m. Dismounted & Mounted Gymkana in afternoon.
11-3-18		Training in Counter-attack formation & musketry. Officers Rifle Competition V.18th Div. Q.Q.s officers won by the Bn.
12-3-18		The following working parties found daily from 12/3/18 to 20/3/18. 2 Officers & 140 O.R. attached to 290th Bde. R.F.A. for construction of gun-pits at VOUEL. 2 Platoons "C" Coy. employed on increasing accommodation at NOUREUIL. 5 Officers & 240 O.R. employed on cable burying under 18th Div. Signal Section. Inter Platoon Rifle Competition commenced on this date & won by No.2 Platoon [see Appendix A2.24].
13-3-18 to 17-3-18		Training of Lewis Gunners & other Specialists. Classes for officers & N.C.O's in afternoon.
18-3-18		2nd Lt.Balls (B.H.) joined the Bn. & posted to D Coy.
20-3-18		Capt. R.O.Clark proceeded to England on 6 months tour of duty. "Prepare for Attack" message received at 3 p.m. & all preparations made for Rapid Move.
21-3-18		Enemy Bombardment started at 4.30 a.m. Morning very misty.
	10.50am	Received orders at 10.50 a.m. to move in Buses & rendezvous in HAUTE TOMBELLE WOOD, where Bn. arrived about 12 noon.
	3pm	received orders to occupy & hold the MONTESCOURT SWITCH, 7th Bedfords being in Brigade Reserve.
	4.40pm	Bn. moved forward & got into position about 7.30 p.m. "C" & "D" Coys supporting Royal Fusiliers & "A" & "B" Coys supporting Northamptons. Bn. Details left out of action were formed into 6 Platoons & occupied position just East of ROUEZ CAMP.
	11pm	Bn. received orders to fall back & take up position south of CROZAT CANAL.

CROZAT CANAL

22-3-18	7am	Bn. in position, but all attempts to blow up bridge failed owing to lack of explosive.
	5.45pm	Heavy attack by enemy on LA MONTAGNE BRIDGE, "C" Coy. on left flank came under very heavy M.G. fire & were forced to retire, enemy crossing Bridge. Counter-attack by 2 Coys Northants, assisted by "C" Coy, restored situation & by 7.30 p.m. all enemy were thrown back across Bridge. Details engaged in fighting in neighbourhood of ROUEZ CAMP.
23-3-18		Morning very misty.
	7am	Enemy attacked again & effected crossing on right & left flanks of Brigade front.
	10am	owing to flanks being turned order received from brigade to retire to ridge in front of FAILLOUEL.
	1pm	Retirement successfully carried out & position taken up.

FAILLOUEL

	4pm	Position in front of FAILLOUEL became untenable owing to high ground of left flank falling into hands of enemy. Order therefore received to fall back to high ground West of village.
	7pm	Received orders to rendezvous Bn. & march back to CAILLOUEL. Details heavily engaged in fighting near ROUEZ CAMP, finally falling back on VILLEQUIER AUMONT.

CAILLOUEL

24-3-18	10am	Took up position in wood North of village: "B" & "D" Coys in front, "A" Coy in reserve. Enemy still advancing & pushing back French in front.
	7pm	Heavy attack on GUIVRY on our left flank: French fell back & left our flank exposed.
25-3-18	3am	Orders received to fall back to CREPIGNY line, which was successfully carried out. Enemy now about 2 miles in rear of left flank.
	10am	Fell back again to MONT DU GRANDU to safeguard left flank.
	12 noon	Heavily fired on by French Artillery & M.G's & forced to retire to high ground West of GRANDU.

GRANDU

	3pm	Received orders to march to VARESNES to take up position South of OISE: orders countermanded while en route & new orders received to counter-attack village of BABOEUF. Counter-attack successful & village retaken, several prisoners being taken & many enemy killed.

BABOEUF

26-3-18	2am	Owing to enemy being in rear of left flank & nearly into NOYON, it was found necessary to evacuate village & retire across OISE; marched about 8 miles & billeted for day.
	3pm	Marched to NAMPZEL & thence to MESNIL where Bn. was accommodated for night in caves. Casualties to date:

(a) <u>Officers</u>

	1 Killed	2nd Lt.Winmill
	4 Wounded	Capt.W.W.Colley
		2nd Lt.R.S.Heard
		2nd Lt.N.C.E.Cockburn
		2nd Lt.C.H.Pierce
	1 Wounded & Missing	2nd Lt.R.A.Stiles
	1 Missing	2nd Lt.R.W.Coutts

(b) <u>O.R.</u>

Killed	22
Wounded	140
Wounded & Missing	4
Missing	99

MESNIL
27-3-18 3pm Marched to ST.AUBIN in reserve to 58th Division.

St.Aubin
28-3-18
to 29-3-18 St.Aubin.

St.Aubin-Boves
30-3-18 3am Marched to NAMPZEL where Bn. embussed & travelled via COMPIEGNE, ST.JUST, AMIENS to BOVES, where Bn. was accommodated for night.

Boves-Gentelles
31-3-18 8.30am Marched to GENTELLES in support to front line.
         4pm   Called out to reject enemy attack, latter did not materialise & Bn. returned to billets at 9 p.m. Casualties: – 2 wounded

GENTELLES
1-4-18 Battalion in billets at GENTELLES. Went up at dusk and relieved 6th Northants in line to left of HANGARD.
2-4-18 Quiet night & morning. Shelled occasionally during day. Carried out an attack in evening in conjunction with Royal Fusiliers. Progress made, but owing to overwhelming superiority of enemy artillery & machine gun fire battalion ordered to withdraw.
Casualties: Officers: Lt.M.C.DUPLOCK killed
Lt.R.L.V.DOAKE, Lt.BALLS, LT.CRAIG and CAPT.STEVENSON wounded.
Other Ranks 2 killed
48 wounded
4 missing
Relieved in line about 10 pm & returned to billets at GENTELLES.
3-4-18 In billets resting, and cleaning of equipment &c.
4-4-18 GENTELLES shelled during day. A and D Coys moved up in Support to 6th Northants but did not go into action. Returned to billets in evening. Casualties. Other Ranks 7 killed 10 wounded.
5-4-18 Battalion in billets. Battalion again moved up in support to 6th Northants, but not need [sic] & returned to billets in evening. Shelled in billets. Other Ranks. 2 killed 13 wounded.
6-4-18 Morning devoted to cleaning of equipment etc. In afternoon marched to billets at BOVES. Casualties. Other Ranks 1 wounded.

BOVES
7-4-18 Battalion in billets and bathed during morning & afternoon.
8-4-18 Morning devoted to cleaning of equipment & refitting. Draft of 52 Other Ranks joined battalion [overwritten in original] of good physique.

9-4-18	Company training during morning. Battalion marched to BOUTILLERIE in afternoon and went into billets.
BOUTILLERIE	
10-4-18	In billets. Kit inspections &c. during day.
11-4-18	In billets. Specialist training & organisation.
12-4-18	In billets. Specialist training & organisation. Promotions as per attached B.O.61 [see Appendix A2.27].
13-4-18 to 15-4-18	In billets training. Specialist training concentrated on. Football in afternoons.
16-4-18	In billets. Draft of 97 Other Ranks joined battalion. Lt.Col.A.E.Percival M.C. proceeded to England on duty for 7 days and CAPT.H.C.BROWNING took over command of battalion. Capt.H.Seys-Phillips took over duties of Acting Adjutant.
17-4-18	In billets. Battalion training & organisation.
18-4-18	In billets. Battalion training & organisation.
19-4-18	In billets. Specialist training & inspection of Transport. Brdg.Genl.H.L.de Vere Sadleir-Jackson C.M.G. D.S.O. presented parchments to number of N.C.O's and men.
20-4-18	Battalion moved to fresh billets in BOUTILLERIE. Draft of 72 other ranks arrived. Mostly of very good physique.
21-4-18	In billets. Battalion attended Brigade demonstration of Tactical Handling of Lewis Guns. Draft of 1 Officer of [sic] 52 Other Ranks arrived. Capt.G.Jarvis Smith C.F. and 2/Lt.W.Hughes awarded M.C.
22-4-18	In billets. Specialist training carried out.
23-4-18	In billets. Specialist training carried out. Reinforcement of 19 officers joined battalion. Capt.W.W.Colley authorised to wear badges of Major. Capt.H.C.Browning appointed adjutant from 11-2-18. Lt.Col.A.E.Percival M.C. returned from England & took over command of battalion.
24-4-18	In billets. Battalion ordered to "stand to" at 4 am. Moved up to line by stages during the day & took up position just South of CACHY. Battalion ordered to do counter attack at 10 p.m. From information received the enemy had penetrated our defences to a depth of 2000 yds (approx.) on a wide frontage. Battalion was formed up in position for attack with Royal West Kents on right and Australians on left. Night was intensely dark. Battalion moved forward to the assault and encountered slight opposition for first 1000 yds. when battalion on our right was held up by heavy machine gun fire. The reserve Company was ordered forward at this stage & thus reinforced the assault was continued & final objective reached in spite of fierce enemy opposition & with two exposed flanks. The left company of battalion was ordered to withdraw in order to conform with line of battalion on left. The right flank still remained exposed. At this stage 2/Lt.Tysoe
(In Action) 25-4-18	was the only Company Officer left. Lt.Tysoe reorganised the line & sent in very clear reports as to the situation as

known to him. As a result of this a section of the 54th Machine Gun Coy was ordered forward to cover the exposed right flank – a weak line being formed of headquarter details. During the whole of the 25th Apl. Lt.Tysoe held this line & repulsed an enemy attack on his right flank, which was launched after a heavy bombardment. Frontage held by battalion 1100 yds. About 10 p.m. the battalion was relieved by French Colonials & marched to bivouacs in Support in rear of our original line. During this action the regiment alone took over 200 prisoners. Many enemy dead were observed on the captured ground. Five enemy machine guns were captured during this action & handed over to the French on relief. Throughout the action 2/Lt.Tysoe displayed the greatest gallantry and leadership & the success of this difficult operation was largely due to his efforts. The bearing of all ranks was most commendable, and deserving of the highest praise.

Casualties: Officers: Capt.O.Kingdon, Capt.A.B.McBride, Lt.C.A.Lawrence M.C. killed
Lt.H.F.Trewman, 2/Lt.S.A.Peerless, 2/Lt.W.Carter, 2/Lt.Kerr, 2/Lt.G.H.Koch D.C.M., 2/Lt.J.W.Partridge and 2/Lt.E.J.Scott wounded.
Casualties: Other Ranks 13 killed 105 wounded 70 missing.

CACHY
26-4-18   In bivouacs. Battalion resting & cleaning.

AVESNES [-CHAUSSOY]
27-4-18   Battalion moved to AVESNES [-CHAUSSOY], marching to AMIENS thence by busses.

28-4-18
to 30-4-18   In billets. Cleaning of equipment, bathing, reorganising & refitting.

1-5-18   Battalion Training. Congratulatory messages received from General Brecard (French Army), G.O.C. 19th Corps & G.O.C. 54th Infantry Brigade. Reinforcements: 15 O.R. from the Base [see Appendix B3.15–17].

2-5-18   Battalion Training. Reinforcements: 66 O.R. from the Base. Honours & Awards.

3-5-18   Battalion Training.
4-5-18   Battalion Training.
5-5-18   Battalion Training.

WARLOY [-BAILLON]
6-5-18   9.30am   Embussed at WARLUS (H.20.c.7.8) & proceeded to CONTAY, marching to WARLOY (AMIENS 17). Battalion relieved 21st London Regt. in Brigade Reserve. "A" Coy in HILL ROW. "B" Coy in DARLING SUPPORT. "C" Coy in VILLA RESERVE. "D" Coy in COPSE TRENCH. Battalion H.Q. in LAVIEVILLE (D.11.a.0.8).

In Reserve

7-5-18		Battalion in same dispositions.
8-5-18		Battalion in same dispositions. Capt.L.H.Keep, M.C. took over duties of 2nd in Command. 3/8112 Sergt.T.A.Smith awarded the Military Medal.
9-5-18		Battalion in same dispositions.
10-5-18		Battalion in same dispositions.
11-5-18		Battalion in same dispositions.
12-5-18		Battalion in same dispositions.
	10 am	Battalion H.Q. heavily shelled with 5.9's & eventually blown in. No casualties. New Batt. H.Q. at N. end of LAVIÉVILLE.
13-5-18		Battalion in same dispositions. LAVIÉVILLE heavily shelled all day with 5.9s & 8 in Hows. Battalion H.Q. moved to shell-slits W. of cemetery & when shelled there moved to Brigade H.Q. in Quarry W. of Cemetery. Battalion relieved 7th Buffs in LAVIÉVILLE line.
14-5-18		Lt.Col.A.E.Percival M.C. awarded the D.S.O. Capt.H.C.Browning awarded the M.C. reinforcements: 2nd Lieut.S.A.Peerless & 52 O.R. from the Base.
15-5-18		Battalion in same dispositions.
16-5-18		"A", "B" & "C" Coys withdrawn from LAVIÉVILLE line to BAIZIEUX. "D" Coy & Lewis Guns of "B" & "C" Coys remained in position till night & then relieved. Capts A.B.McBride and R.L.V.Doake awarded the M.C. Also Capt.T.Stevenson (R.A.M.C. attached) awarded the M.C. 14591 Sergt.A.Scott awarded the D.C.M.

In the Line

17-5-18	Night 17/18th	Battalion relieved the 10th Bn. Essex Regt. in the left sub-sector of the right sector of the Divisional front. "B" Coy in the front line, "D" Coy in support, "A" & "C" Coys counter-attack Coys. 7 O.R. in Base.
18-5-18		Battalion in same dispositions.
19-5-18		Battalion in same dispositions. Reinforcements: – Lieut.W.S.Oliver Jones & 58 O.R. from Base. Chinese attack successfully carried out.
20-5-18		Battalion in same dispositions. 15023 Sergt.S.Walby awarded the Military Medal.
21-5-18		"C" Coy relieved "B" Coy in the front line, & "A" Coy relieved "D" in Support, "B" & "C" Coys. becoming counter-attack companies. Reinforcements: 16 O.R. from Base.
22-5-18		Battalion in same dispositions.
23-5-18		Battalion in same dispositions. Reinforcements: 4 O.R. from Base.
24-5-18		Battalion relieved at night by 22nd London Regt.

WOOD E. of BÉHENCOURT

25-5-18	(AMIENS 17). Reinforcements: 14 O.R. from Base.
26-5-18	Battalion training.

27-5-18	Battalion absorbed by the 2nd Battalion. Casualties during the Month. Lieut.E.A.Hague. Wounded 21-5-18. 4 O.R. Killed. 23 O.R. wounded. 1 O.R. missing. 2 O.R. wounded & remained at Duty.
28-5-18	Battalion at Training and Reorganising. Temp.Sec.Lieut.W.Tysoe awarded the D.S.O. 2nd Lieut.E.J.Scott awarded the M.C. 22361 Sergt.J.Boness & 18570 Sergt.H.G.Robinson awarded the D.C.M.
29-5-18	Battalion training & reorganising.
30-5-18	Battalion training & reorganising.
31-5-18	Battalion moved to valley W. of HENENCOURT WOOD. Strength of Battalion on absorbing 7th Battalion: – 46 Officers & 1000 O.R. Remaining personnel & surplus transport were sent to the Base. Lieut.Col.A.E.Percival, D.S.O. M.C. commanded the Battalion from 28/5/18. Casualties since 27/5/18: – Nil.
25-5-18	The 7th Bn. Bedfordshire Regiment was transferred to the 2nd Bn. Bedfordshire Regiment. The 2nd and 7th Bns then became 2nd Bn. the Bedfordshire Regiment. At 6.30 A.M. a Party consisting as follows was formed into a Training cadre and became known as the 7th Bn. Bedfordshire Regiment. LIEUT.COL.R.O.WYNNE D.S.O. Commanding Officer MAJOR J.T.COE Adjutant CAPT. J.K.BATTEN Company Commander CAPT. F.EVERITT Company Commander CAPT. S.E.CLINE Company Commander CAPT. R.E.OAKLEY M.C. Company Commander 2/LIEUT.J.KEKK Lewis Gun Officer 2/LIEUT.W.ASHTON Scout Officer 2/LIEUT.H.FLAVELL Signalling Officer and 50 other ranks. The 7th Bn. Training cadre left at 6.30 A.M. 26th May to help Train the American Army, entraining at POULAINVILLE for CHÉPY-VALINES, arriving at 3.30 P.M. 27th. We then marched to Billets at ROGEANT about 6½ miles S.W. of ABBEVILLE.

ROGEANT

27-5-18 to 1-6-18	Owing to non arrival of American Units no training was carried out.
2-6-18	H, I and K Companies of 129th Infy. 33rd Division arrived & Training Commenced.
5-6-18	L & M Companies Arrived.
9-6-18	The 33rd American Div. left for EU Area. We remained at ROGEANT.

MONCHAUX

12-6-18	Left ROGEANT at 2.15 pm and marched to billets at

15-6-18	MONCHAUX about 24 Miles E. of DIEPPE ref Map DIEPPE 1/100,000 Arriving at 8 p.m. Left MONCHAUX at 1 pm and marched to billets at YZENGREMER about 7 Miles E of LE TREPORT ref Map ABBEVILLE 1/100,000. Arriving at 4.30 pm & came under 89th Infy Brigade 30th Division.

YZENGREMER

16-6-18	Commenced Training 1st & 2nd Battns of 129th Infy Regt.
17-6-18	Capt.J.K.BATTEN 4/BEDF.R and Captain F.EVERETT 6th N'hants Regt left to join their respective Battalions for Duty.
19-6-18	Transferred from 30th to 66th Division & came under 90th Brigade. Capt.A.F.MACKENZIE 2/A & SII Capt.H.W.WALTER 10/Middlesex Joined for Duty.

BÉHEN

21-6-18	Left YZENGREMER at 8.30 am with 33rd American Div & marched to Billets at BÉHEN about 6 miles SW of ABBEVILLE Arriving at 5 p.m.

ERGNIES

22-6-18	Left BÉHEN at 9 am & marched to billets at ERGNIES about 6 miles NE of FLIXECOURT at Map LENS Arriving at 5 pm.
23-6-18	Continued Training 1st Bn 129th Regt.

OCCOCHES

27-6-18	Left ERGNIES at 9.15 am & marched to billets at OCCOCHES about 3 Miles N.W. of DOULLENS ref map LENS Arriving at 3 p.m.

LE SOUICH

28-6-18	Left OCCOCHES at 9.15 am & marched to billets at LE SOUICH about 5 Miles N. of DOULLENS ref Map LENS. Arriving at 11 am. Came Under 197th Infy Brigade 66th Division.
29-6-18	Commenced training 2nd & 3rd Battns of 107th Infy Regt 27th American Div.

IVERGNY

3-7-18	Left Le Souich at 8.30 a.m. for billets at IVERGNY and BEAUDRICOURT with H.Qrs at IVERGNY arriving at 9 a.m.
6-7-18	2/lieut.J.J.Acton 11th S.Lancs Regt proceeded to join 11th Border Regt for duty.
7-7-18	320th Regt 160th Infy Bde 80th Div arrived.
8-7-18	Commenced training 2nd & 3rd Bns 320th Regt.
18-7-18	Q.Mr.& Hon.Lieut.E.Monks, Royal Scots joined.

CANDAS
21-7-18   Left IVERGNY at 9.45 a.m. for CANDAS arriving at 4 p.m.

SERGUEUX
22-7-18   Entrained at CANDAS at 9.45 a.m. for SERGUEUX about 30 miles S.W. of DIEPPE arriving at 10 p.m.

23-7-18   Left SERGUEUX at 10 a.m. for camp about 1 mile West of ABANCOURT arriving at 4 p.m.

ABANCOURT CAMP
24-7-18   Orders received that the Battalion is to be disbanded and all personnel to proceed to Base

25-7-18   Orders received to cancel disbandment.

29-7-18   Orders received for Battalion to join and be absorbed into the 2nd Battalion.

31-7-18   Entrained at ROMESCAMPS at 3.45 p.m. to join the 2nd Bn Bedfordshire Regt.

Plate 9. Second Lieutenant Henry J. Cartwright, author of the Personal Diary.

PART TWO

The Personal Diary of Second Lieutenant Henry J. Cartwright (1916–1917)

To Olive
MY DIARY
1928
H J Cartwright

Wednesday, 19th April, 1916
The scene of my labours has changed. Peel, Hobson, Carles, Reed and I received our orders on Friday; we are the first officers of the 10th Bedfords[1] to proceed to France. We left Folkestone yesterday and after a terrible crossing, during which I was sick, landed at Boulogne, and are now in that great Camp at Etaples. We are temporarily attached to the 35th Division.

Saturday, 22nd April, 1916
I am all alone now, and not feeling very brave at the prospect in front of me. Reed has left to join the 8th Bedfords. Peel, Carles and Hobson have joined the 6th Bedfords, and I am posted to the 7th Bedfords. I hate being here alone; I am not the sort of fellow to make friends with strangers. As my servant I have one Robbins who, strange to say was my Batman at Dovercourt. For the purpose of training I have the men of the Durham Light Infantry under my command. I took them on the miniature rifle range one day, and yesterday I spent out on the training ground with all the other officers here. We go through all the O.T.C.,[2] training as of old. The training ground is the finest possible, situate at the mouth of the river on the sand dunes, and overlooking Le Touquet, and Paris-Plage. I went today on the tram to Paris-Plage, and had a bain chaud;[3] it is a beautiful watering place.

Sunday, 30th April, 1916
I am now on the verge of the firing line, and for the first time in sound of the guns. At 9.30 last night I left Etaples to join the 7th Bedfords. I shared a first class

---
[1] 10th Battalion Bedfordshire Regiment was a training battalion, based at Dovercourt [Essex] for much of the war; it did not see active service.
[2] Officer Training Corps.
[3] Literally a "warm bath".

compartment with one Warley of the Buffs, and I slept all the way to Abbeville, where we had a stay of several hours. I took the opportunity of having a shave and breakfast, and looking round the town. It is a picturesque town with a very fine Cathedral. Getting back to the train we set off again, and at 1.30 arrived at Mericourt, the rail-head. I spent the night at the Rest Camp, and met two officers from the 7th Bedfords going home on leave. They informed me the Battalion was in the line, and advised me to go to the Quartermaster's billet in Bray.

Monday, 1st May, 1916
This is my first day under fire.

At half past nine I set out and managed to obtain a lift in the mess cart belonging to the Middlesex Regiment. The ride to Bray was not of great interest and though I was all eyes for signs of devastation of war, one or two shell holes by the road side were the only visible signs. It was after eleven o'clock when I reached the Quartermaster's stores, and after explaining my unexpected presence, I decided to join the Battalion in the front line that evening. The Transport Officer (Browning) provided me with a horse, and together we rode up to the reserve trenches. Browning conducts the transport with the Battalion rations up to the lines every evening, a four miles ride, novel and not unexciting for me. Browning pointed out to me our battery positions, our road bristling with guns cleverly concealed. About a mile from the reserve trenches the road comes into full view of the Huns, and as a precaution we opened out to 50 yards interval. The road was all shell holes, and one had to walk one's mount very carefully. The Germans opened fire on a wood on our left. I could hear the shells whistling through the air, and to my surprise I felt little fear; this was perhaps due to ignorance as they were falling less than 200 yards away. Many of the shells appeared to be "duds". It was 9 o'clock when I reported at H.Q.s, in the ruined village of Carnoy, and was introduced to the C.O. (Lt. Col. Price), who, having had no intimation of my arrival, was rather astounded. He was quite pleasant, and gave me a drink. For the night I was posted to "B" Company, who were in reserve. Stewart (late of the 10th Batt) was in that Company and he took me under his wing. I was given a dug-out under the ruins of a house, and though a comparatively safe spot, it appeared to me, not knowing what the future held in store, not at all inviting. My bed was a wire netting bunk, and sleeping in my clothes, I had not much rest. I was the sole occupant of the dug-out, and the loneliness and darkness upset me. Half way through the night there was a bombardment, and imagining I could smell gas, I had to go outside to reassure myself. The day was very quiet, and in the afternoon Stewart conducted me round the trenches. In the evening I was posted to "A" Company, and received orders to join them at once. Preceded by a guide, bearing my kit, I was conducted by tortuous and uninhabited ways ankle deep in mud to the front line of which "A" Company held the right sector some 250 yards in length. My new Company Commander (Percival) received me, if not with open arms, at least kindly, and took me on a tour round the front line, and explained and pointed out things. At 12 o'clock I turned in, sharing a dug-out with Captain Keep, and 2nd Lieut. Colley. My bunk was comfortable and I slept soundly, in spite of mice and rats which ran around and nibbled my hat and my iron rations.

Next morning Percival again took me round the line. Being daylight I was able to grasp more of what my surroundings were like. Trenches are a complicated business, and it takes time to find one's way about. Our sector, the Carnoy sector, was a salient, and having the Huns on three sides made matters very uncomfortable during a "strafe". The trenches were models of their kind, and one felt quite safe. Rifle and machine gun fire troubled us little, and I was surprised to find that one was able to look over the parapet at the Hun lines less than 100 yards away without a shot being fired, provided one did not stay up too long, and got up each time in a different place. During the three days I was in things were rather quiet. I was very glad because I dreaded a heavy bombardment. There were always numerous aircraft overhead, and much anti aircraft firing, but none was brought down.

We were relieved late on Thursday evening by the 18th Liverpools (Pals Battalion). Then began a long march out very slowly by winding communication trenches for quite two miles. We went uphill and downhill through tunnels, through a wood, up steps and down steps, and always creeping creeping at a snail's pace. It seemed hours before we reached the road, in reality it was only an hour and a half. "A" Coy were billeted at Froissy which consisted solely of a river lock (it is on the Somme) three houses and the ruins of a factory. I am attached to No: 3 Platoon and with Colley I saw our men settled and fed at 3.00a.m., and on Friday morning we sat down to our first meal since tea. We were billeted in the "Café Meraut", and all things considered it was quite good. During our meal a terrific bombardment began, and the noise was appalling. Then there was a gas alarm, but it was only lachrymose, and did no more harm than the production of a few tears.

Froissy is quite a pretty place on the Somme on the other bank of which the French are stationed. Five of their officers came into tea one day, and in their honour the band played appropriate music.

11th May, 1916
We are likely to stay at Froissy another week or so and then we expect to go back to some village or other near Amiens, where we shall have a fortnight's so called rest, but in reality shall be kept hard at work rehearsing the part we are to play in the coming push. The general opinion is that the push is coming and that is the reason for our long rest and that when we return it will be for another Loos, only this time we shall hope it may be more successful. Great preparations are being made for this intended push, and we have had several conferences as to our own preparations.

The training we are doing at present is reminiscent of Colchester days. The Adjutant takes an officers' class every morning, and we do every conceivable form of drill and training. It is very boring and I need some lessons in voice production. One morning the Huns shelled a spinney a few hundred yards away; there was such a sudden migration of lorries, horses, etc., parked there.

We usually get the afternoon free and have had some bathing in a lake nearby; the water is surprisingly warm.

The present system of company organisation is that one platoon shall be commanded by a Sergeant, and therefore I am a supernumerary officer under Colley. Colley and I paid an interesting visit to an artillery observation post in our back line trenches one day. It was on the crest of a hill, and commanded an excellent view of the Hun lines from Fricourt to Maricourt. Our visit was made with the object of studying and memorising as far as possible the portion of the enemy line which will be our objective in the coming push. To reach Pommiers Redoubt, our main objective, we shall have to capture eight lines of trenches covering a distance of some 8000 yards. It looks a hot place. Colley and I were rather indiscrete, and the Huns spotted us at the observation post and sent some shrapnel over us; we beat a hasty retreat.

No one expects to come out of this push alive, and all seem to think it will be the end of the officers against whom such a dead hit is always made by the Huns. However, it is surprising how cheerful everyone is, and treats it as a huge joke; nevertheless we think a lot. There is a slight doubt of the push coming off, for it is said that Sir Douglas Haig will not countenance a push unless he is confident of success, but the French are "pressing". Tremendous preparations are being made; miles of trenches dug, cables laid, railways constructed and the whole countryside is bristling with guns. One significant feature is the arrival of O.C. Gravediggers with his men!

We have had to change our quarters. The French have taken over Froissy and are including the Somme in their line. We have moved to Bray-sur-Somme. I prefer the country of Froissy to the town of Bray, deserted, dirty and derelict. Besides I miss our bathing in the lake. I bathed in the river once but it was very cold, muddy, weedy and deep.

The fine weather has returned, and with it the activities of the aircraft. The "Archies"[4] are kept very busy, but I still have to see my first aeroplane brought down. Colonel Price has left to take command of the Divisional School; it is doubtful if he will return to us.

Sunday, 21st May, 1916

Of late my time has been chiefly occupied with supervising fatigues carried out by "A" Coy. The weather has been exceptionally hot, and very sensibly we have been starting work at 5.30a.m., breaking off at 10.30 for a bathe. Principally we have been unloading barges, but yesterday we were road mending, – I shall have to be a road surveyor when I return home. Whilst road mending the Huns shelled Bray with 5.9s, and we had a very hot time. I got the wind up when a shell fell a few yards away on a house, and killed and injured some R.E.'s. It sent up such a column of dust. We expect to be leaving Bray this week, and rumour hath it that we go to Cissy, some 10 miles from Amiens. Preparations for transport are being made, and we shall only be allowed to take very little kit. I have at last got from Ordnance my revolver, – a Webley Mark VI.

I have been fly-fishing with Cathcart-Nicholls today, but we caught nothing on the fly, but firing with a revolver when they rose we stunned some, and in this way caught several.

We have changed our quarters again, and are now very comfortably installed in a house behind the Church, so if the Hun does take it into his head to shell the town, we shall get it in the neck. We have a very good mess, and I share a room with Colley and Hughes.

Barges come up the river every day, and we are kept hard at work unloading. One day we were on from 6.00a.m., to 8.15p.m. I tried my hand at wheeling barrows along the planks. It was tricky work and I soon had blisters. Road metal and timber are the usual cargoes we unload.

[4] Archie was slang for Anti-Aircraft batteries.

Whilst fishing with Nicholls one evening the naked body of a man in the "full knees bend" position drifted down the stream with the top of his head bobbing up and down. Some men in a boat got the body ashore, and it was found to be one of "D" Coy's men.[5] Now we are prohibited from bathing in the river, and a bathing pool has been made. Six new officers have arrived, and one of them, to my great delight was Rednall of the 10th Battalion. He has been posted to "A" Coy, and has been sent away on a signaling course. Keep and Percival are away on courses, Colley is in command, and I have No.2 Platoon.

Saturday, 3rd June, 1916
"A" Coy has become more depleted of its officers than ever. Colley has gone on leave, and Kingdon is temporarily in command of "C" Coy, leaving Hughes in command of "A" Coy and myself. This week we have been taken off the barge unloading, and are now digging trenches behind the lines for cables. The trenches have to be 7 feet deep, so it is case of real hard work. We start about 6.30a.m., and it is usually 2 o'clock before the last Platoon has finished. We have thankfully had little shell-fire, and the only casualties have been caused by accidents with pick axes. Thursday I witnessed an interesting sight. The Huns bombarded the town of Suzanne (occupied by the French) about a mile away on our right. The shells fell fast and furious for about 10 minutes into the centre of the town, and clouds of red brick dust and smoke arose. It was most engrossing to see the shells burst, to hear them whistling through the air overhead, and to see the flashes of the French guns in reply.

Yesterday after digging trenches until 2.0p.m., we had to go out again in the evening to fill in the cable trenches in front of Bonfire Farm and Oxford Copse. We were on the brow of a hill overlooking the Hun lines. The Manchesters were carrying out a raid that night, and our artillery behind us were carrying out an intensive bombardment of the front line; so low was the trajectory of our shells that we had to take refuge in the bottom of the trench and cease work. Some dud shells and premature bursts put the wind up us. One could see red hot masses of metal bounding along the ground, and Hughie had a narrow escape from one piece. It was very unpleasant and terrifying. Shells flew over our heads leaving a streak of light in their wake. The smoke and dust round the Hun lines was intensely dense. Luckily for us the Huns only replied on our first and second lines, but their intermittent machine gun and rifle fire added much to our discomfort. One poor fellow named Slade,[6] a very decent young boy in my Platoon was hit. He died immediately, and the stretcher bearers carried his body to Bronfay Farm. I felt very uneasy at hearing the bullets whizzing past. While standing talking to Hughes a bullet came by and sounded just as though it hit something. Hughie shouted "are you hit?", and he could not believe me when I replied "No". It was 2.00 o'clock before all the Platoons had finished, and Hughie and I stayed to the end, and walked back to Bray together along the road.

This morning I attended Pte. Slade's funeral at Bronfay Farm. A detachment from

---

[5] This was Private Frederick Edmund James Groves from Fulham (Middlesex); he is buried at Bray Military Cemetery.
[6] Private Walter Slade from Trowbridge (Wiltshire), he is buried at Bronfay Farm Military Cemetery.

No.2 Platoon was present, but no volley was fired or bugle sounded as we were too close to the Huns. The cemetery was at the side of the road opposite the Farm, and the service was taken by the Chaplain to the 53rd Brigade. It was a terrible sight, the body being wrapped in sacking and the whole form showing. It was my first meeting with death, and the first casualty in my Platoon. I was very upset. I wrote to the boy's mother this afternoon.

Thursday, 22nd June, 1916
It is twelve days since we left Bray. Our last days were occupied with trench digging, and nothing of much note occurred. Guns both French and English continue to pour in and verily Susanne Valley is "lousy" with them. Every morning the French fire off their 75's and one of their officers explained the gun to me one day. It seems very simple. I have obtained my first trophies, a 75 c.m shell case, and 18 pdr. ditto and a nose cap. Most of the French guns are brazenly lying in the open with a camouflage covering. They appear to dislike gun emplacements, believing that aircraft can spot them too easily.

We left Bray on the 11th instant, Sunday, at 3.0a.m. The reason of our early departure being the practice of the Huns to shell the Bray-Corbie Road during the day, and we wished to make our way out before daylight. At Maricourt L'Abbé, the railhead, we entrained for Picquigny where we detrained about eleven o'clock. Picquigny is a typical old world country town in Picardy on the banks of the Somme about 12 kilos east of Amiens. It is a charming place and remarkably clean, and contains the ruins of an old Norman Chateau. The town is of great historic interest and is honeycombed with underground passages.[7]

Our training here is to practice in every detail every part we may be called upon to play in the coming offensive. We spent the first day in visiting the training area, and having an Officers' Conference with General Shoubridge, our Brigadier, a most charming man. Our main objective in this part is to be "Pommiers Redoubt", and country of a similar contour to the real thing has been selected for our training area. Both our own and the Bosche trenches have been laid out in exact representation on the ground (someone has been very busily employed) and over them we have to rehearse the 54th Brigade attack. For a week we have worked hard at it from early morn to late at night, and our spare time has been engaged in lectures, conferences, etc. It has been interesting but rather tiring. I was in command of No.2 Platoon all the time.

Picquigny found great favour with me and I will remember attending Vespers with Colley, Hughes and Rednall at the Roman Catholic Church. After the service Hughes played the organ, while I worked the bellows; the Curé was quite delighted.

It was at Picquigny I had my first introduction to the new Stokes Trench Mortar. We had a demonstration of the real thing in front of all the "Red Hats" of the Corps; 30 shells a minute and a range of 400 yards. It was here too that I first met our Divisional Commander, General Maxse, a little man of Hunnish appearance and accent, but he inspired in one a wonderful feeling of confidence. A draft from the 10th Bedfords arrived, and in less than 12 hours one fellow committed suicide. At the

---

[7] It was on the bridge of this castle that King Edward IV made a treaty with Louis XI on 29 August 1475 ending a war between the two.

Court of Inquiry I gave evidence of his lack of mental balance. I knew him of old at Colchester.[8]

We Left Picquigny on the 20th and detraining at Heilly we marched to Grovetown, just outside Bray, our billets being tents. After two nights there we moved up to the front line to take over our battle sector at Carnoy. The arrangement was that we should hold the line during our intense bombardment, and go over the top on the 6th day. It was at first decided that 5 officers per Company (of which I was one) should go over the top. How excited and elated I was then, but later that decision was altered, and only 4 officers per Company selected. I was the unfortunate being to be omitted. I was very sick; little I knew then what it meant and what a blessing in disguise that later decision really was.

We had a very bad time in the front line, and the Hun Artillery retaliated on us for all it was worth. "C" Company had their H.Q.s blown in and lost 5 Officers.[9] Three times Rednall and I were detailed to go over the top, with "C" Company, and three times the order was cancelled.

I share a cubby hole in the side of the trench with Colley, and one day that was blown in; fortunately we were both not at home.

Our shell-fire was intense; day and night we gave the Hun no rest, and ceaselessly the shells streamed overhead and destroyed his defenses. It was the biggest thing in gun fire then known, the supply of shells almost limitless, and the number of guns colossal.

The Push was postponed for a few days, and the 7th Bedfords relieved, and eventually we returned to Bray. On the night of the 30th the Battalion moved up again preparatory to going over at dawn next morning. I said au revoir to "A" Coy and saw them off, feeling very sore at heart and wondering how many would return.

July

Shortly after midnight on the 1st the Hun commenced to shell Bray, but he was caught napping for the town was empty. The British had just evacuated it, in order to make room for the French who were taking it over. My Batman, Masson, who had been left behind as his nerves had broken down, awoke me in a terrible scare. He was trembling all over, and to ease him I took him into the fields outside the Town until the shelling was over. Shortly afterwards Rednall returned from fatigue work. In the early morning, 7.45a.m., the Push commenced and every gun was let loose to work its Hell on the Bosche. However, I slept.

After breakfast Rednall and I went up to Grovetown to join the 1st Line Transport where Browning, Dealler and Duggie Keep were. We spent the morning trying to learn how the battle was proceeding. We watched the wounded coming down and from their statements we gathered that the battle was going splendidly. Many prisoners kept coming in. It was there that I saw my first Huns. They were not very pretty specimens of humanity.

During the afternoon Rednall and I spent great labour in making and digging a

---

[8] This was Private John Griffin from Alwalton (Huntingdonshire), he is buried at St. Pierre Cemetery, Amiens.
[9] Second Lieutenant Reginald Baden from Ealing and Second Lieutenant Gordon Beverley Hasler from Barnes (London) were killed; they are buried at Carnoy Military Cemetery. Captain R.L.V. Doake, Captain E. Clegg and Second Lieutenant Evelyn Walter James Johnson were wounded.

bivouac for ourselves, – the only other shelter for Officers being a most evil smelling, and foully used dug-out.

At 9.00 o'clock just as we were preparing to retire an urgent summons came for us. Keep, Browning, Dealler, Rednall and I were all to go up at once to our newly captured position, and take over our Companies. There were only two Company Officers left, – how we speculated as to whom the two were. It was a nasty shock. The Quartermaster hurriedly fitted us out with Tommies' clothes, yellow flashes on our haversacks, rifles, S.A.A., etc., and in the open we changed. it was 10.0 o'clock before we set off very heavily laden with all our equipment. Fortunately we soon managed to secure a lift in an empty ambulance car proceeding up to Carnoy. It was a slow journey for the traffic on the roads was stupendous and blocks were frequent.

At Carnoy we alighted. There an Advanced Dressing Station had been established. It was here that earlier in the day a wounded German Officer had whipped out a revolver and shot the Doctor who was binding his wounds. That Officer was shown no mercy. A crowd of infuriated Tommies set on him, tore every stitch of clothing off him, and kicked him to death. From Carnoy we made our way up to our original front line, and it was there that our difficulties began. Over no man's land and across ground newly won we made our way. Over obliterated Hun trenches, always going up hill, not knowing where our front line had got to, nor how far they had advanced. It was difficult going, and direction was only kept with the aid of a compass, and the North Star. It was like a nightmare, pitch black and dead bodies everywhere. Trenches almost obliterated, and it was a most eerie feeling to tread on the unseen and yielding body of a corpse.

After what seemed hours we stumbled upon some Northants, and found that we were in the "Triangle". We proceeded with a so called guide, but he was worse than useless; after a few yards he had lost us. By devious ways, and by going round three sides of a square we reached Pommiers Redoubt, and reported to B.H.Q.s at 2.00a.m. There we heard the news. A brilliant success, but heavy casualties. The 54th Brigade had over run Pommiers Redoubt and advanced on to Caterpillar Valley, but having no support on the flanks had withdrawn to their final objective in Beetle Alley. Had the cavalry only been close at hand, it appeared that they could have gone right through our positions without opposition from the Hun, and perhaps have cut their lines of communication. A golden opportunity would appear to have been thrown away.

Percival and Colley were the Company Officers remaining. The remnants of the Battalion were somewhere out in front in Beetle Alley, but Colonel Price did not know where they were, and would not let us go to find them. He said he had lost enough officers, and forbade us to go. His nerves seemed badly shattered. The Battalion was being relieved, so we waited to take our Companies back to Carnoy. What a wait it was! How the Bosche shelled that redoubt. I shan't forget it in a hurry. It was broad daylight before we were relieved. What a relief it was to get back to the comparative safety of Carnoy! Our rest was, however, of short duration, and the next evening we were sent up in support. There were no more than two Officers per Company and Rednall and I were parted, – he being transferred to "C" Company, and I to "D" Company commanded then by Lieut. Douglas S.H. Keep. We spent the next week in the Hun trenches which we had just captured, being in "The Bund" and "Austrian Trenches". Keep and I reorganised the Coy, and after a few days we were joined by 2nd Lieut. Howard, newly commissioned from the Bedfordshire Yeomanry. The weather was fairly good, and for the major portion of the time we were able to make ourselves comfortable in the Bosche dug-outs. Never less than 30 feet deep and fitted with beds and all kinds of conveniences. They certainly knew how to build dug-outs, for the labour must have been enormous, and the mystery of it all where they put the excavated earth. We spent many an hour exploring them and hunting for souvenirs. The whole battlefield was dotted with souvenir hunters, even the A.S.C. and M.P. coming up.

There was a number of dead Bosche lying around, and stench and lice were rampant in the dug-outs. It was an interesting week, my first experience of a battlefield and the clearing of it. I buried 2nd Lieut. Cunningham's body which was found by one of his men, and which up till then had been unaccounted for.

Our Artillery had a busy time. All the guns were brought right up, and roads and bridges had to be made for this to be accomplished. It was wonderfully and speedily done. Our last two days were spent in "Bund Support" trench, and there being no dug-outs habitable in our sector, things were not rosy. Howard and I made a cubby hole in the parapet, but the vibration caused by the shell fire made it collapse, and I was buried. On being relieved we spent one night at Bronfay Farm, and then proceeded to a camp in the Bois des Tailles. Duggy persuaded me to be Mess President, and I held this office until I left the Battalion in May [1917].

Contrary to all expectations we were only out for two days, and without any warning at 1.00a.m. one morning we were again moved up to support. The Northants and the Middlesex were in front, and by the brilliant leadership of Colonel Maxwell of the Middlesex they captured the whole of Trones Wood. Seven Brigades had already attempted the capture and failed, and the Royal West Kents had succeeded in obtaining one corner. It was they who got the kudos and the praise which rightly should have gone to the Middlesex and Northampton Regiments. We were in support at Maricourt, where we spent a very uncomfortable six days, the Bosche having got his Artillery up, and shelling us continuously. Whilst here the attack on Mametz and Delville Woods took place, and we saw the momentous sight of our Indian Cavalry going through, but they achieved nothing, our advance not being sufficiently substantial. The 54th Brigade were given no rest, and an attack on Guillemont was contemplated. All we Officers were sent up to Trones Wood to reconnoitre, and it was there that I realised the sterling qualities of Colonel Maxwell.

Trones Wood was the hottest shop on the front, and there Maxwell calmly went about immaculately dressed, living in the open front line with his men. I shall not forget his sangfroid as he stepped out of the trench into view of the Bosche and coolly "pumpshipped". Trones Wood was just a mass of splintered wood and shattered tree trunks. Our reconnaissance was not much value, since Waterlot Farm, which had been captured that morning, was counter-attacked as we were on our way up to it, and we had to beat a hasty retreat. I was glad to regain the comparative security of Maricourt. Each night that we lay down in our dug-out was fraught with the anxiety that our attack on Guillemont would take place at dawn, but each day the attack was postponed until the following morning. There is nothing more nerve racking than the waiting to attack, and our nerves were on edge for days expecting each dawn to be the day. At last after six days the news came through that the attack was cancelled and we were to be relieved. It was then July the 14th and it was not until September the 14th that, after many fruitless attempts, Guillemont was ours. (It was taken by the 2nd Bedfords, and my friend Vaulkhard[10] was killed in the assault.) I dare not contemplate our fate had our unprepared attack taken place. I should never have been writing this today, of that I am certain.

On the 15th July I set off with the advance party to the Bois des Tailles and fixed up the Company billets under canvas, and started fires going. We rested in the wood some days, and for the first time for three weeks we were able to get a bath and change of clothing. It was here that some 14 officers newly arrived from England joined us. To "D" Coy came Capt. Mulligan, who took over the command from Duggie Keep, Petts (who was formerly with the 10th Bedfords, had gone to Gallipoli, and returned home with dysentery), Kay and Bobby Moyse. Thus we numbered seven. After some four or five days we entrained at Maricourt-sur-Somme, and rumour had it that we were to experience a long rest in the neighbourhood of Amiens. It was a real summer's day, and after a very slow run we detrained at Longpré; it was then quite dark. After a very weary march of some 8 miles we arrived at our billets at Citerne about midnight. The villagers expected us, and I remember how we raided a farm and had scores of boiled eggs and coffee. It was here that Dame Rumour proved herself a lying jade, and after only 24 hours stay, we set out before dawn and marched back to Longpré, and entrained. Our journey took us through Boulogne, Calais, St Omer and Hazebrouck, where we detrained and marched to our billets at Wallon Cappel some 5 miles away. It was new country to us all, and our first experience of the pavé roads. The Battalion was in scattered billets, and thus during the days we were here we saw little of Headquarters – a great blessing.

General Maxse inspected us and congratulated us on our brilliant successes on the Somme. We had some great cricket matches in the afternoons, and it was here that I instituted the function of giving a high tea to the Company Sergeants, a proceeding which I hope is still maintained.

After some ten days we marched some 14 kilos to new billets just outside Bailleul. It was a scorchingly hot day, and a march that I shall long remember. Scores of men collapsed and fell out, and it was a worn out Coy that eventually reached the outskirts of Bailleul. We had very good billets. Howard and I sharing one. Bailleul is a smart little town, and everything was procurable there. I visited it several times purchasing delicacies for the Mess. There was a very fine tea place, where we used to sit in the Courtyard overlooking some beautiful gardens. It was a large old world house typically French aristocracy. Our cricket and sports were continued and we spent one of the best rests we have had in France.

August, 1916
All good things must come to an end, and at the beginning of August we trekked to Erquinghem, a mile or two outside Armentieres. Armentieres was the largest town to which we had been, and though only a mile from the Bosche front line, it was very little knocked about. It was too much a home for spies, and it was not until April, 1917, that the Hun started his frightfulness and drove all the civilians out. I

---

[10] Second Lieutenant John Vincent Vaulkhard; he is commemorated on the Thiepval Memorial as he has no known grave.

well remember one day causing some sensation by driving Rednall and myself into the town in an egg-cart. We swerved all over the road, but there was no accident, and we returned successfully with our shopping. In the town there was a most delightful teashop kept by a widow and sa belle fille, where one could partake of the most luscious cream cakes (they were superior to the Waldorf or Regent Street), and sip delicious thick chocolate.

We only had one spell in the trenches in front of Armentieres for a period of six days, and comparatively speaking it was a picnic. In this part of the country it is impossible to dig down, and so a breastwork of sandbags was built up. There was no parados,[11] nor dug-outs, the shelter being only cubby holes built in the side, and only providing protection from rain. "D" Coy struck lucky and were in reserve some 200 yards from the front line. Our "Dug-out" was a three roomed wooden shed, a most delightful affair, but what a death trap if a shell fell in the neighbourhood. It was exactly like a summerhouse with glass windows.

Our days were delightfully spent for the weather was perfect, August at its best, and I used to lie against a bank in a field and read and drowse. Our nights were busier, for Divisional H.Q.s had a passion for wiring, and every evening "D" Coy had to wire right along the front. What competition and rivalry there was between platoons as to who had done the most, and veracity was not rampant. It was not always comfortable work, as the Hun was very apt to use searchlights, and traverse his machine guns along the front. We had to lie low and could hear the ping of the bullets hitting the wire. Again our Artillery were very rife to giving stunts: and dummy raids[12] were made and naturally brother Bosche replied with his guns. A gas attack was made one evening, but with what effect on the Hun I don't know. We always wore our soft caps and Sam Brownes. How different from the pictures one sees in popular papers of Officers fully accoutered with sword, pack, equipment etc.

I well remember one very unorthodox action on my part. One afternoon I left the trenches and went into Armentieres. My way led me along a road in full view of the Hun some 1000 yards away, but he did not trouble to fire. It would have been a waste of useful ammunition. I had tea and returned laden with delicacies for the Mess, and the latest papers.

On being relieved we traveled by motor bus to the Bois de Nieppe, a huge forest, there to practice wood fighting. Then ensued the hardest three nights and four days work we had had. We attacked through that wood scores of times and each time some part of the attack was lost. It forcibly brought home to us the difficulties of keeping touch and direction in a wood, and we returned to Armentieres feeling the impossibility of attacking forests with any success. On the whole it afforded great amusement and night fighting seemed almost ludicrous. To those who have never been in a thick wood at night it is hard to appreciate the impenetrable darkness and the difficulties of progress, but I assure them that a hand held before one's face is invisible, and the rate of progress – usually in the wrong direction – is less than that

---

[11]   A parados served the same function at the back of a trench as a parapet did in front: a raised area to give protection from shell splinters etc.
[12]   In a dummy raid artillery was fired on the enemy positions, as if an attack was about to be made. The enemy would expect an attack when the shelling lifted and would man their trenches. Instead of an attack another round of shelling would occur, hopefully catching the enemy in their trenches and doing some execution among them.

of a tortoise. How well I remember one night when the C.O. discovered one of my men smoking during operations, and how he hauled me over the coals. "God had given me eyes, why did I not use them? I can see better with my one, than you with two." It is as well for me to mention here that Price was blind in one eye over which he wore a black patch, looking like a pirate.

A few days later we left Armentieres, by road to Bailleul and thence by train we reached St. Pol, where I met Peel (with the 6th Bedfords) for the first time since we had parted in April. Our billets were some 10 kilos distant at La Thieuloye. I had dinner with Peel and Hobson one evening at their Mess; after dinner we had some bridge – it was quite like some of our old Colchester days. I made the journey on Mulligans' horse. Rednall and I in our spare time frequently borrowed the Coy Commander's horses, and went for rides round the country. In spite of our hard training I managed in my capacity as Mess President to steal off in the Mess cart on many days to St. Pol and do some provisioning. Petts and I shared a most luxuriant room, and it was a great treat to sleep between sheets again. We were very fortunate in also obtaining a very comfortable Mess at the local schoolmaster's house. We had some three weeks highly intensive training, often being out from 9 in the morning until 7 at night. The training grounds were very extensive, and General Maxse often used to put in an appearance, and it was here that he put into practice his schemes for intensive digging and dug-out building. Many were the competitions we had for the fastest diggers, and invariably that old reprobate Biggs, and L/Cpl Mann, both ex-miners and in my Platoon were the winners.

September, 1916
After some three weeks training we moved to Raincheval in the early part of September where our training continued for another fortnight. At Raincheval we put in the finishing touches to our training; we knew we were in for something big. Mason of the M.G.C., and formerly of the 10th Bedfords came and paid us a visit one day. Our billets were very bad, our Mess being next door to a stable into which a door led, and the effluvia and the flies were beyond words. Beds we had none, and at first we had to be content with a barn and later a tent. It was the third week in September when we left Raincheval, marching by road to Varennes, where we stayed 48 hours; one of the days was a Sunday and many of us partook of Communion at a Service held in our Mess hut, the table providing the Altar. After two days we moved up, the remainder of the Brigade being already in the line. We were in reserve and we rested in the support trenches in Thiepval Wood. We had some busy days carrying materials up to the front line, and some huge dumps were made, but brother Bosche was very wily, and he blew every one of them sky high.

The River Ancre cut us off from the outer world, and all our supplies had to be brought across the river. Times out of number the various pontoon bridges were cut by shell fire and we suffered. The attack on Thiepval by the Middlesex, Royal Fusiliers and Northants Regiments commenced at noon on the 25th September, and in the early hours of that morning we were awakened by the tanks moving into position. How excited we were, it being our first glimpse of them, and their second essay in attack. Our attack waged hard all that day, but only a partial success was obtained. Thiepval Chateau, the first object, then a heap of white stones, was secured, but advance further was impossible.

All that day we waited expectantly, knowing that if the attack did not succeed we should be called up, and I am not above admitting that I prayed that success might be obtained without our aid. It was not to be though. About midnight the order came for us to move up to the Chateau. We had no guides, and the country was foreign to us. What a journey it was! The left half Company lost the right half, and every moment we expected to walk into the arms of the Bosche. However, as so often happens in these cases, we did at length hit upon the Chateau, and we soon knew it, for the Hun shelled it to blazes. Capt. Mulligan met us there, and we learnt that "C" and "D" Coys had been detailed to attack at 5.00a.m. (it was then 4.30a.m.) on the sound of a whistle. There would be no Artillery support, and we were to creep over and endeavour to capture the remainder of the village by surprise. We were extended in shell holes and our direction pointed out, and then began an interminable wait. Gradually dawn broke, and still no whistle blew. A tank embedded in a shell hole attempted to move, and we thought now is the time, but it stuck fast, and after many attempts to move at last gave up the attempt. It drew light, and I went along the line and had a chat with Potts and Major Merrick. It was then the whistle blew, and I hurried back to my Platoon.

Up and over we went, and reaching the Hun front trench, we halted. Capt. Mulligan was hit at the start, so I took matters in hand. I looked at the lay of the land, (it was here that my Platoon Sergeant named Hill,[13] one of the very best, was killed by a sniper), and decided that if we reached the Hun front line – our attack was in the nature of a wheeling movement – we should have reached our objective, so I sent Sergeants Wyatt and Slough with bombing parties down the trench. Immediately then a batch of some 30 Huns came out waving a white flag. These I sent back under Biggs to B.H.Q.s and I regret that I did not get as a souvenir a receipt for them. We made a flank attack along the trench, and Hill's death was avenged by Wyatt bayoneting the sniper.

At last we came into touch with "C" Coy on the right, and how overjoyed I was to meet Capt. L.H. Keep of "C" Coy, and knew that all was well. Then with another bombing party I went down to the left flank, and eventually came in touch with the R. Fusiliers. They danced with joy at the sight of us, having been there unsupported all through the night, and I relieved their bombing post. Then I proceeded to clear the dug-outs and reorganised the Company. Only Bobby Moyse and I were left. Potts had been hit immediately after I had left him, and a few days after he died of wounds.[14] I chose my Coy H.Q.s, and we were no sooner inside than two 5.9s hit the entrance, and L/Cpl Fry my runner was slightly hurt. About noon Duggie came up, and took over command to my great relief, and we moved our H.Q.s to a safer dug-out. Our casualties were not very heavy – some 30 out of a total of 100 – being wounded or killed, but amongst them were some topping boys. My Batman Dorrell[15] was killed, and I often wonder if it was by reason of the fact that he was wearing a

---

[13] This was Sergeant Leonard James Hill, originally of Little Missenden (Buckinghamshire), later Harpenden (Hertfordshire); he has no known grave and is commemorated on the Thiepval Memorial, just a few yards from where he was killed.

[14] Second Lieutenant Henry Potts died of wounds on 1 October 1916, aged 23; he is buried at Boulogne Eastern Cemetery.

[15] This is Private Frederick Thomas Dorrell of Borden (Kent), aged 22; he is buried at Connaught Cemetery, Thiepval.

pair of my cast-off breeches, and also carrying my walking stick, he having picked up the latter when I had thrown it down and armed myself with a rifle. Thus ended my first real battle, and the Division's second objective was gained, and the impregnable village of Thiepval had fallen after resisting all attempts for three months.

The next day[16] Duggie was sent for to attend a Conference at B.H.Q.s, and we surmised that more dirty work was in the offing. He returned at 4 o'clock with the unpleasing information that the attack was to be continued at 5.0 o'clock that evening, and that the Division's 3rd objective was our goal. "D" Coy were to act as moppers up to "A" and "B" the assaulting Coys. My Platoon was to assist "A" Coy and go over with the second wave. We had a tremendous struggle to get into position in time, and I never reached mine as the trench being blown in, we had to cross the open, and a sniper was fixed in the gap. It was here that L/Cpl Horley was hit. With our hearts in our boots we waited for the barrage to open – our signal for attack – we waited and waited . . . and then the news came round that the attack was postponed until the morrow. How gaily we went back to our dug-outs. Food and water were getting scarce, as they had been unable to bring any rations up, all the bridges over the Ancre having again been blown up. I well remember sharing my iron rations with Jack Fletcher, Keep's servant. We found a good supply of soda water left by the Huns, and filled our water bottles with that. Howard came up to take Potts' place, and so we had our full battle complement of Officers again. It was a long sleep we had that night.

The new attack was timed for 1.0p.m. the next day, our objective being Schwaben Redoubt, and we took care to be in a position well to time. No supplies had come up and rations and bombs were very scarce. We had collected all the Hun stick and egg grenades to make use of them. Prompt to the hour the barrage opened, and over the top we went. Once we had started I had no great fear. The barrage was easy to follow by watching the shrapnel hitting the dry ground and raising clouds of dust. After some 500 yards, more by luck than judgement, I came straight to the trench which it was my duty to clear. It ran away from us in the direct line of our advance. I collected the men around me, there seemed to be very few of my platoon though, and down the trench we went. My system was to place a sentry over each dug-out to keep the Bosche inside, and then to follow down the trench immediately behind the barrage, and prevent any Bosche from coming out. This plan answered splendidly, and we put three machine guns out of action, and prevented them enfilading our attacking waves as they went past. We were held up at one point and there ensued a rifle fight. The Bosche was facing us some 50 yards away, and at each other we blazed away, volley after volley, but the shooting was atrociously bad. My aim was terribly erratic. Then the fight pushed on. My party had run out of bombs, and his [Howard's] party, who were just behind went through and carried on. That action saved my life. Howard was one side of a traverse, and I the other when a shell landed instantaneously, and I received a scratch on my cheek and a dent in my shrapnel helmet. Thus I cannot help feeling that I was the cause of Howard's death.

---

[16] Either Lieutenant Cartwright's language here is slightly misleading (he may be referring back to the paragraph beginning "All that day we waited", i.e. 26th) or he is misremembering. The final capture of Thiepval occurred on 27 September with the assault on the Schwaben Redoubt occurring next day on 28th.

A mere boy and an only son.[17] I carried on in Howard's place. Our objective was reached and exhausted we sat and dazedly dozed with no thought of consolidating. Then L. H. Keep came up and took over command, and he sent me on a bombing stunt. We continued down the trench and drove the Huns before us. They threw egg bombs at us, and three of my men were killed. In return I threw at them some of their own hand grenades, and at length the Bosche scurried away.

We advanced some 70 yards and there built a bombing stop. It was a most beautiful position overlooking St. Pierre Divion and the valley of the Ancre. I manned it with some 10 men and put two Lewis guns in position, for it was a most important strategical position. Then I went back to report to Coy H.Q.s where I found the two Keeps, Colley and Brown, the sole survivors of the Battalion Officers already installed, and there I slept until it was my turn for duty at midnight. There was no thought of food but our throats were parched, and of water there was none. The wounded Hun and British were piteously crying for water. Then news came through that we were to be relieved by the West Kents and never, never was there more welcome news. With what anxiety we awaited that relief and when dawn came, and no relief having arrived, we felt we were doomed for another 24 hours in the front line. Eventually when it was daylight, the West Kents did arrive, and there being a ground mist I was able to lead out "D" Coy over the top to our former dug-outs.

We were only just in time, for the Hun counter-attacked, and two Platoons had to stand to ready to support. However, they were not called upon, though the West Kents lost my bombing post. After two or three days in support we were at last relieved. But what an anxious time we had moving out. The Hun put a barrage on our trench, and I had a narrow escape. A shell landed on the trench, knocked me over, killed Humphreys,[18] who was just behind me, and who, if he had lived, would have had the D.C.M., and wounded the next three men, including my new Batman, Meeks. We took shelter, I sheltering in an old Hun latrine which smelt like, well it was indescribable. When the barrage ceased we moved off again, and I took the Coy, some 50 strong, to our billets in Mailly Mallet, some six miles back. There we were reunited, all that was left of us, and the Officers who had stayed behind joined us. Of the Officers who went over the top, only Keep (L.H.), Brawn and myself had survived the two days battle.

For my bombing exploit and the capture of "Cartwright's Post" the C.O., recommended me for the M.C. There were not enough decorations to go round, however, for our capture of Thiepval, which was one of the strongest positions of the Western Front, and which had resisted since July 1st all efforts of capture, and I was very disappointed when my name did not appear in the list of honours.

After a couple of days rest we went back by train, alighting at Candas, and marching to Gorges where we secured good billets.

October, 1916
We rested at Gorges for a little more than a fortnight. Sir Douglas Haig paid us a

---

[17] Second Lieutenant Cedric Stewart Howard, from Cutcliff Place, Bedford, aged 22, is buried in Mill Road Cemetery, Thiepval, which lies on the battlefield where he died.
[18] This is actually Private William Humphrey from Hertingfordbury (Hertfordshire); he has no known grave and is commemorated on the Thiepval Memorial.

visit, and I met him one day in Bernaville where I was shopping. Price, who was acting as Brigadier, also met me, and wanted to know what I was doing in the Town, but he was quite affable. Duggie went away on leave from here, and I was in command of "D" Coy. I took advantage of having the use of a horse in trying to improve my horsemanship. A few days later we trekked by road back to the Somme, spending a night at a village in billets, until we reached Bouzincourt. I felt very proud of myself riding at the head of the Company on Mrs Digby, as my horse was named. At Bouzincourt I attended a conference at Brigade H.Q.s when the Brigadier laid before us the plans of our attack on Miraumont, which was to take place in a few days. After the Conference we motored through Albert, where I saw for the first time the Madonna on the tower of the Cathedral, and which, due to the effect of the Hun's bombardment leans over at right angles. Superstition has it that it will crash to the ground when peace is declared. One cannot help but gaze upon it with awe, and with feelings of the supernatural. We motored as far as the notorious village of Pozieres, where we met General Maxse. We spent the whole day reconnoitering the front line, but nothing of any note occurred, and we profited little for our labour.

The next day we moved from Bouzincourt to billets in Albert. The town was not knocked about to a great extent, but of windows and doors there were none, woodwork having been utilised for fuel. Contrary to all regulations we continued the practice, for it was bitterly cold in those rooms, destitute of all furniture. We carried out our training within reach of the guns, and practiced the form of our attack on Miraumont. This could not take place until the 55th Brigade had taken Regina Trench, which was to be our jumping off point. Thus we had a pleasant week in Albert, though for me it was very worrying. I had many Conferences to attend, and if Duggie did not return, I was to lead "D" Coy into action. Piercy, Waddy and Kay were my Platoon Commanders, and Sergeant Cowling had No: 15 Platoon. On the day following the capture of Regina Trench by the 55th Brigade we moved up, and took over the line from the East Surreys. "C" and "D" Companies were in front. Duggie had not returned and I was in command. What a poor sector of line it was; a trench with no dug-outs, and all the sides blown in. It was impossible to dig as the earth would collapse. For Coy H.Q.s I had a shaft of some 10 steps, but it was at the junction of the West Miraumont Road, and was a constant target for the Hun. Over another portion of the trench a Hun aeroplane had been brought down practically intact, and as the Hun made a practice of using it as a target, that also was a place to avoid. Numbers of dead Huns were lying all around, and I cannot help recalling one who was lying on his back with his pipe in his mouth, and another with his hands up in the position of "Kammerad". Then began that nerve racking period before going over the top. All preparations had been made, and each night we waited for the zero time to be announced. For 48 hours, during which time the Hun shelled us to blazes continuously, we waited, and then at last the news came through that the attack was postponed, on account of the weather. It was well that it was, for the rain had been almost continuous, and the ground was a quagmire, and movement almost impossible. We were relieved by the 6th Northants. I sent what was left of the Coy out at once, and there I waited until the Northants Lewis gunners, who had got lost, were found. Very sportingly Waddy waited with me. We managed to get away at last, and what a journey it was. The trenches were impassable, being knee deep in mud, it was pitch dark, and the way unknown. We stumbled on and on, over what seemed an interminable distance. At last we ran up against some gunners, and they gave us some whiskey, and put us on the right road. Waddy was exhausted, and once he collapsed altogether, and I had a terrible, trying time getting him along. Time after time we slipped down into shell holes, and I had to exercise all my strength to get Waddy out of the clinging mud.

Eventually we came to the light railway, and I rode a mule for some distance with Waddy on the trolley; then another journey on the motor railway, and so to Pozieres. On the Bapaume-Albert Road I treated with a lorry driver to find room for us, and so at midnight we at length struggled to our billets. Duggie had returned that day, and had prepared a grand fire, supper and champagne for us. All the Coy had straggled home worn out and overwrought. We had suffered some 25 casualties, an occurrence for which Mills – I have omitted the promotion of Colonel Price, who had been given command of the 55th Brigade, and so Mills was now in command with Bridcutt 2nd in Command – never forgave me, and for which he blamed me. Unjustly I always think, for he never came up the line to see what the conditions were like. The line was very thinly held, and as we had every reason for believing that the Hun would counterattack, in his endeavour to recapture the newly lost trench, it had to be manned.

November, 1916
For the next month we had an uneventful but worrying time. We did three tours in the trenches, and every dawn we expected to go over the top and attack Miraumont, but day after day the attack was postponed. At Albert we rested in the intervals. There were a few civilians left in the town, and there were one or two canteens, and a very poor and expensive café for Officers only. It was here that Kay fell ill, and was eventually evacuated to Blighty with appendicitis. It was unfortunate for me, as now that Duggie had returned, it was my turn to have a rest from warfare, and it was his intention that I should remain behind with the 1st Line Transport, but the loss of Kay meant that I had to take over No: 15 Platoon again. Another misfortune for me was that Driver, our D.S.O., came out from England and rejoined "D" Coy as 1st in Command, a position which I had enjoyed for two months. Our attack never came off, though a minor attack took place on November 14th in conjunction with the Naval Division[19] on our left. The 55th Brigade captured Desire Trench, some 300 yards in front of Regina Trench. The Naval Division met with great success, taking Beaumont Hamel, etc., North of the Ancre. About the 20th November, the 18th Division was relieved, and we had a happy trek back to a training area at Crecy, just outside Abbeville. On the way we spent a night at each of the following: Monchy, Breton, Beauval, Doullens (where we had a most sumptuous dinner including the delicacy of tripe), Domqueur, Bernaville, Agenvillers and Millencourt. The last named proved to be our final resting place, and we spent three weeks there.

Billets were very fair, and we had an enjoyable rest. We worked in the mornings and devoted the afternoons to sport, having Platoon Company and Battalion Soccer contests, tugs of war, etc. Our training ground closely resembled the features of the

---

[19] 63rd (Royal naval) Division included two brigades of naval troops, in Battalions with appropriately nautical names such as Nelson and Hood and one brigade of army troops, including 4th Battalion Bedfordshire Regiment.

neighbourhood of Miraumont, and we still assiduously practised the attack on that village. We rehearsed all the various parts we might be called upon to play, and never were we more pleased than when we were allotted the role of Brigade Reserve. That was a happy and easy role. On one morning all the G.O.C.s and their staffs came down and witnessed our attack. General Gough and all his satellites and a gorgeous array of brass hats were present.

On December 14th, we moved our quarters to the neighbouring village of Domvast, and on the same day I set out on my journey homewards for leave. I had to walk all the way to Abbeville, some eight miles in the rain, but what did I care? The morrow would see me home. Of that happy time I do not propose to write in my diary. It was unfortunate that I had to leave London on Xmas morning, and my Xmas dinner was eaten at the Officers' Club, Boulogne. I rejoined the Battalion at Domvast, and immediately was sent on a Trench Mortar Course at Conchy. It was supposedly a week's course, and I was three days late. It was the most pleasantly easy course I have ever been on, and was quite interesting.

January, 1917
We had a further three weeks rest at Domvast before we moved up again to the line, and much football was played. We even had some Rugger matches, in which I took part, and Corps Steeplechases. After our eight weeks rest we at length got our movement orders, and we trekked off to the line. We again spent a night at Domqueur, and then two nights at Candas. There things began to hustle and on the second morning we were hastily despatched to Rubempré, which we reached in the dark after a very long and tiring march in the snow.

Next morning we were up before it was light, and we embussed on motor buses towards the line. After some 5 hours travelling we alighted at Aveluy where we lunched. The remainder of our journey had then to be made on foot. We crossed the Ancre by the Pontoon bridge, and nightfall found "D" Coy in the front line again. We relieved a Territorial Battalion of the Warwicks, and though they had held the line for a week not one of them knew the positions of their posts. They were frightfully windy. Before the last Platoon had been relieved it was almost daylight. Our guides were more than useless, and our mode of progression seemed to be by circles. The front line, which was the old aforementioned Desire Trench, was very lightly held by isolated posts of about 10 men, each some 150 yards apart. I had three very lonely posts to man, and was on the left of the Coy. Where the next post on my left was the Warwicks did not know, except that it was somewhat in the rear, as the line ran back very sharply. We had no maps marked, and I never succeeded in finding that post. The left hand post had been raided a few nights previously, so that the outlook in front of us was not very cheerful. There were no defenses, barbed wire entanglements or dug-outs, and Sergeant Cowling and myself shared a cubby hole dug in the side of the trench. It was very damp and cold, and to make matters worse the morning brought with it snow. There was no communication between posts by day for the trench had fallen in, and the muddy bottom was impassable. Besides the two months old corpses were too numerous to be pleasant. Visiting my detached posts at night, one had to move in the open all the time. It was eerie work, for one never knew quite if one was going in the right direction, and a meeting with a Bosche patrol was not at all improbable. I used to take two stalwart lads, Wynne, a professional rugger player and Shadbolt (Military Medal) to accompany me as a bodyguard. The snow in one respect proved a boon, as after a time a beaten track showed out black along the whole line, and one had no fear then of missing one's way. Some 400 yards away in rear situate in Regina Trench was an enormous galleried dug-out, where Coy H.Q.s and two Platoons remained. On the third night my Platoon was relieved by No 18 Platoon, and my left hand post taken over by "B" Coy. Thus I was able to have a long and good night's rest in the dug-out. The Huns had had a latrine downstairs, but we moved it up to the trench outside. Unfortunately, it overflowed, and the muck and urine flowed down the stairs. The next morning I relieved Waddy, who was feeling the effects of a trying time in the line, and I looked after his Platoon for him, and the whole of the front line for the next day and a half. Nothing very eventful occurred, except that the Lewis gun post manned by a section of my Platoon on the extreme left of the line was surprised by the Hun, whom they had taken for men of the Middlesex Regiment, who were relieving us. It was rather an unfortunate contretemps, and 3 of the Section were taken prisoners. Our rest billets were Nissen Huts on the Nab Road, near Aveluy and Aveluy Wood. We usually occupied those named Warwick Huts after their late occupants. It was intensely cold weather, and fuel became increasingly difficult to obtain, and the huts were very draughty. Here we were in Brigade Reserve, and the nights used to bring us many fatigues of carrying up to the front line. To be in charge of a carrying party is no sinecure, for it is a difficult matter to find one's way about in the dark, and if one gets a guide! Well, who has ever yet met with a guide who knew his way? To make matters worse the ground was like sheet ice, the men were not easy to handle, and the Bosche delighted in shelling all communications. After some days in Warwick Huts, we spent another turn in the line. This time "D" Coy were in support in Vancouver Trench, and there was accommodation for all. Our nights were very unpleasant as we had to man Regina Trench, which was untenable by day. It was bitterly cold spending the nights in the open, and patrolling the line. On being relieved we went back to huts in Martinsart some three or four miles back, and from there I was sent to the Brigade Bombing School at Hedeauville. Wightman of the Royal Fusiliers was in charge, and altogether we were a very cheery crowd. It was a pleasantly spent week, and at the termination of it I became a qualified instructor. I rejoined "D" Coy who were on detachment living under canvas. Each night we had carrying fatigues, but only one officer a night was needed, so that it was not so bad. Later we moved into huts, and were employed on the light railway pushing trolleys up to the Rifle Dump.

February, 1917
Whilst out at rest this time, we met the 4th Bedfords, and some of them came to tea. During this time we continued, as ever, our preparations for the coming attack, still having Miraumont for our objective. On me was devolved the responsibility of taking "D" Coy into action, it having been decided that Duggie Keep should remain behind with the Transport. Many were the Conferences I had to attend at Battalion and Brigade Headquarters. It was only a few days before the show was scheduled to begin that we were made acquainted with our separate tasks. By great good fortune we were the Brigade Reserve, the Royal Fusiliers and the Northants were assaulting Battalions, and the Middlesex were mopping up. The attack was timed for dawn on

the 17th February and on the night of the 16th–17th we moved up into position. "D" Company occupied that notorious spot, Mouquet Farm, and there we soundly slept. We turned out at dawn, Waddy, Angas and Piercy were my subalterns, to watch things, but there was a thick ground mist, and we could see nothing. The barrage was intense and the air vibrated with the screaming shells. Until noon we remained undisturbed. From the wounded we gathered news of how things were going, and all seemed well. It was during our scratch lunch that an urgent call for all Company Commanders was received from Brigade H.Q.s. I went up with Leslie Keep, and on our way we met the Padre, and learnt that, after all, things had not gone as well as expected. Boom Ravine had been captured early in the day, and the Division had reached Miraumont, but the Division on our right had however failed to make a material advance. This necessitated the 18th Division falling back to the crest of the hill a few hundred yards beyond Boom Ravine, and in this withdrawal, it lost very heavily. At Battalion H.Q.s., we conferred, and the intention was that the attack should be taken over by the Bedfords at dawn next day, and in preparation we were to move up to Grandcourt Trench. Before moving up the Company, I reconnoitered Grandcourt Trench, and finding that it provided no cover, and was being heavily shelled, I reported to the C.O., and obtained permission to put my Coy in Fabian Trench. In Fabian Trench there was good cover for the men, and the move took place without a hitch. All night long we waited for details of the coming assault on Miraumont, and it was anxious waiting. Dawn broke and we heard then that the Brigadier had appealed to the G.O.C., Division that his Brigade had suffered too heavily to attack again and he desired to keep the Bedfords intact, and we were to be relieved. It was a happy crowd that returned to rest billets in Martinsart. After a few days we moved up to St. Pierre Divion into tents. It was frightfully cold and we were damned uncomfortable. We were occupied with road-making most of the time.

March, 1917
In the last days of February, I in company with Kydd of "B" Coy was detailed for a Course at the 18th Divisional School at Buigny St. Maclou, a few kilos from Abbeville. There we suffered 3 weeks intensive training and instruction under Colonel Fiennes of the Royal West Kents. Weekends were a great relief, and were spent in Abbeville at the Officers' Club. There were some topping men at the School, and we formed quite a clique in the ante-room telling stories and playing bridge after dinner. It was in the last days of March that I rejoined my Battalion, who had just come into rest billets after having taken part in the pursuit of the Hun in his retreat to the Hindenburg Line, a picnic affair which I was sorry to have missed. After spending a night in Hazebrouck – the Battalion having moved up North – I found the Battalion at Steenbeck, a village on the outskirts of the Bois de Nieppe, whose acquaintance we had already made in August. We spent a quiet fortnight training, the most memorable incident which I can recall, being a rugger game. "C" and "D" Coys and "A" and "B" Coys. I was responsible for the former's team, and though "A" and "B" Coys were considered to possess all the supposed talent of the Battalion, we beat them 6 points to nil. I was very bucked, more so, as I scored a try. Percival, Bull, Clegg and several new officers rejoined us here.

April, 1917
When the Arras show commenced we were moved up close to Lillers as Army Reserve, and all our hopes were that the Battle would be eminently successful, and that we might not be called upon. However, we were doomed to disappointment, and gradually we moved by road closer up to the battle zone, finally entraining one early morning at Pernes. Night found us detraining at Arras railhead. We set out on the road for billets at Neuville Vitasse, and at the end of a weary march, we were sorely disgusted to find that our billets were shell holes and trenches. There was no cover and Piercy, Angas, Lingwood and I slept together for warmth in one shell hole. The next night we took over the front line in front of Héninel St Martin. My Platoon was in support, and our trench was only a foot deep, so that before daylight broke we had to get busy and dig down. We only spent three days in the line, and things were very quiet and the weather quite delightful. On being relieved we returned to Neuville Vitasse, and managed this time to obtain dug-outs. However, so mild was the weather that, in spite of spasmodic shelling, I slept outside in my valise. All our meals were taken al fresco.

May, 1917
Final preparations were made for our impending attack on the Hindenburg Line along a twelve mile front. To gain our final objective we had to cover three miles of ground, and thereupon the Cavalry were to come through and carry on. It was an ambitious programme, and if successful real open fighting, of which there had been none since the Marne, would have been renewed. Alas, the scheme failed. On May 1st "D" Company, as assaulting Company, took up their battle position in the front line. Driver was in command, Angas, Lingwood (a newcomer) and myself were Platoon Commanders. Everything seemed favourable, and the general opinion was that it would be easy going. From a sap in our front line we commanded a view over the Bosche lines for miles, a green undulating country that looked most inviting, and made us eager to get there. I was not anxious and windy as on previous occasions.

Zero was timed for dawn on the 3rd, and at 4.0 o'clock the barrage opened; our signal; out of the trenches we scrambled up a slope and down into the valley. It was pitch dark, and to make matters difficult, there was a ground mist in the low-lying land; touch and direction were soon lost, and there were large gaps in our line. As we approached to their lines near Chérisy the wire in front could be seen uncut. The ranks were wavering. Captain Bull and C.S.M. Brand, ("B" Coy) came up and just as we were discussing the line of advance, I saw a blinding flash, my rifle, smashed to smithereens, was knocked out of my hand, and I was hit in the leg. With C.S.M. Brand, wounded in the leg also, I crawled back, and just as we reached a trench, Brand was killed by a shell.[20] The most popular and daring man in the Battalion; it seemed ironic that he should have been killed just as he had reached some cover. The M.O. found me, and after putting on a field dressing, I hobbled to a dressing station. Via Boulogne, where I spent a few days in Hospital, and Newcastle-on-Tyne, where a few more days were spent, I eventually reached London with a month's sick leave to gladden my heart, and a sore leg.

---

[20] Company Sergeant Major Richard Maurice Brand DCM, MM from Hertford has no known grave and is commemorated on the Arras Memorial.

Appendix A1. Table of the Battalion's Moves and Locations

25-7-15	Codford St Mary [Wiltshire] Transport already abroad
26-7-15	Ostronove Rest Camp, Boulogne
27-7-15	Flesselles
28-7-15	Talmas
8-8-15	La Neuville
22-8-15	Ribemont
23-8-15	Companies being acclimatised to trenches by taking in turns to enter and man them over the next twelve days
5-9-15	Bécordel Trenches
21-9-15	Méaulte (B Company at Bécordel; C Company at Point 107 until 24-9-15; A Company at Point 107 from 25-9-15)
5-10-15	Sector D2 Trenches (Fricourt)
15-10-15	Méaulte
25-10-15	D2 Trenches
6-11-15	Méaulte
14-11-15	D2 Trenches
22-11-15	Méaulte
30-11-15	D1 Trenches (Fricourt)
8-12-15	Méaulte
16-12-15	D1 Trenches
24-12-15	Méaulte
31-12-15	D1 Trenches
8-1-16	Méaulte
16-1-16	D1 Trenches
24-1-16	Méaulte
3-2-16	La Houssoye
1-3-16	Corbie
5-3-16	Bray-sur-Somme
6-3-16	A2 Trenches (Carnoy)
11-3-16	Bray-sur-Somme
15-3-16	A2 Trenches
19-3-16	Bronfay Farm, near Bray-sur-Somme [A, B, & D Companies at adjoining Billon Wood]
25-3-16	A2 Trenches
27-3-16	Bray-sur-Somme
2-4-16	A2 Trenches
8-4-16	Bronfay Farm and Billon Wood
15-4-16	A2 Trenches
20-4-16	Bray-sur-Somme
26-4-16	A2 Trenches
4-5-16	Bray-sur Somme (A and B Companies at Froissy; B and D Companies at Corbie from 4-6-16; B & D Companies moved to Picquigny 10-6-16)
11-6-16	Picquigny
23-6-16	Grovetown Camp
24-6-16	A2 Trenches (Carnoy)
29-6-16	Bray-sur-Somme

30-6-16	A2 Trenches
2-7-16	Pommiers Redoubt (and surrounding trenches, Beetle Alley and New Trench, reached in attack of 1-7-16; moved to Carnoy at 2a.m., returning to Emden and Austrian Trenches, with HQ at Piccadilly)
3-7-16	Piccadilly (with companies in Emden and Austrian Trenches)
4-7-16	Suicide Corner, Montauban Road (2 Companies in German first line trenches, rest in Caftet Wood, Carnoy)
6-7-16	The Loop (companies in Pommiers and Caterpillar Trenches)
9-7-16	Bronfay Farm
10-7-16	Bois des Tailles
13-7-16	Trigger Wood
14-7-16	Maricourt
18-7-16	Bois des Tailles
21-7-16	Citerne (actually arrived 12.30a.m. 22-7-16)
23-7-16	Wallon Cappel
28-7-16	Steam Mill, Bailleul
5-8-16	Erquinghem
6-8-16	B2 Trenches (Armentieres)
16-8-16	Rue Marle (near Erquinghem)
18-8-16	Bois de Nieppe, La Motte
21-8-16	Rue Marle
23-8-16	Erquinghem
24-8-16	en route to St Pol
25-8-16	La Thieuloye
9-9-16	Ternas
10-9-16	Ivergny
11-9-16	Raincheval
23-9-16	Varennes
25-9-16	North Bluff, Authuille (C & D Companies in Paisley Avenue, Thiepval Wood)
27-9-16	Thiepval
28-9-16	Schwaben Redoubt, Thiepval
29-9-16	Thiepval
30-9-16	Mailly-Maillet Wood
2-10-16	Vacquerie (C & D Companies at Gorges)
15-10-16	Beauval
16-10-16	Vadencourt Wood
17-10-16	Bouzincourt
19-10-16	Albert
23-10-16	Regina Trench near Courcelette
26-10-16	Albert
3-11-16	Regina Trench (C Company Vancouver Trench, D Company Zollern Trench)
6-11-16	Tara Hill near Albert
12-11-16	Regina Trench (A & B Companies Zollern Trench)
16-11-16	Ovillers
20-11-16	St Riquier
26-11-16	Agenvillers
27-11-16	Millencourt
14-12-16	Domvast
11-1-17	Prouville
12-1-17	Candas
14-1-17	Rubempré
15-1-17	Trenches near Pozieres (HQ at Zollern Redoubt)
20-1-17	Warwick Huts, Martinsart (C Company at Thiepval)
24-1-17	Trenches near Pozieres (HQ at Zollern Redoubt)
28-1-17	Martinsart Wood (C Company at Stuff Redoubt from 9-2-17 to 13-2-17)
10-2-17	Thiepval

13-2-17	Warwick Huts, Martinsart
16-2-17	Zollern Trench (A & B Companies in Farback Trench, C & D Companies at Moucquet Farm)
17-2-17	Zollern Trench (A Company at The Gulley, B Company in Regina Trench, C & D Companies at Moucquet Farm)
18-2-17	Gloucester Huts, Martinsart
1-3-17	St Pierre Divion (A Company, Warwick Huts, Martinsart)
13-3-17	Loupart Line and Hill 130
17-3-17	Bihucourt Line and Achiet le Grand
19-3-17	Ervillers
20-3-17	Loupart Line
21-3-17	Marlborough Huts
22-3-17	Contay
23-3-17	Bertangles
24-3-17	Bovelles
26-3-17	Entrained at Salieux
27-3-17	Steenbecque le Bas
21-4-17	La Pierriere
26-4-17	Bailleul les Pernes
27-4-17	Arras
28-4-17	Trenches near Neuville Vitasse
29-4-17	Neuville Vitasse
1-5-17	Front line trenches west of Chérisy
4-5-17	Rear trenches east of Neuville Vitasse (N.14.d)
13-5-17	Different set of trenches near Neuville Vitasse (N.32.a)
27-5-17	Camp at S.23.a. near Bovelles
2-6-17	Support trenches opposite Fontaine [HQ and D Company in Hindenberg Support [Shaft] Trench, C Company in Concrete Trench, A & B Companies in the Rookery]
9-6-7	Front line trenches opposite Fontaine
17-6-17	Camp at S.17
18-6-17	Monchy-au-Bois
19-6-17	Hénu
3-7-17	Entrained at Doullens and heading for Godewaersvelde [D Company travelling separately]
4-7-17	Scattered billets 1½ miles from Abeele
6-7-17	Palace Camp, near Ouderdom
22-7-17	Connaught Camp, Wippenhoek
24-7-17	Billets 2 miles NW of Stenvoorde
29-7-17	Connaught Camp, Wippenhoek
30-7-17	Palace Camp, Ouderdom
31-7-17	New Canal Reserve Camp
1-8-17	Château Segard Area No.4 near Ypres
3-8-17	Railway Dugouts, Shrapnel Corner near Hooge
7-8-17	Front line near Hooge [D Company at Surbiton Villas, A Company and Battalion HQ in Hooge Tunnel, C & D Companies in Ritz Trench]
10-8-17	Glencourse Wood near Hooge
11-8-17	Dikkebus New Camp
12-8-17	Railway Dugouts [HQ, C & D Companies; A & B Companies in Crab Crawl]
14-8-17	Stirling Castle near Hooge
17-8-17	Dikkebus Railhead
18-8-17	Buysscheure
3-9-17	Scattered farms around Arneke
22-9-17	Tunnelling Camp, near Sint-Jan-ter-Biezen

THE PERSONAL DIARY

16-10-17	Canal Bank Camp, Boezinge
18-10-17	Front Line near Ypres
20-10-17	Irish Farm en route for Tunnelling Camp
21-10-17	Tunnelling Camp near Sint-Jan-ter-Biezen
24-10-17	Cane Trench near Ypres
25-10-17	Front Line near Ypres
27-10-17	Dirty Bucks Camp
29-10-17	Putney Camp
4-11-17	Box Camp, Ondank
10-11-17	Baboon Camp, Boezinge
13-11-17	Front Line, Houthulst Forest
17-11-17	Box Camp, Ondank
22-11-17	Canal Bank Camp, Boezinge
26-11-17	Front Line, Houthulst Forest
29-11-17	J Camp, International Corner
4-12-17	Baboon Camp, Boezinge
8-12-17	Front Line, Houthulst Forest
16-12-17	Claude Chappe Camp, Roesbrugge Haringe
4-1-18	J Camp, International Corner
10-1-18	Baboon Camp, Boezinge
15-1-18	Front Line, Houthulst Forest
18-1-18	J Camp, International Corner
24-1-18	Baboon Camp, Boezinge
26-1-18	Front Line, Houthulst Forest
28-1-18	Larry Camp, Elverdinge
30-1-18	Headquarters Camp, Krombeke
9-2-18	Noyon
10-2-18	Salency
14-2-18	Caillouel
15-2-18	Remigny
26-2-18	Béthencourt
28-2-18	Rouez Camp [C Company at Noureuil]
21-3-18	Montescourt Switch (Details at Rouez Camp)
22-3-18	La Montaigne Bridge, Crozat Canal (Details at Rouez Camp)
23-3-18	Faillouel or Caillouel (Details at Villequier Aumont)
24-3-18	Caillouel
25-3-18	Babouef
26-3-18	Mesnil
27-3-18	St Aubin
30-3-18	Boves
31-3-18	Gentelles
1-4-18	Front Line near Hangard
2-4-18	Gentelles
6-4-18	Boves
9-4-18	Boutillerie
24-4-18	Front Line just south of Cachy
25-4-18	Bivouacs in support of Front Line near Cachy
27-4-18	Avesnes-Chaussoy
6-5-18	Laviéville (A Company Hill Row, B Company Darling Support, C Company Villa Reserve, D Company Copse Trench)
13-5-18	Front Line near Laviéville
16-5-18	Baizieux
17-5-18	Front Line near Laviéville
25-5-18	Wood E of Béhencourt

132 THE SHINY SEVENTH

On 25-5-18 the Battalion was absorbed by the 2nd Battalion. The following moves are for the 7th Battalion Bedfordshire Regiment cadre.

26-5-18	En route for Chépy Valines
27-5-18	Rogeant
12-6-18	Monchaux
15-6-18	Yzengremer
21-6-18	Béhen
22-6-18	Ergnies
27-6-18	Occoches
28-6-18	Le Souich
3-7-18	Ivergny and Beaudricourt
21-7-18	Candas
22-7-18	Sergueux
23-7-18	Camp 1 mile W of Abancourt
31-7-18	Cadre absorbed by the 2nd Battalion Bedfordshire Regimen

From 25 July 1915 to 25 May 1918 the Battalion spent 1,036 days in France and Belgium. During that time the Battalion, or parts of it, spent about 320 days (or parts of days) either in the trenches, in close support or moving against the enemy – about 30% of its total time.

Appendix A2. Selected Operational Orders

1. Operational Orders for relieving another battalion in the front line: this Operational Order has been selected as an example of the orders which interleave the War Diary sheets and thus is transcribed in its entirety. The other Operational Orders listed below will not include the information at the beginning and end, simply the points of the Order (here numbered 1–8).

OPERATION ORDERS   No.1
by   Copy No.4
Major G.P.Mills,
Commanding 7th (S) Battalion Bedfordshire Regt.
4th March 1916

1. INTENTION.	The 7th Bn. Bedfordshire Regt. will relieve the Regiment in A.2. Sector Trenches on 6th March, 1916 The distribution of the Battalion on taking over will be as follows: – Right Sub.Sec. A Coy. Centre Sub.Sec. B Coy. Left Sub.Sec. D Coy. C Coy. in Bn. Reserve at CARNOY. The line will be held by 3 platoons of each company in the fire trench, and 1 platoon of each company in support.
2. RATIONS.	Supporting platoon of each company will be responsible for the drawing and carrying up of rations for their respective companies, from CARNOY. All cooking is done at CARNOY. Hot meals can only be taken up at night time. <u>Water</u> is brought to CARNOY in watercarts and each company must send down 12 men every night after dark with 12 empty petrol tins to bring up 12 tins of water. It is essential that as many empty tins as possible be taken down as full tins will only be issued in exchange for empty ones.
3. BILLETS.	Billeting accommodation is bad, so kits should be reduced to a minimum.
4. RELIEFS.	The Battalion will probably be relieved by the 6th Battn. Northants Regt. every 5 or 6 days. Rest billets are at BRONFAY Farm.
5. VICKERS M.G.	1 Section of the Vickers M.G. Coy. will be lent to the Battalion by the 54th Brigade Machine Gun Coy.
6. EXTENT OF LINE	The Battalion frontage consists of trenches 45 to 54 inclusive. Right Sub.Sec. 45–48 inclusive. Centre Sub.Sec. 49–50 inclusive, Left Sub.Sec. 51–54 inclusive.
7. FROSTBITE.	The usual precautions are to be taken for the prevention of Frostbite and Trench Feet. As there is a shortage of Gum Boots rigid supervision is essential as regards the changing to socks, etc.
8. ROUTE OF RELIEF.	The Battn. will relieve via CARNOY AVENUE, LA GUERRE WOOD, and BERWICK AVENUE. O.C.Companies, O.C.Snipers, M.G.Officer and Battn.Bombing Officer will proceed to the trenches by 9a.m. on morning of 6th inst., to take over their respective sectors, &c. Trench stores Lists to be forwarded to Battn. Headquarters by 12 noon Monday, or earlier if possible.

(signed) P.R.Meautys,
Capt. & Adjutant
7th Bn, Bedf. R.

134 APPENDIX A: BATTALION MOVES

        Issued at 12 noon 4.3.16 by Trench Runner
        Copy No.1 File
        2 54th Brigade
        3 War Diary
        4 War Diary
        5 O.C. "A" Coy.
        6 O.C. "B" Coy.
        7 O.C. "C" Coy.
        8 O.C. "D" Coy.
        9 Transport Officer & Qr.Mr.
        10 Battn.Bombing Officer
        11 Battn.Sniping Officer
        12 6th Northants
        13 Machine Gun Officer
        14 Regtl.Sergt.Major
        15 Spare

2. Operational Order regarding relief of the 6th Battalion Northamptonshire Regiment – 14 March 1916: given as example of a relief order. Note mention of the introduction of steel helmets; previous to this soft peaked caps had been worn at all times.

1. Intention	The 7th Bn.Bedf.Regt. will relieve the 6th battalion Northants.Regt. in Sector A.2.Trenches, tomorrow, 15th instant. The relief will take place after dark. Time of departure from BRAY will be notified later.
2. Trench Stores.	Company Commanders, the Bn.Bombing and Bn.Sniping Officer and the Regimental Sergeant major will proceed to the trenches on the morning of the 15th inst. to take over Trench Stores. Duplicate copies of Trench Store Lists will be submitted to the Adjutant as soon as possible after handing over stores is completed.
3. Transport.	The Bedford Transport will bring back the kit and stores of the Northants from A.2. Kit and stores should be kept down to a minimum.
4. Distribution of Companies	D Company will take over the Left Sector A Company will take over the Right Sector B Company will take over the Centre Sector. C Company will be the Company in Reserve.
5. Personnel to be left in BRAY.	The following men will be left in BRAY, under the Supervision of the Quartermaster. 4 Drummers, and 1 N.C.O. in charge. 1/2 the pioneer Section. Shoemakers & Tailors. The Armourer Sergeant will proceed to the trenches with the Headquarter Company.
6. Steel Helmets.	Until the Battalion is fully equipped with Steel Helmets the Company which is in reserve will hand over their steel helmets to the Centre Sector Company.
7. Spare Kit.	All spare kit not being taken to the trenches will be handed over to the Quartermaster before 4 p.m. and must be stacked in the places selected for the respective companies.
8. Kit for Trenches.	All stores and kits which are for the Trenches must be ready for loading on the limbers by 5 p.m. at latest. The Regimental Provost Sergeant will personally supervise the loading up of Headquarters Stores & Kit. He will also march Headquarter Company to the trenches
Note.	The usual precautions regarding the intervals between platoons and the strength of parties proceeding to the trenches must be observed.

SELECTED OPERATIONAL ORDERS   135

3. Operational Order regarding relief of the battalion in the front line by the 6th Battalion Northamptonshire Regiment 18 March 1916: given as an example of an Order regarding relief of the Battalion. Note the Trench Stores list.

1. <u>Intention</u>	The 7th Battn, Bedfordshire Regt. will be relieved by the 6th Bn.Northants Regt. In Sector A.2 Trenches tomorrow, 19th instant. The relief will take place after dark. The time of relief will be notified later.
2. <u>Information.</u>	The leading Coy. of the Northants will leave BRAY at – p.m. Northants Coys. will leave BRONFAY FARM at intervals of 1/4 hour.
3. <u>Order of Relief.</u>	Companies of the Bedfords will be relieved in the following order: – Left Sub.Sector, Centre Sub.Sector, Right Sub.Sector, Reserve Coy. & Bn.H.Q.Coy.
4. <u>Trench Stores.</u>	In addition to the usual trench stores, the following Battalion property will be handed over, under the separate heading of "BATTALION TRENCH STORES"
	Trench Stretchers 8
	1 1/2″ Very Guns 4 (All Bedfords)
	Periscopes All
	Signalling lamps, visual 4 (All Bedfords)
	Stands for same 4 (all Bedfords)
	Telescopes 2 (all Bedfords)
	Stands for same 2 (all Bedfords)
	Discs 12 (all Bedfords)
	12 way Commutator 1 (Northants)
	Magazines 324 (216 N'Hants & 108 Bedfords)
	Tripods – 4 (2 Bedfords, 2 N'Hants)
	Panniers 16 (All Northants)
	Boilers, complete 8 per company = total 32
	Camp Kettles – 2 per company = total 8
	Camp Kettles – 10 Bn.H.Qrs
	Fryers 4 per company = total 16
	Special attention must be paid to the handing over of Battn.
	Property on this occasion in order to avoid any possibility of confusion or doubt arising later on.
	Steel Helmets will not be handed over, but taken out of the trenches by the men. The DUPLICATE Trench Store List (1 copy only is required) will be forwarded to Orderly Room by 3 p.m. 19th inst.
	<u>TAKING OVER PARTY.</u> Company Commanders, Bn.Bombing Officer, Battn.Sniping Officer and the Regimental Sergeant Major 6th N'Hants will arrive in A.2. on the morning of the 19th to take over Trench Stores.
5. <u>Transport</u>	Transport of the 6th Northants will take to BRONFAY FARM the kits etc. of the 7th Bedfords. The Regimental Provost Sergeant will personally supervise the loading of the kits, etc. and will march H.Q.Coy. to BRONFAY FARM.
6. <u>Distribution of Companies</u>	Battn.H.Qrs. and "C" Company will take over BRONFAY FARM; A, B & D Companies will take over BILLON WOOD. 1 Officer per Coy., Coy.Q.M.Sgts., and 1 N.C.O. per platoon, with 1 Pioneer from Bn.H.Q. will parade after dinner tomorrow to take over their respective company dugouts.
7. <u>Details</u>	Police & Stretcher Bearers at present with their companies will remain with their companies. Company Quartermaster Sergeants and Storemen at present in BRAY will rejoin their companies tomorrow night. The Drummers at present in trenches will proceed under an N.C.O. to BRONFAY FARM by 10am tomorrow, 19th inst., to unload Bn. transport on arrival of limbers, and take charge of baggage until

Battalion Headquarters arrives. They will report to Bn.H.Qrs. at 9.30am for orders

4. Operational Order regarding fatigues – 3 June 1916: fatigues were the bane of life for battalions supposedly resting from duty in the front line.

1. Intention
   B & D Companies are to proceed to CORBIE tomorrow and take over fatigues from 1 company of 6th Northants and 1 platoon of 12th Middx. Regiment.
2. Order of March
   The detachment will march by platoons at 300 yards interval to the BOIS DES TAILLES. The first platoon of B Company will march off at 7.30 a.m. and the last platoon of D Company will march off at 7.55 a.m. The column will close up there and march as a whole to CORBIE.
3. Billets.
   2nd Lieut.J.H.R.Rawes R.Q.M.S. Kerrison and the two Company Quartermaster-Sergeants will proceed by horse and cycle, starting at 6 a.m. 2nd Lieut.Rawes will be responsible for taking over billets.
4. Rations.
   The rations for consumption on the 4th instant will be carried on the travelling kitchens.
5. Transport.
   Transport will move independently of the troops. A guide must be sent to meet it on arrival in CORBIE. The following vehicles and animals will remain there: – 2 cookers, 1 water cart, and 2 Officers horses.
6. Pioneers.
   1 N.C.O. and 3 men of the pioneers will march with the Transport.
7. Surplus kit.
   Surplus kit will be stored at the Qr.Mr.'s Stores pending transport becoming available. Each man should place the spare shirt and pants inside the cape waterproof. These will be done up in bundles of 20 and labelled.
8. Detachment.
   The Detachment Staff will be as follows: –
   Commanding officer: – Capt.W.H.Bull.
   Acting Quartermaster: R.Q.M.S.Kerrison.
   Sergeant Major: C.S.M. E.E.Amos.

5. Operational Order regarding fatigues – 3 June 1916

Subject – Fatigues etc.   18th Div. No. 76/71
"A"

7th Bedford Regt.
Owing to 30th Division taking over some of the fatigues now found by troops of 18th Division, the following moves and changes will take place on 4th and 5th instant.

(1) A battalion of 90th Infantry Brigade will take over the work of burying H.A. Group cables from 7th Bedfords on 4th inst.
On same day 2 companies 7th Bedfords will take over the work of burying telephone lines under orders of O.C. 18th Divisional Signals from 1 Company 6th Northants, and will remain billeted in BRAY. Headquarters, 7th Bedfords will also remain at BRAY.
2 Companies 7th Bedfords will march to CORBIE on 4th instant rationed for consumption on 5th inst., and will take over the fatigues at present found by 1 company 6th Northants and 1 platoon 12th Middlesex on the 5th instant. Billets to be obtained from O.C., XIIIth Corps. Rations to be drawn for consumption 6th et seq from 21st Division refilling point.

SELECTED OPERATIONAL ORDERS   137

The fatigues consist of: –	Off.	O.Rs.
Quarrying at point 102 BRAY-CORBIE Rd (Middx)	1	50
Corps Fatigues under C.C.	–	50
Guard at CORBIE Stn. Under R.T.O.	–	13
Unloading barges at CORBIE	–	50
Fatigue at Ammn. Railhead	–	17

A party to be prepared to make up the ammn. Railhead fatigue to strength of 1 Officer 4 N.C.Os. and 90 men at very short notice.

(2) 1 Company <u>6th Northants</u> at BRAY will march on 4th instant rationed for 5th instant, to join the company 6th Northants at CORBIE. On 5th instant these 2 companies 6th Northants will proceed to SAISSEVAL as follows: –
(a) personnel not exceeding 9 Officers 420 O.Rs. by rail from CORBIE to PICQUIGNY and thence by march route.
(b) 1st. line Transport, baggage and Supply Wagons by road.
(c) Excess baggage and party in charge by barge from CORBIE to PICQUIGNY whence arrangements must be made by unit to transport baggage to SAISSEVAL.
Parties (a and b) will carry rations for 5th instant on the man and vehicles respectively, and rations for 6th inst. will be drawn on 5th inst at 54th Brigade Refilling point under arrangements made by 54th Infantry Brigade direct with S.S.O.

Etc. etc.

(remainder of memo. of no interest to this battn).

6. Operational Order regarding a move to billets at Picquigny – 9 June 1916: this has been selected due to the large number of names of private soldiers included.

1. <u>Intention</u>
   The Battalion will move into billets at PICQUIGNY as follows: –
   <u>B & D Companies</u> – by rail on 10th instant, train leaving CORBIE at 6.53 a.m. arriving PICQUIGNY at 9.12 a.m.
   <u>A & C Companies and Bn.Hd.Qrs</u>. – from BRAY on 11th inst. and proceed by road to MERICOURT and thence by train leaving MERICOURT at 7.32 a.m. and arriving at PICQUIGNY 9.12 a.m.
   All 1st line transport and baggage wagons by road on 11th inst.
2. <u>Meals</u>
   Haversack rations of bread and cheese will be carried; waterbottles will be filled with tea. Dinner meal will be on arrival of cookers at PICQUIGNY. Party proceeding by road will make their own arrangements about dinner. The regimental transport will move by road to PICQUIGNY moving off at 4 a.m. 2 Cooks per company will accompany the cookers and prepare dinner which will be cooked en route and served to the Battalion at PICQUIGNY.
3. <u>Baggage</u>
   All baggage other than the authorised kits will be taken to PICQUIGNY by barge. This baggage must be packed and properly marked with the Coy. to which it belongs and handed in at Qr.Mr. Stores by 7 a.m. on the 10th instant. (Saturday). The Transport Officer will arrange to remove this baggage to the Barge Head at MERICOURT so as to [be] loaded on the boat by 12 noon on the 11th inst.
   <u>Baggage Guard</u>. 2nd.Lieut.O.Kingdon Will command the Baggage Guard and will be responsible for the removal of all Stores, kits, etc. to go by barge. He will arrange his loading and off loading parties at each end and see that the kits and stores are delivered at PICQUIGNY to the companies etc. to which they belong, report to the Adjutant on completion of this duty. Barges must not be delayed more than necessary. Rations for tomorrow will be carried in

Haversacks and ration for 11th and 12th inst. will be drawn from the Quartermaster for the party in bulk. The following will compose the baggage guard and will be under the orders of 2/Lieut.O.Kingdon from 9/6/16 until handed over by him to their companies at PICQUIGNY after all baggage has been delivered.

A Company Baggage Guard.

Cpl.Kitchener, H.J.	Pte.Bird, L.	Pte.Brace, A.
Pte.Bennett, W.F.	Pte.Burton, F.C.	Pte.Clarke, G.
Pte.Collins, J.	Pte.Cosgrove, A.	Pte.Denny, G.
Pte.Manning, W.	Pte.O'Neil, A.	Pte.Purser, N.F.
Pte. Tearle, E.	Pte.Trayner, J.	Pte.Turvey, A.E.
Pte.White, W.S.		

C Company's Baggage Guard

Sgt.Cooper, W.F.	Pte.Chapman, W.F.	Pte.Wells, W.
L/Cpl.Etty, T.	Ptc.Cother, J.	Pte.Lawrence, G.
Pte.Millison, J.T.	Pte.Uren, E.	Pte.Arnold, S.
Pte.Underwood, W.	Pte.Cook, A.G.	Pte.Worby, W.
Pte.Plume, F.	Pte.Turner, G.J.	Pte.Mason, A.
Pte.Tribe, W.	Pte.Lewin, A.	

4. Transport
No lorries will be available.
Transport will be utilised as follows: –
4 limbers and 8 pack animals for Ammunition.
2 limbers for tools.
2 limbers for Machine Guns & Equipment, and Transport Cooking Utensils.
1 limber for Signal Equipment and H.Q. Cooking Utensils.
2 G.S. Wagons will carry officers kits, small shops for Tailors, pioneers, shoemaker, armourer, Orderly Room sufficient for temporary office, Transport kit as laid down in Field Service Manual and part of Qr.Mr. Stores, also Coy. and Headquarters brooms.
Travelling Kitchens will carry the unconsumed rations for the 11th inst., spare camp kettles, company officers mess kit, food necessary for short periods.
Headquarters Cart will carry Headquarters Officers Mess Kit and any extra Orderly Room kit required. Maltese Cart will carry Medical Equipment and M.O.'s kit.
The only spare kit of men which will be sent by barge is 1 shirt and 1 pair drawers per man. These will be done up in bundles of 50 and tied at both ends. They will not be packed in sacks. The Regulation kit of men must be carried in the packs.
Brushes must be tied up in Bundles, scrubbing brushes, men's shorts, gloves hedging, periscopes, Very pistols, oil lamps, company officers necessaries, Practice Tube Helmets and other essential company stores must be packed in sandbags or small boxes. A few bass and soft brooms per company will be kept for cleaning up; these can be put on the 2 G.S. wagons.
Labels
Every package must be labelled with Company or Headquarter letter. Wooden labels are best.
O.C. Companies should by every means reduce spare kits and all unnecessary stores.
Furniture. Tables, forms, chairs, braziers, bath tubs, wire beds, etc. will not be taken, but will be left in the billets in which they are at present, and will be handed over.

5. Billets
All billets are to be left scrupulously clean – properly swept up, and all refuse

6. Meals of Headquarter Company.
   On the 11th inst. Headquarter N.C.Os. and men will have dinner at PICQUIGNY with companies as under, for that day only
   A & B Companies – B Coy.   C & D Companies – C Company.
7. Barge Party.
   The party under 2/Lieut.Kingdon (3 N.C.Os. and 30 men) will proceed via Barge to PICQUIGNY in charge of Stores, proceeding to the bargehead tomorrow with the Transport conveying stores.

7. Operational Order regarding the battalion's move to North Bluff, immediately prior to the assault on Thiepval – 24 September 1916

1. INTENTION	The Battalion will move to dugouts in N.BLUFF Q.36.c.60 tomorrow.
2. PARADE	The Battalion will parade, in Service Marching order, at 6.45 a.m. Order of March: H.Qrs. B: C: D: A.
3. ADVANCE PARTY	One N.C.O. per company and 1 for Bn.Hd.Qrs. under 2/Lieut.F.E.Dealler, will parade at the Orderly Room at 6 a.m. – dress Service Marching Order, carrying 1 days rations. This party will report to the Staff Captain at the west end of BLACK HORSE ROAD W.5.a.40 at 9.30 a.m. to take over dugouts for the Battalion. Route will be explained to 2/Lieut.F.E.Dealler.
4. RATIONS	Rations for tomorrow, 25th inst. must be carried by each individual. Waterbottles must be filled and should be preserved as there may be a scarcity of water in the area where the Battalion will be billeted.
5. SPECIALISTS	All Officers and Specialists detailed to remain behind with 1st. Line Transport will join 1st. Line Transport tomorrow morning at 8.30 a.m. This party will be rationed by the Quartermaster. Each Officer should take sufficient utensils with him for his own use.
6. OFFICERS FOR DIVL. SCHOOL	Instructions regarding these officers will be issued later to all SCHOOL concerned.
7. ROUTE FOR BATTALION	BOUZINCOURT – W.7.Central – W.2.b.60 – S. end of MARTINSART WOOD – W.9.b.80 – through C in Cemetery (in W.16.b.) – W.6.a.40 – BLACK HORSE ROAD. The Battalion must not enter BOUZINCOURT before 10 a.m. and must be clear of the same village by 10.30 a.m. After BOUZINCOURT the Battalion will march by companies at 10 minutes interval.
8. REPORTS	O.C. Companies will report to Battalion Headquarters immediately their companies arrive at their destination.
9. STRETCHER BEARERS	All Stretcher Bearers will march with their respective companies, each party carrying its own stretchers.

140   APPENDIX A: BATTALION MOVES

8. List of recommendations for awards sent to 54th Brigade – 2 October 1916

OFFICERS	Recommended For
2/Lieut. Tom Edwin Adlam	VC
Capt. Leslie Howard Keep	DSO
Capt. William Joseph Wellesley Colley	DSO
2/Lieut. Harold Agnew Reaney	DSO
Lieut. Douglas Scrivener Howard Keep	MC
Capt. John Henry Bridcutt	MC
Capt. John Wright Turner	MC

OTHER RANKS

16176 Coy.Sergt.Maj. Richard Maurice Brand	DCM
6466 Coy.Sergt.Maj.Charles Hall	DCM
15080 L/Corp. Arthur William Harris	DCM
16540 Pte. George Goldhawk	DCM
21343 Sergt. Alfred Wyatt	DCM
14626 L/Sergt. Albert Turville	DCM
15318 Pte. Alfred Pratt	DCM
3/8402 Battn.Sergt.Maj. Frederick Antcliffe	DCM
15153 Pte. John James Winterbourne	MM
17442 Pte. Albert Goodliff	MM
12615 Corpl. Peter Relhorn	MM
14354 Pte. Arthur Frederick Baker	MM
43318 Pte. William Lewis	MM
18267 Pte. Henry Brett	MM
14681 Pte. Albert Gilbert Bailey	MM
12735 L/Sergt. George Frederick Cowling	MM
17317 Pte. Charles James Perkins	MM
15436 Pte. William Wall	MM
14878 Pte. Arthur James Palmer	MM
14644 Pte. Harry[?] Horgan	MM
16002 Pte. Jesse Meeks	MM
43293 L/Cpl. Thomas Fitzgerald	MM
9140 Pte. Henry Erskine	MM
14805 L/Cpl. Herbert John Gammons	MM
15558 L/Cpl. John Joseph Cousins	MM
15684 Pte. William Sidney Mason	MM
8089 Sergt. Robert Hanson	MM
2/7597 Pte. William Inns	MM
43263 Pte. Robert Willacy	MM
15044 Pte. Frank Bayford	MM

9. Battalion Orders – November 1916: these weekly Orders are very infrequently interleaved with the War Diary and this particular example is given as it notes a large number of wounded men.

1475	DUTIES	Orderly Officer for tomorrow.
		2/Lieut. C.B.Kydd. "B" Company
		Next for Duty
		2/Lieut R.B.Rednall, "C" Company
1476	ORDERLY ROOM	Orderly Room will be at 10-0 a.m.
		Company Commanders will attend.
1477	PROMOTIONS	Lieut D.S.H.Keep and Lieut.H.C.Browning

SELECTED OPERATIONAL ORDERS 141

		are authorized to wear the badges of the rank of Captain.
1478	ALARM	In case of alarm, Companies will form up in front of their huts and send an Officer to report to Battalion Headquarters (in the original hut) for orders.
1479	CASUALTIES	The Commanding Officer regrets to announce the following casualties

No.14161 L/Cpl Hobbs F[rank] A Coy Killed 16-11-16
28991 L/Cpl Dungay R[obert] A Coy Killed 16-11-16
15760 Pte Turney, A[rthur] A Coy Killed 16-11-16
40532 Pte Ward, W[alter] A Coy Killed 16-11-16
40506 Pte Osborne, F[rederick Charles] A Coy Killed 16-11-16
40508 Pte Thompson, H[erbert William] A Coy Killed 16-11-16
40535 Pte Hickmore, A[mos] B Coy Killed 16-11-16
16524 Pte Cain, N[athan] C Coy Killed 15-11-16
29774 Pte Halls, H[erbert] R[olfe] C Coy Killed 14-11-16
43309 Pte Johnson, R[obert Marshall] C Coy Died of Wounds 15-11-16
27348 Pte Pitts, W[illiam] C[harles] B Coy Missing 16-11-16
29786 Pte Moore, J.W. A Coy Wounded 16-11-16
28039 Pte Fuller, H. A Coy Wounded 16-11-16
28084 Pte Berry, H[erbert] E[ric] A Coy Wounded 16-11-16
40501 Pte Saunders, J.B. A Coy Wounded 16-11-16
40519 Pte Ovenden, F.A. A Coy Wounded 16-11-16
14135 Cpl Dean, W. B Coy Wounded 16-11-16
10034 Pte Hammond, J. B Coy Wounded 16-11-16
26234 Pte Bottomley, G. B Coy Wounded 16-11-16
29793 Pte Parker G.S. C Coy Wounded 15-11-16
18255 Pte Ellis, W.G. C Coy Wounded 15-11-16
29859 Pte North, W. C Coy Wounded 15-11-16
15491 Pte Miles, A. C Coy Wounded 14-11-16
4366 Pte Hughes, F.H. C Coy Wounded 14-11-16

142   APPENDIX A: BATTALION MOVES

		27855 Pte.Swain, T. C Coy Wounded 14-11-16
		3/8636 L/Cpl Holmes, J. D Coy Wounded 14-11-16
		3/7661 L/Cpl Smith, R. D Coy Wounded 14-11-16
		27627 L/Cpl Skevington, M. D Coy Wounded 13-11-16
		13581 Pte Dillingham, A. D Coy Wounded 13-11-16
		14854 Pte Hargford, W. D Coy Wounded 17-11-16
		29772 Pte Selsby, C. D Coy Wounded 14-11-16
		still at duty 2/Lieut. L.E.Taylor C Coy Wounded 14-11-16
		29796 Pte Redding, B[ertie] KILLED 15-11-16 C Coy
1480	INCREASES	The following having reported from Field Ambulance are taken on the strength from 15-11-16
		20359 Pte North, W. C Coy.
		15491 Pte Miles, A. C Coy
		3/8636 L/C Holmes, J. D Coy
		3/7661 L/C Smith, R. D Coy
		13581 Pte Dillingham, A. D Coy
		29772 Pte Selsby, C. D Coy
1481	DECREASES	The following have been struck off strength in accordance with G.H.Q. Letter No O.B. 181 of 13th October 1916
		18557 Pte Allan, G. A Company
		14861 Pte Lewis, S. D Company
		43348 Pte Meacham, J. D Company
		10328 Pte Thomas, E. A Company
		15392 Pte Rowell, S. C Company
		14596 Pte Plume, F. C Company
		43289 Pte Eggitt, H. D Company
		20344 Pte Dunham, W. B Company
1482	GALLANTRY	The Corps Commander has been pleased to award THE MILITARY MEDAL to the undermentioned N.C.O's and men
		No.15400 C.Q.M.S. Fountain, A.
		12827 Private Silsby, B.F.
		15198 Private A.Chandler
		18176 Sergeant [Major] Brand, R.M.
		17642 L/Corpl Clarke, G.S.
		15333 Pte Fuller, G.B.
1483	RETURN	Companies will render a certificate to-night [in margin an asterisk and at bottom of page "Early tomorrow morning please"] that they are complete with the following.
		S.A.A.
		Bombs
		Bomb Buckets
		Cutters Wire Hand
		Cutters Wire Rifle

SELECTED OPERATIONAL ORDERS   143

		Very Pistols
		Very Pistols 1"
		Gloves Hedging
		Cups Rifle Grenades
		and complete with rifles, bayonets, entrenching tools, smoke helmets, equipment etc.
1484	LETTERS	Some irregularity in receipt of mails from ENGLAND must be expected during the next few days owing to Admiralty restrictions in connection with Cross Channel Services.

10. Operational Order regarding relief of the 2/6th Battalion, Royal Warwickshire Regiment in the front line – 14 January 1917: this order is given here as it mentions the care of feet in an effort to prevent Trench Foot, a condition that could cripple many men in a battalion due to standing around in cold, wet conditions.

1.	MOVE	The Battalion will move into the line and occupy the Left Sub Sector of the 54th Bde front relieving the 2/6th Royal Warwickshire Regiment on the night of 15/16 January 1917.
2.	DISPOSITION OF COMPANIES	Disposition of Companies in the Line. "A" Coy Left of Front Line "D" Coy Right of Front Line "B" Coy Left Support "C" Coy Right Support
3.	RELIEF	The relief will be carried out by Platoons at 5 minutes interval. The leading Platoon not to pass the junction of Pozieres-Ovillers Road before 4 p.m.
4.	BUSES	Companies will be taken as far as Aveluy by buses time to parade to embus will be A Co. 8.5 AM, B Co. 8.10 AM, C Coy 8.15 AM, D Coy 8.20 AM, Bn.H.Q. 8.25 pm.
5.	COOKING	All cooking will be done in the line at a spot known as the Gravel Pits.
6.	GUIDES	Guides will meet the Companies at the junction of Nab Valley and the Pozieres Road at time to be notified later.
7.	TRENCH STORE LISTS	Trench Store Lists will be made out on taking over, one copy to be sent to Adjutant at Battn Headquarters in Zollern Redoubt.
8.	RATIONS	"B" and "C" Companies will each furnish one platoon to be accommodated at the Gravel Pits for carrying food etc. to the front line Companies (only). Companies in support do their own carrying.
9.	GUM BOOTS	The two Companies holding the front line (A. & D) will draw a pair of Gum Boots per N.C.O. and man at Crucifix Corner any Gum Boots remaining after A & D have been supplied will be drawn by "B" and "C" Companies. These boots will be carried over the shoulder into the trenches and then taken into rear.
10.	FEET CARE OF	O.C. Companies will ensure that every man changes his socks once every 24 hours and that the feet are well rubbed with whale oil at least once every day.
11.	WATER BOTTLES	Water is a difficulty and care should be taken to see that every man arrives in the trenches with a full waterbottle.
12.	LEWIS GUNS	Lewis Guns will be attached to Companies in accordance with instructions issued direct to the Company Comdrs and Lewis Gun Officer.
13.	MEALS	Midday meal will be served to the men when they get out of the

144   APPENDIX A: BATTALION MOVES

14. TRANSPORT	buses at AVELUY, food for 16th must be carried by every man. Two limbers will proceed to Aveluy to carry up Lewis Guns and Cooking Utensils from the buses forward.
15. MESS BOXES OFFICERS	Officers Mess Boxes required for the trenches should be sent by the cookers to Aveluy in the morning.

11. Operational Order regarding a training exercise in attack – September 1917: this Order is given as an example of how exercises were undertaken.

1. GENERAL IDEA	On September 15th the 7th Bn Bedfordshire Regiment in co-operation with "X" Battalion on its Right and "Y" Battalion on its left will attack and Capture. 1st Objective. Red Line H.6.b.0.8. – B.30.c.5.6. 2nd Objective. Blue Line. High Ground B.30.d.8.1. to B.30.b.6.0. "X" and "Y" Battalions will be represented by BLUE FLAGS
3.a. ROLE OF COYS	"C" Coy will be the Right assaulting Company. "D" Company will be the Left assaulting Company. "B" Coy in Close Support, covering the Battalion frontage. "A" Coy will be in reserve at the disposal of the Battalion Commander.
3. INTENTION	The Assaulting Coys will fight their way through to the Final Objective after the capture of which they will each push forward posts and consolidate the Final Objective. The Reserve Company will move to the Old German Front Line H.6.a.5.4. to B.30.c.1.3. They will not move from here without orders from O.C. Battn except in case of great emergency.
2. INFORMATION	Enemy is known to be holding a trench line from H.6.a.5.4. to B.30.c.1.5. with a series of strong points in echelon behind. His defences have been much knocked about by Artillery fire. The only known strongpoints are "A" B.30.c.4.0. "B" B.30.c.9.5. "C" B.30.d.3.1.
4. MOPPING UP PARTIES	Two Coys of the 11th Royal Fusiliers will be attached to the 7th Bedfords and will clear up and consolidate. One Coy will be attached to each of the assaulting Coys and will find both area and special point mopping up parties. 1ST LINE OF MOPPERS UP. Will be detailed to all ground between first objective and railway. 2ND LINE OF MOPPERS UP. Will be detailed to all ground WEST of 1st objective and up to and including 1st Objective. On completion of their task all Area Moppers Up will rendezvous at the MILL B.30.d.3.3. where they will remain in close support to the front line under the orders of the Senior Officer or N.C.O. present. Lewis Gun Section of Area Moppers Up will move with the Reserve Coy until the Final Objective is taken when they will join their platoons at the MILL B.30.d.3.3. SPECIAL POINT MOPPERS UP. Will supply 2 sections to consolidate and garrison each of the strong points A B and C, remainder will be divided into groups to consolidate and garrison any unknown strong points.
5. 54TH M.G.COY.	One gun will move to each of the Strong points A.B.& C as soon as these positions have been captured. One gun remaining at B.H.Q.
6. BN SCOUTS AND SNIPERS.	Orders will be issued separately

7. 54th T.M.BTY.	Two guns will [too faint to read] Reserve Company and proceed to 1st Objective near B strong point. On the capture of the Final Objective one gun will move forward to the railway cutting about B.30.d.5.4.
8. ENEMY.	Will be provided by two Coys of the 11th R.Fusiliers. They will either wear white cap bands or Steel helmets.
9. BARRAGE.	Artillery barrage will open 200 yards in front of assembly trenches and will swell for 1½ minutes and then move forward at the rate of 100 yards in 2 minutes for 1st 200 yards and afterwards at the rate of 100 yards in 3 minutes. There will be a halt of 15 minutes on a line 100 yards beyond 1st objective. Barrage will remain on a line 400 yards behind final objective until it is no longer required. Artillery Barrage will be simulated by the rolling of drums.
10. TOOLS.	Picks and Shovels will be carried by 35% of the assaulting and Support Coys and by 50% of the Reserve Coy. One pick to six shovels. Moppers up 50% will carry tools. Tool Cart at Rendezvous H.5.b.3.7 at 9.30 a.m.
11. ASSEMBLING	The attacking troops will form up in four imaginary trenches which will be marked out on the ground. Nos 1 and 2 trenches will be occupied by assaulting Coys and area moppers up. 3 Support Coy and Strong Point Moppers Up. 4 Reserve Coy, M.G.Co. T.M.B. and B.H.Q. All troops to be in position by 10.30 a.m.
12. BN HD QRS	Will be at H.5.b.3.7. until the first objective has been taken when they will move to old German front line about H.6.a.2.8. Advanced Battalion Signal Station will be established at Strong Point B as soon as 1st Objective has been taken.
13. BDE HD QRS	At Mill B.28.1.3.0.
14. ZERO HOUR	11 a.m.
15. RENDEZVOUS	7th Bn Bedfords and Moppers up 11th Royal Fusiliers, H.5.b.3.7. at 9.30 a.m. ENEMY MILL B.30.1.3.3. at 9.30 a.m. O.C.Coy providing enemy will report to Major Percival M.C. at 9 a.m. at Mill B.30.1.3.3.
16. MEDICAL	Advanced Dressing Station will be established at I.6.a.4.4.
17. DRESS	Battle Order less Steel Helmets and Box Respirators. No live ammunition to be carried. Pouches must be thoroughly examined and Lewis Gun Drums emptied. 500 rounds blank per Coy will be issued. On Standfast sounding all troops will remain in the positions they have reached, until either "continue" or "dismiss" is sounded. Should the "Officers" call be sounded, followed by the Dismiss all Officers and Platoon Commanders will rendezvous at Centre of Final Objective and Companies will be marched home by the Sergt Major. Both in consolidating Strong Points and the Final Objective, actual digging must be carried out on the intensive system.

11a. Note as to points to be brought out in the exercise detailed as 11 above – September 1917

With reference to Operation Orders No 152 issued herewith the chief points which it is hoped to bring out in this exercise are: –

1. Forming up with several lines in the same trench and the advance from same.
2. Action of Supports and Reserves when the front line is held up by unknown Strong Point.

146 APPENDIX A: BATTALION MOVES

3. Re-organisation and further advance after the lines have become mixed up.
4. Action of Subordinate Commanders in re-organisation and consolidation immediately after the final objective has been captured.

12. Training programme for 1 November 1917: this is given as an example of the exhaustive training undertaken in the winter of 1917/1918.

9 a.m.	to 9.30 a.m.	All Officers will parade with rifles under Captain Ferguson on the Battalion Training Ground for Musketry Instructions.	

Subject: Muscle Exercises

Coy	9.30/10.30	10.30/11.30	11.30/12.30
A	Company Drill	Musketry	Platoon Drill
	Sec 86 I.T.	Muscle Exercises	Sec 78 I.T.
B	Musketry	Platoon Drill	Bayonet Fighting
	Muscle Exercises	Sec. 78 I.T. [Infantry Training]	
C	Company will fire on the range.		
	Platoons will exercise instruction in muscle exercises before firing.		
	Aiming instruction must be carefully taught.		
D	Bayonet Fighting	Company Drill	Platoon Drill
		Sec 86 I.T.	Sec 78 I.T.

DRESS. Drill Order.
Drums will attend.
R.E.Platoon will be inspected at 10.30 a.m.
Scouts will parade under 2/Lt Davies.
Signallers will parade under 2/Lt Partridge

13. Training Orders for the Christmas period 1917

24 Dec	10–11 a.m.	"A" and "B" Coys Plat.Drill (Close order) "C" and "D" Coys P.T. & Bay F'ing Musketry
	11 a.m.–12 noon	"A" & "B" P.T. & Bay F'ing
	11 a.m.–12.45 p.m.	"C" and "D" Companies Platoon Drill (Close Order)
	12–12.45 p.m.	"A" & "B" Musketry.
	12.45–1 p.m.	Coy Drill
25 Dec	CHRISTMAS DAY CHURCH PARADE	
26 Dec	10 a.m.–12 noon	ROUTE MARCH – Demonstration – by Companies
27 Dec	10–10.30 a.m.	"A" & "B" Bombing "C" & "D" Plat: Drill (Close Order)
	10.30–11 a.m.	"C" & "D" Bombing "A" & "B" Platoon Drill
	11.30 a.m.–12.45 p.m.	"A" and "D" Coys Wiring and Digging "C" and "B" Coys Musketry Aiming & Muscle Exercises. Trigger Pressing.
	12.45–1 p.m.	Coy Drill.
28 Dec.	RANGE IF AVAILABLE ALTERNATIVE	
	10–11 a.m.	"A" and "B" Companies Platoon Drill – Extended Order.

		"C" and "D" Companies P.T. and Bayonet Fighting.
	11.30–12.45 p.m.	"A" and "B" Coys P.T. & Bay.F'ing "C" and "D" Coys Platoon Drill – Extended Order
	12.45–1 p.m.	Lecture Officers and Coy. N.C.O's Drill OUTPOSTS.
29 Dec.	10–11 a.m.	"C" and "B" Companies Wiring and Digging. "A" and "D" Companies P.T. and B.F.
	11.30 a.m.–12.45 p.m.	SHORT ROUTE MARCH Demonstration OUTPOSTS
	12.45–1 p.m.	C.O's conference on week's work.

NOTES: (1) Short Running Parade daily 8 am to 8.10 am under Pn.Cmdrs.
(2) 9.15 to 9.45 daily Conference by Coy. Commanders of Platoon Commanders and Senior N.C.Os on morning's work.
(3) Training of Lewis Gunners in mechanism (except those fully trained) and training of qualified Lewis Gunners in firing at Aeroplanes to be carried out daily from 9.15 to 10.
(4) Signallers, T.M.B. and Scouts will be trained under arrangements made by Officers commanding these sections.

14. Operational Order regarding inspection by the General Officer Commanding 54th Infantry Brigade – 29 December 1917

1. INTENTION	The G.O.C. will inspect the Battalion tomorrow, 29/12/17 at 8 a.m. on Battalion Training Ground. Afterward Tactical Scheme
2. HOUR OF START	Companies will move off in time to be on parade ground by 7.45 a.m.
3. GENERAL INSTRUCTION	(a) The Battalion will be formed up in Mass Battalion Hd.Qrs. on right Coy.Hd.Qrs. in rear of Companies. (b) R.E.Platoon will parade with Battalion Hd.Qrs. under Sergt.Weston. They will draw 1 pick and 1 shovel for every three men, from the Quarter-masters Stores. (c) Stretcher Bearers and Vickers Gun Section will parade with Battalion Head Quarters. (d) S.A.A. All live ammunition will be left in huts. Pouches must be inspected before moving off. (e) Lewis Guns. 4 Drums per TEAM will be carried.
4. DRESS	FIGHTING ORDER. Haversacks to be worn resting on shoulder. Mess Tins with covers, handle of Mess Tin through strap of haversack. Steel Helmets will be worn with strap under point of chin. Box respirators at the "Alert" Position. No Rifle or Breech Covers will be carried.
5. GUIDE	2/Lieut.R.A.Stiles will meet the G.O.C. at Bde.Hd.Qr.Mess at 7.40 a.m. and guide him to Bn.Parade Ground.
6. MEALS	REVEILLE 6 a.m. BREAKFAST 6.30 a.m. DINNERS on return to camp.
7. SIGNALLERS	Will carry Signalling Lamps, and dress will be Rifle, Box Respirators and water Bottle.

148   APPENDIX A: BATTALION MOVES

8. TRANSPORT   1st Line Transport with Cookers, will be formed up by 7.45 a.m. in rear of the Battalion on Battn. Parade Ground.
(Note: Battn. Parade Ground READ Northants Parade Ground)

15. Training programme for week ending 6 January 1918

Battn	30/12/17	CHURCH PARADE	
Battn	31/12/17	Battalion will parade at 10 am on Battn Parade Ground	
"A" & "B"		Demonstration of Company Organisation	10.30 am to 11.30 am
		Practice Formation – Company in Attack	11.30 am to 12.30 pm
"C" & "D"		Same as "A" and "B"	Hours reversed
"A"	1/1/18	Range Practice	9.30 am to 10.30 am
		Company Drill & Organisation	11 am to 12.30 pm
"B" & "C"		Company Drill	9.30 am to 10.30 am
		Tactical handling of Company in attack	10.30 am to 12.30 pm
"D"		Range Practice	10.30 am to 1 pm
"B"	2/1/18	Range Practice	8.30 am to 10.30 am
		Company Drill & Organisation	11 am to 12.30 pm
"D" & "A"		Company Drill	9.30 am to 10.30 am
		Tactical Handling of Company in attack	10.30 to 12.30 pm
"C"		Range Practice	10.30 am to 1 pm
Battn	3/1/18	Battn will parade at 9.30 on Battalion Parade Ground.	
		Demonstration and Practice of an Advanced Guard to a small Force	10 am to 12 noon

All Coys		Extended Order Drill	12 noon to 1 pm
Battn Lewis Guns	4/1/18	All Lewis Guns on Range	10 am to 1 pm
"A" & "B"		Range Practice	8 am to 9 am
"C" & "D"		Range Practice	9 am to 10 am
All Coys		Demonstration & Practice Guard Mounting on Battn. Parade Ground	10.30 am to 1 pm
Battn	5/1/18	Battn will parade on battn. Parade Ground at 10 am	
		Battalion Drill	10.30 am to 11.30 am
		Tactical Exercise	11.30 am to 1 pm
<u>NOTES</u>		Football and Sports in the Afternoons.	
		Coy. Comdrs. will attend Hd.Qrs. mess daily at 4.30 pm for Conference Company Conferences in Evening	

16. Operation Orders for 54th Trench Mortar Battery – 8 January 1918: this stray Order for the 54th Trench Mortar Battery is given as it shows 7th Battalion men attached to the Battery's 7th Bedford section; 54th Trench Mortar Battery was, as the number suggests, attached to 54th Infantry Brigade.

(1) Gun teams will move to the line on the following dates 11th Royal Fusiliers & 6th Nthants on night of 9th
Fusilier Section to consist of
L/C Smith
L/C Hedgecock
Pte.Hopson
Pte.Jenner
Pte.Joyce
Pte.Stacey
Pte.O'Shea
Pte.Taylor
Pte.Howard
Northants Section to consist of
L/C.Wooley
L/C.Harrison (12th Mx)
Pte.Currall
Pte.Hartfree

Pte.Williams
Pte.Whiting
Pte.Turnham
Pte.Dunn (11th R.F.)
These sections to be at ONDANK SIDING at 11.30 a.m. to entrain at 12 noon for BOEZINGE. They will meet guides at EGYPT HOUSE at 5.30 pm. Each man will carry unconsumed portion of days rations, 2 days rations, iron rations, 2 waterbottles & 4 sandbags to be drawn from Battlns. No.26302 L/C.Jolly 6th Nthants will change over with No.7573 L/C.Harrison (12th Middx) at 5 pm 8th inst.

(2) 7th Bedford & 12th Middlesex Sections will take over from above at same time date to be notified later. 12th Middlesex Section will move to BABOON CAMP with 7th Beds on 10th inst & will be accommodated & rationed by them, they will report to 2nd LT.CURTICE. Bedford Section will consist of
2nd LT.CURTICE
L/C.Reed
Pte.Sawkins
Pte.Swain
Pte.Tatnall
Pte.Taylor
Pte.Hudson
Pte.Chubb (12th Mx)
Pte.Harper
12th Middlesex section will consist of
L/C.Jolly (6th Nthants)
Pte.Elliott (7th Beds)
Pte.Newman (7th Beds)
Pte.Pettifer (6th Nthants)
Pte.Hedges (12th Mx)
Pte.Walden (6th Nthants)
Pte.Davey (12th Mx)
Pte.Froggart (12th Mx)
No.43119 Pte Pettifer & No.30990 Pte.Walden 6th Nthants will report to 2nd LT.CURTICE 7th Beds on 9th inst & be rationed by above Battln.
(3) Two guns & 20 boxes of Ammunition will be taken to EGYPT HOUSE from ATN BOMB Store by 5.30 pm of the 9th under Brigade arrangements.
(4) Battery Hd.Qtrs will close at "H" Camp at 9 am & reopen at SIGNAL FARM at 12 noon 9th inst.
(5) ACKNOWLEDGE

17. Operational Order regarding wiring of 54th Infantry Brigade front – 12–13 January 1918: this Order shows the efforts taken to set up reasonable defensive positions for 5th Army; in the event the positions were not strong enough to prevent the German breakthrough on 21st March 1918

1. Intention	On the night 12th/13th inst. the whole Bde front will be wired. The right sector will be wired by the 12th Middlesex Regt. and the left sector by the 7th Bedfordshire Regt.
2. Wiring Party	The party to be detailed by 7th Bedfordshire Regt. will be found by "C" Coy. and will consist of 3 Officers 8 N.C.O's and 72 men. This party will be sub-divided into 4 platoons, each platoon consisting of 2 squads of 1 N.C.O. and 9 men each. The whole party will be under the command of 2nd Lieut N.C.E.COCKBURN.
3. Frontage	The frontage to be wired is the outpost line from U.6.a.18 to

SELECTED OPERATIONAL ORDERS   151

	U.6.b.61. Exact position of the wire has been marked out by the 92nd Field Coy. R.E.
4. Tasks	Each squad will put up 100 yds of Double Apron wire. Work will commence at 9.30 pm and will be carried on until completed. As soon as the work has been passed as satisfactory by an Officer of the 92nd Coy. R.E. each platoon will return to BABOON CAMP under orders of its platoon Commander.
5. Material	All material has been dumped at COLOMBO HO. Each platoon will report here and will pick up one load. A special carrying party of 1 officer and 40 other ranks from the Bde Details will be at the disposal of the O.C. wiring party for the purpose of carrying material from COLOMBO HO to the wiring parties.
6. Guides	Each squad will be guided from COLOMBO HO to the left of its task by one of the Bn observers. These observers will subsequently guide the special carrying party to their destination.
7. Covering Party	The covering party strength 1 Coy will be found by A Coy. under 2nd Lieut W.CARTER. They will be met by guides on the scale of 1 per platoon supplied by 11th Royal Fusiliers at AJAX HO at 8 pm. They will take up positions as shown on map issued specially to all concerned and will be in position by 9 pm.
8. Stretcher Bearers	On the scale of 1 per platoon will be taken by both wiring and covering parties.
9. Action in case of attack by enemy	
	(a) <u>Covering Party</u>: will hold to ground at all costs and under no circumstances are they to withdraw.
	(b) <u>Wiring Party</u>: will at once lie down directly fire is opened and await orders from their platoon commander.
	All troops working in the sector will come under the orders of the O.C.Sector.
	In the event of it becoming necessary to withdraw the wiring party owing to general attack by the enemy, the party will withdraw as complete units under their platoon commanders and proceed to BABOON CAMP via CLARGES ST.
10. Report Centres	The covering party and wiring party will both establish report centres at COLOMBO HO. Advanced Bn.H.Qrs will be established at AJAX HO.
11. Completion of Work	As soon as the work on either sub sector (i.e. West or East of the COLOMBO HO Road) has been completed the O.C. covering party will be informed by the O.C. wiring party and the party covering that sector will be withdrawn. The front line posts and the Advanced Bn. H.Qrs. will be informed as soon as this has been done.
12. Dress	<u>Wiring Party</u> Box Respirators and Steel Helmets.
	<u>Covering Party</u> Battle order less Haversacks.
13. Lewis Guns	Will not be taken by the covering party.

18. Battalion Orders – 18 January 1918: another example of Battalion Orders.

1. DUTIES	Battalion orderly Officer 2/Lieut.H.W.Haward. "D" Coy.
2. INCREASES	2/Lieut.Ernest James Scott, embarked 31/12/17, joined Battalion for duty 11/1/18, is taken on strength accordingly.

The undermentioned having joined the Battn. on dates stated are taken on strength and posted to companies as under.
Joined 9/1/18
23591 L/Cpl.Brunt, W. "D" Coy.
43153 Pte.Stott, R. "A" Coy.
12730 Pte.Cooper, F. "C" Coy.
Joined 11/1/18
271066 L/Cpl.Brown, F. "A" Coy.
33643 Pte.Judge, W. "D" Coy.
21842 Pte.Stratford, H. "D" Coy.
Rejoined 11/1/18
21546 Pte.Bawden, R. "A" Coy.
6936 Pte.Waldock, G. "B" Coy.
31404 Pte.Shortland, W. "B" Coy.
33769 Pte.Shailer, S. "C" Coy.
13416 Pte.Crossman, A. "C" Coy.
23639 Pte.Richardson, P. "D" Coy.

3. CASUALTIES DECREASES

The Commanding Officer regrets to announce the following casualty.
KILLED IN ACTION
43365 L/Cpl.Spinks, C. "B" Coy. 11/1/18
17010 Pte.Ferris, A. "C" Coy. acc. w'ded 13/1/18
41357 Pte.Hemsley, E. "C" Coy. w'ded (self-inflicted) 12/1/18
The undermentioned having been evacuated on dates stated are struck off strength accordingly
16201 Pte.Tyler, B. "A" Coy. 6/1/18
12860 Pte.Goss, W. "A" Coy. 8/1/18
31069 Pte.Burnham, H. "A" Coy. 12/1/18
43153 Pte.Stott, R. "A" Coy 13/1/18.

4. NEW YEAR'S HONOURS

His Majesty the KING has been pleased to award the undermentioned Officers the following Decoration in recognition of their valuable Services rendered with the armies in the field during the present war
THE MILITARY CROSS
T/Lieut. E.W.Benson (attchd.Sig.Coy.)
T/2/Lt. C.A.Lawrence
(Auth: Div. Routine Order No.367 d/9:1:18)

5. PROMOTION

T/Lieut.C.A.Lawrence is hereby authorised to wear the Badges of the higher rank of Captain pending confirmation by superior authority. (Auth: 18th Div.No.19.353 "A" dated 10/1/18. 54th Inf.Bde.No.A/273/3 dated 12/1/18).

6. LEAVE

The undermentioned have been granted leave as per dates specified below.
11/1/18–25/1/18
20030 Cpl.Ely, R. "A" Company
15156 L/C.Swain, H. "B" Company
31336 Pte.Phillips, A. "B" Company
30930 Pte.Sains, A. "B" Company
7876 Pte.Cooper, A. "D" Company
12/1/18–26/1/18
17234 L/C.Abrams, T. "C" Company
15130 L/C.Sturgeon, H. "B" Company
14535 Pte.Haines, G. "B" Company
37079 Dmr.Field, A. "B" Company

SELECTED OPERATIONAL ORDERS   153

	14/1/18–28/1/18
	23070 L/C.Weeks, R, "B" Company
	26470 Pte.Collins, W., "B" Company
	15/1/18–29/1/18
	202387 Pte.Cross, A. "A" Company
	200339 Pte.Wordley, W. "A" Company
	14237 Pte.Favell, J. "B" Company
	16/1/18–30/1/18
	23648 Pte.Walker, J. "A" Company
	43306 Pte.Hudson, G. (att.T.M.Btry)
7. HOT COCOA BAR	(Extract D.R.O. No.306 dated 8/1/18)
	A Bar for the sale of hot cocoa and biscuits has been erected at the Divisional Baths ELVERDINGE CHATEAU. Cocoa will be on sale to all men after they have bathed.
	(Extract D.R.O. No.368 dated 11/1/18)
	Owing to the continual pilfering of enamelled mugs Os.C.Units are requested to instruct all bathing parties who wish to purchase cocoa to bring canteens with them.

19. Appendix to training programme notes regarding trench foot – 20 January 1918

TRENCH FOOT

PROGRAMME	Jan.21st	Wash feet carefully in tepid water (not hot). Dry thoroughly, especially between the toes. Rub vigorously for 10 minutes (each foot) in upward direction, i.e. toward knee, commencing with the calf and working downwards. Put on dry socks.
	Jan 22nd.	As for 21st.
	Jan 23rd.	Use of Pedicuria according to instructions.
	Jan 24th.	As for 21st, but without washing feet.

20. 7th Bedfords football team for a match against the 12th Battalion Middlesex Regiment – January 1918

		Bidmead (A)	
	L/Cpl.Sewell (A)	Tingey (B)	
	Sgt.Mears (A)	Cpl.Machin (A)	Cpl.Spring (H.Q.)
Sgt.Reed (A)	2/Lt.Donovan	Cpl.Butler (A)	Dmr.Clarke (Drums)
		Dmr.Skipper	

RESERVES   Defence Sgt.Worrell (B) Sgt.Chapman (C)
Forward Pte.Pudney (A)

KICK OFF 2 p.m.

21. Training programme – 1–7 February 1918

Fri 1st Feb	Clothing	9.15 am-10 am "A"; 10-10.45 am "B"; 10.45–11.30 am "C"; 11.30 a.m.–12.15 pm "D"; 12.15–1 pm B.H.Q.
	Specialists	9.15–10 am "B"; 10-10.45 am – "A"; 10.45–11.30 am "D"; 12.15–1 pm "C"

APPENDIX A: BATTALION MOVES

	Organisation	9.15–10 am "C"; 10–10.45 am "D"; 11.30 am–12.15 pm "A"; 12.15-1 pm "B"
	Platoon Close	9.15–10 am "D"; 10–10.45 am "C"; 11.30 am–12.15 pm
	Order Drill	"B"; 12.15–1 pm "A"
Sat. 2nd Feb	Cleaning Kits	12.15–1 pm All Coys.
	Marching & Saluting	9.15–10 am All Coys
	Squad Drill & Speed in turning out	10–10.45 am All Coys
	Specialists	10.45am–12.15 pm All Companies
Sun 3rd Feb	CHURCH PARADE and inspection of Lines by Commanding Officer.	
Mon 4th Feb	C.O.'s inspection	9.15–10 am "D"; 10–10.45 "C"; 11.30 am–12.15 pm "B";
	in organisation	12.15–1 pm "A"
	Guard Mtg.	10–10.45 am "D"; 10.45–11.30 am "C"; 11.30 am–12.15 pm "A"; 12.15–1 pm "B"
	Squad Drill by Sections	9.15–10 am "A" & "D"; 11.30 am–12.15 pm "B" & "C"
	Platoon Drill	10–10.45 am "A" & "B"; 12.15–1 pm "C" & "D"
Tues 5th Feb	C.O.'s inspection	9.15–10 am "A"; 10–10.45 am "B"; 10.45–11.30 pm "C";
	in Turn-out	11.30 am–12.15 pm "D";
	Squad Drill by Sections	9.15–10 am "C" & "D"; 10.45–11.30 am "A" & "B"
	Specialists	10–10.45 am "C" & "D"; 11.30 am–12.15 pm "A" & "B"
	Packing kits Marching and Fighting Order 12.15–1 pm.	
Wed 6th Feb	ROUTE MARCH	ALL COMPANIES Fighting Order
Thurs 7th Feb	Squad Drill by Sections	9.15–10 am "A" & "B"; 11.30 am–12.15 pm "C" & "D"
	Specialists	9.15–10 am "C"; 10–10.45 am "D"; 11.30 am–12.15 pm "A"; 12.15–1 pm "B"
	Speed in Turning-Out	9.15–10 am "D"; 10–10.45 am "C"; 11.30 am–12.15 pm "B"; 12.15–1 pm "A"
NOTES	(1)	Running Parade under Platoon Commanders daily 7.45 am– 8 am
	(2)	Specialist Training will be carried out as under
	BOMBERS RIFLE GRENADIERS	Under Coy. arrangements, one Officer per Company being detailed to supervise this training.
	LEWIS GUNNERS	Under Coy. arrangements and in accordance with programme drawn up by Battalion L.G. Officer, who will supervise training.
	RUNNERS	Under Battalion Signal Officer.
	STRETCHER BEARERS Under Medical Officer.	
		Specialist Classes for backward men will be arranged in each company 2 p.m. –

SELECTED OPERATIONAL ORDERS   155

	3 p.m. in each of above subjects and will be supervised by an Officer. Each Company will detail 4 Reserve Stretcher Bearers (including those already semi-trained) to parade under the M.O. at 2 p.m. daily.
(3)	The object of all training is to be development of smartness, improvement in turn-out and discipline. The men's closest attention is to be obtained so as to prepare their minds to receive advanced instruction in the field.
(4)	No time is to be wasted when men are on parade. Parades are to be short and pithy.
(5)	Officers, N.C.O's and men called out by their seniors on parade will always come <u>at the double</u>

22. Operational Order regarding move to Noyon – 7 February 1918: this Order is given as it details a move by train.

1. <u>INTENTION</u>	The Battalion will move to NOYON to the 5th Army by Strategical train on the 9th FEBRUARY 1918
2. <u>TIME OF DEPARTURE</u>	The Train will leave PROVEN station at 10.40 am.
3. <u>PARADE</u>	The R.S.M. will report to the Adjutant with one Marker per Coy., H.Q. and Drums at 7.45 a.m. Coys will march on to their markers at 7.50 a.m. on the "Advance" sounding. The Battn will be formed up in Mass ready to march off at 7.55 a.m.
4. <u>DRESS</u>	Full Marching Order. Leather jerkins will not be worn. They will be carried on top of the pack.
5. <u>ORDER OF MARCH</u>	Hd. Qrs. "D" "A" "B" "C".
6. <u>ENTRAINING & DETRAINING</u>	2/Lieut.N.C.E.Cockburn will act as entraining and detraining Officer. he will proceed to PROVEN one hour before the Battalion to reconnoitre the Station, its approaches and its entraining facilities. He will also arrange for hot tea to be ready on the arrival of the Battalion, when he will report to the Adjutant. On the arrival of the Battalion at the station, one N.C.O. per Company and Hd.Qrs. will report to 2/Lieut.Cockburn for instructions regarding trucks and entraining.
7. <u>CYCLIST ORDERLIES</u>	The Signalling Officer will detail L/Cpl.Brett and one Runner with bicycles to report to Captain V.D.CORBETT, 12th Middlesex Regiment at PROVEN STATION at 7.40 a.m. L/Cpl.Brett will obtain a marching out state from the Orderly Room and hand it to Capt.Corbett on arrival.
8. <u>RATIONS</u>	Every man will carry the unexpended portion of the day's rations, rations for the following day and iron rations.
9. <u>DISCIPLINE</u>	(1) Hd.Qrs and "C" Coy. will each detail a picquet of one N.C.O. and 6 men to prevent troops leaving the train without permission during halts (2) All doors on the right hand side of the train must be kept closed.
10. <u>BAGGAGE</u>	(1) All Coy. Stores and Workshops will be dumped across the road near Transport Lines by 3 p.m. on the 8th instant.

156   APPENDIX A: BATTALION MOVES

	(2) As much Officers Kit and Officers' Mess kit as possible will be dumped at the same place and time. (3) The remainder of the Officers' kits, Bn. O.R. stores will be dumped across the road near the Transport Lines by 5.45 a.m. on the 9th inst. (4) All Lewis Guns & L.G.Equipment, together with Trench Mortars and Vickers Guns and their equipment will be packed on the limbers by 1 p.m. 8/2/18. (5) All Blankets, rolled in bundles of 10, will be dumped at the same place and time.
11. <u>DUMP GUARD</u>	The Quartermaster will arrange for a guard over the Battalion dump at PROVEN STATION. He will also arrange to accommodate and ration them.
12. <u>REAR PARTY</u>	2/Lieut.G.S.Richards and 15 N.C.Os and men to be detailed by him from the R.E.Platoon will remain behind to clean up the Camp. They will not move off from the Camp until Lieut.E.D.Alcock, M.C. Staff Captain's representative, is satisfied that the Camp is scrupulously clean. The party will then proceed by No.18 train leaving PROVEN at 1.40 p.m.
13. <u>AREA STORES</u>	Stoves, Stove Piping, tables, forms etc., will be handed over to the Camp Warden and a receipt obtained from him.
14. <u>TRANSPORT</u>	(1) the Transport will be conveyed on the same train as the personnel of the Battalion. Supply and Baggage Wagons will also move on the same train. (2) The Transport Officer will arrange to move off so as to arrive at PROVEN STATION at 7.40 a.m. (3) Animals will carry the unexpended portion of the day's rations for the following day. (4) Water Carts will travel <u>Full</u>. They can be filled at PROVEN, near the station. (5) Animals will be watered before entrainment. (6) Head ropes must be taken for tying up animals in the trucks. (7) Animals will be unharnessed and harness stacked in the middle of the trucks. Two men will travel in each truck. (8) Buckets for watering Horses will be taken to water them en route.
15. <u>HALT</u>	The train will halt for one hour at TINCQUES, where (1) Horses will be fed and watered. (2) Hot tea will be made and distributed to the men. (3) A Buffet canteen is open for Officers and men.
16. <u>MARCHING OUT STATE</u>	Headquarters and Coys. will render an accurate marching out state by 6 p.m. 8/2/18 showing separately the number of Officers, other ranks and bicycles proceeding by train on 9/2/18. This will not include Transport men. The Transport Officer will render a Marching-out state by the same time, showing in detail the number of Officers, other ranks, animals, G.S.Wagons, Limbered G.S.Wagons and two-wheeled carts entraining on 9/2/18.

23. Operational Order regarding the action of the battalion while 54th Infantry Brigade was in Corps Reserve – March 1918: this order is interesting given what was to happen on 21 March.

1. While the 54th Infantry Brigade is Brigade in Corps Reserve it may be warned to be in a

state of readiness to move at 15 minutes notice. On this notice being issued, the following action will be taken: –
(1) No man will leave the Camp without orders from the O.C.Company.
(2) Men to be left out of Battle will be detailed in accordance with V/946. They will remain at ROUEZ CAMP.
(3) The unexpired portion of the day's ration will be issued and water bottles filled.
(4) Surplus kit will be left in Billets and stacked by details.
(5) Lewis Gun Limbers and the Tool Cart will be parked in the Camp.
(6) Watercarts will be filled.
(7) The Battn. Orderly Officer will post himself near the Telephone to receive instructions from brigade.
(8) Fighting Order equipment will be put together and every man will be issued with one bandolier of S.A.A.
(9) Company Commanders will report to Bn.Hd.Qrs. for instructions.
2. The Brigade may be called upon: –
(a) to carry out a deliberate and organised counter-attack.
OR (b) to man positions in the Battle Zone.
3. the Brigade may be ordered to a position of readiness in any of the following places, when the Battalion will move by the routes shown: –
(1) <u>PIERREMANDE – AUTREVILLE.</u> (Southern Sector)
Route: – Main CHAUNY – PIERREMANDE Road.
Alternative Route: – CHAUNY – Cross Roads – K.12 – DAMPCOURT – QUIERZY – MANICAMP.
(2) <u>LIEZ – BOIS de VIEVILLE.</u> (Centre Sector)
Route: – VILLEQUIER-AUMONT – FAILLOUEL – FRIERE-FAILLOUEL – MENNESSIS – CANAL BRIDGE – N.31.c. – LIEZ.
(3) <u>MONTESCOURT – CLASTRES.</u> (Northern Sector)
Route: – VILLEQUIER AUMONT – FAILLOUEL – JUSSY
4. The Battalion will move either: –
(a) By Bus.
or (b) By Route March.
In the event of (a) being ordered, the following action will be taken: –
(1) The Battalion will march to X.30.c.9.6., south of VILLEQUIER AUMONT, where it will embus.
(2) Lewis Guns, and 30 Drums per gun, will be carried by the teams.
(3) Picks and shovels will be issued in the proportion of 3 shovels to 1 pick
In the event of (b) being ordered: –
(1) Lewis Gun Limbers will proceed with Companies and Guns and drums will be carried on them.
(2) Picks and shovels will be carried on the Tool Cart, which will accompany B.H.Q. to destination.
(3) Officers Chargers will accompany the Battalion.
5. (1) First Line Transport will be Brigaded and divided into 2 Echelons.
(2) Echelons will be disposed as follows: –
"A"
All G.S. L-Wagons
1 Water Cart (Full)
Maltese Cart
All Pack Animals
"B"
1 Water Cart (Full)
Officers Mess Cart
4 Cookers
(3) "A" Echelon under 2/Lieut.GALE, 11th Royal Fusiliers, will proceed along routes as laid down, according to the Sector to which the Brigade is being despatched. If the Battalion moves by Route March, L.G.Limbers will proceed with their respective Companies, and

rejoin "A" Echelon after disposing of the Guns etc. The position of "A" Echelon will be arranged by Brigade Headquarters. Immediately the order to move forward is issued, the Transport Officers will at once despatch two mounted Orderlies to Battn. Hd.Qrs. for instructions. These orderlies will go to Bde.H.Q. and will be employed for liaison purposes between Bde.H.Q. and "A" Echelon.
(4) "B" Echelon will remain at ROUEZ Camp.
(5) After the Battalion has moved forward 1st Line Transport will be controlled by Brigade, and all requirements for ammunition etc. will be notified direct to Brigade Headquarters.
6. In the event of the Battalion having to move forward Companies will march out in the following order: –
"B" "A" "D" "C" Hd.Qrs. Companies will march at 200 yards distance

24. 7th Bedfords rifle competition result – 12 March 1918

	Appl.	Rapid	TOTAL
No.2 Platoon	99	139	237
No.3 Platoon	99	100	199
Bn.Hd.Qrs.	97	98	195
No.7 Platoon	92	92	184
No.9 Platoon	77	102	179
"B" Coy. H.Q.	83	94	177
No.4 Platoon	82	85-4	163
"A" Company H.Q.	90	71	161
"C" Company H.Q.	78	78	156
No.11 Platoon	68	84	152
Scouts & Q.M.Stores	72	80	152
No.12 Platoon	77	73	150
"D" Company H.Q.	73	73	147
No.6 Platoon	84	61	145
No.10 Platoon	75	58	133
No.16 Platoon	66	66	132
No.1 Platoon	61	74-4	131
No.14 Platoon	71	55	126
Runners	62	64	126
Drums	65	60	125
No.13 Platoon	58	64	122
No.15 Platoon	60	57	117
No.5 Platoon	46	67-4	109
Transport	59	39	98
R.E.Platoon	45	52	97
No.8 Platoon	56	38	94

25. Arrangements for a rapid move while in Corps Reserve – 13 March 1918: this order shows that the German attack was, to some extent, expected.

The following additions and amendments are made to our W/153 of 3/3/18 [see Appendix A2.23]
(1) <u>TOOLS</u> 200 additional Shovels have been drawn. On receipt of message "Prepare for Attack", Transport Officer will at once send all tools to ROUEZ CAMP. These are allotted to Companies as under: –
SHOVELS "A" 75 "B" 75 "C" 75 "D" 75 Hd.Qrs. 10
PICKS "A" 18 "B" 18 "C" 18 "D" 18 Hd.Qrs. 4
On receipt of the order to move forward, the following procedure will be adopted: –

(a) If the Battn. is to move by lorries, the tools will immediately be drawn by Companies and Bn.H.Q. and issued to the men. Those for "C" Company being picked up on the road outside ROUEZ CAMP.
(b) If Battn. moves by Route March tool limbers will accompany Battalion.
(2) LEWIS GUNS. In event of the Battn. moving forward by Route March, Lewis Gun Limber will follow each Company. In any case 24 Drums per Gun will be carried instead of 30 as stated in our W/153 of 3/3/18.
(3) ARMOUR PIERCING AMMUNITION; will shortly be issued to Companies on the following scale: – 10 rounds per man. 1 Drum per Lewis Gun. These will be kept in Companies' Stores and issued on receipt of the message "Prepare for Attack". The Drums set aside for this ammunition will be marked with a yellow circle. 2/Lieut.KELF will report to Orderly Room when this has been completed.
(4) TRANSPORT Transport Officer will send as many men as possible to reconnoitre the route to the 3 rendezvous laid down in B.M.197.
"B" ECHELON. On receipt of the order to move forward "B" Echelon will proceed under the Quartermaster to CAILLOUEL, also all details who are not taken forward. They will report to Captain HAGGARD, 6th Northants.
(5) STORES AND BAGGAGE. These will all be dumped in hut at present occupied by "D" Company at ROUEZ CAMP. Transport Officer will arrange to move "C" Company's Baggage to ROUEZ CAMP. On arrival of the Baggage Wagons these will be loaded up with Q.Ms. Stores, Officers Valises (not exceeding 50 lbs each) Workshops, etc. and will join "B" Echelon at CAILLOUEL. The R.Q.M.S. will remain in charge of Stores until loaded. The Q.M. will detail 2 men to be in charge of all kits, etc. left a ROUEZ CAMP.
(6) PROCEDURE IF ORDERED TO MOVE BACK. It is possible that the Battn. may suddenly be withdrawn for strategical reasons. In this case the allotment of motor Transport would be limited. The procedure to be adopted would be as under: –
(a) Men would parade in Full Marching Order.
(b) Arrangements for dumping of Baggage and Kits would be as for para.5. Q.M's Stores, Workshops. Officers Valises and as many Blankets as possible would be loaded on the available lorries and baggage wagons. All surplus kit would be moved by the Transport Officer and a dump formed in the cellar of the CHATEAU at VILLEQUIER AUMONT. The Q.M. would be responsible for detailing a loading party for these lorries, and also 2 men to take charge of the dump at VILLEQUIER AUMONT. In this event the S.A.A. now in possession of Companies would be collected by the Transport Officer.

26. Order for details – March 1918: these "details" were elements of the battalion on fatigues and working parties, i.e. detailed to carry out the tasks involved.

1. INTENTION   The Battalion Details will be formed into 4 Platoons, a Drummer Platoon and a Hd.Qr.Platoon, and will take up a position at 10 minutes notice on the following lines: –
"C" Platoon will hold the Trench which was pointed out at the reconnaissance, running through S.29.c. "B" Company will be echeloned 100 yards on and on "C" Platoon's left to the road about S.29.b.5.6. "D" Company will form the left flank on the road near S.29.b.5.6. in the trenches reconnoitred this afternoon, to about S.29.a.1.9. "A" Company will be in support of "C" Company's right flank, and will take up a position about A.4.b.9.7., with one section in advance keeping in touch with "C" Coys. right flank, and one section acting as patrol on the eastern outskirts of NOUREUIL, and two sections in Sunken Road in S.28.d. The Drums will occupy the trench running through S.28.c.7.5. to S.28.a. central. The Shoemakers Tailors, etc. will hold the redoubt on the top of the hill in S.28.c.7.4.

160 APPENDIX A: BATTALION MOVES

	HEADQUARTERS will be at S.28.c.7.7. in the dugout on the crest of the hill.
2. TIME	The time of "Battle Positions" will be notified later.
3. ORDER OF MARCH	"C" Platoon, "B" Platoon, "D" Platoon, "A" Platoon, Drums, Shoemakers, tailors etc. and Hd.Qrs.
4. DRESS	Battle Order.
5. BAGGAGE	Packs and Blankets will be dumped in the Camp Store Hut on receipt of the Order to Move.
6. REPORTS	Reports to ROUEZ CAMP Orderly Room until the Order to Move is given, then to Battn.Hd.Qrs. on the crest of the hill, S.28.c.7.7.
7. WORK	Platoons will forthwith consolidate the above reconnoitred positions.

27. Promotions and appointments – April 1918

PROMOTIONS & APPOINTMENTS	The Commanding Officer has been pleased to make the following Promotions and Appointments. 15937 Cpl.L/Sgt.Chandler F.C. "A" Coy. to be Sgt vice 14827 Sgt.Rugman C. "C" Coy. Killed 22.3.18. To date 23.3.18. 19446 Cpl.L/Sgt.Chapman W.A. "C" Coy. to be Sgt. vice 33776 Sgt.Buckingham, W. "B" Coy. Killed 23.3.18. To date 24.3.18. 40120 Cpl.L/Sgt.Kemble H. "B" Coy. to be Sergt vice 14397 Sgt.Whiting J. "D" Coy. To England 23.3.18. To date 24.3.18. 20454 Cpl.L/Sgt.Cooper W.J. "A" Coy to be Sgt. vice 290208 Sgt.Colbert W. "D" Coy. Died of Wds. 26.3.18. To date 27.3.18. 16475 Cpl.L/Sgt.Phypers H. "A" Coy. to be Sgt. vice 12471 Sgt.Dring J. "D" Coy. Killed 4.4.18. To date 5.4.18. 15083 Cpl.Swannell H. "B" Coy. to be Act.Sgt. vice 33459 Sgt.Odell W. "C" Coy. Missing 21.3.18. To date 22.3.18. 22361 Cpl.Boness J. "B" coy. to be Act.Sgt. vice 13772 Sgt.Morris J. "B" Coy. Wounded and Missing 23.3.18. To date 24.3.18. 14446 Cpl.Jaggard S.W. "C" Coy to be Act.Sgt. vice 14780 Sgt.Mears J. "A" Coy. Wounded 23.3.18. To date 24.3.18. 40689 Cpl.Buxton W. "C" Coy. to be Act.Sgt. vice 14554 Sgt.Blake, W. "A" Coy. Wounded 23.3.18. To date 24.3.18. 32631 Cpl.Trussell A. "C" Coy to be Act.Sgt. vice 17767 Sgt.Bradfield F. "D" Coy. Wounded 23.3.18. To date 24.3.18. 16540 Cpl.Goldhawk G. "D" Coy to be Act.Sgt. vice 16553 Sgt.Dawbon W. "B" Coy. Wounded 23.3.18. To date 24.3.18. 8736 Cpl.Butler W. "A" Coy. is appointed L/Sgt. vice 15196 Cpl.L/Sgt.Poole W.E.G. "A" Coy. Killed 22.3.18. To date 23.3.18. 19152 Cpl.Williams A. "D" Coy. is appointed L/Sgt. vice 15957 Cpl.L/Sgt.Chandler W. "C" Coy. Promoted Sgt. 23.3.18. To date 24.3.18. 13459 Cpl.Baker G.R. "A" Coy. is appointed L/Sgt. vice

SELECTED OPERATIONAL ORDERS   161

19446 Cpl.L/Sgt.Chapman W. "C" Coy. Promoted Sgt. 24.3.18. To date 25.3.18.

15141 Cpl.Osmond J.J. "C" Coy is appointed L/Sgt. vice 40129 Cpl.L/Sgt.Kemble H. Promoted Sgt. 24/3/18. To date 25.3.18.

13695 Cpl.King R.G. "C" Coy. is appointed L/Sgt. vice 20454 Cpl.L/Sgt.Cooper W.J. "A" Coy. Promoted Sgt. 27.3.18. To date 28.3.18.

15195 Cpl.Goodwin S.R.M. "D" Coy is appointed L/Sgt. vice 16475 Cpl.L/Sgt.Phypers H. "A" Coy. promoted Sgt. 5.4.18 To date 6.4.18.

15459 Cpl.Collins D. "B" Coy. is appointed Act.Pd.L/Sgt. vice 3/7662 Cpl.L/Sgt. Smith R. "D" Coy. Missing 23.3.18. To date 24.3.18

18419 L/C.Moss B.S. "B" Coy. to be Corpl. to complete establishment. To date 24.3.18.

15975 L/C.Turner W. "B" Coy. to be Corpl. vice 33849 Cpl.Wale L. [sic, actually Oscar George] "B" Coy, Killed 23.3.18. To date 24.3.18.

29884 L/C.Fleckney A.J. "B" Coy. to be Corpl. vice 15139 Cpl.Seabrook A. "B" Coy. Killed 23.3.18. To date 24.3.18.

3/7525 L/C.Holton A. "A" Coy. to be Corpl. vice 43327 Cpl.Mortimer W. "D" Coy. Killed 23.3.18. To date 24.3.18.

240594 L/C.Webb A.J. "D" Coy. to be Corpl. vice 15937 Cpl.L/Sgt.Chandler, F.[sic]"A" Coy. Promoted Sgt. 23.3.18 To date 24.3.18.

18267 L/C.Brett, H. "C" Coy. to be Corpl. vice 19446 Cpl.L/Sgt.Chapman W.A. "C" Coy. Promoted Sgt. 24.3.18. To date 25.3.18.

270920 L/C.Talbot F. "C" Coy. to be Corpl. vice 40129 Cpl.L/Sgt.Kemble H. "B" Coy. Promoted Sgt. 24.3.18. To date 25.3.18.

23070 U.P.L/C.Weeks R.C. "B" Coy. to be Corpl. vice 16475 Cpl.L/Sgt.Phypers H. "A" Coy. promoted Sgt. 5.4.18. To date 6.3.18.

15722 U.P.L/C.Squire T.J. "B" Coy. to be Corpl. vice 20454 Cpl/L/Sgt.Cooper W.J. "A" Coy. Promoted Sgt. 23.3.18. To date 28.3.18.

10034 U.P.L/C.Hammond J. "B" Coy. to be Corpl. vice 19796 Cpl.Parles B. "C" Coy. Died of Wds. 6.4.18. To date 7.4.18

15610 U.P.L/C.Halsey R.C. "D" Coy. to be Act.Cpl. vice 15083 Cpl.Swannell H. "B" Coy. promoted Act.Sgt. 22.3.18 To date 22.3.18

14351 U.P.L/C. Ravenscroft C. "D" coy. to be Act.Cpl. vice 22361 Cpl.Boness J. "B" Coy. promoted Act.Sgt. 24.3.18. To date 24.3.18.

10359 U.P.L/C.Slatter G. "B" Coy. to be Act.Cpl. vice 14446 Cpl.Jaggard S.W. "C" Coy. Promoted Act.Sgt. 24.3.18. To date 24.3.18.

13212 U.P.L/C.Smith H.G. "D" Coy. is appointed Pd.L/C. vice 201981 L/C.Turvey E. "A" Coy. Died of Wds. 21.3.18. To date 22.3.18.

27598 U.P.L/C.Moulster W. "D" Coy. is appointed Pd.L/C. vice 15975 L/C.Turner W. "B" Coy. Promoted Cpl. 24.3.18. To date 24.3.18.

19260 U.P.L/C. Emery W.S. "C" Coy. is appointed Pd.L/C. vice 29824 L/C.Fleckney A.J. "B" Coy. Promoted Cpl. 24.3.18. To date 24.3.18.
16595 U.P.L/C.Batchelor F. "B" Coy. is appointed Pd.L/C. vice 3/7535 L/C.Holton W. "A" Coy. Promoted Cpl. 24.3.18. To date 24.3.18.
20296 U.P.L/C.Tearle T. "A" Coy. is appointed Pd.L/C. vice 24034 L/C.Webb A.J. "D" Coy. promoted Cpl. 24.3.18. To date 24.3.18.
19231 U.P.L/C.Wilsher J. "C" Coy. is appointed Pd.L.C. vice 18267 L/C.Brett H. "C" Coy. Promoted Cpl. 25.3.18. To date 25.3.18.
13145 U.P.L/C. Weston L. "B" Coy. is appointed Pd.L/C. vice 270930 L/C.Talbot F. "C" Coy. Promoted Cpl. 25.3.18. To date 25.3.18
14797 U.P.L/C. Pope W. "C" Coy. is appointed Pd.L/C. vice 13581 L/C.Turney H. "C" Coy. To England 24.5.18. To date 25.3.18.
15730 U.P.L/C.Sturgeon H.G. "B" Coy. to be Act.Pd.L/C. vice 14852 L/C.Bull J. "A" Coy. Missing 23.3.18. To date 25.3.18.
15763 U.P.L/C. Tarburr E. "C" Coy to be Act.Pd.L/C.vice 22752 L/C.Meadows A. "D" Coy. Missing 23.3.18. To date 25.3.18.
10879 U.P.L/C. Neale W.J. "A" Coy. to be Act.Pd.L/C. vice 14625 L/C.Chapman W.J. "B" Coy. Missing 25.3.18. To date 26.3.18.
16210 U.P.L/C.Tucker H. "A" Coy. to be Act.Pd.L/C. vice 33455 L/C.Chapman A. "C" Coy. Wounded 23.3.18. To date 26.3.18.
33108 U.P.L/C.Wright H.E. "B" Coy. to be Act.Pd.L/C. vice 43301 L/C.Hurlock E. "A" Coy. Wounded 23.3.18. To date 26.3.18.
29983 U.P.L/C.Dungar W. "B" Coy. to be Act.Pd.L/C. vice 32287 L/C.Cox C. "B" Coy. Wounded 23.3.18. To date 3.4.18.
12785 U.P.L/C.Stokes F. "B" Coy. to be Act.Pd.L/C. vice 6698 L/C.Nash A. "B" Coy. Wounded 2.4.18. To date 3.4.18.
25812 U.P.L/C.Deal W.C. "B" Coy. to be Act.Pd.L/C. vice 28407 L/C.Appleby E. "C" Coy. Wounded 2.4.18. To date 3.4.18.
14775 U.P.L/C.Stiles H.M. "B" Coy. to be Act.Pd.L/C. vice 15401 L/C.Miles A. "B" Coy. Wounded 4.4.18. To date 5.4.18.
31075 U.P.L/C.Cole H.T. "D" Coy. to be Act.Pd.L/C. vice 15770 L/C.Welch E. "C" Coy. Wounded 8.4.18. To date 9.4.18.
40170 Pte.Clarke J.S. "A" Coy. to be Act.Pd.L/C. vice 14434 L/C. Clarke E. "C" Coy. Evacuated 8.4.18. To date 9.4.18.
41532 Pte.Newell W.T.W. "D" Coy. to be Unpaid L/Cpl. To date 11.4.18.
31670 Pte.Smith A. "A" Coy. to be Act.Pd.L/C. vice 33798 L/C.Clifton H. "C" Coy. Evacuated 8.4.18. To date 9.4.18

CONFIRMATION

14845 Act.Pd.L/C.Watts E.J. "B" Coy. is confirmed in his

SELECTED OPERATIONAL ORDERS   163

                  rank 23.2.18 vice 12701 L/C.Birch F. Category
                  B.111.23.2.18.
TRANSFERS   16475 Sgt.Phypers H. is transferred from "A" to "C"
                  Company with effect from 11.4.18.
EMPLOY   15083 Act.Sgt.Swanell H. "B" Coy. Employed as Gas Sergt.
                  14446 Act.Sgt.Jaggard S.W. "C" Coy employed as Scout
                  Sergt.
                  40129 Sgt.Kemble H. "A" Coy. P.&.B.T. Instructor attached
                  to "B" Company.
                  10358 Act.Cpl.Slatter G. "B" Company employed as Scout
                  Corpl.
                  240584 Cpl.Webb A.J. "D" Coy. employed on Sanitary
                  Duties.

Appendix 2.

Bar to Military Medal: –	15084 Sgt.H.Swannell.
	14782 Sgt.G.C.Stuckey.
Military Medal: –	13780 C.Q.M.S. J.W.Pollard.
	3/7825 Cpl.A.Holton.
	15850 Pte.A.G.Smith.
	15755 Pte.A.Thorby.
	3/8485 Sgt.W.Renny.
	433275 Pte.H.Brunt.
	29695 Pte.F.Cootes.
	22631 Sgt.H.Trussell.
	15626 Pte.F.Fyson.
	14787 Pte.W.H.Dyer.

Appendix B1. Battle Operational Orders

1. Operational Order for the assault on the Pommiers Redoubt, 1 July 1916

1.	INTENTION	The 7th Bn. Bedfordshire Regiment will form part of the assaulting line of the 54th Inf.Brigade in an attack on the German position in which the 18th Division will take a prominent part.
2.	UNITS ON OUR FLANKS	The Berkshire Regiment of the 53rd. Brigade will be on our immediate right; the 11th R.Fusiliers (54th Brigade) will be on our immediate left.
3.	ARTILLERY PREPARATION	The attack is being preceded by a five days bombardment which will last up to the moment of the infantry assault on the 6th day. Guns of all calibres will take part in the bombardment and will fire both day and night.
4.	FRONT, AND FORMATION	During the whole of the artillery bombardment the 7th Bn. Bedfordshire Regiment will hold the battle front of the 54th Infantry Brigade. The allotted frontage of the 7th Bedfordshire Regt. and the area of assault are as follows: – B & C Companies will occupy the forming up trenches 1 & 2, with two platoons in each trench, respectively. A Company will occupy No.4 Trench and will be held in battalion Reserve. D Company will occupy No.3 Trench and cover the entire Battalion Front, and will act as support to B & C Companies.
5.	METHOD OF ADVANCE	The Method of advance will be as practiced in previous training.
6.	OBJECTIVES.	The 7th Bedfordshire Regiment will attack on the following objective.

<table>
<tr><td>FIRST Objective</td><td>The German front line and support trenches. EMDEN TRENCH, BUND TRENCH, POMMIERS TRENCH.</td></tr>
<tr><td>SECOND Objective</td><td>point A.1.b.8.1 POMMIERS LANE – Junction of POMMIERS Lane and MAPLE Trench – POMMIERS Redoubt – MAPLE Trench to its junction with Western point of POMMIERS REDOUBT.</td></tr>
<tr><td>THIRD Objective.</td><td>A line from point S.26.a.2.3. to point S.25.b.70.15.</td></tr>
</table>

In capturing these objectives the following factors are of vital importance: –
(a) To secure BLACK ALLEY as a defensive flank to the 18th Division, and, should occasion arise, to hold it at all costs.
(b) To consolidate and hold the second objective at all costs

BATTLE OPERATIONAL ORDERS 165

even if MONTAUBAN and MAMETZ should not be captured.
(c) To consolidate that portion of BEETLE ALLEY between S.25.d.98.17 – A.1.b.28.60.
(d) On reaching the third objective to construct a series of strong points on that line and push detachments of Infantry with Lewis Guns rapidly forward to over-look CATERPILLAR Valley and prevent the enemy from removing any guns.
The compass bearing for the first objective will be notified later.

7. BARRAGES. The advance of the Battalion will be covered by a barrage of Field and Heavy Artillery, and Machine Guns. The object of these barrages is to prepare every step of the infantry advance and to allow of the infantry to get within assaulting distance of the enemy's trenches before he can man his parapets. The leading waves must work forward to within 60/100 yards of each barrage so that immediately it lifts they are within charging distance. The closer the barrage is followed the greater the possibility of success. This is particularly essential in the advance from the line MAPLE Trench – POMMIERS REDOUBT to the final objective as direct observation is not possible after the line is crossed. The 18th Divisional Field Artillery will fire 5 rounds H.E. shell per gun immediately before each lift.

8. TIMES OF BARRAGES

First objective –	EMDEN TRENCH	0.5
	BUND TRENCH	0.10
	POMMIERS TRENCH	0.20
Second objective	point A.1.b.8.1 – POMMIERS LANE – Junction of POMMIERS Lane & MAPLE TRENCH – POMMIERS REDOUBT – MAPLE TRENCH to its junction with BEETLE ALLEY	1.0

9. MACHINE GUNS 2 Vickers Guns have been allotted to the Battalion. The Lewis Guns will be at the disposal of Company Officers. They should not, unless urgently required, be with the first two leading waves.
The 54th Machine Gun Company will cover the advance of the Battalion from a position in CAFTET WOOD with overhead fire.

10. STOKES BATTERIES. The 54th Stokes Battery and attached Stokes Battery will be distributed as follows: –
(a) 12 guns in position in front line. To be employed for final barrage. As soon as strong points II, III, IV, V, VI and VII are consolidated one gun will move forward to each. The remaining 6 guns will be retained in Brigade reserve in our own trenches.
(b) Two guns at the disposal of each assaulting battalion. these guns will not proceed beyond MAPLE TRENCH until the final objective is consolidated.

11. BATTN. HD.QRS. Battalion Headquarters will move into its initial position at the junction of NEW CUT and LIVERPOOL STREET. All reports will be sent to TRIANGLE after the first objective has been gained. It will move to POMMIERS REDOUBT

12. DUMPS. when the Battalion moves forward to its final objective. The supply of all ammunition, grenades, R.E. material etc. will be worked from a series of Dumps. There will be dumps at Junction of COOPER STREET and Front Line Trench, KING STREET and Front Line Trench, Advanced Brigade Reserve Dump – PICCADILLY. Brigade Dump – CARNOY. The guiding principle will be that Advanced Dumps move forward by stages as objectives are gained; that the Brigade will be responsible for keeping Dumps full; and that Battalions will be responsible for drawing stores from these dumps. A dump will open at the TRIANGLE as early as possible after the first objective is gained.

A special party will be detailed for carrying all ammunition and bombs for use of the assaulting battalions, irrespective of the dumps. This party will move with D Coy.

13. RATIONS AND WATER
Rations and water will be carried forward after night fall. Special instructions for their carriage will be issued as occasion demands.

14. TOOLS.
(a) 50% of the 3rd. platoon of the two leading companies will carry large tools.
(b) 50% of the 3rd. and 4th Companies (assaulting battalions) will carry large tools.
(c) 50% of all garrisons detailed for strong points will carry tools.

Tools will be carried in the proportion of 2 shovels to 1 pick, and will be carried in a vertical position on the man's back.

A reserve of picks and shovels will be kept at C Dump from which the Battalion may draw to meet their requirements.

15. AMMUNITION CARRIERS
Each Lewis Gun team will be strengthened by 4 Lewis Reserve Gunners to carry S.A.A.

16. WATER
The provision of water during and after the assault will be extremely difficult. Steps must therefore be taken to ensure that all water bottles are full at zero hour and that all ranks practice the greatest restraint in drinking water. The normal supply will be from the well in CARNOY and from the stand pipes in CARNOY ALLEY. Reserve storage tanks have been placed in the Russian saps at A & B Dumps. 250 petrol tins will also be placed at each of these dumps.

17. MEDICAL ARRANGEMENTS.
The 55th Field Ambulance will be responsible for the collection of all wounded in the Division. It will establish an advanced dressing station at the following points: –
(a) In dugouts at west end of BRICK ALLEY, CARNOY for wounded of the 53rd. and 54th Inf.Bdes. (Accommodation for 200 stretcher cases).
(b) In dugouts at BRONFAY FARM for local and walking cases (accommodation 50).

All walking cases will be directed to the Advanced Dressing Station at CARNOY and from there will proceed via CARNOY to BRONFAY FARM Dressing Station.

Regimental aid posts will be established as shewn on the special map. Wounded will be conveyed from these posts to the nearest advanced Dressing Station by regimental stretcher bearers.

Wounded cases occurring in the enemy's trenches will be collected into suitable dugouts by regimental medical officers. Such dugouts must be marked and their position notified to the 55th Field Ambulance who will arrange for the removal of these cases to the Advanced Dressing Station in CARNOY VALLEY by the R.A.M.C. Stretcher bearers. In addition to the 8 battalion stretchers with units 16 additional R.A.M.C. stretchers will be stored near each regimental aid post and used by both R.A.M.C. and regimental stretcher bearers for bring in cases.

18. <u>PRISONERS.</u> Prisoners will be sent back in batches to the Bde. Dump and thence to the Advanced Divisional Collecting Station at BILLON FARM. They will be marched <u>across the open</u> and not down communication trenches. Escorts to BILLON FARM will be found by the Battns. which take the prisoners, the men rejoining their units under proper control as soon as possible. Batches of 100, with about 10 per cent escort have on previous occasions been proved suitable for despatch as one party. Slightly wounded men can be used as escorts. Prisoners must be disarmed and searched for concealed weapons and documents, immediately after capture before being marched off. <u>Officers must be separated from the rank and file immediately</u>. Prisoners will be searched for documents and examined under Divisional arrangements, at the Divisional Collecting Station.

<u>It is most important that immediate information should be sent back concerning the identification of regiments opposed to us.</u>

19. <u>CAPTURED GUNS.</u> When hostile guns are captured the following procedure will be adopted: –
(a) Report to Battn.Hd.Qrs. the number and nature of guns captured.
(b) Detail parties to man handle them to the nearest position where our gun teams can be hooked in.
(c) Report exact position where teams are required, and number of teams necessary.

20. <u>COLLECTION OF INTELLIGENCE.</u> Two men will be attached to each assaulting Battn. (under Brigade Arrangements) for the purpose of collecting documents, etc. in the enemy's trenches. They will go forward with the dug-out clearing parties and will carry a distinguishing mark which will be a Red White and Blue bull's-eye painted on either side of the sack which each man will carry.

21. <u>STRAGGLERS.</u> Regimental police will be employed under Brigade arrangements to control traffic in the trenches and to check stragglers moving to the rear.
Posts will be established as under: –
1 N.C.O. and 4 men in CARNOY) To be
1 N.C.O. and 4 men in CAFTET WOOD) detailed by
) Brigade.
They will be required to take the number, names, and units of all stragglers and march them back in parties to their units.

22. <u>UP AND DOWN COMMUNICATIONS TRENCHES</u> The Main Up Trench will be PIONEER AVENUE, commencing at BRONFAY FARM. The Main Down (evacuation) trench will be MAIDSTONE – CARNOY AVENUES. Steps out of these trenches have been cut on alternate sides at 50 yards interval.

168 APPENDIX B: BATTLES

23. <u>COMMUNICATION</u>.

Under no circumstances will individuals be allowed to use either of these trenches in the wrong direction.
All companies will go over the top accompanied by their respective Signallers and runners. B & C Coy. Hd.Qrs. are due to arrive in BUND TRENCH at 20 minutes after zero. C Coy. will have with the 2nd. Wave 2 Signallers who will immediately open up communication, if possible, with the PERONNE ROAD. Their station will be the top left hand corner of the TRIANGLE. All telephone lines will endeavour to reach this point, which will be marked by a triangular piece of tin, white with a black stripe on one side and black with a white stripe on the other side.
By the time C Coy. advances from the TRIANGLE i.e. 30 minutes., D Coy. H.Q. will have arrived and D.Coy. Sigs will have taken over the station and so freed C Sigs., thus enabling them to move on with their company.
D Coy. will run this Signal station (TRIANGLE) with 2 men detailed from A Coy. to accompany them with that object in view. When D Coy. advances from the TRIANGLE "A" Coy. Sigs. will remain to run the station.
A Coy. H.Q. are due in the TRIANGLE at 1.00 after zero hour and will continue to staff the station until arrival of Bn.Hd.Qrs. who will then take over this station.
By the time Bn.H.Qrs. are ready to move on the Northants Bn.H.Qrs. will have arrived in the TRIANGLE and will take over the station from the Bedfords entirely.
PICCADILLY CIRCUS will be kept open permanently. The "New Cut" Office will be closed when Bn. reaches the REDOUBT.
B & C Coy. Hd.Qrs. are due in POMMIERS Trench at 30 minutes after zero, when the Signallers will open Signal Stations. If casualties have been heavy "D" Coy. will reinforce these 2 stations. B & C Companies will remain in the POMMIERS TRENCH forty minutes.
POMMIERS TRENCH is the last point for Visual Signalling to the PERONNE ROAD.
B & C Companies Hd.Qrs. arrive in the REDOUBT at 1.00 after zero. As no visual Signalling is possible from the Redoubt to PERONNE ROAD all messages will have to go by runner to the station at S.p.VI or other station in POMMIERS Trench. B & C Coys. Remain for 1 hour in the REDOUBT.
B & C Hd.Qrs. advance to BEETLE ALLEY at 2.15 after zero and remain there, taking all their Signallers with them less 8 left in the REDOUBT to carry on a RELAY Station. D.Coy sweep on right through to the intermediate line, taking their Signallers with them. A Coy. sweep round the right flank of the redoubt and take up position on the front line ridge taking their signallers with them.
By the above method, economy is affected in the use of runners, who instead of running say from REDOUBT (B Coy.) to TRIANGLE (Bn.Hd.Qrs.) would only run to the POMMIERS TRENCH STATION, hand in the message there and return at once to their companies. POMMIERS Trench Station would then endeavour to visual the M/s and if impossible, would send on by runners to the TRIANGLE.

Messages would, in other words, be dealt with in "RELAYS". No runner would be long away from his Coy. and so be available for a further message. White and Black Triangles are being made at the proportion of 3 per coy. Immediately a Signaller opens a station, one of these triangles will be placed in the ground near him as a mark to guide runners from other directions. Signalling will be done by "discs" until REDOUBT is taken, when flags may possibly be used with safety, from POMMIERS TRENCH to PERONNE AVENUE.

TELEPHONES.

Each Coy. will have two telephones allotted to them, these being taken across after A Coy. One of these will be accompanied by a man carrying a coil of cable which he will reel out as he goes along. These lines will all converge on the TRIANGLE and be connected up. As Coys. Advance endeavours will be made to continue laying telephone lines, and to keep them in repair. Each Coy. as it goes over takes with it 2 miles of black enamel wire for use whenever practicable.

2 Signallers will be detached from Bn.Hq.Qrs. to take over Station in POMMIERS TRENCH.

All messages to be as short as possible; indelible pencils should <u>not</u> be used for writing messages.

CONTACT AEROPLANE PATROLS.

Each Battalion will have a supply of red flares. One flare must be carried by each man. One special signalling lamp, one panel and one ground signal will be taken with each Battn.Hd.Qrs. The ground signal must be put out as soon as Battn.Hd.Qrs. reaches its new position, but should only be unfolded when one of our own aeroplanes is over the line. XIII Corps and XV Corps aeroplanes will be of type B.E.2.c. and have a broad black band under each lower plane. The method of working these contact aeroplanes will be that already practised.

General.

Officers should always, when possible, speak on the telephone themselves, or else write down their messages and sign them. Signallers are ordered not to accept messages unless signed by an officer or N.C.O. or man in command of a unit. It is essential that all messages should have time and place on them and that they should be as short and concise as possible

24. ARTILLERY DISTINGUISHING <u>FLAGS</u>.

Every platoon will carry two red and yellow artillery flags. These flags will be waved for a short period by the leading line to show our artillery how far the attack has progressed. <u>On no account will any flags be stuck into the ground</u>. These flags Will not be waved at any position in advance of the POMMIERS REDOUBT.

25. EQUIPMENT TO BE TO BE CARRIED ON <u>THE MEN</u>

Every man will carry: –
Rifle and equipment less pack.
1 Bandolier in addition to his equipment amn. (170 rounds in all).
1 days ration and 1 iron ration.
1 waterproof sheet.
2 sandbags.
1 yellow patch on haversack on his back.

		2 Smoke Helmets.
Grenadiers will only carry 50 rounds S.A.A.
26.	MAPS, DOCUMENTS	No maps showing our own trenches or important papers will be carried by officers and men taking part in the attack.
27.	STRONG POINTS.	Apart from the strong points constructed on the final objective, the strong points marked I, VI & VII on the special map will be commenced immediately the objectives in which they are situated are reached. 7th Bedfords will construct strong points at THE TRIANGLE and POMMIERS REDOUBT.
All strong points must be prepared for all round defence, and wired. They must hold out even if the troops on either side of them are driven back. Strong points No.1 and No.7 will be garrisoned by the 3rd. Battalion.
28.	BOSCH COUNTER ATTACKS.	Recent experience has shown that the Bosch delivers small counter attacks with platoons or companies immediately hostile troops gain their objective. These small counter attacks have had far reaching results and must be specially guarded against. To meet these counter attacks the reserves in the hands of platoon and coy. commanders will be of the greatest value.
29	RELIEFS.	All troops must clearly understand that no reliefs can be expected until their final objectives have been efficiently consolidated. Units who first complete the consolidation of their objectives will be considered first for relief.
30.	Dugout clearing parties	The 6th Northamptonshire Regt. will furnish Dugout Parties as follows: –
4 sections will be in No.2 Trench.
Two of these Will stop at AUSTRIAN TRENCH and two in AUSTRIAN SUPPORT TRENCH.
4 sections in No.3 Trench. Two of these will stop at EMDEN TRENCH and two at BUND TRENCH. The four sections in No.2 Trench will move out with 3rd. wave, the four secs in No.3 between 3rd. and fourth waves.

2. Operational Orders for an attack on Petit Miraumont which did not, in fact, take place.

Map reference LE SARS
57D S.E.2 & 57c S.W.1 (parts of)
1/10,000.
30/10/16

1. INTENTION
   The Battalion in conjunction with units on its right and left is to capture the village of PETIT MIRAUMONT and the bridge over the ANCRE.
2. INSTRUCTIONS
   The Battalion will be formed up for the attack as follows:
   "C" Coy. on the right in REGINA TRENCH
   "D" Coy. on the left in REGINA TRENCH
   "B" Coy. on the right in HESSIAN & VANCOUVER
   "A" Coy. on the left in HESSIAN & VANCOUVER
   "C & D" Companies will have their first two waves in shell holes in front of REGINA TRENCH before Zero hour.
3. ROLE OF THE BATTALION
   The Battalion will form the right attack and fight its way through to PETIT MIRAUMONT. It will seize the bridges at R.5.b.25, R.5.a.46 and the railway bridge at

R.5.a.55. Strong points with Vickers and Lewis Guns will be made covering these bridges. A party will be sent forward to destroy the telephone exchange at R .5.d.28. The Battalion will also form a defensive flank from the left of the 11th Canadian Brigade to the bridge at R.5.a.55, these points are marked on special map. On obtaining its final objective the Battalion will by means of Active patrolling be responsible for cutting off the retreat of any Germans retiring from South West Corner of MIRAUMONT towards IRLES.

4. 12TH BATTALION MIDDLESEX REGIMENT

The 12th Battalion Middlesex Regiment will furnish one company for dugout clearing, with the 7th Bedfords. 2 sections will follow each of the first four ways [sic] on either flank. The 4 Sections with the first wave will be responsible for clearing Courcelette trench on the right and west MIRAUMONT ROAD on the left up to trench in 17 central and also any dugouts in 17 central trench. The 4 sections with the second wave will be responsible for clearing Courcelette trench from 17 central trench to GRANDCOURT trench, gun pits about R.12.c.2.0. and ravine in E.MIRAUMONT ROAD in R.12 up to junction with GRANDCOURT trench also W MIRAUMONT ROAD and short trench starting at R.11.d.20.15. The 8 sections with the 3rd and 4th waves will support the leading sections up to GRANDCOURT trench and then clear any dugouts in it, clearing up new trench on R.17.B on the way. The Company is to reform in GRANDCOURT trench, consolidate and hang on to it.

5. LEWIS GUNS

During the advance Lewis Guns must take every opportunity of covering the advance on defended positions. They are to be used boldly. A Lewis Gun must be detailed for each strong point before the attack.

6. 54TH MACHINE GUN COMPANY

One Section will be attached to the 7th Bedfords. One gun to railway bridge at R.5.a.5.5. and one gun to strong point at R.5.d.0.8.

7. TRENCH MORTAR BATTERY

One Mortar will be attached to the Battalion to proceed down COURCELETTE TRENCH and assist if necessary at any point where attack is held up, eventually proceeding to railway embankment at R.5.a.5.5. prepared to cover attack on bridge.

8. STRONG POINTS

In addition to the strong points referred to in para.3 the Battalion will establish strongpoints along the E.MIRAUMONT ROAD at R.5.d.6.3. R.5.d.0.8. R.5.a.8.0. R.5.d.6.7. and R.5.a.6.4. All strong points to be wired with concertina wire.

9. ARTILLERY BARRAGE

a. Commencing from Zero hour there will be fixed barrages on the following lines.
1. The new trench from R.18.a.0.1. to R.16.c.0.6.
2. GRANDCOURT TRENCH.
3. MIRAUMONT TRENCH.
4. Railway Embankment.

The Field Artillery shrapnel barrage will be supplemented by 60 pounder shrapnel on the lines 2, 3 & 4 above. there will also be a rolling barrage which, up to the first objective will move at the rate of 50 yards a minute, and from the first objective onwards at 25 yards a minute. The fixed barrage will be joined by the rolling barrages and the two will then lift simultaneously.

b. The rolling barrage will open on the line approximately 200 yards north of REGINA TRENCH and remain steady till plus 4. It will then roll forward at the rate of 50 yards in one minute on to the first objective – GRANDCOURT TRENCH. It will lift from GRANDCOURT TRENCH to form a defensive barrage approximately 200 yards to the North, and to let the Infantry into that trench at plus 28. At plus one hour 28 minutes the advance to the second objective will commence. The defensive barrage will intensify its fire at plus one hour 28 minutes on its defensive lines and remain steady till plus one hour 32 minutes to enable the Infantry to leave GRANDCOURT TRENCH and to get up under the barrage preparatory to following it. At plus one hour 52 minutes the barrage will lift from MIRAUMONT TRENCH and roll on towards the second objective. From the moment the Infantry enter MIRAUMONT TRENCH and continuing during their advance to the second objective, a defensive barrage will be established on the right flank of the 54th Infantry Brigade. This barrage will be approximately on a line through L.35.d. – R.6.a. in the neighbourhood of which it will be joined by the Canadian defensive barrage. This right flank defensive barrage will remain on and join the defensive box barrage which will be finally placed round MIRAUMONT after the capture of the third objective.

At plus 2 hours 8 minutes, the barrage will commence to lift off the second objective by rolling up from the West end (the embankment at R.4.d.05.05) to R.5.a.4.6, which it is timed to reach at plus 2 hours 24 minutes, when it will lift off the whole of the remainder of the objectives to form a defensive barrage along the whole front of the Division approximately 200 yards north of the railway embankment. At plus 3 hours 24 minutes, the defensive barrage will intensify its fire on its defensive lines and remain steady till 3 plus 28 minutes to enable the Infantry to leave the second objective and to get up under the barrage preparatory to following it. The barrage will then roll on and finally establish a box barrage round the village of MIRAUMONT.

In order that the time for the first advance from the first and second objectives after the hours halt may be quite clear to the Infantry, there will be a complete cessation of 18 pounder fire for the five minutes immediately previous to the moment at which the further advance is to take place. The reopening of the heavy shrapnel barrage at the end of this five minutes will be the signal for the advance.

FROM THE ABOVE IT WILL BE SEEN THAT IT BEHOVES THE INFANTRY TO FOCUS THEIR ATTENTION ON THAT PORTION OF THE BARRAGE IMMEDIATELY IN FRONT OF THEM AND CONFORM TO ITS MOVEMENTS. A STEADY AND ORDERLY ADVANCE MUST BE MAINTAINED[.] THE OPENING OF THE BARRAGE AT ZERO AND ITS INTENSIVE REOPENING AFTER EACH HOUR HALT ON THE FIRST AND SECOND OBJECTIVES WILL BE THE SIGNAL TO ADVANCE. IT MUST BE IMPRESSED ON ALL COMMANDERS DOWN TO THOSE OF SECTIONS THAT THE ORGANIZATION FOR THE NEXT ADVANCE MUST BE COMPLETED WELL BEFORE THE EXPIRATION OF THE HOURS HALT AND THAT TROOPS MUST GET AS CLOSE TO THE BARRAGE AS POSSIBLE BEFORE IT COMMENCES TO MOVE FORWARD. IF THE PSYCHOLOGICAL MOVEMENT [sic MOMENT?] FOR THE FORWARD MOVEMENT IS MISSED IT WILL BE DETRIMENTAL TO THE SUCCESS OF THE UNDERTAKING.

c. In addition to the shrapnel barrage the Divisional howitzers and Corps heavy Artillery will, from zero onwards, keep under fire all points and localities forward of the rolling barrage, in which the presence of the enemy is suspected.

10. TOOLS
50% of the 3rd and 4th platoons of each company will carry large tools, one pick to three shovels.

11. GRENADES & BOMBS ETC.
Every man will carry 150 rds S.A.A. (Specialist 50 rds) and two grenades, these grenades to be kept as a Company reserve and are not intended to be thrown by the men carrying them. Grenade Sections will carry ten grenades per man and in addition each man will carry one and the section Commander ten No.23 Rifle grenades.

12. COMMUNICATIONS
All communication possible will be maintained by the Signal Section in accordance with instructions issued direct to O.C. Signals by Brigade Signalling Officer. Communication between Companies and battalion headquarters will be kept up by runners. The Bde. runners will wear a red armband.

13. ROLE OF COMPANIES
"C" Company will be on the right, its objective being the GRANDCOURT TRENCH,

its right flank to keep in touch with the 11th Canadian Brigade, moving along the E.MIRAUMONT ROAD it will reform in the GRANDCOURT TRENCH and act as support to "B" Company in the attack on PETIT MIRAUMONT, halting in South MIRAUMONT TRENCH and consolidating there. A party to be detailed to destroy the telephone exchange at R.5.d.2.8. The Signalling Officer will detail two Signallers to accompany this party it will also form strong points at R.5.d.6.3. and R.5.d.6.7 "D" Company will be on the left of "C" Company its right in touch with the left of "C" Company and its left in touch with the 11th Royal Fusiliers. The W.Miraumont Road (inclusive) being the left flank, its objective being the GRANDCOURT TRENCH. It will reform in GRANDCOURT TRENCH and act as a support to "A" Company in the attack on PETIT MIRAUMONT it will take up a position in support of "A" Company about R.5.d.6.8. "B" Company will follow "C" Company halting at a convenient distance from the GRANDCOURT TRENCH until Barrage time when it will pass through "C" Company, over GRANDCOURT TRENCH and continue the attack on PETIT MIRAUMONT. It will tell off dug out clearing parties to clear any dugouts encountered. After taking SOUTH MIRAUMONT TRENCH it will take up a defensive flank from R.5.d.6.3. exclusive to R.5.a.8.O. forming strong points at R.5.a.8.0 R.5.b.25.10 and at R.5.d.0.9. These points must be held at all costs. In the attack the right flank will move by the E.MIRAUMONT ROAD and keep touch with the 11th Canadian Bde. "A" Company will follow up "D" Company in Support halting at a convenient distance from the GRANDCOURT TRENCH until barrage time, when it will pass through "D" Company over GRANDCOURT TRENCH and continue the attack on PETIT MIRAUMONT. It will tell off Dug Out clearing parties to clear any Dugouts encountered and will press resolutely on through PETIT MIRAUMONT and take up defensive line from R.5.a.8.0. (exclusive) along the PETIT MIRAUMONT ROAD to the River Ancre and endeavour to secure the RIVER BRIDGE at R.5.a.4.6. forming strong points at R.5.a.4.6 R.5.a.5.5 and R.5.a.6.4. It will keep in touch with "B" Company on its right and the 11th Royal Fusiliers on its left. the W.MIRAUMONT ROAD (inclusive) being its left flank.

14. FORMATION
    All Companies will move in four waves at the usual distances.
15. In order to keep our attacking troops clear of hostile artillery fire directed from the map and at the same time to adapt new defences to the lie of the ground, troops will, when consolidating positions gained, avoid, so far as possible, old trenches.
16. FLARES
    Every man, of all four Companies will carry one aeroplane flare. The leading line of Infantry will light Red flares at the following times: –
    Zero plus one hour.
    Zero plus three hours.
    Zero plus five hours.
    and at any other time on demand being made by contact aeroplanes sounding Klaxon horns or dropping white VERY lights.

3. Operational Orders for the attack at Chérisy, 3 May 1917

1. GENERAL PLAN   The 7th Bedfordshire Regt with the 9th Leicesters on its right and 12th Middlesex Regt on its left. The objectives of the 7th Bedfordshire Rgt are: – 1st trench from O.33 c.7.2 to U 3.a.1.3. 2nd Line running through U 4.a.1.5. – U.4.c.3.3. the 7th Bedfordshire Regt to attack on a frontage of two companies with "A" Company on the right and "D" Company on the left, "B" Company in support and "C" Company in reserve. Boundaries between companies through O 31.b.3.6. O 31.b.9.1. O 32.c.2.6. U 3.a.4.7 and U 4.c.2.9.

APPENDIX B: BATTLES

2. DISTRIBUTION OF COMPANIES at ZERO HOUR	"A" Company on right, "D" Company on left in 4 lines. First 2 lines not more than 100 yards forward of front trench. 3rd and 4th line in front trench. "B" Company between 1st and 2nd Trench. "C" Company behind 2nd trench.
3. ROLE OF COMPANIES	"A" and "D" companies will follow the barrage starting at Zero hour and will fight their way to the first objective making strong points as per appendix 1. "B" Company will follow in close support and take up a position in the River Bed also making strong points as per appendix 1. "C" Company will be in reserve and move up to trench running through O.32 a central to O 32 c.5.2; being prepared to form defensive flanks whether to the right or to the left. At Zero plus 2 hours "A" and "D" Companies will continue to follow the barrage fighting their way to final objective and dropping points as per appendix 2. "B" Company will follow in close support and render what help is necessary and dropping points as per appendix 2. "C" Company will advance to original first objective 1st and 2nd objectives to be at once consolidated.
4. M.GUN Co.	One Vickers Gun will proceed with "B" Company under Capt Bull and when 1st objective is taken will take up a position at U 3.a.2.3 covering the right flank of the battalion. One gun will proceed with "C" Company under Captain Keep and when the 2nd objective is taken it will be sent forward to U.3.d.6.5.
5. T.M.BTY	One Mortar with 60 rounds will be attached to the Battalion and will move with "C" Company to trench in O.32.c. taking up a position at O.32.c.7.3.
6. DUGOUT CLEARING PARTY	Dugout clearing parties, 2 platoons of 11. Royal Fusiliers will be attached to the Battalion. One platoon will follow the 2nd line. 2nd platoon will follow the 4th line. 1st platoon will clear trench running from O.32.a. central to O 32.c.5.2. They will block trench at O 32.c.5.2. and cover block with their Lewis Guns. 2nd platoon will clear the Sunken road running thro O 32.central to O.32.c.7.2 and will install their Lewis guns to cover their right flank.
7. ARTILLERY BARRAGE	The advance will be preceded by a rolling barrage which will open 200 yards in front of our present front line. The rate of advance will be 100 yards in 2 minutes up to the Western outskirts of CHÉRISY thence to the 1st objective at 100 yards in 6 minutes beyond which it will rest. At Zero plus 2 hrs it will proceed to the final objective at 100 yards in 3 minutes, barrage lines and times of lifts may be seen on barrage map at Bn Hd Qrs. 60 pounder batteries will search the ground 600 yards beyond the rolling barrage for Machine Guns and other likely targets will be dealt with by Corps Heavy Artillery. The Brigade Commander will have a direct call on one 18 pounder battery to take on hostile counter-attacks or deal with enemy strong points.
8. SIGNAL COMMUNICATION	See appendix 3.
9. COMMUNICATION with contact AEROPLANES	Every man will carry a flare. Flares will be lit at all times when called for by the sounding of the Claxton Horn or the dropping of a white light by the aeroplane and definitely at Zero plus 1½ hrs and Zero plus 3½ hrs. Flares may only be lit by troops in the front line.

10. LIAISON OFFICER	Major E.Clegg with 2 runners will report to Bde Hd Qrs N 22.d.4.2. at Zero hour.
11. MOVEMENT OF Hd Qrs.	Bn Hd Qrs will be situated in the front trench at Zero hour and will move into German dugouts at O.32.c.8.4 after the 1st objective has been taken. Z day, Zero hour and synchronisation of watches will be notified later.
12. ADMINISTRATION AMMUNITION	Following dumps have been formed. Bde Dump N.29.c.8.9 Forward Bde Dump N.36.b central. The 2 assaulting coys will each form a small dump of S.A.A. in front line (these to be collected in surrounding trenches). As soon as possible after Zero hour these dumps will be moved forward to O 32 c.9.7. coys in 1st objective.
13. CARRYING PARTIES	2/Lieut.Piercy will undertake to supply Bombs. S.A.A. throughout the operation. The Drum Major i/c of the Drums will form a dump of water at O.32.c.9.7. as soon as possible.
14. AMM. PACK TRAIN	Bde Transport Offr will be responsible for the Brigade ammunition and water supply.
15. L.G.DRUMS.	Reserve drums will be dumped N.36.b central.
16. RATIONS & WATER	The iron ration and unconsumed portion of the days rations will be carried on the man, All water bottles must be full at Zero hour. 2/Lieut Piercy will undertake the carrying forward of rations from Héninel. Across country track will be staked out – N.29.c.8.9. N.30.c.00. N.36.b.central N.31 central O.33.c 8.5. 2/Lieut Piercy will send back 4 guides for the ration party and will report at Bde H.Qrs N.22. d central before 6 p.m. Transport Offrs and Quarter Masters will report to Staff Captain Bde H.Qrs N 22 d central after 6 p.m. to obtain latest information with regard to the situation and also to pick up their guides. Water carts can be filled at Héninel at N.28.b central. Companies must supply rations to detached sections of M.G.Coy and T.M.Bty.
17. MEDICAL	Arrangements for evacuation of wounded see appendix 4.
18. PRISONERS	Bde Collecting post Cross roads N.29.b.8.0.
19. POLICE	L/Cpl Sturgess and Pte Raynor will be posted at N 36.b.central to direct wounded to collecting post N 30.a.1.3. March all prisoners and direct escorts to Bde Collecting Post N.29.b.8.0., to take the Nos Ranks names and Units of all stragglers, send those who are fit back to their units, pass the remainder to the rear to the line of evacuation

APPENDIX 1
"A" Coy Strongpoint U 2.b.10.1 L/C till Vickers gun arrives.
"D" Coy Strongpoint E U.3.a.5.7.
"B" Coy Strongpoint C O.32.c.9.6. O.32.d.5.4.

APPENDIX 2
"A" Coy Strongpoint U.3.d.6.5.
"B" Coy Strongpoint U.3.a.9.8.

APPENDIX 3.
Signal Communication.
Divided into the following headings.
1. Visual. 2. Telephone System 3. Pigeon 4. Power buzzer 5. Aeroplane Contact 6. Runners.
1. A Bn H.Q. visual post will be pushed out after the support Coy (B) to gun pit at O.31.b.8.0. for the purpose of receiving visual signals from the 4 Coys. This station will answer and

in urgent cases will send messages forward. There will also be Bde visual post at O 31.b.14. When "A" and "D" Coys reach the 1st objective they will open visual communication from (roughly) U.3.a.0.7. and U 3 a 2.9. respectively. On moving forward to the final objective "A" Coy will open visual from the trees at U.3.c.9.7. and later from U 3 d 6.5. "A" Coy will man this last place with lamp during the ensuing night. These special orders will not prevent any coy from sending an urgent message by visual wherever they may be.

2. When Hd Qrs subsequently move forward lines will be laid to Coys.

3. 2 pigeons will be carried forward by "A" Coy and 2 by "B" Coy. 2 will remain with Bn H Qrs.

4. Power Buzzer set will remain at battle H.Qrs. O 31 b.0.5. during the attack.

5. No aeroplane signalling will be attempted.

6. Bde runner posts will be attached at Bn H Qrs at O.31.b.0.5. and O.31 b.3.8. When Bn H.Qrs moves forward the posts at the latter place will move forward to O.32.c.8.5. Runner posts will be marked by a triangular red flag.

APPENDIX 4.
As arranged at Conference.

4. Operational Orders for the assault on Glencorse Wood, 10 August 1917

Information

1. The II Corps will capture and hold at an early date INVERNESS COPSE, GLENCORSE WOOD and the Southern end of WESTHOEK RIDGE.

2. "Z" day and "Zero" hour will be notified later.

3. The attack will be carried out by the 18th Division on the right, 25th Division on the left, 7th Brigade will attack on our left.

4. The 54th Brigade will attack on a two Battalion and the 55th Brigade on a one Battalion frontage.

5. The 11th Royal Fusiliers will form the right assaulting Battalion and will form up on a general line J14.c.1.5.55 – J14.a.0.0. – J13.b.9.3. They will fight their way through to the final objective, consolidate and hold it.

Instructions

6. The Battalion (7th Bedfords) will form up along a line J.13.b.9.3. J.7.d.95.15. road exclusive and fight their way to final objective, consolidate and hold it.

7. Disposition of Companies

"C" Coy. will be the right assaulting Company.
"B" Coy. will be the left assaulting Company.
"A" Coy. will be in Support.
"D" Coy Reserve Company.

8. Dividing Line

The approximate dividing line between Fusiliers and Bedfords is J.13.b.9.3 – J.14.a.90.55 – J.14.b.65.65.

9. Mopping Up

One Company Northants will be attached to the Battalion for Mopping Up, this Company will not proceed beyond the road running from J.9.c.6.2 through J.8.c.7.1 Companies will do their own mopping up after crossing this road

Task of Assaulting Coys

The two assaulting Coys ("C" & "B") will fight their way through to the final objective (YELLOW LINE) consolidate and hold it.

"A" COMPANY will follow in close support to the assaulting Companies ready to give them any assistance to gain their final objective. This Company must lose no opportunity to push the assault forward until the final objective (YELLOW LINE) is reached. If the assaulting Companies are not held up or checked, the Company will follow them, fighting in close support and be ready to render them any assistance on the YELLOW LINE, they may require – they will also act as counter-attack Company should the necessity arise. After the YELLOW LINE has been gained and all is quiet, this Company should be tucked away in close support to the front line.

"D" COMPANY will be in Reserve and will move up as the attack goes forward to a position in JARGON TRENCH, ready to render any assistance that may be required, should the situation become critical they will support the front line Companies in such a manner that no ground that has been once gained is lost. If the attack is successful orders will be sent to this Company from the Battalion Commander, but this does not prevent the Company Commander from issuing his own instructions to prevent any ground being given up after once it has been gained.

MACHINE GUNS Two Machine Guns will be attached to the Battalion, these Guns will move forward with the Reserve Coy ("D" Coy) until the objective is gained, they will then be placed in position in Strong Points 4 and 5.

FORMING UP The lines for forming up will be marked out by Y-Z night with telephone wire and tape in accordance with verbal instructions given to all concerned.

THE ADVANCE The signal for the advance will be the opening of the Shrapnel Barrage when Bayonets will be fixed and the attack carried out.

DRESS Fighting Order plus one day's rations including the Iron Rations.

RIFLEMEN: 170 rds S.A.A.

BOMBERS: 5 No.5's, 120 rds S.A.A.

RIFLE BOMBERS: 5 No.23, 120 rds S.A.A.

MOPPERS UP: 5 No.23's or 5 No.5's, 120 rds S.A.A.

All Other ranks will carry their usual complement.

EXPLOITING SUCCESS After reaching the objectives on the YELLOW LINE patrols will be pushed out to reconnoitre the S.W. portion of NONNE-BOSSCHEN from about the Western end of the Track running through the SCH in BOSSCHEN to the track running along the southern border of the wood NONNE-BOSSCHEN – this will be carried out in conjunction with similar patrols of the 11th Royal Fusiliers.

WATER All Water Bottles must as far as possible be kept filled.

PRISONERS Brigade collecting points at J.13.a.9.13

LIAISON Lt.H.B.Stewart will act as Liaison Officer between Bn. Headquarters and the 8th Loyal North Lancs on our left.

Appendix B2. Battle Reports

1. Battle report for the attack on the Pommiers Redoubt, 1 July 1916

Enclosed herewith report on operations 1/2 July for information of G.O.C. 54th Brigade

Sir. I beg to forward herewith report on the operations carried out by the Battn under my Command on 1/2 July 1916.

In a report of this nature, in order to arrive at a clear understanding of the various incidents that took place, where the advance was held up, and where it proceeded, it appears advisable to divide the front allotted to the Battn into right and left attack. The dividing line was roughly between the assaulting Battns Coys ran roughly through the triangle and left of Pommiers Redoubt. The right started on Bay Point then swung half right on to Poppof Lane. The Left keeping in touch with 53rd Brigade. The left was directed on Austrian Junction to a point about 80 yds west of Pommiers Redoubt.

Assaulting Coys.	Right attack – B Company – under Capt Bull Left attack – C Company under Capt Clegg
Supporting Company	D Company under Capt Lloyd supported the attack of the two assaulting Companys [sic]
Reserve	A Company under Captain Percival was held in Battalion Reserve
Formations	The Battn was formed up in four forming up trenches each coy of the assaulting Coys on a two platoon frontage of 175 yds each, with one platoon in support and one in Company Reserve. No.3 Company acted as support to the two leading Coys company was in No.4 Company in Battn Reserve.

The first three waves of each Coy were moved in extended order. The 4th way [sic. wave] in sections.

No.3 Coy moved in Sections in Artillery Formation.

No.4 Coy moved in Platoons in Artillery Formation.

I would here call attention to the fact that although Nos. 3 & 4 Coys moved in what would appear to be close formations yet their losses while remaining in their formations was extremely small. Their losses really began when called into the final stages of the attack.

As this formation is more mobile and infinitely more under the control of their leaders it is one that might be adhered to on future occasions and the fact that they are not so vulnerable as would appear at first sight might with advantage be made known more widely known.

Touch was maintained from rear to front. The result was good especially as regards the 3rd & 4th Companies and saved permitted the leaders of the assaulting coys to devote all their attention to the forcing of the enemy's position, in addition to keeping the largest number of rifles in the front waves.

The vital responsibility of keeping touch with units on right and left remained with the leaders of the assaulting coys.

Right Attack   At 7.28 the Right Attack started to move out, Zero being 7.30. I considered this most necessary, as it had some distance to traverse before reaching the 1st Line German trenches. 2ndly in order to get straight on its first line of advance, it had to move half left before the right of the Company could rest on Bay Point. 3rdly Previous to the intense bombardment enemy machine guns had been particularly active and I wished to get the men through our wire whilst this bombardment continued. 4thly It seemed of vital necessity not to run any risks in being late for the prearranged barrage up to the Pommiers Redoubt.

As the machine gun fire even on cessation of intense bombardment was still very galling. The waves hurried through the gaps in the wire and <u>doubled</u> down the slope. It was on the gaps and the top of the slope that the machine gun fire was principally directed. There was practically none at the foot of the slope. Here the Right attack formed up in deliberate formation, making absolutely certain of its true line of advance. It then advanced as if on parade. The waves were perfectly dressed, intervals and distances as it seemed to me from our trenches, kept extraordinarily well.

The machine gun fire still continued very active and casualties were seen to occur before Austrian Trench was reached, but the waves still continued on their way, seemingly without a check.

Between the Austrian Trench & Emden Trench the Company was practically leaderless as regards officers, all having been either killed or wounded. There was practically no opposition except from machine gun fire. This principally came well away from our right flank which from the early commencement of the fight was most exposed owing to the Battn of the 53rd Brigade on our right being unable to advance at the same rapid rate as our right attack. Severe machine gun fire seemed to come from Poppof Lane, which did considerable execution. It was not until reaching the ground between Bund & Pommiers Trench that a real check occurred. Here the wire in front of Pommiers was not cut and a mixed party of the right attack with men of the Berkshire Regt proceeded to cut the wire in a most methodical way. In the words of Capt Bull in a letter to me. "The ½ hour outside that trench will be a nightmare for years to come and this was our expensive time. There were about 20 Berkshires & about the same numbers of my lot. [blank] were splendid, the way they cut the wire just as if there was nothing doing["].

---

1. The Comp. Sergt. Major of the right attack states that the German front line when he crossed it was filled with barbed wire around spiked stakes. From previous ~~experience~~ reports, which this statement confirms, it would appear as if the Germans hold only <u>parts</u> of the front line, ~~preferably~~ and those parts are defended with machine guns only. As their second line was so close and contained deep dug outs this method appears to be quite possible and has its advantages in the event of a sudden raid. The C.S.M. further states that the wiring and spikes seemed to have been recently put in. This may have been the case as a guard against our continual raids during the preliminary bombardment. The left of the right attack was held up by a machine gun in the right corner triangle, firing across front of right attack ~~but this~~ and was put out of action by the bombers of the left attack and by men of the right attack crawling up the right side of the triangle. ~~This gun was in~~

    I would here call attention to the close co-operation of the assaulting companies, from the triangle to the redoubt this was from all accounts most marked, resulting which enabled all engaged to keep to the timetable laid down. The right attack or in all events large portions of it arrived at Pommiers Redoubt roughly at 8.30 am.

As regards the actual storming of the Redoubt, this was carried out piecemeal, elements of B, C & D companies the latter having pushed in sections here and there, all taking part. It is quite clear that the front face was forced by parties swinging round to the flanks. Here many individual acts of great gallantry & devotion to duty were performed, as the German front trench which was held very tenaciously by the enemy was filled with their dead. Here too our losses were heavy, many of the dead lay round the front and flank of the redoubt. It is unquestionable that the Germans who remained in the Redoubt were either ordered or fully prepared to defend this last vital point in their line of defences to the last. ~~It is also. The attack~~ The fight at this point was therefore extremely obstinate and costly to both sides, for the redoubt was not in our hands entirely until roughly about 9.30 a.m. Our first elements having arrived at 8.30 a.m. which hour was the scheduled time. Before the Redoubt was taken men of all 3 coys had pushed on to the Maple Trench, which was subjected to a heavy shrapnel fire, and here it was that Captain Bull who had done splendid work, was wounded severely and had to retire.

Beetle Alley was next to be occupied, by that time, though platoons had been reorganized, and were under the control of very junior N.C.O.s the coys were still mixed ~~especially~~ This applied especially to the right attack whose losses had been very heavy in the taking of part of Pommiers Trench & the Redoubt.

Those that were left were used in bombing attacks along the Montauban Alley & the eastern part of Beetle Alley, and during the latter part of the day, were among those who occupied White Trench until the relief of the Battn on the morning of July 2nd.

~~To follow the account~~

From all reports from it would appear that the taking of the Redoubt was made by elements of all three companies and it is impossible to follow closely the operations of the right attack as such, from the time of their leaving the Pommiers Trench.

Left Attack The ~~purpose~~ left attack crossed our line wire on the stroke of zero. Then It was straight opposite its line of advance and as regards direction had not the same difficulties to contend with as the right attack. It has been difficult to get exact details of what happened to the first two waves. From observation it appeared as if the lines of both assaulting companies were moving on at exact intervals. From a sergeant who in the 4th wave who eventually took command of the Company it seemed to him that the 1st & 2nd wave became merged before reaching the Emden Trench. It is certain that the left attack passed quickly through our wire and doubled down the slope – reforming in the valley below. It is equally certain that their losses were heavier in the ~~earlier part~~ initial stages of the attack than the company on its right, for between Austrian & Emden a section of the company reserve had to be thrown in to make good a gap. Somewhere in the vicinity of Emden this part of the attack came under the German barrage but the men dashed through it suffering very few casualties, as they put it behind them. After Emden Trench the left attack was left without an officer. Between Bund & Pommiers the line became very ragged and there was some difficulty in keeping the formations as the fire was very heavy. The barrage on Pommiers Trench was so hot that the left attack pushed on and lay in the open beyond it and the Maple Trench.

Whilst waiting there this attack came under fire of machine guns & snipers. Men were laying in shell holes and any cover they could get, and there was again some considerable difficulty in reorganizing the line. Relief eventually came from the right which had got ahead of the left attack. For the latter were able to get at ~~the machine gun & snipers~~ those who were holding up the left. As

BATTLE REPORTS 181

the Germans fell back the left attack followed closely on them, and some made their way into the Redoubt and some outside. The bulk of the left only remained about 20 minutes in the Redoubt and being scattered had once more to be reformed in the open Here they and came under another barrage under shell fire which was avoided by their pressing on, but unfortunately they ran into our own barrage which compelled them to fall back. Thus they waited and on the barrage lifting rushed forward & took Beetle Alley without opposition at the place they entered it. Patrols were then pushed forward and the work on consolidation proceeded with.

~~What was left of C Coy~~ Those of the left attack who got into Beetle Trench apparently remained there, for from Emden Trench they were without officers, the company being under command of a sergeant.

It is to be regretted that no one either officer or N.C.O. who can could be relied on was left with the first three waves, for further details explaining the reasons of their losses and cause of their being behind the right attack ~~might~~ would have been of very great value, and a more concise view of the situation from the beginning obtained.

Supporting Company
This went over 2 minutes after zero. Its losses in parts were nil, for there was no machine gun fire at the time it crossed our wire. Their losses commenced at German 2nd Line Trench from a machine gun in the Emden trench brought up after first waves had passed from a dug out. This gun was actually put out by the 3rd Company. An officer was with it, who shot Sergt. Newton [corrected in the margin to Laughton] and was in turn killed just a second too late by Sergt.Slough. Between Emden & Bund Trench the right flank of the Fusiliers overlapped our left platoon. Before reaching Bund Trench all the officers of this Company were out of action. In the advance between Bund & Pommiers Trench, the Fusiliers eased off to their left leaving our front free, and here it was that a machine gun from left of Pommiers held up the ~~line~~ whole attack . It was being used on the parapet & moved about. This gun must apparently have been taken on by the Fusiliers for it stopped firing ~~and as one~~ for when the men rushed forward after being reinforced, they found heaps of ammunition but no gun. It was here that the elements of all three companies became mixed up, before taking the Redoubt and getting into Maple Trench. There is no doubt that the supporting company carried on those elements of B & C that had been severely handled. It is also quite certain that between the edge of Pommiers and Maple Trench certain parts of the line ran into our own artillery barrage and came under Heavy German barrage. ~~Our own fire ceased across~~ Flares were lighted, which were acknowledged by an aeroplane and five minutes afterwards our fire ceased. Here as far as possible elements of the Coys were reorganized and Sergt.Slough took charge of the 3rd Company. On reaching Beetle Trench bombing parties were organized and they proceeded to clear the eastern edge of same, while others went on with work of consolidation. About 4 pm parties of Fusiliers & Bedfords occupied the White Trench, the latter remaining until recalled on the morning of July 2nd

---

Reserve Company
Went through our wire at 7.40. This company came under quite a heavy barrage of shrapnel & machine gun fire. This latter seemed to come from direction of Black Alley. Half the losses of this company occurred while passing through the wire and two officers were put out of action before crossing our own fire trench. Times of reaching the German Trenches were as follows. Austrian Trench 7.50. Emden trench 7.55. Bund 8.20. Between Austrian Support & Emden a German barrage was encountered.

Company was reorganized in Bund Trench, leaving it at 9.15, and moved up towards Pommiers Trench. At 9.30 I gave orders while in the Δ for the Reserve to push through and make for final objective as word was brought that the Redoubt was taken.

Before reaching the Redoubt this company went through a 3rd Barrage. The statement of Capt.Percival on his arrival at Redoubt is as follows.

"On arrival at Redoubt, ~~there was~~ a great state of confusion reigned. Men of four different Battalions (Bedfords, Fusiliers, Essex & Berkshires) no officers and no N.C.O.s. As the Fusiliers were making for the Beetle Trench I at once sent forward 3 platoons under Lt.Colley, with instructions not to go beyond it until arrival of 53rd Brigade on our right flank. I then set about the consolidation of Redoubt and told off men of the 53rd Brigade into bombing parties to clean up Montauban Alley. At 10.15 there were no signs of the main attack of the 53rd Brigade. A strong party of Germans were holding Montauban Alley at this time. The first attempt to clear it was not successful but a fresh party of men of the Essex Regt & ~~Bedfordshire~~ accomplished the clearing of it by 2.30 p.m. About 3.30 pm the same platoon of the Essex Regt. cleared Montauban Alley as far as Loop Trench. About 6 pm the Norfolk Regt. made good the remainder of Montauban Alley. Our machine guns assisted very materially during the whole time by flanking fire. At 6.15 pm White New Trench was occupied by one platoon of Bedfords & 2 platoons Fusiliers. At 10 p.m. the construction of strong points S.W. of New Trench was commenced. At 10.30 covering party reported advance of Germans coming over ridge, these when fired on retired. The Coy was brought out of the line at 3.15 a.m.["]

The above is a description of what happened as far as can be gathered from the most trustworthy sources now available. Had the losses in officers ~~not been so very~~ & senior N.C.O.s not been so heavy further details would have been available.

On my arrival at the Redoubt the confusion mentioned by Capt.Percival was still very evident. My time of arrival was about 9.50.

Pommiers Lane was choked with men, principally 53rd Brigade, and I had considerable difficulty in thinning the men out as at any moment there was danger of heavy shell fire from the Germans.

The consolidation of our right flank especially was being rapidly put in hand, and was strongly held by Vickers & Lewis Machine Guns.

The situation at this time was ~~somewhat~~ critical. On the right the 53rd Brigade ~~we~~ seemed solidly held up with no signs of any advance of their main attack though considerable numbers of Essex & Berkshires had in some manner made their way into the Redoubt. Similarly on our left flank, the advance of the 91st Brigade had not made headway beyond Fritz Trench. The two assaulting Battns of the 54th Brigade had made good as far as Beetle Trench which was being consolidated. The Northampton Regt was close up in support. We were thus in a salient, on our right neither Montauban or Caterpillar Alleys were clear of Germans and there appeared to be heavy fighting in the direction of Montauban village. On our left Fritz Trench was held but to our left flank there was the wood of Mametz which might easily have harboured a large force for counter attack. Under the circumstances I deemed it more prudent to consolidate the positions already gained and to endeavour as far as possible to clear Montauban Alley in order to relieve the pressure on the 53rd Brigade.

The New Trench was therefore not truly occupied until our right flank had been made good, roughly about 6 pm though elements had reconnoitered it some time previously.

Strong points were at once put in hand at the places previously ordered.

The chief reasons of the success of the operations are in my opinion as follows.

1. The work of the artillery, with very few exceptions the wire was beautifully cut and the trenches filled up. The shooting was wonderfully accurate.

2. The training of the Battn at Picquigny. The time and attention to every detail that was carried out there was repaid a thousand fold. As an example I may quote that only three officers in the entire Battn got beyond Emden trench, most of the platoon and very many section leaders had gone, yet so thorough was the training beforehand that the men carried on entirely by themselves, knew where to go to and what to do when they got there.

3. The clear & concise orders that were received, nothing had been forgotten and provision made for all emergencies.

4. The good work done by the clearing up parties. The work done by the Northampton Regt was splendid and we had no shooting from behind. I would suggest that these parties, so absolutely necessary should be increased in strength.

5. The good work of the carrying up parties. In addition to those provided under Brigade arrangements, another party made up from odd men in the Battn about 30 in number, carried up with the 4th company a supply of SAA & bombs. This party then returned to the most advanced dump and continued during the whole day to keep the supply to maintain the supply. A large number of bombs were used in clearing Montauban Alley and without the supply furnished by this advanced party matters would have come to a standstill. They did most excellent work and never ceased carrying until a large stock of bombs & SAA had been accumulated.

I would suggest this advanced carrying party going with the 4th Company whenever possible.

6. The quickness with which the assaulting Battns left our Trenches. Where a prearranged timetable barrage is arranged, it seems imperative that the men should be quick off the mark. In the assault the two companies left previous our trenches before cessation of intense bombardment. They were thus able to take full advantage of the scheduled artillery barrage and consequently arrived at the Pommiers Redoubt at 8.30 a.m.

It would thus appear safer to risk a few casualties from our own guns than to miss the effect of the barrage and so come under the fire of enemy machine guns which are without doubt kept in dug outs until the barrage has stepped forward. This point has continually been insisted by all those who were in the first waves.

7. The close co-operation of all units in the assaulting waves. This was very marked, both between our two companies and the company of the Fusiliers on our left. With regard to the latter I can only s both at the Pommiers Trench and Redoubt they rendered most invaluable assistance at very critical times. Their help was very deeply appreciated and remarked on by the men of my Battn.

I would suggest also that in clearing Montauban Alley as far as the Loop Trench considerable assistance was given to the 53rd Brigade which enabled them to make good their final objective.

8. A sustained & continual advance.

This seems highly important and is exemplified in the taking of the Redoubt. Those immediately facing it were held up but ~~the outflanking~~ elements which outflanked it pressed on, made use of their bombers & machine guns all then killing or forcing the defenders to fall back. Those held up immediately pressed forward and allowed the lines to maintain their formations. An advance of this nature has no doubt a big effect on the morale of the enemy.

Communications   Though minute and detailed arrangements were made for visual signalling and communication by runners, neither were very successful. ~~The length of time taken in getting messages through was very~~ Messages took a very long time in getting through, and the varying aspect of operations could not be brought quickly enough to the notice of higher authority.

Perhaps some form of small portable wireless telegraphy might be arranged for in future operations

Losses

		Killed	Wounded	Missing	D of Wo.	
	Officers	2	13			= 15
	O.R.s	79	212	6	9	= 306

In conclusion I would bring to your notice the wonderful steadiness and coolness of all ranks under heavy shell and machine gun fire. As before mentioned from Emden Trench to the taking of the Redoubt the men worked practically without officers and the majority of their senior platoon & section commanders. A truly wonderful performance when it is taken into consideration that their training had not reached its second year.

Both during the preliminary bombardment, when the weather was very bad, and the men were living in trenches filled with water day and night and during and after making good their final objective, the cheeriness and high morale of all ranks was remarkable.

~~Where all did so well it is indeed difficult to bring forward the names of officers & men deserving of special recognition.~~ I would bring to your notice for special recognition the following names –

Capt. Bull – who led the right attack with conspicuous gallantry, until severely wounded at the Maple Trench.

Capt. Lloyd – who was in charge of the 3rd Company until very severely wounded at the Emden Trench.

Capt. & Actg. Adjt. Bridcutt – This officer was my right hand man during the previous to and during the assault. He took five German prisoners single handed – arr organized and led two bombing parties agst Montauban Avenue. He was tireless in seeing to the organisation of the strong points and arranging for the comfort of the men.

Lt. Benson. This officer never ceased in his exertions to ~~maintain~~ touch with keep up communications. The difficulty of keeping laying down wires was enormous, for the enemy shell fire was heavy and the wires were continually being cut. ~~His system of runners was very good but unfortunately the casualties among them were very heavy.~~ Six separate efforts were made by him personally to lay wires while exposed to this fire but without success, until it had to be abandoned.

Lt. Fleming Brown. This officer did remarkably good work ~~as machine~~ in charge of the machine guns. He personally superintended the placing of the machine guns in all strong points in the Redoubt, in Beetle Alley and in the New Trench. In addition he acted as orderly officer to me and rendered valuable assistance in letting me know the exact situation whenever it required clearing up.

The names of the officers, N.C.O.s & men were submitted for recognition in my [ends here].

I have the honour to be

Sir

2. Battle report of the assault on Thiepval and the Schwaben Redoubt, 26–28 September 1916

[C.O.'S REPORT – ACTION AT THIEPVAL AND SCHWABEN REDOUBT]

September 25th, 1916
Battalion moved from Varennes by route march to act as Brigade Reserve and was posted as follows: – A & B Companies – Battalion Hd. Quarters in North Bluff, C & D Companies in Thiepval Wood.

About 8 p.m. I left Battalion Headquarters to receive instructions from G.O.C. 54th Brigade. Before doing so, orders were issued for all Companies to stand by in a state of instant readiness.

The route to Thiepval had been reconnoitred as well as was possible during the day. The situation was very fully discussed and it was not until midnight of 26th–27th that orders were issued to companies to make their way to Thiepval and there await orders – as the situation demanded.

CD [27 Sep] 1.25 am – I left Brigade Hd.Quarters about 12.30 a.m. 27th. the companies had already started the crossing was quite a tiglish [sic] operation as the Boche had ringed Thiepval round with a very heavy Barrage of H.E. and shrapnel. The night was particularly dark, but all companies reached their objective with comparatively small casualties – A Company only suffered in this respect, B Company on the other hand had no casualty of any kind. I arrived at the Chateau sometime before the arrival of the Companies and so had time to confer with Col.Maxwell and get an idea of the general situation. It was as shewn on attached map [not attached]

The plan of the attack that was adopted on Col.Maxwell's knowledge of the ground was as follows.

Two companies to take over defensive line then held by men of all three Regiments of the 54th Brigade. This had to be done at night. The Companies to be drawn up in two lines, dividing the front 83-08 roughly between them. Thus as soon as day broke. 5.30 a.m. was given as a provisional zero hour. The whole area enclosed by 83, 34, 08, 19, 40 was to be stormed with one rush and cleared at the point of the bayonet.

The extremely difficult operation of getting the line into position was carried out under the guidance of Captain Johnson & Lt.Lubman, Royal Fusiliers. Too great credit cannot possibly be given to these Officers, as the night was extremely dark and the ground beyond all powers of description.

The time was also strictly limited as my first company did not arrive at the Chateau until the attack being arranged for dawn.

At 5.45 "C" Company was in position all ready to move. As it was getting light it started on the attack, without waiting for "D" Company on the left. "D" Company owing to greater difficulty did not get off the mark until 6.50 a.m. I attach a report of what happened sent us by Capt.Keep who was in command of the operations. It is very full and explicit. See attached report marked A. [not attached]. While this attack was being carried out the position of "A" & "B" Companies was as follows – "A" Company occupied their line 60-72 and had orders to occupy the trench 83 to 34 as soon as it was cleared by "C" Company and hold it at all costs in event of a counter attack by enemy. This was done and this Company remained on this line until further operations on 29th. [sic] "B" Company were in dug-outs in and around 72.

After giving the fullest credit to the skill shewn by Captain Johnson and Lt.Lubman of the Royal Fusiliers in getting the Bedfords into position I think that the carrying out of this extremely delicate operation to a successful issue deserves the highest praise. When it is taken into consideration that the Companies received their orders to move from Thiepval Wood and North Bluff at about midnight 26/27, that the route to the Chateau baffles all description, that they had to go through an extremely heavy barrage, without being rattled, that they then had to get into position immediately on arrival and attack an unknown and uneven terrain which they knew to be held by a determined enemy with machine guns – is rare proof that the discipline, determination and morale of the men was of a very high order. In my opinion the ensuing operations, successful though they were, in no way compares with those of the 26/27th.

The positions of Companies on this date was as follows: –
"A" 83 to 33 with blocking posts on Martins Lane, this latter handed over sector to Essex Regt.
B Dug-outs in and around Pt.72.
C Holding trenches: – 33-47-36-34-23 with bombing posts and stops 50 yds North of 47 & 36.
D. Holding German first line trench from 13 to 08.

Preliminary orders were received that the Battn was to be in readiness to assault and taken in conjunction with the 53 Brigade on our right the final objective – Probable Zero Hour 5 o'clock.

A conference of Officers was held, formation discussed and final orders issued.

The 5th Battn. West Yorkshire Regt. came up during the afternoon and were in reserve, north of the Chateau.

After the whole Battalion had got into position the orders for the attack were cancelled and companies got into their formed positions "B" Company relieving "C" Company as the former had been detailed as an assaulting Company. The 5th West Yorkshire Regt. hurried to its former position.

Sept. 28th – The attack postponed from previous day was carried out at 1 p.m. In order to conform with the barrage, bombing stops and the forward line previously held, were brought back on the line 34, 33, 43, 83.

A & B Companies were the assaulting companies and formed up on the line 34 to 83, their 4th line being between points 13-60.

"D" Company detailed as clearing up company formed up with the two assaulting companies.

"C" Company in support were formed up on the roads 67-19, two machine guns were detailed with supporting Company.

"A" Company 5 West Yorks was used as a Battalion Reserve with remaining 3 Coys in support of main attack.

The forming up by mid-day was an exceedingly difficult operation as the trenches in question were in full view of the enemy and the light was very good. It was however successfully carried out.

The Artillery barrage which opened at 1 pm was very effective, very little fire was met with until lifts occurred. The waves followed the Barrage very closely and went in beautiful formation until points 29 & 49 were reached.

"A" Company on the right made for the Cemetery and from thence to swing on to Market Trench but unfortunately, the right platoon got knocked right out by machine gun fire from Schwaben Redoubt before reaching Market Trench.

The whole line from here on appears to have commenced to lay to the left – partly forced there by pressure of the Queens on their right. The supports hereabouts joined the assaulting Companies, who were suffering severely from machine gun fire from R.19.c.

*From this point the Boches could be seen streaming away in full flight towards St.Pierre Divion along trenches 19-63-54 and towards 69.

*About 2.30 Captain K[eep] arranged with an Officer of the Queens to relieve him of trench 22-45 and his bomb stop in trench 45-19.

About 3 pm 22-45 was taken over by C.S.M.Brand who had with him men of "A" Coy and West Yorks the latter on the right.

Sergt.Patterson West Yorks held strong point 45 with a platoon of his men and the above mentioned bombing stop.

After arranging with the Queens officer, Captain K hurried back to point 86 and found that the party at 19 had fallen back towards 86 making a bombing stop half way up that trench. There was great confusion reigning at this time and the troops available had to be retold off. Men of the West Yorkshire Regt. under 2/Lt.Brawn were told off to hold the Line 19-86 with a bombing stop and line 19-63 while 2/Lt.Cartwright with 2 Lewis guns and a Stokes mortar gun was put in charge of a strong point 50 yds West of 86 on trench 86.4 This point was immediately counter-attacked, but as quickly driven off.

About 4pm the shortage of Mills bombs and ammunition was acutely felt. Boche bombs from dugouts were of immense value. The situation at this point was somewhat precarious. It appeared as if the Queens had failed to reach point 65 and to clear the dug-outs in second line trench from that point to point 45.

From 45 to 19 the situation was uncertain except that we held points 45 and 19 but the intervening trench had not been exploited. No bombs were available to do this work.

At 7.15 the clearing up of this trench 15-19 was taken in hand by a Platoon of D Company under Lt.D.Keep but was held up by strong resistance on the enemy's part and a lack of bombs, and it was not until 9.30 when bombs and reinforcements were sent up that Lt.Keep managed to win through and join hands with a party of the West Yorks who had been holding Pt.19 and had established bombing stops in and around Pt.39.

It was at 11.30 pm that the situation in the square 22, 45, 19, 86, 95, 13 was definitely held with bombing points round 39 and West of 86.

All night there were constant bombing fights north of Pt.45 the Boches coming out of their dug-outs in the 2nd Line. About midnight 28/29th the trench 45/19 was reinforced by men of "D" Company & West Yorks, as it appeared to be too lightly held.

In order to ensure that the men who were very weary were kept on the alert the square above mentioned was continually patrolled by 2 Officers in reliefs starting from 11.30 to 1 a.m. Capt.Colley & Lt.Keep 1 to 3 Lt.Brawn, C.S.M.Hall 3 to 5 Lt.Cartwright and C.S.M.Brand.

Point 39 was held all night but was lost about the time the relief took place – the Boche making a strong counter attack with bombs under cover of a smoke cloud. At 6 a.m. the West Kents relieved the Bedfords and the West Yorks, Lt.Keep taking "B" Coy R.W.K. up trench 86-19 with their right on 19 and Capt.Keep taking "C" Company R.W.K. along trench 13-22-45-19. On arrival at point 19 it was found 30 had been evacuated but a bombing point had been established along trench 19-39. Point 39 was held by bombers of the West Yorks under their Battn. Bombing Officer. Lt.Keep & 2/Lt.Brawn personally saw the relief & posting of sentries in both trenches 19-86, 45 to 19 with Officers from the R.W.K.

Capt.Keep did not leave the position until 9 a.m.

The attack on extreme left advanced very quickly as the bomb stops at 36 & 47 were left until just a few minutes before Zero. They had flanking bombing parties posted forward which proved to be invaluable.

The L.Guns advanced on left flanks through points 36, 29, 22.

Very few casualties or serious opposition until reaching points 29, 49, 72.

At 29 the Boche had a machine gun implacement covered by strong bombing party of some 40 men. The flanking bombing party was held up and had to wait until the dugout clearing party came to their assistance.

It was here the first three waves suffered losses – 2nd Lt.Adlam organised a strong party, told the men to cheer and they charged the strong point with him as leader, in one big rush, overbore all resistance and completely wiped out the enemy.

The Lewis Guns did great execution at this point. Two more strong points between 29 & 91 were taken at point of bayonet after a bomb preparation.

The situation hereafter became very difficult as it was impossible to recognise any trenches owing to the intensity of the Artillery preparation which had obliterated everything.

The final objective was almost impossible to locate accurately.

This may account for parties of men over reaching by far the final objective – some patrols pushing as far as 47 and 35.

The final objective was held early on in the day and the whole of the Boche front line by parties of Lancashire Fusiliers, Bedfords & West Yorks. until the two latter were withdrawn at dawn, 29th.

The whole of this operation was carried out with great dash, personal cases of daring bravery were very numerous.

The taking of strong points with a determined rush came off every time both on 27th & 28th.

The fact that there were two points numbered 45 led to great confusion and accounted for the lagging of the line away from what was after all the true objective viz. the Schwaben Redoubt.

The fact that the right of the right attack was blotted out by machine gun fire may have led to the Queens filling in the gap and causing them to lose their real line.

This loss of direction is to be regretted, but on the other hand the 54th Brigade certainly made its objective and held it until handed over to the R.W.K. As there seems to be some doubt on this point I attach statement from my Officers, who held points 19-45 and 86 [not attached]. I have described how it was won.

I was fully prepared to hold line won by us till day light or even later.

Considering the great difficulties and the continuous barrage communication though slow was good. The work done by all the runners of the Battalion was beyond all praise. They were run off their legs from Zero until day light next morning and yet were ready to go on.

As inevitable the question of water was one of extreme difficulty, by far the larger majority of the men fought on without fluid of any sort from Zero.

The courage, resolution & endurance displayed by all ranks was quite wonderful. They were out to kill and the Battlefield is a witness that they carried out to the full their intentions.

Even when the Battalion had been relieved by the R.W.K. and volunteers were called for in the event of a counter attack being successful on the ground they had so dearly won the preceding day, every man declared his willingness to return at once if needed.

I might mention the extreme need for more stretchers. The Regimental stretcher bearers were absolutely inadequate to cope with the numberless cases of all Regiments, some means might be devised to alleviate the sufferings of the wounded and perhaps save many valuable lives. As it was the stretcher bearers of every Battalion worked right through the night and into the morning still leaving many men untended, who might have been brought in were more bearers available.

During this attack Capt.Bridcutt who was observing the operations through a very excellent Boche periscope noticed that the Boches had run down the front and immediate [intermediate?] trench between 91 & 29 had lined their parados and shot into the left flank of the advancing troops. All available men consisting of servants, runners, signallers etc. were lined up in front of the Battalion Head Qrs and commenced rapid fire into the flank of the Boche doing great execution and causing them to retire hastily

3. Battle report of the assault on Glencorse Wood, 10 August 1917

From: Officer Commanding 7th (S) Battalion Bedfordshire Regt.
To: Headquarters 54th Infantry Brigade.

In accordance with B.M.465 I have the honour to forward herewith a brief account of the operations undertaken by the 7th (S) Bn.Bedfordshire Regiment on the 10th August 1917

13/8/17 J.H.Bridcutt, Major
Comdg 7th (S) Bn.Bedfordshire Regt.

On Y/Z night the Battalion was distributed as follows: one Company ("D" Coy Company Commander Capt.J.C.M.Ferguson) was holding the battle front, one Company ("A" Coy Company Commander Capt.R.J.Clark) was in close support sheltered in tunnel on MENIN road (about J.13.a.9.3) two Coys ("B" & "C" Companies Commanders Capt.H.Driver & Capt.O.Kingdon respectively) were quartered in the RITZ area (RITZ trenches).

Zero was fixed for 4.35 a.m. and all troops were to be in their jumping off position by 3.30 a.m.

At about 11.50 p.m. the first platoon of "B" Coy (left assaulting Coy) arrived at a point on the MENIN Road about J13.a.9.3. here they were checked by two Officers (Capt.W.J.W.Colley, Lieut.H.B.Stewart & the Regtl.Sergt.Major).

Each platoon was counted by one Officer.

Each man was given a cup of hot tea & Rum as he passed.

Each platoon Commander & Sergt. was handed copy of situation map.

Each platoon Commander given his guide to conduct him to SURBITON VILLAS.

The remaining platoons of the assaulting Companies "B" & "C" arrived at this point at about one or two minutes interval and were checked and passed as already described.

A Tape was laid previously from this point to SURBITON VILLAS (this tape was independent of the forming up tapes) along which each platoon moved and could not possibly miss their way.

As each platoon arrived at a spot near SURBITON VILLAS they were met by a platoon guide and the Company Commanders and were conducted to their battle formation – here they laid down in perfect quietness until the first note of the guns sang out.

"A" Company (the Company in immediate support) moved from their cover in the MENIN road tunnel by platoons to their place in battle formation, under the same arrangements as the assaulting Companies.

"D" Company (already in and holding the line) furnished a covering party (one platoon) who were posted about 150 yards in front of the forming up tapes, pieces of trench which were almost identical to their forming up position afforded this Company protection in case of

Bosche barrage being turned on; this they occupied, moving forwards to JARGON trench as previously ordered as the attack went forward.

THE BATTLE
The arrangements for forming up went without a hitch and at the appointed time (4.35 a.m.) the guns opened and the attack went forward in a most determined manner to the final objective which was reached at 5.13 a.m. Some 100-150 Bosches were in GLENCOURSE WOOD on the Battalion front and two machine guns, these were knocked out & the teams destroyed in such a rapid manner that any organised resistance by the Bosch was at once overcome and most of the Bosch that had not been killed at once cried "KAMERAD" and ran forward into our lines most of them wounded & fearfully frightened.

After the objective had been reached battle patrols were sent out & posts established in usual way, along the South Western end of NONNE-BOSSCHEN WOOD as near to the protective barrage as it was safe to get. (i.e. about 200 yards).

The Battalion then commenced to consolidate.

"A"–"B" + "C" Coys = front line "D" Coy – Reserve Coy = JARGON TRENCH and a Battalion carrying party was sent forward with S.A.A. and Lewis Gun drums etc.

During the day the Bosch made repeated attempts to form up & deliver what appeared to be a counter-attack of some strength, he was prevented time after time from doing so by rifle and machine gun fire, but owing to the expenditure of S.A.A. and the difficulty of replenishing same, care rose to anxiety and probability of our foremost line & right flank being overcome.

At this stage of the operation I considered it advisable if the position was to be held with any degree of certainty it required artillery support in the form of a few shots every few minutes on the only places the Bosch could use to form up under cover from view i.e. NONNE BOSSCHEN, INVERNESS & SOUTH WESTERN portion of POLYGON WOOD.

This was suggested over the telephone but so far as could be understood it could not be arranged, consequently it appeared to me & others at the front that it was a question of S.O.S. for Artillery or nothing at all. And this signal was repeatedly seen in the air at various points along the line but no S.O.S. was asked for by the 7th Bedfords until towards the evening when it was too obvious that the Bosch intended to have a final struggle to get back the ground we held, as troops were seen emerging from each of the three woods above mentioned, and a dense cloud of smoke & gas was being sent over which obscured everything from view. At this time I cannot state the exact clock hour the artillery opened and with terrible execution, but the Bosch line came on delivering their attack on the right flank of the Battalion.

The advanced posts were either killed or captured, it is impossible to say which, but judging from the very intense barrage which the Bosch rolled over GLENCORSE WOOD they were undoubtedly killed, a certain amount of confusion set in on our right and it was only by firm determination that the strong point at J.14.a.4.2. which I had taken over from the right Battalion (11th Royal Fusiliers) and JARGON TRENCH was held.

When the attack was fully developing re-inforcements (two Coys) of the Royal Berkshire Regt arrived and were sent forward to hold our original front line in case the Bosch succeeded in his object to gain the strong point and high ridge STIRLING CASTLE – STRONG POINT J 14.a.4.2. – JARGON TRENCH.

The attack however did not materialise and only his advanced line got near the position. The situation quietened down and the relief of the Battalion by the Royal Berkshire Regt was carried out by 2 A.M. and the Battalion withdrew to CHATEAU SEGARD.

Established line handed over was JARGON TRENCH – LADY'S LEG – STRONG POINT J14.a.4.2. Situation of forward posts was somewhat obscure.

It us worthy of record the splendid manner in which the two Coys of the Royal Berkshire Regt came up to re-inforce.

The Bosch had a terrific barrage on the support line through which they travelled without a waver, shells falling into and all round each platoon. Major Longhurst of this Regt. arrived in advance of these two Coys and rendered most valuable assistance in establishing a second line of defence in case of necessity.

Lessons

1. I venture to think had a fresh Battalion been close at hand when the situation on the right became obscure and pushed in, in attack formation a good deal more ground would have been taken and the Boche routed from his position.

2. Artillery should not cease firing on protected lines until Battalion Commander is satisfied all is well. Artillery ceased on the 10th without any reference to Battalions (at least not to 7th Bedfords). I consider it of great importance that Battalion Commanders should be able to convey to Artillery which fire other than S.O.S. is required.

3. No telephone wire to be laid beyond Brigade HQ as it is used for all kinds of things that hopelessly give away arrangements, and too many other ranks have access to it and the Commanders of the sector having no knowledge of many things happening on the wire unless he or his Adjutant sits by it. The telephone was a nuisance and not the least assistance to the Battalion on the 10th inst.

4. It took from 5 to 6 minutes before the Hun Barrage got really going on our lines, it was severe when it did do so.

5. The 54th Brigade arrangements for ordering up the reserve Coys from RITZ area and the Coys for mopping up was excellent, timing was also extremely good.

6. To avoid any Platoon going astray I placed Battalion Police posts 100–200 yds apart along the ATN track from RITZ area to MENIN road passing point.

7. Our own Artillery inflicted many casualties on our troops by firing very short what appeared to be one 8″ gun in particular.

8. The Boche attack was guided by a line of his men at a few paces apart firing very lights, during the advance these were with the first wave.

Appendix B3. Congratulatory Telegrams

1. 30 April 1916

COMPLIMENTARY ORDER.

At the request of the General Officer Commanding 54th Infantry Brigade, the Commanding Officer has great pleasure in notifying to all ranks the Communique published in the "Times" of April 29th 1916 which referred to the recent raid.

"Last night the Bedfordshire Regiment carried out a very successful raid near CARNOY. The raiding party rushed the trenches and after fierce hand to hand fighting drove the remaining Germans into their dugouts and bombed them there. Our casualties – eight wounded, all brought in. German loss considerable."

The General Officer Commanding 54th Infantry Brigade is of opinion that in publishing the name of the Regiment in the newspaper, which up to now has scarcely ever been done, a high honour has been conferred on the Battalion.

The British Communique has also been published in all French papers.

2. 1 July 1916

From Fourth Army:

In wishing all ranks good luck the Army Commander desires to impress on all Infantry units the supreme importance of helping one another and holding on tight to every yard of ground gained. The accurate and sustained fire of the Artillery during the bombardment should greatly assist the task of the Infantry.

3. 1 July 1916

From XIII Corps:

General CONGREVE wires – Please convey to all units my intense appreciation of their splendid fighting which has attained all asked for from them and resulted in heavy losses to the enemy, nearly 1000 prisoners have already passed through the cage.

From General MAXSE to 18th Division (in continuation of above)

Well done; it's what I expected; now hold on to what you have gained so splendidly

4. 2 July 1916

From Fourth Army:

Following message received from 18th Div. Begins

Following received from Fourth Army – "please convey to 18th Division my best congratulations and thanks for their dashing attack yesterday. They have done excellent work and I desire to thank them most heartily."

5. 5 July 1916

It is difficult for the Commanding Officer to add to the great praise bestowed on the Battalion by the higher commands. While we all deplore the loss of our brave comrades fallen in the great fight, the knowledge that the Battalion won its objective in spite of stubborn resistance ~~encountered~~ and with such steadiness, determination and gallantry, is a great compensation for those who have fallen on the slopes of the POMMIERS REDOUBT.

It is a great honour to command a Battalion which has shown such fine fighting qualities and the Commanding Officer, in tendering his heartfelt thanks to Officers, Non-commissioned officers and men, feels sure that whenever called upon the Battalion will live up to the high reputation it has earned on the field of battle.

6. 10 July 1916

Following message received from 18th Div. Begins:

Commander in Chief desires his warm congratulations conveyed to XIIIth Corps for their good work and especially to 30th Division for gallant defence of TRONES WOOD yesterday and last night by 90th Brigade against such heavy counter-attacks. XIII Corps has not only captured all its objectives including many strong and important positions against all hostile efforts to retake them [sic]. This is a record to be proud of. Such performances lead to certain & complete victory

7. 22 July 1916

Fourth Army

The part which the 18th Division has taken in the battle of the SOMME reflects the highest credit on every Officer, Non Commissioned Officer and Man, and I desire to tender to one and all my gratitude and congratulations.

The gallantry and determination displayed in the assault of the enemy's first system of defence, together with the night attack on, and final capture, of TRONES WOOD, were feats of arms which will rank amongst the best attainments of the British Army. Nothing could have been finer than the behaviour of those men of the West Kent Regt. who held their position throughout the night when surrounded by the enemy at the Northern end of the wood.

The heavy fighting in the village of LONGUEVAL and DELVILLE WOOD in which portions of the Division were engaged was an example of discipline, valour, and endurance which was wholly admirable.

It is with great regret that I hear the Division is to be transferred to another Army and I trust at some future time I may be honoured by again having it under my command.

8. 26 September 1916

Telegram from Lieutenant General C.W.Jacob C.B., Commanding IInd Army Corps

To 18th Division

Corps Commander wishes to thank you and all ranks of your Division for their admirable work today. Thiepval has withstood all attacks upon it for exactly 2 years and it is a great honour to your Division to have captured the whole of this strongly fortified village at their first attempt. Hearty congratulations to you all

9. 27 September 1916

Personal congratulations of General Sir Douglas Haig G.C.B., G.C.V.O., K.C.I.E., Commander-in-Chief British Armies in France.

The Commander-in-Chief personally called today on General Maxse to congratulate the Division on its success at Thiepval.

10. 28 September 1916

The Corps Commander again thanks and congratulates all ranks of 18th Division on further gallant and successful work today. He specially commends the good organisation, training and Staff work displayed and the methodical and determined manner in which all orders and plans have been carried out and all prearranged objectives reached and consolidated.

11. 28 September 1916

Telegram from General Sir H.de la P.Gough K.C.B. Commanding Reserve Army

Congratulate you very heartily on success of today's attack as well as of previous operations. Reflects greatest credit on you and your troops.

12. 28 September 1916

Telegram from General Sir Herbert C.O.Plumer G.C.M.G., K.C.B., Commanding Second Army

Many congratulations to you and your Division from Commander & Staff Second Army

13. 3 December 1916

The Corps Commander congratulates all ranks who took part in the operations of the 18th ult on the successful results attained.

That the 18th Division has once again gained a success is only what the Corps Commander expected of a Division which has for so long been consistently successful in all the operations it has undertaken.

14. 31 October 1917

The XVIII Corps Commander sends his hearty congratulations on the success of the 18th Division on the 22nd instant. He adds that this success was gained in spite of bad weather, bad mud and hot artillery fire, and that all concerned deserve great credit from highest to lowest.

A.E.Percival, Major a/Brigade Major

15. 27 March 1918

The following letter has been received from Monsieur le General BREGARD, Commanding 1st Division, Dismounted Cavalry: –

"During the Operations of the 24th/25th March, the 18th Division with two Brigades of Artillery, commanded by General LEE has been put under my orders.
With regard to this, I wish to bring to your notice the splendid attitude and the brilliant bearing [of] the 54th Brigade and the 8th and 83rd Artillery Brigades.
I wish to bear testimony to the perfect "camaraderie" which those General Officers and their units placed under their commands have never ceased to show, as also to the superb bearing of their troops.
It is thanks to their splendid and dogged defence that I have been able to free on my right a situation often difficult, especially at the time of retirement on to the South Bank of the Oise on the night of 25th/26th March."

sd C.BRECARD

(Translated from French)

16. 3 April 1918

Dear Colonel

I am enclosing you the result of the operation yesterday evening. I cannot express to you my admiration for the determination, and gallantry displayed by your Battalion. Although the attack made by your Regiment was unable to make headway in the face of overwhelming Artillery and Machine Gun Fire, the manner in which they held their ground is beyond praise and drew the whole of the enemy's strength, so that the troops co-operating on your left were able to get on to the objective. The Northamptonshire Regt. have pushed up on the right, and the whole objective is now in our possession. I mourn with you, for the loss of so many gallant Officers and men, which I fear was inevitable in so stiff an engagement. I hope you will convey to all ranks under your Command, the information that all the objective has been gained, and this is entirely due to their magnificent steadiness and behaviour in the face of overwhelming odds in artillery and machine guns. I hope you will convey the contents of this letter to all ranks in your Battalion The Northamptonshire Regiment have now direct observation on AUBERCOURT.

Yours very truly

sd/ L.W.SADLEIR JACKSON,
Brigadier General
3.4.18 Commanding 54th Infantry Brigade

17. 5 April 1918

18th Division No.G.563
Following message received from XIX Corps:-

"Please accept on your behalf and that of all ranks of the 18th Divn my heartiest congratulations on the splendid work done by the Division since joining the Nineteenth Corps. The results achieved by the fine fighting spirit and powers of endurance displayed have been of the greatest importance and I am most grateful to all concerned:

Lieutenant General Commanding XIX Corps"

Appendix B4. Battlefield Walks

Introduction

Walking the battlefields of the First World War is a popular pastime encouraged by a number of very good and detailed guides which have been published in the last few years. A large part of the attraction is that in many areas the landscape now is little different to the way it was in 1914. In compiling these walks I have been able to blow up modern French Série Bleu 1:25000 maps to the same scale as the First World War Trench Maps and have found that the course of most of the roads now is exactly the same as then. Even many of the woods are the same size and shape. This makes pinpointing spots where certain actions took place comparatively easy.

The Somme, in particular, seems almost untouched by the last eighty years or more. It was originally intended by the French government to turn the wasteland into a National Forest, as was done with the Verdun battlefield. However, the returning locals beat them to it and quickly began replacing their smashed houses and farms, replanting shattered woods and mending broken roads. It is a blessing for the amateur historian and battlefield walker that they did. Because this corner of France remains rural and traditional, still an agrarian culture which has not experienced any kind of economic boom to attract many immigrants from other areas of France, the landscape remains much the same. This is true, also, of Chérisy, though the areas closer to Arras have begun to disappear under roads and industrial estates. The entire area around Ypres is quite different. There has been extensive development here in the last two decades or so as is evidenced by the brand new housing estate on the site of Jargon Trench and Glencorse Wood and the amusement park in the area just behind Surbiton Villas.

The areas of the 7th Bedfords' major battles are, by and large, pleasant if unspectacular. I have walked each of them myself, as the photographs demonstrate, and one can do anything from simply driving around the area to quite strenuous walks. Perhaps the most satisfying thing to do is to walk them in combination with visits to other areas of interest, the Thiepval Memorial, Newfoundland Memorial Park or Museum des Abris in Albert, while on the Somme, for example, or the Menin Gate and Cloth Hall Museum in Ypres or Tyne Cot Cemetery in Passchendaele whilst in that vicinity.

The soil on the Somme is heavy clay, overlying chalk, and that of Ypres and its surrounding area can still be as wet as in 1917, so good walking boots and old trousers are thus essential! The walks can all be achieved by sticking to main roads and tracks to avoid trespassing on private land. Finally, you should be careful not to go near any unexploded ammunition. This tends to get piled up by the sides of roads, particularly during the ploughing and harvesting seasons and can be very unstable. The French and Belgian armies have specialist bomb squads who destroy it under safe conditions.

1. Attack on the Pommiers Redoubt, 1 July 1916

See Figs 1 and 2, Plates 10, 11 and 12
Some parts of the Somme battlefield are much visited – Thiepval, the Newfoundland Memorial Park and the area of the Pals' Battalions attacks around Serre, for example. The scene of the 7th Bedfords' first battle is in a little visited area and consists of open, rolling fields in and around the Vallée de Carnoy.

This walk is best done in two distinct phases, which may be taken in any order, but which I did in chronological order, so to speak. If arriving at the battlefield by car it is easy to park by the side of the road, so long as you do not block any tracks and leave sufficient room for tractors to get past.

The positions of the 7th Bedfords on the morning of 1 July are best reached by taking the minor road south-west out of Montauban towards Carnoy. You will need to find the track (which is metalled where it meets the road) about two thirds of the way along the road on the left. It is almost opposite a track on the other side of the road. Follow this track to the point where it makes a right angled turn to the left and keep walking. At the point where the track dips south-east, or a few metres away, was the crater of the Casino Point Mine. As the illustration at Fig. 2 shows, the 7th Bedfords' positions were about half way along this track as you head towards the minor road from Carnoy to Mametz. Their actual starting positions were a little way to the north-west of the track which was bisected by the British front line running roughly east-west. As you walk along you will see that the Vallée de Carnoy is surprisingly deep and its sides comparatively steep. It is important to remember that the German front line angled sharply away from this track which it touched in the vicinity of Casino Point Mine so that by the time the 7th Bedfords' positions were reached there was quite some distance to cross.

It is now best to return to your car, drive to the outskirts of Carnoy and take the road to Mametz. Again look for a track opening off the road on the right, park the car and follow this track. This runs along the other side of the valley bottom from the 7th Bedfords' positions, which you will see as you walk along (though the ground is fairly featureless, contours apart, so it may be best to fix the Bedfords' positions in your mind by their relationship to quite temporary features you may spot such as heaps of vegetables, earth etc.!). After a while you will come to another track leading left and this is the area of The Triangle which contained the machine gun which caused serious casualties during the advance and which became the temporary Battalion Headquarters in the later stages of the day. Walk on to the point where the next track leads off left and take this track. A few yards along the track was the meeting point of Poppoff Lane and Pommiers Trench. As you continue on, you are now more or less following in the footsteps of 7th Bedfords as they attacked towards the Pommiers Redoubt, the southern face of which lay at right angles to this track a few yards from the D64 Mametz-Montauban road. It is thought provoking to stand on the line of the Pommiers Redoubt and look back towards the Bedfords' position to see just how far they had come, under heavy shell and machine gun fire.

But they had further to go. You can cross the road and look north to see the approximate furthest point their advance reached and then either retrace your steps or walk along the road towards Mametz, stopping at Dantzig Alley British Cemetery, where a large number of the 7th Bedfords are buried (including Sergeant George Laughton who is mentioned in Colonel Price's report of the battle), entering Mametz and turning right along the road to Carnoy to reach your car.

Alternatively, you can walk along the road towards Montauban and take the first track which opens out on the left. Taking this you will cross both Montauban Alley and Beetle Alley before reaching a T junction where the track splits both left and right. You are now more or less on the line of White Trench and a few metres north in the field is the final extent of the Bedfords' gains on that day. Walking this you will appreciate what a feat it was to fight across this terrain during a hot July day (the temperature that day was recorded as 72°F but that would have been in the shade!).

You will now need to retrace your steps to the D64 and either take the return route via Mametz or return the way you came.

2. Capture of Thiepval, 27 September 1916

See Figs 3 and 4, Plate 13
The fields around the tiny village of Thiepval are some of the busiest on the entire battlefield. There always seems to be someone visiting the majestic Memorial to the Missing and others visit the Mill Road and Connaught Cemeteries and the Ulster Tower. The Memorial is dedicated to all those British and South African officers and men who died on the Somme before March 1918 but have no known grave. There are around 72,000 names carved on the pillars that support the monument and it would be terrible enough if these represented the total crop of those killed. What makes a visit here truly sombre is the knowledge that the roll here does

not include all those buried under named headstones in all the cemeteries round about, or Canadians, or Australians or New Zealanders; or indeed French or Germans. There are a number of names on the Memorial that will be familiar to those who have read the 7th Bedfords' War Diary, particularly the sections dealing with the fighting just a few hundred yards away in Thiepval itself and around the Schwaben Redoubt. These include Second Lieutenant I.H.M.Ross-Taylor and Second Lieutenant Herbert Merchant from Luton as well as those mentioned in Lieutenant Cartwright's diary such as his platoon sergeant Leonard Hill and Private William Humphrey.

The Thiepval Memorial is the best place to park to see both the area of the capture of Thiepval on the 27th and the attack on the Schwaben Redoubt the next day. You should make for the church and then the crossroads of D73 (Hamel-Pozieres) and D151 (Authuille-Grandcourt). You should stand with your back to the church and look out towards Mill Road Cemetery which you will see in the distance. Before the War Thiepval was much bigger than it is now (lack of readily accessible water has kept numbers low) and the field immediately in front of you was covered in houses which, of course, by September 1916 were smashed to the ground. As you will see from the sketch map, the Bedfords were facing much the same direction as you, though their line was some yards in front of you. The left flank of D Company cut the road down to Hamel, Mill Road and Connaught Cemeteries and Ulster Tower and the right flank of C Company cut the road towards Grandcourt and the farm you can see about a quarter of a mile away (La Grande Ferme).

The field itself is now featureless and so you will need to imagine the trenches as they are shown on the trench maps but it was here that 52 men of the Battalion died in that short but desperate action to clear the village at bayonet point and push the front line some way towards the Schwaben Redoubt which occupied a large part of the crest of the slope in front of you. It was here too that Tom Adlam did so much of the good work that won him his Victoria Cross. His platoon, part of D Company, was held up by heavy machine-gun and rifle fire. Realising that time was of the essence, Adlam rushed from shell hole to shell hole gathering his scattered platoon for a charge. Whilst doing this he collected a number of grenades and was wounded in the leg. Adlam had been a keen cricketer and had a good arm for throwing in from the boundary. He used this, in throwing the grenades he had captured, to out throw the enemy, peppering their positions. He then led a charge on the German position which captured it and killed the occupants. He continued to lead his platoon for the rest of the action.

3. Attack on the Schwaben Redoubt, 28 September 1916

See Figs 5 and 6, Plates 14, 15 and 16
Standing in the same place as you stood to see the area of the attack of 27 September you will see Mill Road Cemetery on the slope in the distance, with the top of the Ulster Tower some way behind. This cemetery lies on what was the axis of advance of the 7th Bedfords on 28 September, indeed Point 84 is now the northern corner of the cemetery itself. All the slope between the cemetery and the road towards La Grande Ferme was a maze of trenches, with deep dugouts beneath which constituted the Schwaben Redoubt and its outer perimeter. The dugouts and underground tunnels are still there, causing the ground to be unstable, necessitating some tombstones in Mill Road Cemetery to be laid flat instead of their normal, upright position. From here it will be seen how skilfully the Germans had used the lie of the land to their advantage and, as you walk further towards the area of the Redoubt itself, that will become even more apparent.

The best way to see how the land lies and to follow what happened is to take the following route with the sketch maps and the War Diary account in hand. Walk up the D151 towards Grandcourt and La Grande Ferme. You will see that the battalion was facing the same direction as you and that you are walking down their right flank. C Company, in support, was lined up roughly along the D73 towards Mill Road Cemetery. After a hundred yards or so you come to the positions of reserve platoons of A, B and D Companies. Carrying on you will see the village cemetery in front, with a footpath branching off left from the road at about 45 degrees. The front line positions of A, B and D Companies were some yards on the Thiepval side of this turning as the sketch map shows.

The position of the village cemetery is very useful for orientation as the cemetery has not moved and shows as plainly on modern maps as on the trench maps of the time. The track you are about to follow heads towards St Pierre Divion and, before 1914, was much more important than it is now.

As you head along the St Pierre Divion track you go uphill, then enter a dip before climbing uphill again. As you can see from the sketch maps you will cross both Market Trench and Price Street before reaching the area of the Redoubt proper. The 7th Bedfords' attack was conducted partly in the open, as the machine-gun casualties received by A Company from the Schwaben Redoubt just after leaving the area of the Civilian Cemetery make clear. However, much of the attack was conducted up the German trenches leading towards the Redoubt.

To determine the extent of the 7th Bedfords' advance here on the right perhaps the easiest thing to do is to look across to Mill Road Cemetery. When the right-hand wall of the cemetery (as you look at it) running NE-SW (i.e. towards Connaught Cemetery and the D73) appears to run directly away from you, then you will have more or less reached the point at which the Bedfords' advance was ended and consolidated. Their right flank lay roughly on the track and their left ended some way short of Mill Road Cemetery. As you can see, you have a wonderful view of the Ancre Valley looking towards Hamel and Beaumont Hamel, emphasising the wonderful placement of the Redoubt.

It would be best, before leaving, either to retrace your steps to you car and drive down to the two cemeteries or to walk back to the crossroads and walk down to them on foot. Connaught Cemetery is on the road itself and the path up to Mill Road Cemetery lies opposite. A number of the Shiny Seventh are buried in each cemetery including, in Connaught Cemetery, Lieutenant Cartwright's batman, Private Frederick Dorrell, and at Mill Road Lieutenant Robert Hunston, Second Lieutenant Thomas Wilson, William Andrews from Luton, a lance corporal at age seventeen, and Second Lieutenant Cedric Howard from Bedford, about whose death Cartwright writes so movingly. The walk up to Mill Road Cemetery is worth it to look back at the line of advance of the left flank of the 7th Bedfords who moved through here to a point just past the Ulster Tower and some way to its right – Point 47 – overrunning the objective by some distance before falling back to the line eventually consolidated. Take a look back towards the crossroads near the church. About a third of the way from Mill Road Cemetery to the crossroads was Point 29 which was taken at a rush by a party under Tom Adlam which, combined with his feats the day before in the final capture of Thiepval, earned him his Victoria Cross. Finally, Cartwright's post lies just a few yards from the north-west corner of the Cemetery.

4. Attack on Achiet le Grand, 13–17 March 1917

See Fig 7, Plate 17

If Thiepval is one of the most visited places on the Somme battlefield, the ground of the 7th Bedfords' attack on Achiet le Grand must be one of the least frequented. This is, in large part, due to the fact that it did not form part of the Battle of the Somme, occurring, as it did, in March 1917 as the Germans fell back to the Hindenburg Line. Consequently, it does not figure in any guide book.

However, in spite of this, the battlefield is a very rewarding place to visit as it is just as it would have been at the time. Indeed, the absence of other people is refreshing, giving one time to think about what happened here. I visited it early on an April morning, with a heavy frost on the ground and blue sky above and found the loneliness of the spot and the silence, broken only by the forlorn cry of the curlew and the occasional lark, helped bridge the river of years that lay between those different mornings in a way I have seldom experienced.

The general area is easy to find but the battlefield itself is easy to miss. It is important to drive along the D163 between Irles and Grévillers. If driving from Irles you are looking for the second track on the right after the cemetery, a distance of over a mile. If driving from Grévillers the track is the second on the right. The Série Bleu maps show the track as a road, but it is only a track and so easy to miss. This track leads to the area described in the War Diary as the Star Roads, the area where five ways intersect. As you turn off the D163 you are more or less on the right flank of the 7th Bedfords' position consolidated on the evening of 13 March after their advance. It was from here that C Company attacked the sunken road after dark on 13 March, occupying it in the early hours of the next day. To reach the sunken road, move up the track to the point where the tracks all converge and the sunken road will be very obvious as the first road on the left. The road sinks from a few inches below the bank to eight feet or more down, forming a kind of natural trench and C and D Companies occupied the whole stretch of it from the crossroads to the railway line. Given that each Company would have been around 150–200 strong you can see that they were quite extended. This would have been even more pronounced when just one Company, D, took over the whole line on the evening of 14 March.

The abortive attack on the Bihucourt Line by C Company on 15 March would have taken place with the men scrambling up the bank of the sunken road and heading directly towards Achiet le Grand which you will see in front. Doing this today leaves one feeling very exposed on the shallow slope and one can see how the attack failed in the face of determined opposition. It is possible to envisage C Company digging-in around 200 yards down the slope and spending a very uncomfortable and dangerous time before being withdrawn in the early evening under cover of darkness. In some ways it is surprising that only 17 men were killed. It was during this attack that the 7th Bedfords won their second and last Victoria Cross of the war, a fact not mentioned in the War Diary.

As C Company attacked and began to suffer heavy casualties, Private Christopher Augustus Cox from King's Langley [Hertfordshire], a stretcher bearer with B Company, which was in reserve, went over the top and, ignoring the shell and machine-gun fire, single-handedly rescued four men. The War Diary does not note any attacks other than that by C Company, but the neighbouring battalion was also attacking because Private Cox also rescued a number of men belonging to it. His Commanding Officer, Lieutenant R.J. Clarke noted in the citation: "Heedless of the fire Private Cox went from shell hole to shell hole and bound the wounded up and after he had finished with them started back with another man, with the most severe case. For the first 200 yards he was under MG fire, but without hesitating once he completed his journey and I saw him come back for a second load a few hours later." Private Cox was a very strong man as well as a very brave one, as he would have needed to be for such work.

The successful attack on Achiet le Grand took place two days later on 17 March. The attack saw C Company go, once more, down the slope in front of you. This time Achiet was taken and the furthest limit of the village reached. Meanwhile, B Company occupied the railway line as a defensive flank from the sunken road right up to Achiet le Grand. By returning to the five way crossroads referred to as the star roads from the sunken road one should take the first left as you approach it and walk or drive along the track into Achiet to give some idea of the distance the attack went. On reaching the first road on the right on the outskirts of the village and looking along it a hundred or so yards you will see where Battalion Headquarters was established. Eventually, the Battalion occupied the northern and eastern edge of Achiet as well as the railway line leading back to the sunken road. Again, this shows how extended the line was and there must have been considerable gaps between men or between platoons. It is interesting to note that this attack on 17 March only produced one death in action, Private William Rowell from Sawtry (Huntingdonshire) who is buried in Achiet le Grand Communal Cemetery along with nine others from the attack two days earlier. This surprising lack of casualties on 17 March, together with Lieutenant Cartwright's description of the battle as "a picnic affair which I was sorry to have missed" shows that the Germans were in retreat towards their Hindenburg Line positions some way further east and so had decided, some time after the attack on 15 March, not to defend Achiet le Grand with any vigour.

5. Attack on Chérisy, 3 May 1917

See Figs 8 and 9, Plate 18
Like Achiet le Grand, Chérisy is an area little visited by First World War buffs. It is set in quietly attractive countryside and the battlefield may be driven, if desired, saving tired feet. It is an easy battlefield to understand.

To find the battlefield it is important to use the right set of roads and tracks, since there are any number in the area. Perhaps the best thing to do is to approach Chérisy northwards from Fontaine-les-Croisilles along the D9. Before you enter the village you will reach a crossroads like an inverted Y of which you are on the right most fork. Go straight on and a little way along you will see a small road on your left. Take this and follow it for some distance until you see a crucifix. A little way after the crucifix a road opens out on the right. Ignore this and a little way further on a metalled track opens out on the left. Take this as it runs parallel to the 7th Bedfords' front line, which was on the reverse side of the slope on your right.

Continue along the track until you come to a dirt track on your left. This leads straight down towards the 7th Bedfords' objective. Take this track and you are advancing with the 7th Bedfords, in the face of heavy shell and machine-gun fire. To your right you will see a line of straggly bushes. These mark the rough position of Wood Trench, from where the infamous tank cut across the advance, throwing it into disorder.

Fontaine Trench, where the wire remained uncut, ran along the slightly raised contour near the end of the track where it joins the road, as the sketch plan shows. Imagine small groups of the Bedfords lying in front of this in shell holes all day. The furthest point reached by a small group of the Battalion was somewhere in the field to your right.

The first objective, never reached, of course, lies in front of you across the road from Fontaine along which you came and across another road beyond that. As you can see, to advance this distance across uncut wire in the face of determined opposition was asking the impossible, a similar position to that faced by most British battalions on the first day of the Somme some ten months earlier.

6. Attack on Glencorse Wood, 10 August 1917

See Figs 10 and 11, Plate 19

Of all the 7th Bedfords' battlefields, Glencorse Wood is the most disappointing to the modern visitor. This is because the Ypres area is growing and, within the last five years, a small housing development has been built right on Jargon Trench and Glencorse Wood behind it. The visitor will find that they will not spend very much time at the site and so it is best incorporated into a day doing more satisfying things such as visiting the Menin Gate, Hill 60 or Tyne Cot Cemetery.

At least the site is easy to find, as the map shows. The site is just off the famous Menin Road (now the N8). It is best approached from Ypres as this was the direction of the Third Battle of Ypres and you will be following the British troops forward. The road you need is just after the Bellewaarde Amusement Park which is on your left. Take the road to the left as shown in the sketch map and then the first road again on you left. Surbiton Villas is just behind you and you are looking along the 7th Bedfords' line as they drew up for the attack, C Company nearest to you and B Company further on, its flank resting, roughly, on the road to the left leading back in the direction of the Amusement Park.

The attack was made straight across the field on your right as you travel up the road, towards Jargon Trench. The line of this trench is marked, roughly, by the line of the modern development. Glencorse Wood lay behind.

If you turn around and head back to the junction and turn left (i.e. on the minor road leading towards the modern housing estate) you will be, more or less, following the extreme right flank of C Company's advance. About three quarters of the way to the housing estate, roughly on the road, would have been the strong point referred to in the battle report and shown on the sketch plan. Remember that 11th Royal Fusiliers, on your right, failed in their attack and formed a defensive flank from the corner of Glencorse Wood in front of you, diagonally back towards Clapham Junction (for which see below).

As you drive past the housing estate you will be driving along the southern edge of Glencorse Wood and, when another estate is reached, you will be at the southern edge of Nonne Bosschen, as shown on the sketch plan. The 7th Bedfords penetrated some distance into this Wood before suffering a heavy counterattack by the Germans towards dusk. This attack was successful in pushing the Bedfords, reinforced by two companies of Royal Berkshires, back to Jargon Trench, but was held there.

Retrace your steps to the Menin Road and turn left towards Menin. The obelisk on the right side of the road is to the memory of the 18th Division, including the 7th Bedfords, and is on the site of Clapham Junction. The position of the strong point in Inverness Copse, at which B and D Companies were thrown without success on 16th August, is near the point at which the wood meets the Menin Road, as shown on the sketch plan.

BATTLEFIELD WALKS 203

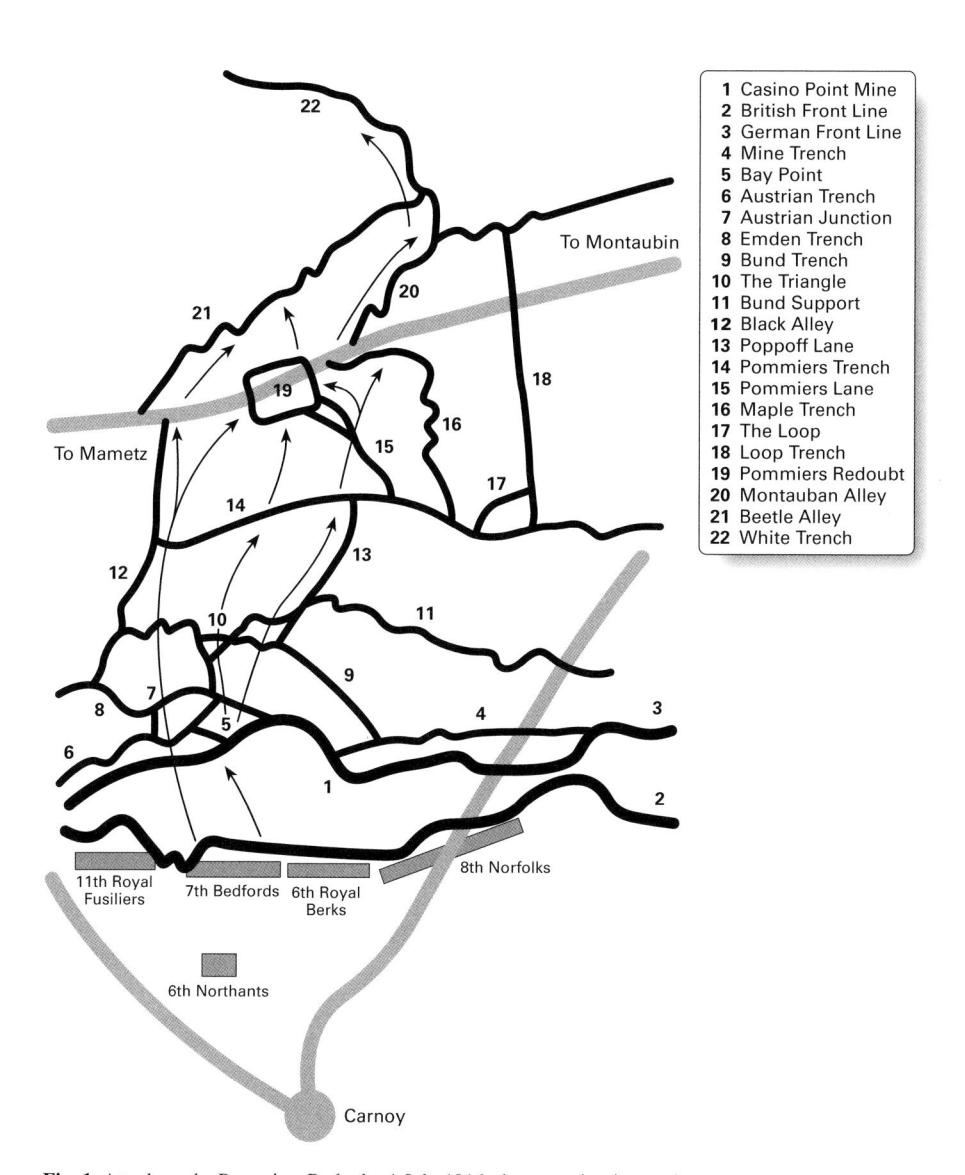

Fig. 1. Attack on the Pommiers Redoubt, 1 July 1916: the ground as it was then.

1 Casino Point Mine
2 British Front Line
3 German Front Line
4 Mine Trench
5 Bay Point
6 Austrian Trench
7 Austrian Junction
8 Emden Trench
9 Bund Trench
10 The Triangle
11 Bund Support
12 Black Alley
13 Poppoff Lane
14 Pommiers Trench
15 Pommiers Lane
16 Maple Trench
17 The Loop
18 Loop Trench
19 Pommiers Redoubt
20 Montauban Alley
21 Beetle Alley
22 White Trench

204   APPENDIX B: BATTLES

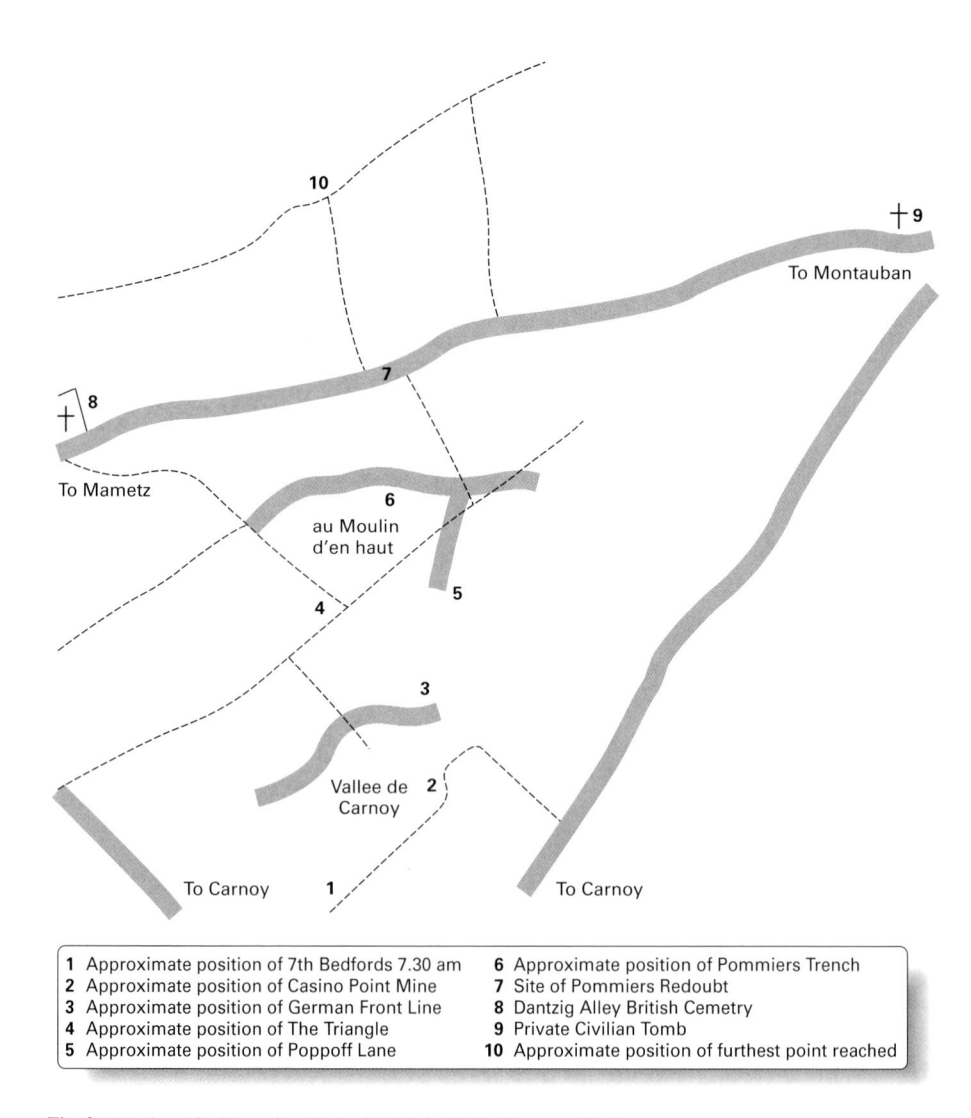

1 Approximate position of 7th Bedfords 7.30 am
2 Approximate position of Casino Point Mine
3 Approximate position of German Front Line
4 Approximate position of The Triangle
5 Approximate position of Poppoff Lane
6 Approximate position of Pommiers Trench
7 Site of Pommiers Redoubt
8 Dantzig Alley British Cemetry
9 Private Civilian Tomb
10 Approximate position of furthest point reached

Fig. 2. Attack on the Pommiers Redoubt, 1 July 1916: the ground today.

Plate 10. A view from the 7th Bedfords' trenches towards the German lines attacked on 1 July 1916. The Pommiers Redoubt lay just to the left of the row of trees on the high ground in the far distance. The German front line lay along the lower parts of the opposite slope, with support trenches higher up.

Plate 11. A view from the front trench of the Pommiers Redoubt towards the 7th Bedfords' starting positions on the slope in the middle distance.

Plate 12. A view from the bank above the Mametz-Montauban road towards the furthest point reached by 7th Bedfords on 1 July, White Trench, about halfway down the nearest slope. The woods seen are, closest to the camera, Bois des Montagnes (called Caterpillar Wood by the British) with Bois de Mametz (Mametz Wood) and Bois de Bazentin (Bazentin Wood) behind it.

208 APPENDIX B: BATTLES

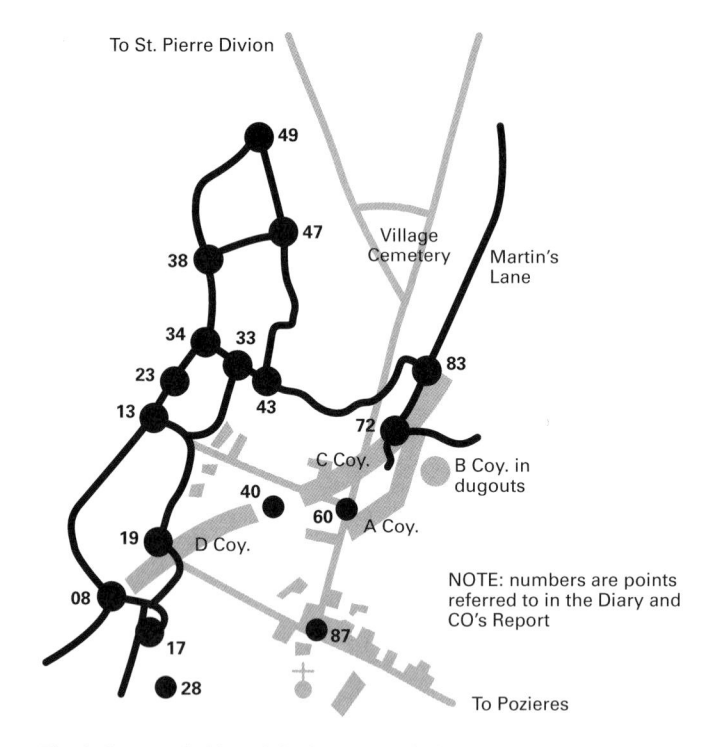

Fig. 3. Capture of Thiepval, 27 September 1916: the ground as it was then.

BATTLEFIELD WALKS 209

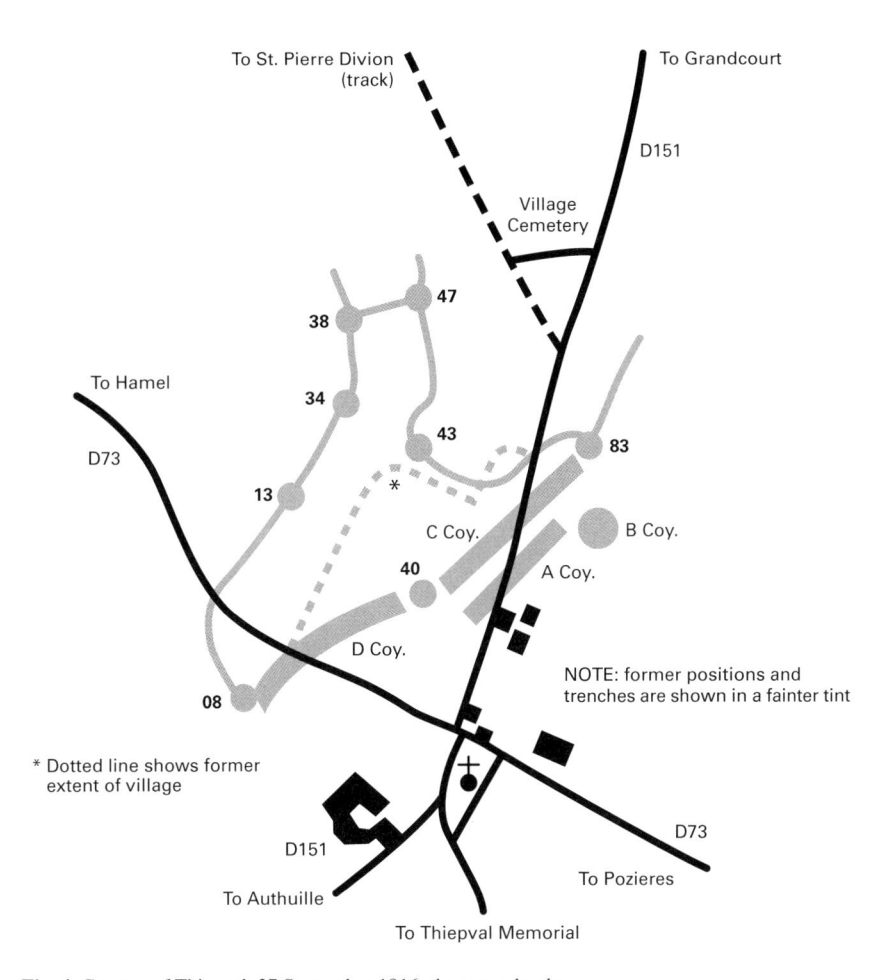

Fig. 4. Capture of Thiepval, 27 September 1916: the ground today.

210   APPENDIX B: BATTLES

Plate 13. The view from the crossroads of the D73 and D151. The ground immediately in front of the camera contained streets and houses before the First World War and was the last portion of Thiepval to be captured, by 7th Bedfords, on 27 September 1916. Here Tom Adlam did much of the work that won him his VC, and Lance Corporal Atkins and Private Billington died. The building on the extreme right is La Grande Ferme; the wall and trees on the extreme left mark Mill Road Cemetery; between them, along the top of the ridge, lay the Schwaben Redoubt.

BATTLEFIELD WALKS 211

SCHWABEN REDOUBT

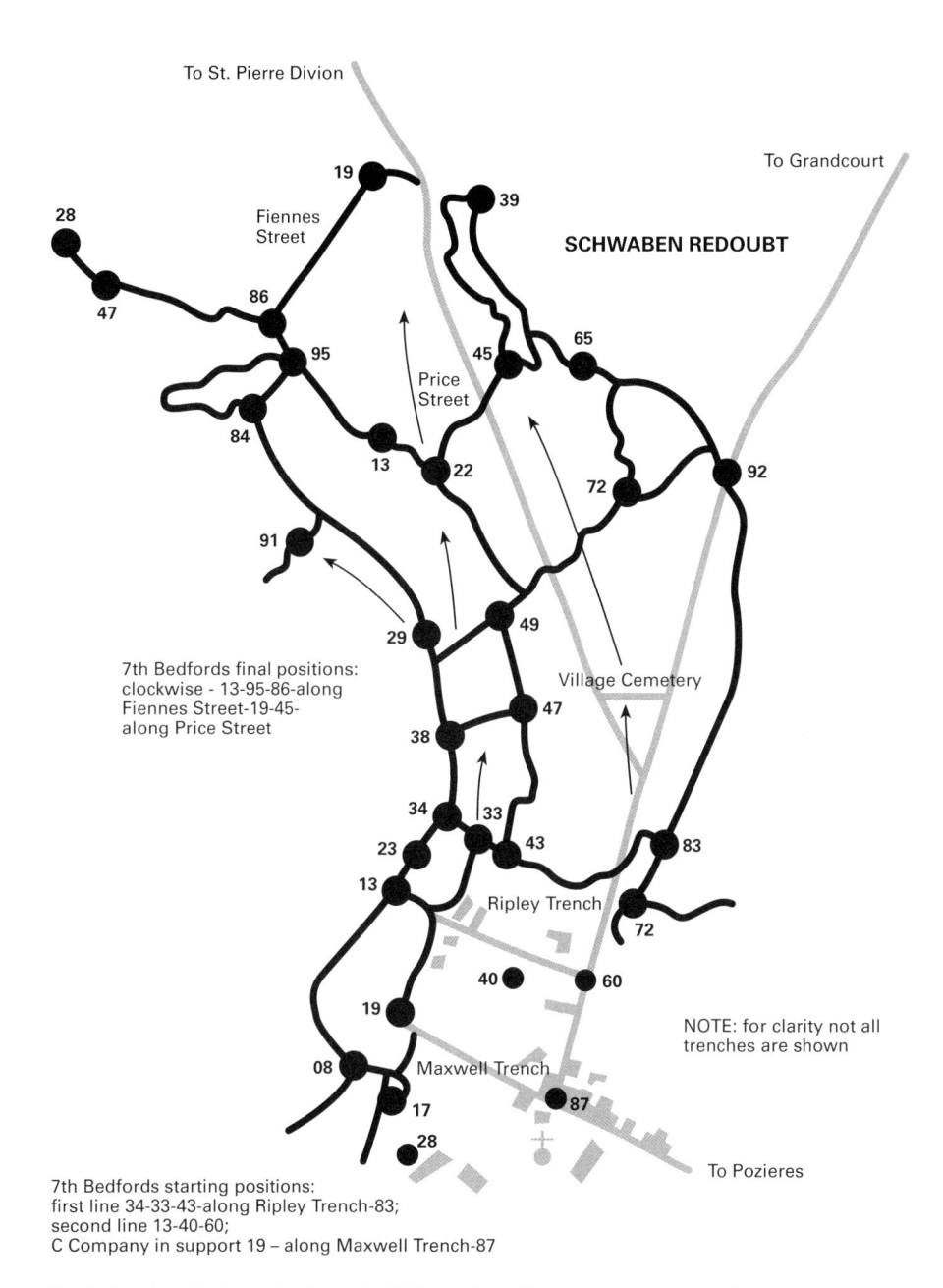

To St. Pierre Divion

To Grandcourt

Fiennes Street

Price Street

Village Cemetery

Ripley Trench

Maxwell Trench

To Pozieres

NOTE: for clarity not all trenches are shown

7th Bedfords final positions: clockwise - 13-95-86-along Fiennes Street-19-45-along Price Street

7th Bedfords starting positions:
first line 34-33-43-along Ripley Trench-83;
second line 13-40-60;
C Company in support 19 – along Maxwell Trench-87

Fig. 5. Attack on the Schwaben Redoubt, 28 September 1916: the ground as it was then.

212 APPENDIX B: BATTLES

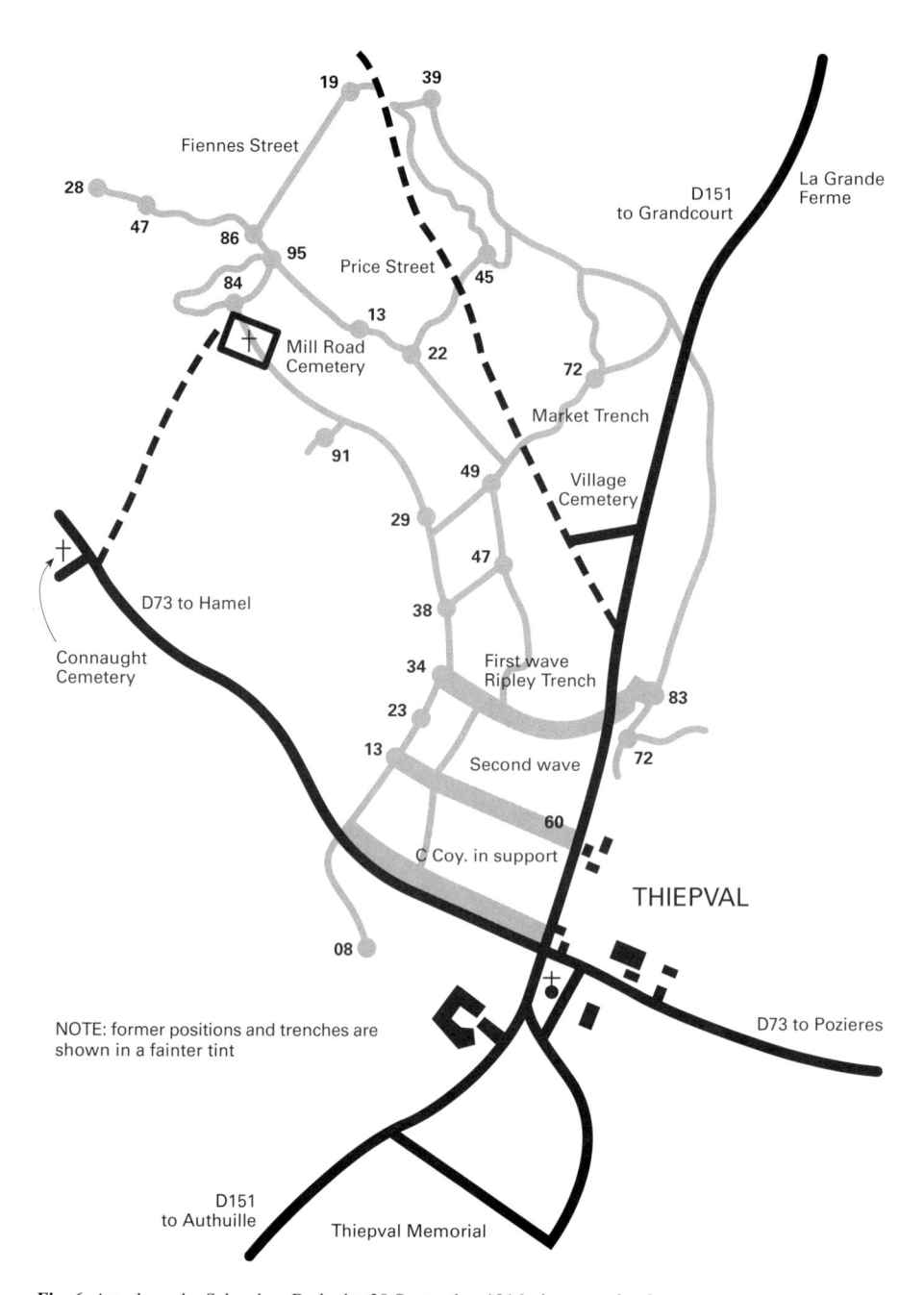

Fig. 6. Attack on the Schwaben Redoubt, 28 September 1916: the ground today.

Plate 14. The view from the road towards La Grande Ferme, looking towards the Schwaben Redoubt (which ran along the crest of the ridge). The trees on the right mark the Thiepval civilian cemetery, those in the far distance Mill Road Cemetery. It was from about this position that the 7th Bedfords' front line began the attack on the Schwaben Redoubt on 28 September 1916.

214   APPENDIX B: BATTLES

Plate 15. The view of the axis of advance by the right flank of the 7th Bedfords' attack on the Schwaben Redoubt, 28 September 1916. Note how the ground dips before rising again, the redoubt being along the highest contour. It is in this vicinity that the right-flank platoon of A Company was knocked out by machine gun fire.

Plate 16. The view from the rough location of "Point 19 on Fiennes Street", the furthest extent of the 7th Bedfords' advance in the attack on the Schwaben Redoubt on 28 September 1916. At the bottom of the slope is the River Ancre and its attendant marshes; the village beyond that in the middle distance, towards the right of the photograph, is Beaumont Hamel, held by the Germans until November 1916. The British line curved around here so that the high ground seen directly behind the village was in British hands; it was known as "White City".

216   APPENDIX B: BATTLES

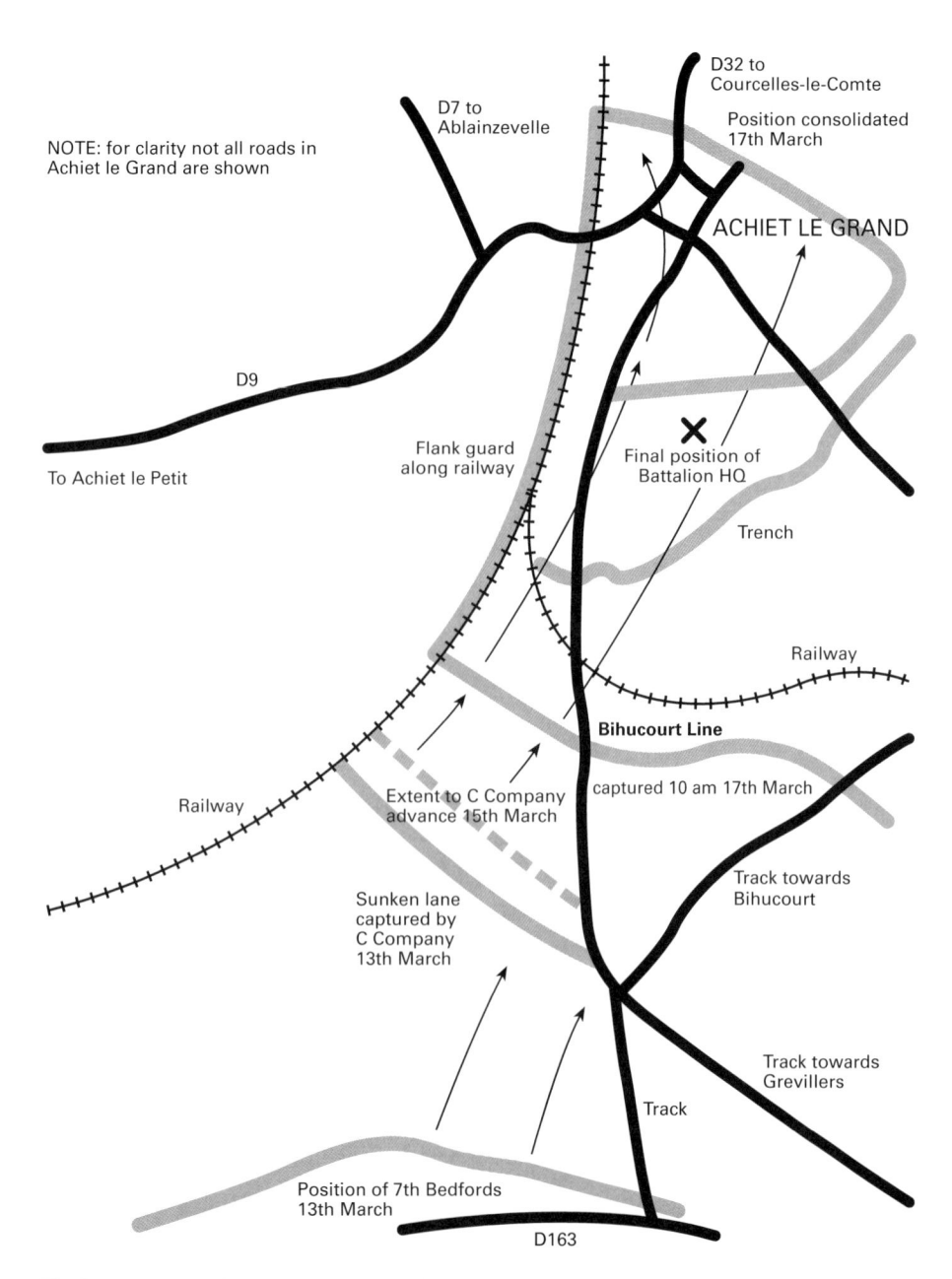

Fig. 7. Attack on Achiet le Grand, 13–17 March 1917.

Plate 17. The view from the top of the sunken lane looking towards Achiet le Grand. This was the area of the abortive attack by C Company on 15 March 1917, and where Christopher Cox won his Victoria Cross. It was also the line of C Company's successful attack on 17 March.

218   APPENDIX B: BATTLES

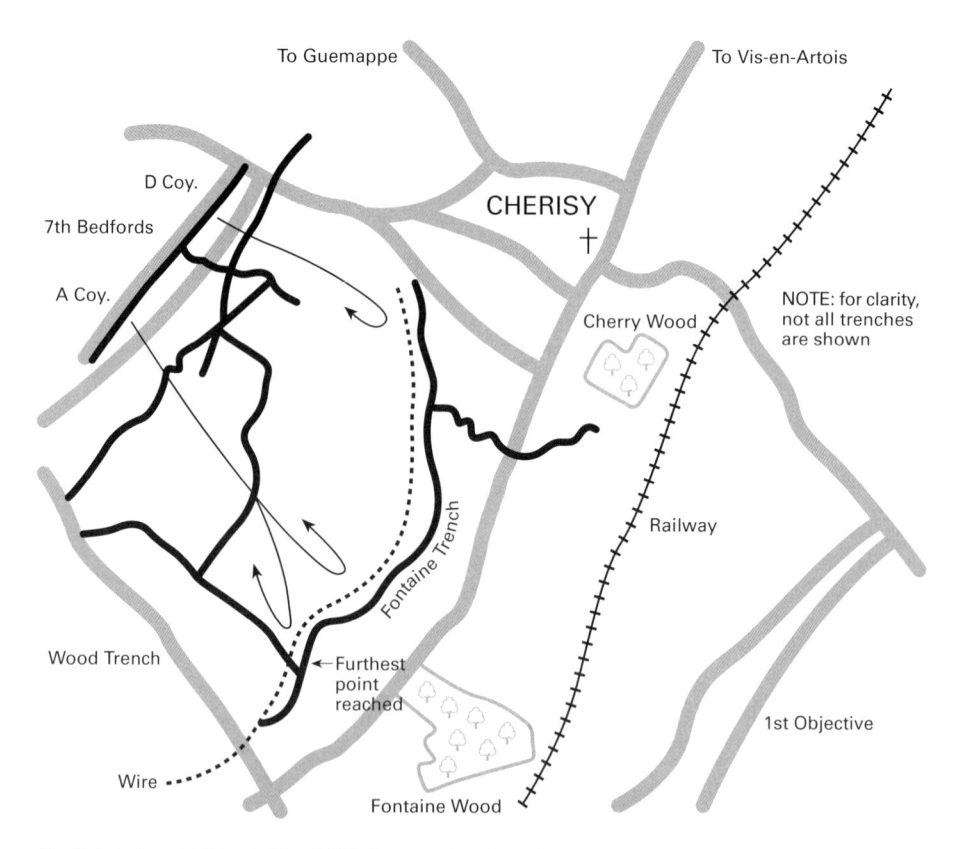

Fig. 8. Attack on Chérisy, 3 May 1917: the ground as it was then.

BATTLEFIELD WALKS   219

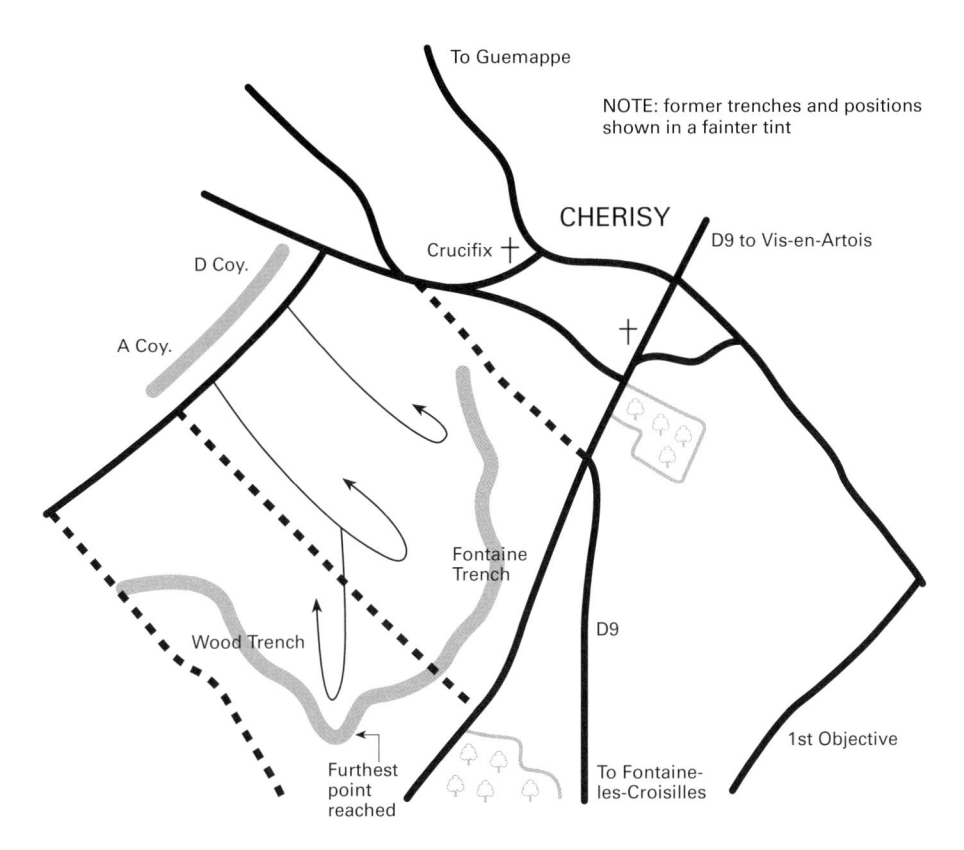

Fig. 9. Attack on Chérisy, 3 May 1917: the ground today.

Plate 18. A view from the top of the slope of the area attacked by A Company in the Battle of Chérisy, 3 May 1917. The right-hand corner of the wood marks the approximate position of the furthest point reached, at the junction of Fontaine Trench and Wood Trench. The church spire is Fontaine-les-Croisilles.

BATTLEFIELD WALKS 221

1 Menin Road
2 Stirling Castle
3 Surbiton Villas
4 Clapham Juction
5 C Company along line of modern road
6 B Company along line of modern road
7 Jargon Trench
8 Glencorse Wood
9 Strong Point
10 Strong Point
11 Inverness Copse
12 Nonne Bosschen

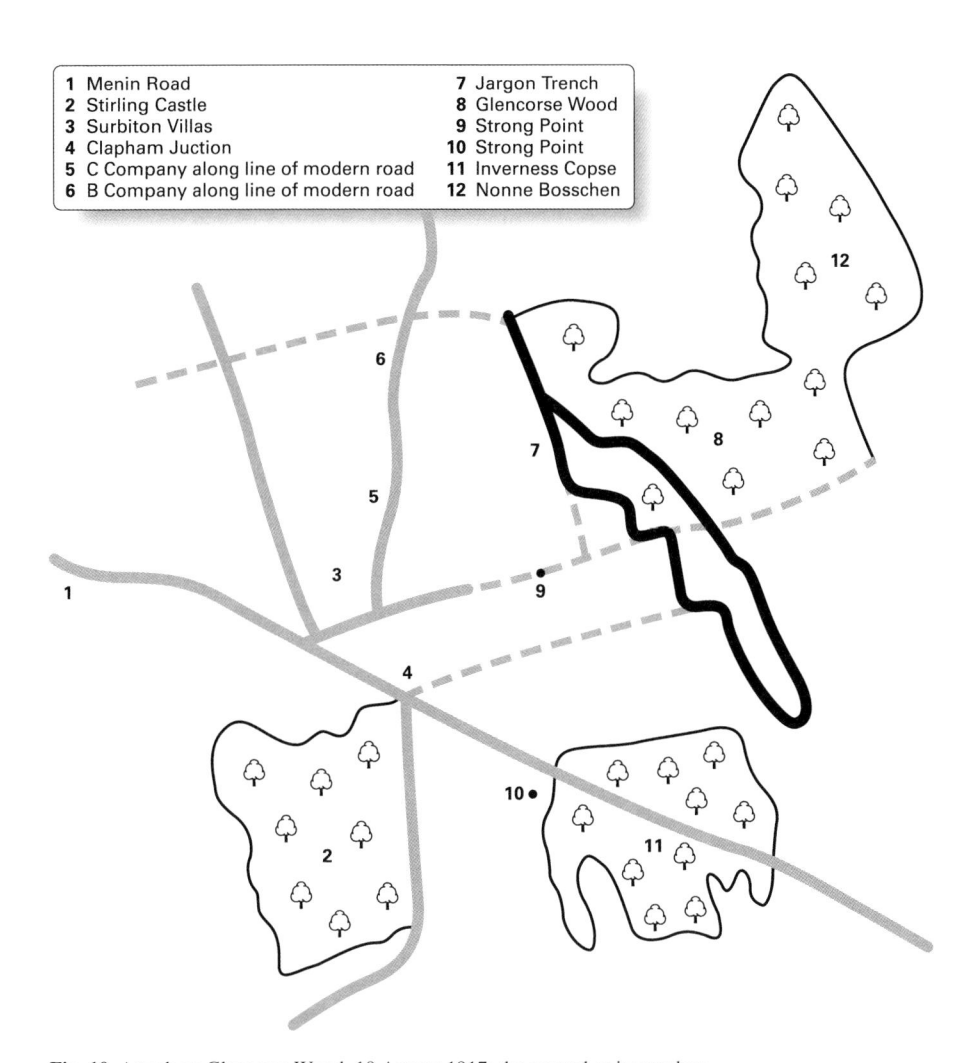

Fig. 10. Attack on Glencorse Wood, 10 August 1917: the ground as it was then.

222 APPENDIX B: BATTLES

1 Menin Road
2 Stirling Castle
3 Bellewaarde Amusement Park
4 Surbiton Villas
5 18th Division Memorial at site of Clapham Junction
6 C Company along line of modern road
7 B Company along modern road
8 Site of Jargon Trench, now a road and area of new housing
9 Site of Strong Point
10 Site of Strong Point
11 Inverness Copse
12 Glencorse Wood, now with modern housing
13 Nonne Bosschen

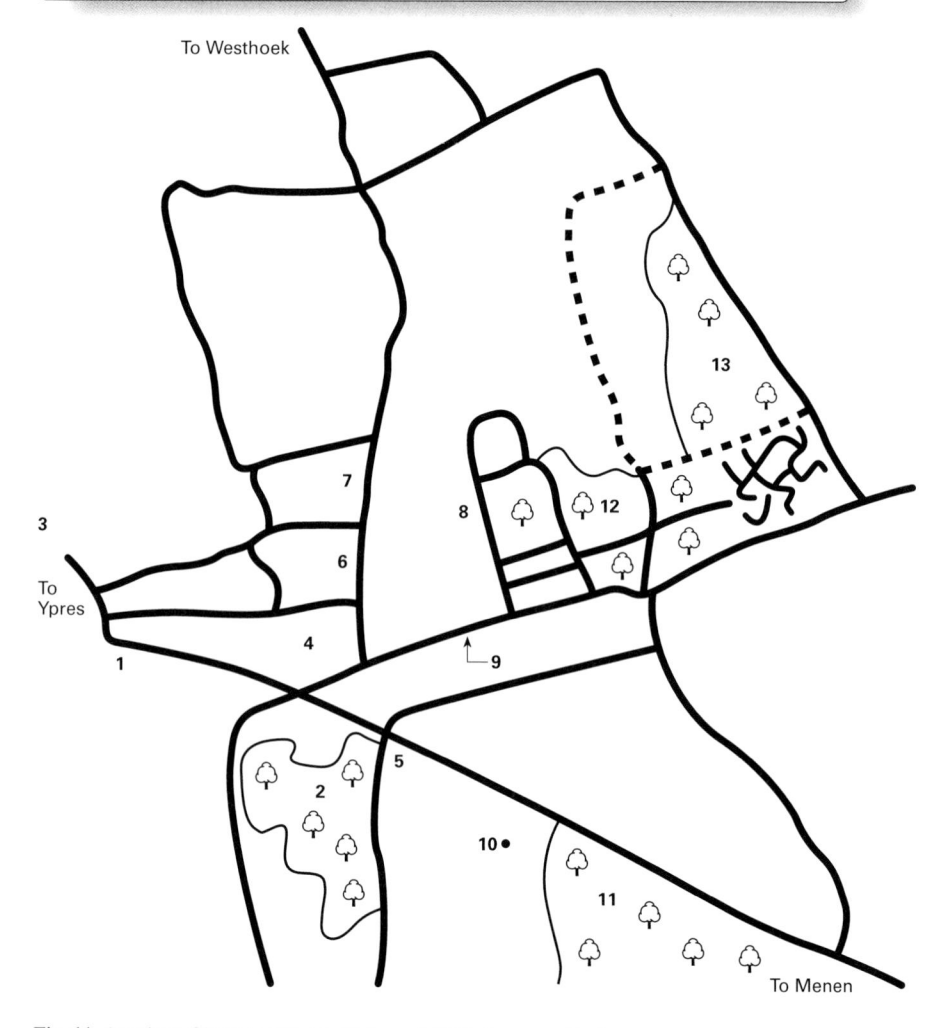

Fig. 11. Attack on Glencorse Wood, 10 August 1917: the ground today.

Plate 19. The view from the 7th Bedfords' front line towards what is left of Glencorse Wood, near Ypres, attacked on 10 August 1917. The new houses mark the approximate position of Jargon Trench, the German Front Line.

Appendix C1. Casualty Lists

1. Attack on Pommiers Redoubt, 1 July 1916

Killed 27-6-16

A Company
Haynes, A[lbert] E[dward], 3/8156, Sgt

C Company
Stokes, C[harles], 14819, Pte

Killed 1-7-16

A Company
Adams, E[dward], 15942, Pte
McGrane, W[alter], 12686, L/Cpl
Perkins, E[rnest] G[eorge], 3/7867, L/Cpl
Freeman, H[erbert] E[dward], 16466, Pte
Palmer, E[rnest] S[tanley], 14828, Pte
Titchmarsh, A[rthur], 3/8227, Pte

B Company
Bargioni, E[ugenio], 22865, Pte
Clarke, W[illiam] G[eorge], 16535, Pte
Dawes, H[enry], 22907, Pte
Fensome, S[tanley] W[illiam], 15296, Pte
Foley, H[erbert] J[ohn], 13989, Sgt
Green, G[eorge], 12750, Cpl
Lewin, H[orace], 18411, Cpl

Chandler, W[illiam], 3/8191, L/Cpl
Cutler, A[rnold], 13541, Pte
Fawkes, A[lan], 13268, Pte
Field, C[harles] W[illiam], 19177, Pte
Fox, J[ames] W[illiam], 15427, L/Cpl
Knapp, B[ert], 15028, L/Sgt
Mapley, T[homas] H[arry], 14712, Pte [sic 7/7/16]

Paton, I[an] V[alentine], 7964, L/Sgt
Ruffhead, F[rederick] C[harles], 16998, Cpl
Smail, W[illiam], 13538, L/Cpl
Stokes, L[eonard], 13297, Cpl
Tridgett, A[rthur] A[lbert], 13656, Pte
Westlake, T[homas] R[ichard], 14940, Pte
Worsley, L[ionel] R[alph], 3/7730, Pte

Rickard, P[ercy] E[dward], 3/8141, Sgt
Sibthorpe, J[oseph], 14862, Cpl
Smith, S[idney] T[homas], 26549, Pte
Stone, L[eonard] V[ictor], 15546, Pte
Tuck, F[rederick] G[eorge], 17263, Pte
Wilkinson, W[illiam] T[homas], 12532, Pte

C Company
Armstrong, F[rederick] W[illiam], 19794, Pte
Bateman, J[oseph], 17270, Pte
Brett, G[eorge] J[ohn], 18195, Pte
Clark, W[illiam] G[arner], 15748, Pte
Cook, A[lbert] G[eorge], 12752, Pte
Cornell, A[rthur] E[rnest], 15354, Sgt
Dawbon, G[eorge] W[illiam], 17279, Pte
Ginger, J[oseph], 19820, Sgt
Howlett, W[alter], 25551, Pte
Mead, W[illiam] A[lbert], 15307, Pte
Parish, W[illiam], 23151, Pte
Stancliff, H[erbert] P[rior], 16184, Pte
Thurley, F[rederick] G[eorge], 15215, Pte

Atkins, E[dward] W[illiam], 20789, L/Cpl
Bowles, A[lec], 15050, Cpl
Brown, H[enry] G[eorge], 20097, L/Cpl
Coleman, A[lbert] F[rancis], 14685, Pte
Cooper, W[illiam] P[ercy], 15704, Sgt
Croft, E[dward], 17236, L/Cpl
Gates, F[rank], 13335, Pte
Hewitt, F[rank], 12816, L/Cpl
Legate, G[eorge], 20284, Pte
Missenden, R[eginald] W[illiam], 16200, Sgt
Partridge, B[ert], 22404, Pte
Stratton, E[dmund], 3/8248, Pte

CASUALTY LISTS

D Company
Ansell, W[alter], 19803, Pte
Carter, F[rederick] H[erbert], 15249, Pte
Darrington, P[eter], 20317, Pte
Foreman, W[illiam], 15383, Pte
Goebel, R[ichard] H[enry], 3/7975, L/Cpl
Hardie, S[idney] D[uncan] G[rellier], 15367, Cpl
Jowett, C[harles], 14867, Pte
Lovatt, A[lbert] W[illiam], 20075, Pte
Peach, C[harles] F[rederick], 19571, Pte
Watson, J[ames], 3/8143, Sgt

Benson, W[illiam], 16052, Pte
Cox, C[harlie] G[eorge], 19213, L/Cpl
Drury, G[eorge], 15766, Pte
Godfrey, A[rthur], 15325, Pte
Graves, H[erbert], 20098, Pte

Laughton, G[eorge], 19470, Sgt
Oakley, E[dward], 12791, Pte
Ranson, R[ichard], 12665, Pte

Died of wounds

A Company
Bullard, W[illiam] R[alph], 10430, Pte, 8-7-16
Catlin, A[lbert], 15674, Pte, 2-7-16
Lincoln, A[rthur] G[eorge], 15979, Pte
White, S[ydney] C[harles], 22335, 3-7-16

Carr, T[homas] B[urges], 18200, Pte
Hensman, H[orace] A[lfred], 13015, Pte
Swift, S[tanley], 20735, L/Cpl, 6-7-16

B Company
Brown, W[illiam] G[eorge], 19810, Pte, 1-7-16
Curchin, H[arry], 26576, Pte
Harrison, F[rederick] G[eorge], 25661, L/Cpl, 1-7-16
Martin, A[rthur] H[enry], 3/7638, Pte, 4-7-16
Shadbolt, B[ertie], 14388, Pte, 15-7-16
Smith, H[arry], 15272, Pte, 1-7-16

C Company
Goodfellow, G[eorge] W[illiam], 17259, Pte, 13-7-16
Purser, A[rthur] W[illiam], 13857, Pte
Vickery, W[illiam], 14941, Pte, 8-7-16

D Company
Gurney, F[rank], 19182, Pte, 5-7-16
Johnson, A[rthur], 16283, Pte.
Perry, J[ames] E[mmings], CSM, 9-7-16

Hyde, W[illiam], 13379, Sgt, 2-7-16
Johnson, C[harles], 14506, Pte, 18-7-16

Wounded

A Company
Archer, J., 22273, Pte
Barton, F.W., 25268, Pte
Bird, L., 20246, Pte.
Blowes, C.R., 14827, Pte
Brace, A., 15273, Pte
Burton, F.C., 15696, Pte
Clark, B.J., 14826, Pte
Cox, A., 17425, Pte

Coxwell, E.A., 17890, L/Cpl
Darlow, A., 12764, L/Cpl
Deal, W.C., 25812, Pte
Ellins, S.T., 13782, Sgt
Harrison, W., 17369, Pte
Holiday, H., 3/8337, Pte

Baker, F., 15705, Pte
Birch, T.M., 14756, Pte
Birdsey, W.T., 15562, Cpl
Bolton, F.W., 17345, Pte
Burgess, A[lbert], 4/7223, Pte.
Byford, A., 7332, L/Cpl
Coventry, D., 17401, Pte
Cox, C.A., 13909, Pte [awarded VC in 1917 for bravery at Achiet-le-Grand]
Cutmore, W.H., 13374, Pte
Dawson, S.C., 15349, Pte
Duller, C.W., 15237, Cpl
Hammond, H.T., 12369, Pte
Hastler, A.C., 15236, Pte
Hopcroft, F., 15718, Pte

226 APPENDIX C: CASUALTIES

Howard, C., 15180, Pte
Lewis, F.J., 14169, L/Cpl
Munns, G., 12804, Pte
Pantlin, H.P., 16316, Pte
Pratt, W., 20367, Pte
Saville, T., 22260, Pte
Sibsby, B.F., 12527, Pte
Smith, J., 22075, Pte
Tearle, J., 16521, Pte
Thody, H., 19531, Pte
Whelan, R., 15335, Pte

Johnson, C., 3/7693, Pte
Luff, A.T., 12824, Sgt
Norman, F., 23791, Pte
Pipkin, G., 3/7764, Pte
Purser, H.F., 3/8471, Pte
Seabrook, R., 14449, Pte
Smith, E.T., 24519, Cpl
Sweeting, E., 17423, Pte
Tearle, T., 24296, Pte.
Warwick, B., 5502, Pte
Wilson, J., 19533, Pte

B Company
Allen, J.W., 3/7623, Sgt
Coleman, E., 14576, Pte
Costin, W., 22822, Pte
Custer, E., 17473, Pte
Downing, F., 13829, Pte
Faulkner, N[oah], 13944, Pte
Fleet, W., 12775, Pte
Foskett, F.G., 14118, Pte
Gage, R., 12552, Pte
Hack, A.J., 25785, Pte
Harrington, G., 14465, L/Cpl
Innes[?], W.H., 12572, L/Cpl
Kinch, H., 26564, Pte
Lambert, A., 14764, Pte
Langley, J., 14997, Pte
Lewin, A., 16932, Pte
Maling, F., 17149, Pte
Martin, A.W., 16211, Pte
McInnes, S.A., 15071, Pte
Morris, E.H., 18566, Pte
Munns, C., 3/8373, Pte
Nicholson, F.T., 12675, L/Sgt
Peach, W., 19431, Pte
Powell, J., 13347, Pte
Ramsdon, E.R., 13765, Pte
Robinson, N., 17264, Pte
Seaman, B., 14866, Pte
Simpkins, E., 15492, Cpl
Smith, A., 19826, Pte
Smith, G., 17017, Pte
Sturgess, A.J., 3/8104, Pte
Taylor, C[harles], 15341, L/Cpl
Tridgett, W., 13673, Pte
Waldron, H.E., 15667, Pte
Waters, L.W., 13646, Pte
Wilbury, H., 15204, Pte
Williams, T.F., 14119, Pte
York, C., 26545, Pte

Bunce, F., 12204, Pte
Coote, H.E., 15607, Pte
Crawford, J., 18400, Cpl
Dewey, F.J., 17344, Pte
Eardley, A., 13106, Pte
Fenwick, G[eorge Alfred], 15065, Pte
Folkes, T., 12749, Pte
French, J., 14378, Pte
Gregory, W., 17432, L/Cpl
Harding, G., 4/7115, Pte
Hayes, S., 16730, Pte
Jolly, C.P., 19543, Pte
King, B., 15387, Pte
Langdon, L.H., 18565, Pte
Lawes, G., 23414, Pte
Lillington, E.A., 25806, Pte
Mansfield, W., 7097, Pte
May, C., 12692, Pte
Meadows, R[eginald], 17265, Pte
Morris, J.H., 15727, L.Cpl
Munns, R.J., 13293, Pte
Peach, W., 4/7178, Pte
Peters, A.A., 12714, L/Cpl
Quarry[?], W.J., 26223, Pte
Ricks, G.H., 13249, L/Sgt
Seabrook, C., 14933, Pte
Shadbolt, C., 15238, Pte
Simpson, C.R., 25664, Pte
Smith, E., 14677, Pte
Stone, V.C., 14817, Pte
Sutton, E., 15603, Pte
Tozer, A.J., 14544, Pte
Tyler, F., 15797, Sgt
Walton, H[arry], 15226, Pte
Watts, J[ohn], 13966, Pte
Wilde, E., 15300, Pte
Wolsey, J.K., 14754, Pte

C Company
Alwin[?], H.J.[?], 14806, Pte.
Butler, G., 3/6444, Pte.
Carron, W., 17111, L/Cpl.

Bailey, A.G., 14681, Pte.
Butterfield, G., 17090, Pte.
Chapman, C.F., 14633, Pte.

Clark, S., 14623, Pte.
Cope, A., 16542, Pte.
Dennison, C.J., 17367, Pte.
Field, M[artin] E[dgar], 14808, L/Cpl.
Griffiths, G., 18194, Pte.
Hurlock[?], G., 14370, Pte.
Martin, J., 23449, Pte.
Mitchell, R.H., 22626, Pte.
Peariman[?], C.F., 15668, Pte.
Sleet, W., 14482, Pte.
Stone, H.J., 15850, Sgt.
Underwood, W., 16203, Pte.

Clarke, W.F., 16587, L/Cpl.
Covington, G.B., 19852, Pte.
Ellis, W.G., 19123, Pte.
Gordon, A., 3/8433, Sgt.
Hill, A., 20904, Pte.
Kethridge, H., 18177, Pte.
Matthews, E.E..[?], 25821, L/Cpl.
Partridge, E., 15908, Pte.
Piercy[?], T., 15340, Cpl.
Smith, A.L., 19798, L/Cpl.
Tibbett, C., 19558, Pte.
Young, F., 17519, Pte.

D Company
Andrews, S., 14325, Pte.
Barton, A., 16599, Cpl.
Canham, J., 19737, Pte.
Cobb, J.A., 19151, L/Cpl.
Cook, F[red] J[ames], 19209, Pte.
Dilks, H.W., 14140, Pte.
Dring, J[oseph], 12741, L/Cpl.
Evans, G., 14186, Pte.
Field, A.H., 18408, Pte.
Foldo[?], S., 19547, Pte.
Harris, E., 15732, L/Cpl.
Hollister, J., 14829, Pte.
Hutton, G.H., 3/8352, Pte.
Ives, P., 15679, Pte.
Jeffs, W.J., Pte., 26283
Johnson, A.S., 14802, Pte.
Jones, A.W., 19822, Pte.
Lawrence, V[ernon] A[lan], 14301, Pte.
Maddox, E.J., 15573, Pte.
Maxall, W., 14886, L/Cpl.
Miles, D., 15609, L/Cpl.
Smith, K., 3/7661, L/Cpl.
Titmuss, A.J., 14215, Pte.
Williams, A., 19152, Pte.
Wootton, F., 12787, Sgt.

Archer, C.J., 14531, Cpl.
Butcher, W., 15727, Pte.
Clark, S.B., 14912, Pte.
Colman, J., 19216, Pte.
Croft, J.W., 19189, Pte.
Doyle, J., 15059, Pte.
Dwight, J., 19150, Pte.
Ewer, W., 13963, Pte.
Fitzgerald, J., 15960, Pte.
Ginger, E., 19128, Pte.
Hewitt, B.R., 15514, Pte.
Huggett, J., 14871, Pte.
Impey, S., 15115, Sgt.
Jackson, E., 15959, Pte.
Jennings, R., 15444, Pte.
Johnson, R.J., 15670, Pte.
Josling, A., 15609, Pte.
Lawson, H.A., 14896, Pte.
Mason, G., 14916, Pte.
Mead, A[lfred], 3/7974, Pte.
Sapsford, H., 13543, Cpl.
Stringer, A., 19112, Pte.
Wheeler, F., 7207, Pte.
Winch, S.J., 14931, Pte.

Missing

A Company
Clerk, G., 12634, Pte.

Merry, F., 12825, Pte.

C Company
Pratt, S[idney], 28702, Pte [killed]
Worley, W., 14612, Pte.

West, F[rank], 20400, Pte [killed]

2. Attack on Thiepval and Schwaben Redoubt, 26–30 September 1916

Officers killed in action

2nd Lieut. Cedric S. Howard (28.9.16)
2nd Lieut. Robert Donald Hunston (28.9.16)

228　APPENDIX C: CASUALTIES

2nd Lieut. Herbert George Merchant (28.9.16)
2nd Lieut. Ian Henry Munro Ross-Taylor (27.9.16)
2nd Lieut. Thomas Percy Wilson 28.9.16

Officers wounded in action

2nd Lieut. Tom Edwin Adlam (28.9.16)
2nd Lieut. Samuel Lawrence Cannon (27.9.16)
2nd Lieut. Camille Floutier (27.9.16)
2nd Lieut. Henry Cheney Malone (28.9.16)
2nd Lieut. Robert Edwin Moyse (28.9.16)
Captain Thomas Reginald Jack Mulligan (27.9.16)
Captain Arthur Ernest Percival (28.9.16)
2nd Lieut. Ernest George Pernet (28.9.16)
2nd Lieut. Henry Potts (27.9.16)
2nd Lieut. Harold Agnew Reaney (28.9.16)

Other Ranks killed in action

A Company – 27.9.16
Andrews, F[rederick], 15856, Pte.
Blackmore, W[illiam], 14910, Pte.
Brown, J[ohn] W[alter], 15435, Pte.
Deighton, R[euben], 19816, Pte.
Gladding, F[rederick], 4/6940, L/Cpl.
Hunt, A[lbert] V[ictor], 17450, Pte.

Bennett, W[illiam], 14671, Pte.
Bowers, R[ichard], 17012, Pte.
Cowland, E[dward], 22040, Pte.
Evans, W[illiam], 43366, Pte.
Higgs, J[ohn] F[rederick], 7665, Pte.

B Company – 27.9.16
Fudge, W[alter] G[eorge], 43292, Pte.

Gurney, J[ames], 14225, Pte.

C Company – 27.9.16
Arnott, F.H[erbert], 12256, Cpl.
Brown, J[ohn] W[alter], 15319, Cpl.
Cracknell, F[rederick], 15040, Pte.
Edwards, F[rank] H[enry], 23198, Pte.
Knowles, J[ohn] N[orman], 43369, Pte.
Lane, P[ercy], 16416, Pte.
Oldfield, F[rederick] H[inton], 43326, Pte.
Shelford, F[red], 27815, Pte.
Warner, H[arry], 43346, L/Cpl.

Bayford, L[eonard] J[ohn], 25979, Pte
Canham, C[harles] W[illiam], 22819, L/Cpl.
Elliott, W[illiam], 18230, Pte.
Jordan, J[ohn], 13367, Pte.
Mitchell, R[ichard] C[harles], 16777, Pte.
Lee, A[lbert Victor], 43351, Pte.
Seward, W[illiam] H[erbert], 23790, Pte.
Sylvester, H[arry], 15433, Pte.
Winfield, G[eorge], 16985, L/Cpl.

D Company – 27.9.16
Atkins, A[rthur] E[dward], 16133, L/Cpl.
Dorrell, F[rederick] T[homas], 14660, Pte.
Hill, L[eonard] J[ames], 14683, Sgt.
Taylor, V[ictor] C[harles], 15692, Pte.
Tompkins, J[oseph] W[illiam], 27589, Pte.
Williams, J[ohn] H[enry], 27884, Pte.

Billington, W[illiam Charles], 15229, Pte.
Fountain, A[rthur], 15400, CSM
Nice, P[ercy], 43324, Pte.
Terry, F[rederick Abraham], 23363, Pte.
Waterton, S[idney], 19171, Pte.
Wright, P[ercy] H[arry], 27830, Pte.

A Company – 28.9.16
Andrews, W[illiam], 22020, Cpl.
Marshall, W[alter], 3/8751, Sgt.

Holloway, J[oseph] J[ohn], 14792, Pte.
Turner, H[erbert] W[alter], 15465, Cpl.

B Company – 28.9.16
Hodge, W[alter] F[red], 3/7497, Cpl.
Payne, T[homas], 27836, Pte.

Miles, W[alter], 8289, L/Cpl.
Quartermass, R[obert Alfred], 16419, Cpl.

C Company – 28.9.16
Field, M[artin] E[dgar], 14808, L/Cpl.
Robinson, F[rank] C[harles], 18202, Pte.

D Company – 28.9.16
Humphrey, W[illiam], 43339, Pte.
Kingham, A[rthur], 15292, Pte.

Parsons, E[rnest] A[rthur], 14872, Pte.
Shepherd, R[eginald] W[alter], 16208, Sgt.

James, H[erbert] W[illiam], 13742, Pte.
Miller, C[harles] H[enry], 43320, Pte.

Other Ranks wounded in action

A Company – 26.9.16
O'Neil, A., 17431, Pte.

C Company – 26.9.16
Allen, L., 13232, Pte.

D Company – 26.9.16
Allen, W.S., 16261, Pte.

A Company – 27.9.16
Atkinson, J.H., 43273, Pte.
Burge, O[liver] S[amuel], 14796, Pte. [died 27.9.16]
Carter, W[alter], 25626, Pte. [died 27.9.16]
Freeman, G., 43367, Pte.

Hill, E[dward], 20817, Pte. [died 28.9.16]
Payne, W.G., 15030, Pte.

B Company – 27.9.16
Gibbard, A., 6436, Pte.
Tripp, A., 15329, Pte.

C Company – 27.9.16
Alderman, G., 43557, Pte.
Bean, W., 10638, Pte.
Clark, W.P., 22910, Pte.
Cornell, V.H., 16083, Pte.
Farey, R., 19925, Pte.
Mellor, J., 22830, Pte.
Rands, T., 15680, Pte.
Rubnett, F.H., 17462, Sgt.

D Company – 27.9.16
Gamage, H., 15399, Sgt.
Horsted, T., 15644, Pte.
Jones, H., 14934, Pte.
Pearson, A., 43332, Pte.
Shanks, H., 43340, Pte.
White, W.C., 27866, Pte.
Yearley, R.W., 15126, Pte.

Turvey, A[rthur], 15760, Pte.

Puddephat, P., 14318, Sgt.

Breed, F., 23417, Pte.
Butler, A[rthur], 19357, L/Sgt., [died 24.10.16]
Cripps, C., 16550, Pte.
Furr, E[rnest] W[illiam], 7722, Pte. [died 27.9.16]
Hobby, A., 17409, Pte.
Pearce, C[harles] H[enry], 15357, Pte. [died 27.9.16]

Pavitt, E., 43347, Pte.

Baxter, C.E., 25555, Pte
Bradley, A., 12660, Pte.
Cooper, C., 43283, Pte.
Ettey, T., 18192, L/Sgt.
Gould, F.A., 19930, Pte.
Norris, W., 15232, Pte.
Raynor, A.J., 13822, Pte.

Horley, A.L., 16029, L/Cpl.
Jeffs, J., 20095, Pte.
Mardle, A[lbert], 15118, Pte. [died 28.9.16]
Putman, H[orace], 22192, Pte. [died 27.9.16]
Smythe, J., 19175, Pte.
Woodcock, F., 27772, Pte.

A Company – 28.9.16
Allen, A.W., 15244, Pte.
Allen, J[ohn] R[obert], 16388, L/Cpl [died 31.10.16]

230 APPENDIX C: CASUALTIES

Arborn, W., 43271, Pte.
Banes, F.J., 14836, L/Cpl.
Berry, H[erbert] E[Richard], 20084, Pte. [died 17.11.16]
Blower, C.R., 14894, Pte.
Bradford, R., 26710, Pte.
Clare, G.T., 16810, Cpl.
Cowlin, A., 25627, Pte.
Davis, A., 43285, Pte.
Eversden, G[eorge], 7677, Pte. [died 28.9.16]
Haverson, A.E., 43864, L/Cpl.
Hunt, C., 12405, Pte.
Masson, R., 18567, Pte.
Taylor, G., 19659, Pte.
Tutton, A.P., 19829, Pte.
Watson, E.C., 20980, Pte.
Wilson, A[ugustus] E[dwin], 14499, Sgt.

Bailey, F.J., 15963, Pte.
Batty, J.E., 18559, L/Cpl.
Blakeman, F.G., 12801, Sgt.

Bradbury, W.E., 15683, Pte.
Briers, F.J., 14562, Pte.
Clifton, C[harles], 23280, Pte. [died 5.10.16]
Daniels, W.W., 15232, Pte.
Dorrington, J.W., 20452, Cpl.
Hart, A[lfred], 43261, Sgt. [died 28.9.16]
Holloway, G.A., 14934, Pte.
Kempster, E., 13281, Pte.
Spacey, T., 19757, L/Cpl.
Thornton, T., 18044, Pte.
Watson, A., 15497, Pte.
Waugh, H., 19676, Pte.
York, W.G., 12761, Pte.

B Company – 28.9.16
Bayford, F[rank] W[illiam], 15044, Sgt.
Brookes, T., 12695, Pte.
Chandler, A[lfred], 15198, Cpl.
Chapman, T.J., 43364, Pte.
Honour, B[ruce], 43300, Pte. [died 4.10.16]
Moverley, A., 14673, Pte.
Petifor, G.R., 17276, Pte.
Pimm, A., 20874, Pte.
Rowlings, W.A., 16031, Cpl.
Sewell, H.J., 16215, L/Cpl.
Tippett, A[lfred], 12672, Cpl. [died 30.9.16]
Wilson, A., 16194, Pte.

Bradshaw, E., 14620, L/Cpl.
Cairns, T.F., 43880, Pte.
Chandler, C., 17375, Pte.
Hammond, J., Pte.
Meeks, J., 16002, Pte.
Murray, E.J., 15956, Pte.
Pickford, G., 43362, Pte.
Rowland, R., 27904, Pte.
Seabrook, A[rthur], 15138, Pte.
Tebbutt, W[alter], 43363, Pte.
Wagstaff, H., 17273

C Company – 28.9.16
Andrews, J.E., 18275, Pte.
Aylott, J[ohn], 18171, Pte.
Docwra, W., 43443, Pte.
Ingrey, C.R., 17206, Sgt.
Marchant, H.W., 13969, Sgt.
Peacock, G.R., 26539, Pte.
Tinsley, E., 14874, Pte.
Wilsher, W., 18230, Pte.

Arnold, S., 14222, Pte.
Butler, J., 4/7334, Pte.
Greenhill, D[ennis], 17292, Pte.
Lawrence, G., 19131, Pte.
Payne, A.C., 14880, L/Cpl.
Piercy, T[homas] V[ictor], 15340, Cpl.
Tribe, W., 17016, Pte.

D Company – 28.9.16
Adams, T[homas] I[saac], 43370, Pte. [died 28.9.16]
Cooper, G[eorge] A[lbert], 3/8441, Pte. [died 28.9.16]
Knock, H., 43315, Pte.
Line, B.C., 22666, Pte.
Prew, F., 43329, Pte.
Slough, J.W., 19210, Sgt.
Wyatt, A., 43340, Sgt.

Clayton, W., 23409, Pte.

Halsey, G., 16261, Pte.

Land, F[rederick], 23531, Pte. [died 9.10.16]
Lord, H., 43316, Pte.
Simpkins, A.H., 19141, Pte.
Wright, S.W., 26326, Pte.

B Company – 30.9.16
Head, S., 8365, Pte.
Lewis, H., 43267, L/Cpl.

Land, A.L., 16173, Pte.

D Company – 30.9.16
Hughes, A., 13970, Pte.
Showler, G., 27819, Pte.

Other Ranks missing

A Company – 27.9.16
Cornish, J.A., 17410, Pte.

A Company – 28.9.16
Baxter, G.W., 19003, Pte.
Elwood, W[alter], 13301, Pte. [killed]
Mardel, C[harles] J[ames], 18669, L/Cpl [killed]
Mimms, J[ames], 14405, Pte. [killed]

B Company – 28.9.16
Battison, A., 43358, Pte.
Chapman, W., 43284, Pte.
Dickens, J[ohn] W[illiam], 43365, Pte. [killed]
Doel, S[ydney Herbert], 43286, Pte. [killed]
Fisher, H[arry], 43291, Pte. [killed]
French, W.G., 25665, Pte.
Giddings, J[ohn], 16922, Pte. [killed]
Goodwin, A[ustin], 43297, Pte. [killed]
Hedger, J[ohn], 7002, Pte. [killed]
Hill, W., 14306, Ptc.
Knight, W., 23262, Pte.
Morgan, W[illiam], 27840, Pte.
Pearce, W[illiam James], 4/7178, Pte. [killed]
Pepper, F[rank], 19875, Pte. [killed]
Rollins, J[ohn Henry], 43333, Pte. [killed]
Sims, C.A., 12010, Pte.
Slatter, G., 10358, Pte.
Smith, T.W., 15312, L/Cpl.
Walker, A., 12693, Pte.
Webb, J[ohn] G[eorge], 26230, Pte. [killed]

C Company – 28.9.16
Cochrane, J[ohn], 15754, L/Cpl. [killed]

Missing believed killed

Heley, T[homas] J[ohn], 15743, L/Cpl., D Company, [died 29.9.16]
Whittaker, [Charles] J[esse], 27955, L/Cpl, D Company [killed 27.9.16]

3. Casualties in January 1917

CASUALTIES DURING THE MONTH OF JANUARY 1917

NO	RANK	NAME	COY	CASUALTY
15270	Corpl	Reynolds A	"C"	Wounded 20-1-17
30070	Pte	Dear B	"D"	Wounded 20-1-17
13672	Sergt	Forde J	"D"	Missing 20-1-17
15571	Pte	Major L	"D"	Missing 20-1-17
29700	Pte	Cannell A	"D"	Missing 20-1-17
31345	Pte	Allen W	"D"	Missing 20-1-17

4. Attacks on Achiet le Grand, 13–17 March 1917

Officers going into action

Lieut.Col.G.P.Mills	C.O.
Capt. & Adjt.W.J.W.Colley	Adjutant
2/Lt.R.B.Rednall	Signal Officer
2/Lt.H.B.Stewart	Lewis Gun Officer
Capt.H.C.Browning A Coy	
2/Lieut.R.J.Clarke	A Coy
2/Lieut.J.J.Murray	A Coy
2/Lieut.Oliver-Jones	A Coy
2/Lieut.S.R.Chapman	B Coy
2/Lieut.F.E.Dealler	B Coy
2/Lieut.H.M.Woodyer	B Coy
Lieut.P.P.Steel	C Coy
2/Lieut.G.J.Luscombe	C Coy
2/Lieut.C.A.Lawrence	C Coy
2/Lieut.W.P.Cannell	C Coy
Capt.D.S.H.Keep	D Coy
Lieut.T.M.Elderton	D Coy
2/Lt.E.F.Piercy	D Coy
2/Lt.A.G.Angas	D Coy

Officers with 1st line transport

Major J.H.Bridcutt	2nd in Command
Lieut.E.W.Benson	Signal Officer
Lieut & Q.M. F.Corner	Quartermaster
2/Lt.A.W.Brawn	Transport Officer
2/Lt.S.C.Tremeer	A Coy
2/Lt.C.B.Kydd	A Coy
2/Lt.H.Driver	B Coy
2/Lt.H.F.Trewman	B Coy
Capt.W.G.Chirnside	C Coy
Capt.L.H.Keep	C Coy
2/Lt.H.J.Cartwright	D Coy
2/Lt.A.H.Waddy	D Coy.

Officers & Other Ranks recommended

Lieut.P.P.Steel
Lieut.& Qmaster F.Corner
2/Lt.E.F.Piercy
12702 Sergt. Mulrien, B[ernard]
14782 Sergt. Stuckey, G.
15703 Sergt. Clarke, H[arry] A[lbert]
12826 Sergt. Turville, A.
15321 L/Sgt. Blanshard, H.E.
15514 Pte. Franklin, A.
13908 Pte. Cox, C.A.
Lieut.T.M.Elderton wounded 14-3-17
2/Lt.H.M.Woodyer wounded 14-3-17
2/Lt.S.R.Chapman wounded (still at duty) 14-3-17
Capt.H.C.Browning wounded 15-3-17
Lieut.P.P.Steel wounded 17-3-17

2/Lt.W.P.Cannell wounded 17-3-17
2/Lt.E.F.Piercy wounded (still at duty) 17-3-17

Other Ranks killed in action

13-3-17
Batchelor, G[eorge] H[enry], 29775, Pte, B Coy
Smith, A[rthur] T[homas], 31171, Pte, A Coy
Tucker, H[arold Frederick], 33773, Pte, C Coy
Darvell, A[lfred], 40494, Pte, A Coy

Willacy, R[obert], 43263, Sgt, B Coy

14-3-17
Cook, [Fred] J[ames], 19029, L/Cpl, A Coy
Higby, J[ohn] B[rackley], 29518, Pte, C Coy
Morgan, W[illiam], 27890, Pte, B Coy
Miller, F[rank], 27839, Pte, B Coy

15-3-17
Battram, G[eorge], 21311, Pte, A Coy
Brown, C[harles], 17481, Pte, C Coy
Clark, A[quila], 53419, Cpl, A Coy
Gibbs, P[ercy] S[eaman], 29987, Pte, C Coy
Goble, F[rederick] C[harles], 31670, Pte, C Coy
Mulraney [sic Mulrien], B[ernard], 12702, Sgt, C Coy
Parsons, C[ecil] C[urtis], 16809, Cpl, A Coy
Robinson, C[ecil] C[lement], 16318, L/Cpl, C Coy
Sewell, F[rederick] C[harles], 33440, Cpl, C Coy
Blundell, W[illiam], 40521, Pte, A Coy
Chapman, E[dwin], 15544, Cpl, C Coy

Judd, J[ohn], 29831, Pte, C Coy

Petchey, E[rnest], 30001, Pte, C Coy

Smith, S[olomon], 23121, Pte, C Coy

17-3-17
Rowell, W[illiam], 27837, Pte, C Coy

Other Ranks wounded in action

12-3-17
Inison, F., 43307, Pte, D Coy

13-3-17
Anderson, J[ames Frederick], 10432, Pte, C Coy (still at duty)
Aylott, J[ohn], 18171, C Coy
Bamfield, P.B., 33751, Pte, A Coy (still at duty)
Clifton[?], A.A., 43352, L/Cpl, A Coy
Cronk, J[oseph] W[illiam], 33470, Sgt, C Coy [died 17.3.17]
Desborough, J., 31264, Pte, D Coy
Gay, A., 9872, Pte, A Coy (still at duty)
Halsey, J.W., 29851, Pte, C Coy (still at duty)
Merchant, J., 7562, L/Cpl, C Coy
Murray, J[ohn], 27093, Pte, C Coy [died 20.3.17]
Piercy, J.D., 15340, Pte, C Coy (still at duty)
Presland, E., 16395, Pte., C Coy
Timson, C.P., 12988, C Coy
Vernon, A., 19364, Pte., C Coy (still at duty)

Baker, R., 13609, Pte, A Coy
Brazier, D.A., 22788, Pte, A Coy

Franham, J.S., 18657, Cpl, C Coy
Goldsmith, H., 14445, Pte, C Coy
Matthews, J.A., 25717, Cpl, C Coy

Prentice, R.J., 29726, Pte, D Coy
Randle, H., 19136, Pte, D Coy

14-3-17
Bellamy, A., 18992, Cpl, A Coy
Dry, E.R., 40509, Pte., A Coy
Coote, W.H., 15458, Pte, B Coy
Durrant, 26575, H., Cpl, B Coy

Emery, W., 40510, Pte., A Coy
Glover, J., 43294, Pte, B Coy
Hawkes, A[lbert], 27500, Pte, B Coy
Henley, J., 23758, Pte, B Coy
Johnson, W.J., 43262, Pte., B Coy
Memmott, J.A., 12153, Pte, B Coy
Pantling, A.E., 16518, Pte, A Coy (still at duty)
Rawlinson, J., 40517, Pte, A Coy
Samuels, J., 40425, Pte, B Coy
Weston, L., 13143, Pte, B Coy
Woods, E.A., 29527, Pte, D Coy

Folds, R., 13905, Pte., A Coy
Gough, H., 43295, Pte., B Coy
Hawkes, J.W., 13856, Sgt, A Coy
Henson, A.G., 33759, Pte, B Coy
Leggatt, A., 29970, Pte, D Coy

Peters, A., 12704, L/Sgt., B Coy
Riddle, F., 30845, Pte., B Coy
Smith, A.H., 18232, Pte, B Coy
Woods, A.E., 15021, Pte, A Coy
Woods, W., 30797, Pte, A Coy

15-3-17
Dent, C[harles] E[dward], 15316, Pte, A Coy
Ely, R.A., 20030, L/Cpl, A Coy (still at duty)
Hales, W.G., 23059, Pte, C Coy
Leach, B., 15905, L/Cpl, C Coy
Povey, J.W., 13253, Pte, A Coy
Stebbings, A.G., 31375, Pte., A Coy
West, B.J., 29464, Pte, A Coy
Wilkinson, C.H., 30902, Pte, A Coy
Wood, G[ilbert] H[enry], 29804, Pte, A Coy [died 15-3-17]
York, W.G., 12761, Pte, A Coy

Grief, J.C., 40500, Pte. A Coy
Halsey, R.C., 15610, C Coy
Mason, A., 13652, Pte,
Ravenscroft, C., 14351, L/Cpl, C Coy
Turner, G.A., 31185, Pte, A Coy
West, J.H., 30899, Pte, A Coy

17-3-17
Eggleton, W., 12038, Pte, D Coy
Webb, J., 25880, Pte, C Coy

Neville, F.H., 17325, Pte, D Coy
Young, F., 17519, Pte, C Coy

18-3-17
Brunton, G., 31378, Pte, D Coy
Mason, A., 13652, Pte, C Coy

Missing Believed Killed
Norman, R.S., 14774, L/Cpl, C Coy

Missing – 15-3-17
Barcock, F[rederick], 25417, Pte, C Coy [killed]
Harrison, W., 17369, Pte, A Coy
Wheton, J., 33772, Pte, C Coy

Clarke, G.J., 17642, Pte, C Coy
Jarman, H.L., 29992, Pte, C Coy

5. Attack at Chérisy, 3 May 1917

Officers proceeding into action on 3/5/17 & Casualties.

Lt.Col.G.P.Mills Commanding Officer
Capt.W.J.W.Colley Adjutant
2/Lt.H.B.Stewart Lewis Gun Officer
2/Lt.R.B.Rednall Sig. Officer wounded 3/5/17
Capt.K.H.Nelson Medical officer
2/Lt.S.C.Tremeer wounded 3/5/17 Died of wounds 17/5/17
2/Lt.R.J.Clarke wounded 3/5/17
2/Lt.J.J.Murray wounded 3/5/17
2/Lt.W.D.Oliver Jones wounded 3/5/17
Capt.W.H.Bull killed 3/5/17

2/Lt.H.Driver wounded (still at duty) 3/5/17
2/Lt.E.G.Pernett
2/Lt.C.B.Kydd killed 3/5/17
Capt.L.H.Keep
2/Lt.C.A.Lawrence
2/Lt.G.J.Luscombe killed in action 3/5/17
2/Lt.P.J.Reiss wounded 3/5/17
Capt.D.S.H.Keep
2/Lt.E.F.Piercy wounded 3/5/17
2/Lt.L.G.Angas killed 3/5/17
2/Lt.H.J.Cartwright wounded 3/5/17
2/Lt.E.St.Hilary Lingwood killed 3/5/17

Officers
Killed   5
Wounded   8
Died of Wounds   1

Other Ranks
Killed   19
Missing   48
Wounded   162
Died of Wounds   6
Missing believed Killed   4
Missing & Wounded   3

                          242

6. Attacks at Ypres, 10–17 August 1917

Officers to go into Action

Headquarters
Major J.H.Bridcutt D.S.O. Comdg. Officer.
Capt.W.J.W.Colley M.C. Adjutant.
Lieut.H.B.Stewart Lewis Gun Officer.
Lieut.S.R.Chapman Signal Officer.
Capt.J.A.Vlasto (R.A.M.C.) Medical Officer
"A" Company
Capt.R.J.Clark O.C.Coy.
2/Lieut.F.Halsey
2/Lieut.K.H.Bishop.
"B" Company
Capt.H.Driver D.S.O. O.C.Coy.
2/Lieut.G.R.Craig.
"C" Company
Capt.O.Kingdon O.C.Coy.
2/Lt.C.A.Lawrence.
2/Lt.N.C.E.Cockburn.
2/Lt.S.M.Connor.
"D" Company
Capt.J.C.M.Ferguson O.C.Coy.
2/Lt.G.S.Richards
2/Lt.E.C.H.Conyers.

Casualties

2/Lt.S.M.Connor. Killed in Action 10.8.17
2/Lt.F.Halsey Missing 10/8/17
Capt.H.Driver D.S.O. Wounded 10.8.17
2/Lt.E.C.H.Conyers Wounded 10.8.17
Capt.J.C.M.Ferguson Wounded still at duty 10.8.17
Lieut.H.F.Trewman Wounded still at duty 7.8.17
2/Lt.G.R.Craig Wounded still at duty 8.8.17

Summary of Casualties O.R.s

Killed	35
Wounded	163
Died of Wounds	5
Missing	47
Missing Believed Killed	6
Missing Believed Wounded	3
	259

Incurred from 10/8/17 to 17/8/17 inclusive

Appendix C2. Places Of Birth Of Other Ranks Who Died

Hertfordshire	148 (19.68%)	Oxfordshire	5
Bedfordshire	117 (15.56%)	Durham	4
Middlesex	78 (10.37%)	Hampshire	4
Surrey	43	Ireland	4
Norfolk	38	Lincolnshire	4
Huntingdonshire	36	Scotland	4
Northamptonshire	35	Warwickshire	3
Essex	35	Worcestershire	3
Cambridgeshire	24	Australia	2
Kent	21	Berkshire	2
Staffordshire	20	Derbyshire	2
Gloucestershire	15	Devon	2
Buckinghamshire	14	Northumberland	2
Suffolk	11	Wiltshire	2
Somerset	10	Bohemia	1
Leicestershire	9	Cheshire	1
Yorkshire	9	Herefordshire	1
Sussex	7	Isle of Wight	1
Lancashire	5	London	1
Nottinghamshire	5	Shropshire	1

Major Towns

Luton	18	Northampton	7
St Albans	14	Leicester	6
Watford	12	Paddington	6
Bedford	12	Battersea	5
Bristol	9	Bermondsey	5
Wolverhampton	9	Hertford	5
Lambeth	8	Hitchin	5
Sandy	8	Kempston	5
Hemel Hempstead	7	Ware	5

Appendix C3. Comparative Battle Casualties – Other Ranks Only

With other battalions in the Division

53rd Bde.	
8th Norfolks	673
8th Suffolks	398
10th Essex	1,072
6th Royal Berkshires	629
Brigade Total	2,772
54th Bde.	
11th Royal Fusiliers	987
7th Bedfordshires	781
6th Northamptonshires	1,199
12th Middlesex	648
Brigade Total	3,615
55th Bde.	
7th Queens	1,200
7th East Kents	1,062
8th East Surreys	1,091
7th Royal West Kents	1,185
Brigade Total	4,538
Pioneers	
8th Royal Sussex	215
Divisional Total	11,140

Deaths in specific engagements – Other Ranks only, Killed in Action only

1. 1-2/7/16: Pommiers Redoubt

7th Bedfordshire		87
6th Northamptonshire	31	
11th Royal Fusiliers		57
12th Middlesex	2	
Total	177	

2. 14/7/16: Trones Woood

7th Bedfordshire		1
6th Northamptonshire	78	
11th Royal Fusiliers		2
12th Middlesex	30	
Total		111

3. 26-29/9/16: Thiepval & Schwaben Redoubt

7th Bedfordshire	88

6th Northamptonshire	44	
11th Royal Fusiliers		80
12th Middlesex	143	
Total		355

TOTALS FOR 1916

7th Bedfordshire		176
6th Northamptonshire	153	
11th Royal Fusiliers		139
12th Middlesex	175	
Total		643

1. 17-18/2/17 Boom Ravine

7th Bedfordshire		3
6th Northamptonshire	99	
11th Royal Fusiliers		92
12th Middlesex	28	
Total		222

2. 12-18/3/17 Achiet le Petit

7th Bedfordshire		25
6th Northamptonshire	1	
11th Royal Fusiliers		7
12th Middlesex	12	
Total		45

3. 3-4/5/17 Chérisy

7th Bedfordshire		66
6th Northamptonshire	38	
11th Royal Fusiliers		24
12th Middlesex	109	
Total		237

4. 9-16/8/17 Glencorse Wood etc.

7th Bedfordshire		55
6th Northamptonshire	23	
11th Royal Fusiliers		100
12th Middlesex	7	
Total		185

TOTALS FOR 1917

7th Bedfordshire		149
6th Northamptonshire	161	
11th Royal Fusiliers		223
12th Middlesex	156	
Total		689

1. 21-26/3/18 Kaiserslacht

7th Bedfordshire		48
6th Northamptonshire	48	
11th Royal Fusiliers		53
Total		149

2. 2-5/4/18 Gentelles

7th Bedfordshire		15
6th Northamptonshire	43	

APPENDIX C: CASUALTIES

11th Royal Fusiliers 9
Total 67

3. 24-25/4/18 Cachy
7th Bedfordshire 54
6th Northamptonshire 22
11th Royal Fusiliers 2
Total 78

TOTAL FOR 1918 [note 12th Middlesex disbanded February 1918]
7th Bedfordshire 117
6th Northamptonshire 113
11th Royal Fusiliers 64
Total 294

Index of Personal Names

Note: rank given is the highest noted for that individual in the diary; where the name in the index differs from that on the page it indicates a spelling error by the adjutant (see Introduction p.xii for an explanation of the transcription)

Abrams, Thomas W., Lance Corporal 152
Acton, J.J., Second Lieutenant 104
Adams, Edward, Private 224
Adams, G.H.D., Second Lieutenant 85
Adams, Mike J. xii
Adams, Thomas Isaac, Private 230
Adlam, Thomas Edwin VC, Temporary Second Lieutenant xx, 48, 140, 188, 198, 199, 210, 228
Alcock, E.D., Lieutenant (54th Brigade Staff) 156
Alderman, G., Private 229
Allan, G., Private 142
Allen, A.W., Private 229
Allen, John Robert, Lance Corporal 229
Allen, J.W., Sergeant 226
Allen, L., Private, 229
Allen, W., Private 231
Allen, W.S., Private 229
Alwin, H.J., Private 226
Amos, Ernest E., Company Sergeant Major 136
Anderson, James Frederick, Private 233
Andrews, Frederick, Private 228
Andrews, J.E., Private 230
Andrews, S., Private 227
Andrews, William John, Corporal 199, 228
Angas, Lionel George, Second Lieutenant 58, 126, 127, 232, 235
Ansell, Walter, Private 225
Antcliffe, Frederick, Battalion Sergeant Major 140
Appleby, William, Lance Corporal 162
Arborn, W., Private 230
Archer, C.J., Corporal 227
Archer, J., Private 225
Armstrong, Frederick William, Private 224
Arnold, Sydney, Private 138, 230
Arnott, F.Herbert, Corporal 228
Ashton, W., Second Lieutenant 103
Asquith, Herbert Henry, (later Earl of Oxford), Prime Minister 63
Atkins, Arthur Edward, Lance Corporal xxi, 210, 228
Atkins, Edward William, Lance Corporal 224
Atkinson, J.H., Private 229
Aylott, John, Private 230, 233
Baden, Reginald, Second Lieutenant 16, 18, 45, 113
Bailey, Albert Gilbert, Private 140, 226

Bailey, F.J., Private 230
Baker, Arthur Frederick, Private 140
Baker, F., Private 225
Baker, G.R., Corporal 95, 160
Baker, R., Private 233
Balls, B.H., Second Lieutenant 97, 99
Bamfield, P.B., Private 233
Banes, F.J., Lance Corporal 230
Barcock, Frederick, Private 234
Bargioni, Eugenio, Private 224
Barton, A., Corporal 227
Barton, F.W., Private 225
Batchelor, Frederick, Lance Corporal 162
Batchelor, George Henry, Private 233
Bateman, Joseph, Private 224
Batten, Joseph Keith, Captain 103, 104
Battison, A., Private 231
Battram, George, Private 233
Batty, J.E., Lance Corporal 230
Bawden, Robert, Private 152
Baxter, C.E., Private 229
Baxter, G.W., Private 231
Bayford, Frank William, Sergeant 140, 230
Bayford, Leonard John, Private 228
Bean, W., Private 229
Bellamy, A., Corporal 233
Bennett, William, Private 228
Bennett, William F., Private 138
Bennett, W.H., Second Lieutenant 42
Benson, E.W., Lieutenant 18, 20, 37, 152, 184, 232
Benson, William, Private 225
Berry, Herbert Eric, Private 141, 230
Bidmead, Daniel E., Private 153
Biggs, Private 118
Billington William Charles, Private xxii, 210, 228
Birch, Frederick, Lance Corporal 163
Birch, T.M., Private 225
Bird, Leonard, Private 138, 225
Birdsey, W.T., Corporal 225
Bishop, K.H., Second Lieutenant 235
Blackmore, William, Private 228
Blakeman, F.G., Sergeant 230
Blanshard, Arthur Ernest, Corporal 34, 232
Blake, W., Sergeant 160
Blower, C.R., Private 230
Blowes, C.R., Private 225
Blundell, William, Private 233

242 INDEX OF PERSONAL NAMES

Bolton, F.W., Private 225
Boness, John, Sergeant 103, 160, 161
Bottomley, George, Private 141
Bowers, Richard, Private 228
Bowles, Alec, Corporal 224
Brace, Arthur, Private 138, 225
Bradbury, W.E., Private, 230
Bradfield, F., Sergeant 160
Bradford, R., Private 230
Bradley, A., Private 229
Bradshaw, E., Lance Corporal 230
Brand, Richard Maurice, Company Sergeant Major 127, 140, 142, 187
Brawn, A.W., Second Lieutenant 53, 60, 121, 187, 232
Brawn, W.N., Second Lieutenant 85
Brazier, D.A., Private 233
Brecard [or Bregard], General (French 1st Dismounted Cavalry Division) 101, 194
Breed, F., Private 229
Brett, George John, Private 224
Brett, H., Corporal 155, 161, 162
Brett, Henry, Private 140
Bridcutt, John Henry, Major (Adjutant) 43, 44, 49, 52–54, 56, 59, 65, 77–79, 82, 109, 123, 140, 143, 177, 184, 189–191, 232, 235
Briers, F.J., Private 230
Brookes, T., Private 230
Brown, Charles, Private 233
Brown, Frank, Lance Corporal 152
Brown, Henry George, Lance Corporal 224
Brown, John Walter, Private 228
Brown, John Walter, Corporal 228
Brown, William George, Private 225
Browning, Herbert Compton, Captain (Adjutant) 45, 60, 61, 68, 90, 91, 96, 100, 102, 108, 113, 114, 140, 232
Brunt, H., Private 163
Brunt, William, Lance Corporal 152
Brunton, G., Private 234
Buckingham, William, Sergeant 160
Bull, E.E., Captain 48
Bull, John William, Lance Corporal 162
Bull, Wilfred Herbert, Captain 14, 18, 20, 41, 72, 126, 127, 136, 174, 178–180, 184, 234
Bullard, William Ralph, Private 225
Bunce, F., Private 226
Burge, Oliver Samuel, Private 229
Burgess, Albert, Private 225
Burnham, Harry T., Private 152
Burton, Frederick C., Private 138, 225
Butcher, W., Private 227
Butler, Arthur, Lance Sergeant 153, 229
Butler, G., Private 226
Butler, J., Private 230
Butler, William, Lance Sergeant 160
Butterfield, G., Private 226
Buxton, W., Sergeant 160
Byford, A., Lance Corporal 225
Cain, Nathan, Private 141
Cairns, T.F., Private 230
Canham, Charles William, Lance Corporal 228
Canham, J., Private 227

Cannell, A., Private 231
Cannell, W.P., Second Lieutenant 55, 61, 232, 233
Cannon, Samuel Lawrence, Second Lieutenant 228
Carles, R.E., Second Lieutenant (6th Bedfords) 107
Carot, Colonel (French 43rd Regiment) 88
Carr, Thomas Burgess, Private 225
Carron, W., Lance Corporal 226
Carter, Frederick Herbert, Private 225
Carter, Walter, Private 229
Carter, W.G., Second Lieutenant 101, 151
Cartwright, Henry J., Second Lieutenant xi, xii, 29, 41, 106–127, 187, 199, 200, 232, 235
Cartwright, Olive 107
Cathcart-Nicholls, H., Second Lieutenant 27, 45, 110, 111
Catlin, Albert, Private 225
Chandler, Alfred, Corporal 142, 230
Chandler, C., Private 230
Chandler, Frederick Charles, Lance Sergeant 160, 161
Chandler, William, Lance Corporal 224
Chandler, William, Sergeant 160
Chapman, A., Lance Corporal 162
Chapman, C.F., Private 226
Chapman, Edwin, Corporal 233
Chapman, S.R., Captain 79, 232, 235
Chapman, T.J., Private 230
Chapman, W., Private 231
Chapman, W.A., Sergeant 153, 160, 161
Chapman, W.F., Private 138
Chapman, Walter J., Lance Corporal 162
Chase, Captain (Royal Engineers) 53
Chirnside, William Stuart, Captain 232
Chubb, Private (12th Middlesex) 150
Clare, G.T., Corporal 230
Clark, Aquila, Corporal 233
Clark, B.J., Private 225
Clark, R.O., Captain 77, 81, 97, 189
Clark, S., Private 227
Clark, S.B., Private 227
Clark, William Garner, Private 224
Clark, W.P., Private 229
Clerke, Drummer 153
Clarke, E., Lance Corporal 162
Clarke, G., Private 138
Clarke, G.J., Private 234
Clarke, G.S., Lance Corporal 142
Clarke, Harry Albert, Sergeant 232
Clarke, Jack Stanley, Lance Corporal 162
Clarke, R.J., Second Lieutenant 58, 200, 232, 234, 235
Clarke, W.F., Lance Corporal 227
Clarke, William George, Private 224
Clayton, W., Private 230
Clegg, E., Captain 20, 22, 42, 44, 45, 72, 113, 126, 175, 178
Clerk, G., Private 227
Clifton, A.A., Lance Corporal 233
Clifton, Charles, Private 230
Clifton, H., Lance Corporal 162

INDEX OF PERSONAL NAMES 243

Cline, S.E., Captain 103
Cobb, J.A., Lance Corporal 227
Cochrane, John, Lance Corporal 231
Cockburn, N.C.E., Second Lieutenant 98, 150, 151, 155, 235
Coe, J.T., Major 103
Colbert, William, Sergeant 160
Cole, H.T., Lance Corporal 162
Coleman, Albert Francis, Private 224
Coleman, E., Private 226
Colley, William Joseph Wellesley, Major 69, 79, 85, 90, 96, 98, 100, 108–114, 121, 140, 182, 187, 189, 232, 234, 235
Collins, David, Lance Sergeant 161
Collins, John, Private 138
Collins, Walter, Private 153
Colman, J., Private 227
Congreve, Sir Walter Norris VC, Lieutenant General (XIII Corps) 193
Connor, Samuel Maurice, Second Lieutenant 235, 236
Conyers, E.C.H., Second Lieutenant 77, 235, 236
Cook, Albert George, Private 138, 224
Cook, Fred James, Private 227, 233
Cooper, A., Private 152
Cooper, C., Private 229
Cooper, F., Private 152
Cooper, George Albert, Private 230
Cooper, W.F., Sergeant 138
Cooper, William John, Lance Sergeant 160, 161
Cooper, William Percy, Sergeant 224
Coote, H.E., Private 226
Coote, W.H., Private 233
Cootes, F., Private 163
Cope, A., Private 227
Corbett, V.D., Captain (12th Middlesex) 155
Cornell, Arthur Ernest, Sergeant 43, 224
Cornell, V.H., Private 229
Corner, F., Honorary Lieutenant and Quartermaster 17, 19, 79, 85, 134, 232
Cornish, J.A., Private 231
Cosgrove, Albert, Private 138
Costin, W., Private 226
Cother, J., Private 138
Cousins, John Joseph, Lance Corporal 140
Coutts, R.W., Second Lieutenant 96, 98
Covell, H.C., Second Lieutenant 45
Coventry, D., Private 225
Covington, G.B., Private 227
Cowland, Edward, Private 228
Cowlin, A., Private, 230
Cowling, George Frederick, Sergeant 122, 124, 140
Cox, A., Private 225
Cox, C., Lance Corporal 162
Cox, Charlie George, Lance Corporal 225
Cox, Christopher Augustus VC, Private 200, 217, 225, 232
Coxwell, E.A., Lance Corporal 225
Cracknell, Frederick, Private 228
Craig, Gordon Robert, Second Lieutenant 83, 99, 235, 236
Crawford, J., Corporal 226

Cripps, C., Private 229
Croft, Edward, Lance Corporal 224
Croft, J.W., Private 227
Cronk, Joseph William, Sergeant 233
Cross, Albert, Private 153
Crossman, A., Private 152
Cunliffe Owen, Sir Charles, Brigadier (54th Brigade) 85
Cunningham, James, Second Lieutenant 43, 115
Curchin, Harry, Private 225
Currall, Private (6th Northamptonshires) 149
Curtice, R.W., Second Lieutenant 84, 150
Custer, E., Private 226
Cutler, Arnold, Private 224
Cutmore, W.H., Private 225
Daniels, W.W., Private 230
Darlow, A., Lance Corporal 225
Darrington, Peter, Private 225
Darvell, Alfred, Private 233
Davey, Private (12th Middlesex) 150
Davidson, R., Captain (54th Brigade Major) 37
Davies, D., Second Lieutenant 90, 146
Davis, A., Private 230
Dawbon, George William, Private 224
Dawbon, William Walter, Sergeant 160
Dawes, Henry, Private 224
Dawson, S.C., Private 225
Deal, Walter Charles, Lance Corporal 162, 225
Dealler, F.E., Second Lieutenant 27, 43, 44, 113, 114, 139, 232
Dean, Walter, Corporal 61, 141
Dear, B., Private 231
Deighton, Reuben, Private 228
Dennison, C.J., Private 227
Denny, Guy, Private 138
Dent, Charles Edward, Private 234
Desborough, J., Private 233
Dewey, F.J., Private 226
Dickens, John William Private 231
Dillingham, A., Private 142
Dilks, H.W., Private 227
Doake, R.L.V., Captain 45, 99, 102, 113
Docwra, W., Private, 230
Doel, Sydney Herbert, Private 231
Donovan, T.N., Second Lieutenant 84, 153
Dorrell, Frederick Thomas, Private 119, 199, 228
Dorrington, W., Corporal 230
Downing, F., Private 226
Doyle, J., Private 227
Dring, Joseph, Sergeant 160, 227
Driver, Harry, Captain 40, 68, 79–81, 127, 189, 232, 235, 236
Drury, George, Private 225
Dry, E.R., Private 233
Duffin, Company Sergeant Major 73
Duller, C.W., Corporal 225
Dungay, Robert, Lance Corporal 141, 162
Dunham, W., Private 142
Dunn, Private (11th Royal Fusiliers) 150
Duplock, Marten Cave, Lieutenant 99
Durrant, H., Corporal 233
Dwight, A., Private 227

INDEX OF PERSONAL NAMES

Dyer, William Henry, Private 163
Eardley, A., Private 226
Edgerton Hine, S., Lieutenant 10
Edward IV, King 112
Edwards, Frank Henry, Private 228
Eggitt, H., Private 142
Eggleton, W., Private 234
Elderton, T.H., Second Lieutenant 58, 232
Ellins, S.T., Sergeant 225
Elliott, Private 150
Elliott, William, Private 228
Ellis, W.G., Private 141, 227
Elwood, Walter, Private 231
Ely, R.A., Corporal 152, 234
Emery, W., Private 234
Emery, W.S., Lance Corporal 162
Erskine, Henry, Private 140
Ett[e]y, T., Private 138, 229
Evans, G., Private 227
Evans, William, Private 228
Everitt [or Everett], F., Captain 103, 104
Eversden, George, Private 230
Ewer, W., Private 227
Falkenhayn, Erich von, General xiii, 27
Farey, R., Private 229
Faulkner, Noah, Private 226
Favell, Joseph S., Private 153
Fawkes, Alan, Private 224
Fensome, Stanley William, Private 224
Fenwick, George Alfred, Private 226
Ferguson, John Charles Moore, Captain 81, 83, 146, 189, 235, 236
Ferris, Albert, Private 152
Field, Alfred, Drummer 152
Field, A.H., Private 227
Field, Charles William, Private 224
Field, Martin Edgar, Lance Corporal 227, 229
Fiennes, Colonel (7th Royal West Kents) 42, 126
Fish, W.Herbert, Private 55
Fisher, Harry, Private 231
Fitzgerald, J., Private 227
Fitzgerald, Thomas, Lance Corporal 140
Flavell, H., Second Lieutenant 85, 103
Fleckney, A.J., Lance Corporal 161, 162
Fleet, W., Private 226
Fleming Brown, G.F., Lieutenant 184
Fletcher, Jack (batman) 120
Floutier, Camille, Second Lieutenant 228
Foch, Ferdinand, Maréchal 92
Foldo, S., Private 227
Folds, R., Private 234
Foley, Herbert John, Sergeant 224
Folkes, T., Private 226
Forde, J., Sergeant 231
Foreman, William, Private 225
Foskett, F.G., Private 226
Foster, B.C., Lieutenant 37
Fountain, Arthur, Company Sergeant Major 142, 228
Fox, F.H., Second Lieutenant 85
Fox, James William, Lance Corporal 224
Franham, J.S., Corporal 233
Franklin, A., Private 232

Freeman, G., Private 229
Freeman, Herbert Edward, Private 224
French, J., Private 226
French, Sir John Pinkston, Field Marshal 3
French, W.G., Private 231
Froggart, Private (12th Middlesex) 150
Fry, Lance Corporal 119
Fudge, Walter George Private 228
Fuller, George B., Private 142
Fuller, H., Private 141
Furr, Ernest William, Private 229
Fyson, F., Private 163
Gage, R., Private 226
Gale, Second Lieutenant (11th Royal Fusiliers) 157
Gamage, H., Sergeant 229
Gammons, Herbert John, Lance Corporal 140
Gates, Frank, Private 224
Gay, A., Private 233
George V, King 44, 152
Gibbard, A., Private 229
Gibbs, Percy Seaman, Private 233
Gibson, A.H.C., Second Lieutenant 43
Giddings, John, Private 231
Ginger, EW., Private 227
Ginger, Joseph, Sergeant 224
Gladding, Frederick, Lance Corporal 228
Glover, J., Private 234
Goble, Frederick Charles, Private 233
Godfrey, Arthur, Private 225
Goebel, Richard Henry, Lance Corporal 225
Goldhawk, George, Private 140, 160
Goldsmith, H., Private 233
Goodfellow, George William, Private 225
Goodliff, Albert, Private 140
Goodwin, Austin, Private 231
Goodwin, Stanley Robert Marshall, Lance Sergeant 161
Gordon, A., Sergeant 227
Goss, William, Private 152
Gough, George E., Private 61
Gough, H., Private 234
Gough, Sir Hubert de la Poer, General 64, 92, 124, 194
Gould, F.A., Private, 229
Graves, Herbert, Lieutenant 48
Graves, Herbert, Private 225
Green, George, Corporal 224
Greenhill, Dennis, Private 230
Gregory, W., Lance Corporal 226
Grief, J.C., Private 234
Griffin, John, Private xii, 45, 112, 113
Griffiths, G., Private 227
Groves, Frederick Edmund James, Private xii, 42, 111
Gurney, Frank, Private 225
Gurney, James, Private 228
Hack, A.J., Private 226
Haggard, Captain (6th Northamptonshires) 159
Hague, E.A., Lieutenant 103
Haig, Douglas, Field Marshal, Earl 3, 33, 42, 43, 57, 58, 64, 110, 121, 193
Haines, G., Private 152

INDEX OF PERSONAL NAMES

Hales, W.G., Private 234
Hall, Charles, Company Sergeant Major 140, 187
Halls, Herbert Rolfe, Private 141
Halsey, Frederick, Second Lieutenant 235, 236
Halsey, G., Private 230
Halsey, J.W., Private 233
Halsey, Reginald Charles, Corporal 161, 234
Hammond, H.T., Private 225
Hammond, J., Private 230
Hammond, J., Corporal 141, 161
Hanson, Robert, Sergeant 140
Hardie, Sidney Duncan Grellier, Corporal 225
Harding, G., Private 226
Hargford, W., Private 142
Harper, Private 150
Harrington, G., Lance Corporal 226
Harris, Arthur William, Lance Corporal 140
Harris, E., Lance Corporal 227
Harrison, Lance Corporal (12th Middlesex) 149
Harrison, Frederick George, Lance Corporal 225
Harrison, W., Private 225, 234
Hart, Alfred, Sergeant 230
Hartfree, Private (6th Northamptonshires) 149
Hasler, Gordon Beverley, Second Lieutenant 43, 45, 113
Hastler, A.C., Private 225
Haverson, A.E., Lance Corporal 230
Haward, H.W., Second Lieutenant 85, 151
Hawkes, Albert, Private 234
Hawkes, J.W., Sergeant 234
Hayes, S., Private 226
Haynes, Albert Edward, Sergeant 224
Head, S., Private 230
Heard, R.S., Second Lieutenant 98
Hedgecock, Lance Corporal (11th Royal Fusiliers) 149
Hedger, John, Private 231
Hedges, Private (12th Middlesex), 150
Heley, Thomas John, Lance Corporal 231
Hemsley, Edward E., Private 152
Heneker, Sir William Charles Giffard, Brigadier (54th Brigade) 5, 11, 25, 62
Heneker, Mrs.Clara Marion 62
Henley, J. Private 234
Hensman, Horace Alfred, Private 225
Henson, A.G., Private 234
Hersted, L, Lance Corporal 65
Hewitt, B.R., Private 227
Hewitt, Frank, Lance Corporal 224
Heyworth, Frederick James, Brigadier (20th Brigade) 36
Higby, John Brackley, Private 233
Higgs, John Frederick, Private 228
Hill, A., Private 227
Hill, Edward, Private 229
Hill, Leonard James, Sergeant 119, 198, 228
Hill, W., Private 231
Hobbs, Frank, Lance Corporal 141
Hobby, A., Private 229
Hobson, Owen Ellis, Second Lieutenant (6th Bedfords) 107, 118
Hodge, Walter Fred, Corporal 228

Holiday, H., Private 225
Hollister, J., Private 227
Holloway, G.A, Private 230
Holloway, Joseph John, Private 228
Holmes, J., Lance Corporal 142
Holton, A., Corporal 161–163
Honour, Bruce, Private 230
Hopcroft, F., Private 225
Hopper, J.D., Second Lieutenant 43
Hopson, Private (11th Royal Fusiliers) 149
Horgan, Harry, Private 140
Horley, A.L., Lance Corporal 120, 229
Horsted, T., Private 229
Howard family xi
Howard, Private (11th Royal Fusiliers), 149
Howard, C., Private 226
Howard, Cedric Stewart, Second Lieutenant 115, 116, 120, 121, 199, 227
Howlett, Walter, Private 224
Hudson, Colonel 62
Hudson, Mrs. 62
Hudson, G., Private 150, 153
Huggett, J., Private 227
Hughes, A., Private 231
Hughes, F.H., Private 141
Hughes, G.H.A., Second Lieutenant 35, 110, 111, 112
Hughes, W., Second Lieutenant 100
Humphrey, William, Private 121, 198, 229
Hunston, Robert Donald, Second Lieutenant 48, 199, 227
Hunt, Albert Victor, Private 228
Hunt, C., Private 230
Hurlock, Edward, Lance Corporal 162
Hurlock, G., Private 227
Hutton, G.H., Private 227
Hyde, William, Sergeant 225
Impey, S., Sergeant 227
Ingrey, C.R., Sergeant 230
Inison, F., Private 233
Innes, W.H., Lance Corporal 226
Inns, William, Private 140
Ives, P., Private 227
Ivory, James, Corporal 34
Jackson, E., Private 227
Jackson, Sir Thomas Dare, Brigadier (55th Brigade) 27
Jacob, Sir Claud William, General (II Corps) 57, 58, 61, 71, 77, 193, 194
Jaggard, S.W., Sergeant 160, 161, 163
James, Herbert William, Private 229
Jarman, H.L., Private 234
Jarvis Smith, G., Captain 41, 100
Jeffs, J., Private 229
Jeffs, W.J., Private 227
Jenner, Private (11th Royal Fusiliers) 149
Jennings, R., Private 227
Joffre, Joseph, Maréchal 29
Johnson, Captain (RE) 185, 186
Johnson, Arthur, Private 225
Johnson, A.S., Private 227
Johnson, Charles, Private 225
Johnson, C., Private 226

Johnson, Evelyn Walter James, Second Lieutenant 45, 113
Johnson, R.J., Private 227
Johnson, Robert Marshall, Private 141
Johnson, W.J., Private 234
Jolly, Lance Corporal (6th Northamptonshires) 150
Jolly, C.P., Private 226
Jones, A., Lance Corporal 44
Jones, A.W., Private 227
Jones, H., Private 229
Jones, P.Vincent, Major 14, 16
Jordan, John, Private 228
Josling, A., Private 227
Jowett, Charles, Private 225
Joyce, Private (11th Royal Fusiliers) 149
Joyce, A.H.S., Corporal 42, 44
Judd, John, Private 233
Judge, W., Private 152
Kay, J.H., Second Lieutenant 48, 116, 122, 123
Keep, Douglas Scrivener Howard, Captain 60, 61, 68, 71, 78, 113–116, 119–123, 125, 140, 187, 232, 235
Keep, Leslie Howard, Captain 18, 20, 41, 43, 55, 56, 68, 102, 108, 111, 119, 121, 126, 140, 174, 185, 187, 232, 235
Kekk, J., Second Lieutenant 103
Kelf, J.A., Second Lieutenant 159
Kemble, H., Lance Sergeant 160, 161, 163
Kempster, E., Private 230
Kerr, W., Second Lieutenant 96, 101
Kerrison, E.P., Regimental Quartermaster Sergeant 136, 159
Kethridge, H., Private 227
Kinch, H., Private 226
King, Captain 12
King, B., Private 226
King, R.G., Corporal 161
Kingdon, Oliver, Captain xxiii, 79–81, 94, 96, 101, 111, 137–139, 189, 235
Kingham, Arthur, Private 229
Kitchener, Horatio Herbert, Field Marshal, 1st Earl Kitchener of Khartoum 1, 29, 44
Kitchener, H.J., Corporal 138
Knapp, Bert, Lance Sergeant 224
Knight, W., Private 231
Knock, H., Private 230
Knowles, John Norman, Private 228
Koch, G.H., Second Lieutenant 101
Kydd, Chester Bishop, Second Lieutenant 48, 65, 126, 140, 232, 235
Lacey, W.G., Lieutenant 16, 48
Lambert, A., Private 226
Lancaster, Alec, Lance Corporal 42, 44
Land, A.L., Private 230
Land, Frederick, Private 230
Lane, Percy, Private 228
Langdon, L.H., Private 226
Langley, J., Private 226
Laughton, George, Sergeant 181, 197, 225
Lawes, G., Private 226
Lawrence, Charles Alfred, Captain 93, 101, 152, 232, 235

Lawrence, G., Private 138, 230
Lawrence, Vernon Alan, Private 227
Lawson, H.A., Private 227
Leach, B., Lance Corporal 234
Lee, Albert Victor, Private 228
Lee, Sir Richard Philipps, Major General (18th Division) 82, 126, 194
Legate, George, Private 224
Leggatt, A., Private 234
Lewin, Arthur, Private 138, 226
Lewin, Horace, Corporal 224
Lewis, F.J., Lance Corporal 226
Lewis, H., Lance Corporal 230
Lewis, S., Private 142
Lewis, William, Private 140
Lillington, E.A., Private 226
Lincoln, Arthur George, Private 225
Line, B.C., Private 230
Lingwood, Edward St. Hilary, Second Lieutenant 127, 235
Lloyd, T.E., Lieutenant 17, 19, 44, 178, 184
Lloyd-George, David, Prime Minister xii, 3, 63, 92
Long, Captain (RE) 90
Longhurst, Major (Royal Berkshire Regiment) 191
Lord, H., Private 230
Louis XI, King 112
Lovatt, Arthur William, Private 225
Lubman, Lieutenant (RE) 185, 186
Luff, A.T., Sergeant 226
Luscombe, Gridland John, Second Lieutenant 43, 61, 232, 235
MacAndrew, Henry John Milnes, Major General 41
Machin, G.E., Corporal 153
Mackenzie, A.F., Captain 104
Maddox, E.J., Private 227
Major, L., Private 231
Maling, F., Private 226
Malone, Henry Cheney, Second Lieutenant 228
Mangin, Charles, General xiii
Mann, Lance Corporal 118
Manning, W., Private 138
Mansfield, W., Private 226
Mapley, Thomas Harry, Private 224
Marchant, H.W., Sergeant 230
Mardel, Charles James, Lance Corporal 231
Mardle, Albert, Private 229
Marshall, Walter, Sergeant 228
Martin, Arthur Henry, Private 225
Martin, A.W., Private 226
Martin, J., Private 227
Mason (Machine Gun Corps) 118
Mason, A., Private 138, 234
Mason, G., Private 227
Mason, W., Lieutenant 60
Mason, William Sidney, Private 140
Masson, R., Private 113, 230
Matthews, E.E., Lance Corporal 227
Matthews, A., Corporal 233
Maw, Harry, Second Lieutenant 86
Maxall, W., Lance Corporal 227

INDEX OF PERSONAL NAMES 247

Maxse, Sir Ivor, General (18th Division) 5, 23, 29, 32, 38, 44, 49, 53, 54, 57, 112, 116, 118, 122, 192, 193
Maxwell, Sir Francis Aylmer, Lieutenant Colonel (12th Middlesex) 56, 66, 185
May, C., Private 226
McBride, Andrew Best, Captain 101, 102
McGrane, Walter, Lance Corporal 224
McInnes, S.A., Private 226
Meacham, J., Private 142
Mead, Alfred, Private 227
Mead, William Albert, Private 224
Meadows, A., Lance Corporal 162
Meadows, Reginald, Private 226
Mears, J., Sergeant 65, 153, 160
Meautys, Paul Raymond, Captain (Adjutant) xi, 4, 20, 22, 37, 42, 133
Meeks, Jesse, Private 121, 230
Mellor, J., Private 229
Memmott, J.A., Private 234
Merchant, Herbert George, Second Lieutenant 55, 198, 228
Merchant, J., Lance Corporal 233
Merrick, Major 119
Merry, F., Private 227
Miles, A., Lance Corporal 141, 142, 162
Miles, D., Lance Corporal 227
Miles, Walter, Lance Corporal 228
Miller, Charles Henry, Private, 229
Miller, Frank, Private 233
Millison, J.T., Private 138
Mills, George Pilkington, Lieutenant Colonel 5, 23, 37, 42, 53–56, 58, 59, 62, 69, 72, 77–79, 89, 90, 94, 123, 133, 232, 234
Mills Cox, Lance Sergeant 42
Mimms, James, Private 231
Missenden, Reginald William, Sergeant 224
Mitchell, Richard Charles, Private 228
Mitchell, R.H., Private 227
Monash, John, General xii
Monks, E., Honorary Lieutenant and Quartermaster 104
Monro, Sir Charles, General (3rd Army) 4
Moore, Private 141
Morgan, William, Private 231, 233
Morland, Sir Thomas Lethbridge Napier, General (XIII Corps) 5, 23, 47, 53, 57, 136
Morris, E.H., Private, 226
Morris, John Henry, Lance Corporal 65, 160, 226
Mortimer, William, Corporal 161
Moss, B.S., Corporal 161
Moulster, W., Lance Corporal 161
Moverley, A., Private 230
Moyse, Robert Edwin, Second Lieutenant 48, 116, 119, 228
Mulligan, Thomas Reginald Jack, Captain xxiv, 48, 55, 56, 116, 118, 119, 228
Mulrien, Bernard, Sergeant 61, 232, 233
Munns, C., Private 226
Munns, G., Private 226
Munns, R.J., Private 226
Murray, F.J., Private 230
Murray, John, Private 233

Murray, J.J, Second Lieutenant 58, 232, 234
Nash, A., Lance Corporal 162
Neale, William John, Lance Corporal 162
Nelson, K.H., Captain (RAMC) 234
Neville, F.H., Private 234
Newell, W.T.W., Lance Corporal 162
Newman, Private 150
Nice, Percy, Private 228
Nicholson, F.T., Lance Sergeant 226
Nivelle, Robert, General 63
Norman, F., Private 226
Norman, R.S., Lance Corporal 234
Norris, W., Private 229
North, W., Private 141, 142
Nutwyche, G.L.M., Captain 73
Oakley, Edward, Private 225
Oakley, R.E., Captain 103
Odell, W., Sergeant 160
Oldfield, Frederick Hinton, Private 228
Oliver-Jones, W.S., Lieutenant 102, 232, 234
O'Neil, A., Private 138, 229
Osborne, Frederick Charles, Private 141
O'Shea, Private (11th Royal Fusiliers) 149
Osmond, John Berry James, Lance Sergeant 161
Ovenden, F.A., Private 141
Palmer, Arthur James, Private 140
Palmer, Ernest Stanley, Private 224
Pantlin, H.P., Private 226
Pantling, A.E., Private 234
Parish, William, Private 224
Parker, G.S., Private 141
Parles, Bertram, Corporal 161
Parsons, Cecil Curtis, Corporal 233
Parsons, Ernest Arthur, Private 229
Partridge, Bert, Private 224
Partridge, E., Private 227
Partridge, J.W., Second Lieutenant 101, 146
Paton, Ian Valentine, Lance Sergeant 224
Patterson, Sergeant (1st/5th West Yorkshire Regiment) 187
Pavitt, E., Private 229
Payne, A.C., Lance Corporal 230
Payne, Thomas, Private 228
Payne, W.G., Private 229
Peach, Charles Frederick, Private 225
Peach, W., Private 226
Peacock, G.R., Private 230
Pearce, Charles Henry, Private 229
Pearce, William James, Private 231
Peariman, C.F., Private 227
Pearson, A., Private, 229
Peel, Geoffrey, Second Lieutenant (6th Bedfords) 107, 118
Peerless, S.A., Second Lieutenant 101, 102
Pepper, Frank, Private 231
Percival, Arthur Ernest, Lieutenant Colonel 53–55, 72, 77, 79, 89, 90, 93, 95, 96, 100, 102, 103, 108, 111, 114, 126, 145, 178, 182, 194, 228
Perkins, Charles James, Private 140
Perkins, Ernest George, Lance Corporal 224
Pernet, Ernest George, Second Lieutenant 48, 228, 235

248 INDEX OF PERSONAL NAMES

Perry, James Emmings, Company Sergeant Major 225
Petchey, Ernest, Private 233
Peters, A.A., Lance Sergeant 226, 234
Petifor, G.R., Private 230
Pettifer, Private (6th Northamptonshires) 150
Phillips, Arthur, Private 152
Phypers, H., Lance Sergeant 160, 161, 163
Pickford, G., Private 230
Pierce, C.H., Second Lieutenant 98
Piercy, E.F., Second Lieutenant 55, 122, 126, 127, 175, 232, 233, 235
Piercy, J.D., Private 233
Piercy, Thomas Victor, Corporal 227, 230
Pimm,. A., Private 230
Pipkin, G., Private 226
Pitts, William Charles, Private 141
Pizey, H.H., Second Lieutenant 42
Plume, F., Private 138, 142
Plumer, Sir Herbert Charles Onslow (Baron Plumer of Messines & Bilton) Field Marshal 50, 64, 194
Pollard, J.W., Company Quartermaster Sergeant 163
Poole, William Edward George, Lance Sergeant 160
Pope, W., Lance Corporal 162
Potts, Henry, Second Lieutenant 48, 56, 116, 118, 119, 228
Povey, J.W., Private 234
Powell, J., Private 226
Pratt, Alfred, Private 140
Pratt, Sidney, Private, 227
Pratt, W., Private 226
Prentice, R.J., Private 233
Presland, E., Private 233
Prew, F., Private 230
Price, Sir Frederick 62
Price, Lady Alice 62
Price, George Dominic, Brigadier xviii, 23, 29, 30, 37, 40–42, 44, 46, 49, 50, 53–56, 58, 79, 108, 110, 114, 118, 122, 123, 178–189, 192, 193, 197
Prior, Lieutenant 19
Puddephat, P., Sergeant 229
Pudney, Private 153
Purser, Arthur William, Private 225
Purser, Herbert F., Private 138, 226
Putman, Horace, Private, 229
Quarry, W.J., Private 226
Quartermass, Robert Alfred, Corporal 228
Ramsbotham, Herwald (later 1st Viscount Soulbury), Captain 20, 22, 79
Ramsdon, E.R., Private 226
Randle, H., Private 233
Rands, T., Private 229
Rankin, W., Second Lieutenant 48
Ransom, Robert Cyril Starling, Second Lieutenant 85
Ranson, Richard, Private 225
Ravenscroft, Charles, Corporal 161, 234
Rawes, J.H.R., Second Lieutenant 31, 44, 136
Rawlinson, J., Private 234

Raynor, Private 175
Raynor, A.J., Private 229
Reaney, Harold Agnew, Second Lieutenant 55, 140, 228
Redding, Bertie, Private 142
Rednall, R.B., Second Lieutenant 43, 69, 111–114, 117, 140, 232, 234
Reed, Sergeant 153
Reed, Guy Baron, Second Lieutenant (8th Bedfords) 107
Reed, Horace, Lance Corporal 150
Reiss, P.J., Lieutenant 235
Relhorn, Peter, Corporal 140
Renny, W., Sergeant 163
Reynolds, A., Corporal 231
Richards, G.S., Second Lieutenant 156, 235
Richardson, Percy Reginald, Private 152
Rickard, Percy Edward, Sergeant 224
Ricks, G.H., Lance Sergeant 226
Riddle, F., Private 234
Robbins (batman) 107
Robinson, Cecil Clement, Lance Corporal 233
Robinson, Frank Charles, Private 229
Robinson, H.G., Sergeant 103
Robinson, N., Private 226
Roeber, David Arnold, Second Lieutenant xxv, 48, 51
Rollins, John Henry, Private 231
Ross-Taylor, Ian Henry Munro, Second Lieutenant 37, 48, 198, 228
Rowell, S., Private 142
Rowell, William, Private 233
Rowland, R., Private 230
Rowlings, W.A., Corporal 230
Rubnett, F.H., Sergeant 229
Ruffhead, Frederick Charles, Corporal 224
Rugman, Charles George, Sergeant 95, 160
Sadleir Jackson, Sir Lionel Warren de Vere, Brigadier (54th Brigade) 90, 91, 100, 101, 126, 147, 195
Sains, A., Private 152
Samuels, J., Private 234
Sapsford, H., Corporal 227
Saunders, J.B., Private 141
Saville, T., Private 226
Sawkins, Ernest Alfred, Private 150
Scott, A., Sergeant 102
Scott, Ernest James, Second Lieutenant 94, 101, 103, 151
Seabrook, Arthur, Corporal 161, 230
Seabrook, C., Private 226
Seabrook, R., Private 226
Seaman, B., Private 226
Selsby, C., Private 142
Seward, William Herbert, Private 228
Sewell, Frederick Charles, Corporal 233
Sewell, H.J., Lance Corporal 153, 230
Seys-Phillips, Howard, Captain xi, 96, 100
Shadbolt 125
Shadbolt, Bertie, Private 225
Shadbolt, C., Private 226
Shailer, Samuel Theodore, Private 152
Shanks, H., Private 229

INDEX OF PERSONAL NAMES

Shelford, Fred, Private 228
Shepherd, Reginald Walter, Sergeant 229
Sherwell, Ferdinand Nigel, Lieutenant 76
Shortland, W., Private 152
Shoubridge, Thomas Herbert, Brigadier (54th Bde) 25, 38, 40, 41, 43, 44, 52, 55, 57, 58, 62, 67, 72, 112, 185, 192
Showler, G., Private 231
Sibthorpe, Joseph, Corporal 224
Silsby, Bertram Frederick, Private 142, 226
Simpkins, A.H., Private 230
Simpkins, E., Corporal 226
Simpson, C.R., Private 226
Sims, C.A., Private 231
Skevington, M., Lance Corporal 142
Skipper, Drummer 153
Slade, Walter, Private 111
Slatter, G., Corporal 161, 163, 231
Sleet, W., Private 227
Slough, J.W., Sergeant 119, 181, 230
Smail, William, Lance Corporal 224
Smith, Lance Corporal (11th Royal Fusiliers) 149
Smith, A., Lance Corporal 162
Smith, A., Private 226
Smith, Arthur G., Private 163
Smith, A.H., Private 234
Smith, A.L., Lance Corporal 227
Smith, Arthur Thomas, Private 233
Smith, E., Private 226
Smith, E.T., Corporal 226
Smith, F.W., Lieutenant 18, 37
Smith, G., Private 226
Smith, Harry, Private 225
Smith, H.G., Lance Corporal 161
Smith, J., Private 226
Smith, K., Lance Corporal 227
Smith, Reuben, Lance Corporal 142, 161
Smith, Sidney Thomas, Private 224
Smith, Solomon, Private 233
Smith, T.A., Sergeant 102
Smith, T.W., Lance Corporal 231
Smythe, J., Private 229
Spacey, T., Lance Corporal 230
Spinks, Charles, Lance Corporal 152
Spring, F.C., Corporal 153
Squire, Thomas J., Corporal 161
Stacey, Private (11th Royal Fusiliers) 149
Stancliff, Herbert Prior, Private 224
Stebbings, A.G., Private 234
Steel, P.P., Lieutenant 70, 232
Stevenson, T., Captain 99, 102
Stewart, C.C., Captain (RAMC) 73
Stewart, H.B., Second Lieutenant 55, 69, 80, 108, 177, 189, 232, 234, 235
Stiles, H.M., Lance Corporal 162
Stiles, R.A., Second Lieutenant 98, 147
Stokes, Charles, Private 224
Stokes, F., Lance Corporal 162
Stokes, Leonard, Corporal 224
Stone, H.J., Sergeant 227
Stone, Leonard Victor, Private 224
Stone, V.C., Private 226
Stott, R., Private 152

Stratford, H., Private 152
Stratton, Edmund, Private 224
Stringer, A., Private 227
Stringer, George, Lance Corporal 95
Stuckey, George C., Sergeant 163, 232
Sturgeon, H.G., Lance Corporal 152, 162
Sturgess, Lance Corporal 175
Sturgess, A.J., Private 226
Stutfield, Lieutenant (54th Brigade Staff Captain) 37
Sutton, E., Private, 226
Swain, Private 150
Swain, H., Lance Corporal 152
Swain, T., Private 142
Swannell, H., Sergeant 160, 161, 163
Sweeting, E., Private 226
Swift, Stanley, Lance Corporal 225
Sylvester, Harry, Private, 228
Tabor, Sidney, Captain (Adjutant) xxvi, 82, 91
Talbot, F., Corporal 161, 162
Tarburr, E., Lance Corporal 162
Tatnall, Private 150
Taylor, Private 150
Taylor, Private (11th Royal Fusiliers), 149
Taylor, Charles, Lance Corporal 226
Taylor, G., Private 230
Taylor, Victor Charles, Private 228
Tearle, E., Private 138
Tearle, J., Private 226
Tearle, T., Lance Corporal 162, 226
Tebbutt, Walter, Private 230
Terry, Frederick Abraham 228
Tippett, Alfred, Corporal 230
Titmuss, A.J., Private 227
Thody, H., Private 226
Thomas, E., 142
Thompson, A., Private 61
Thompson, Herbert William, Private 141
Thorby, A., Private 163
Thornton, T., Private 230
Thurley, Frederick George, Private 224
Tibbett, C., Private 227
Tilton, F.E., Second Lieutenant 45
Timson, C.P., Private 233
Tingey, Private 153
Tinsley, E., Private 230
Titchmarsh, Arthur, Private 224
Tompkins, Joseph William, Private 228
Tozer, A.J., Private 226
Trayner, J., Private 138
Tremeer, Sidney Charles, Second Lieutenant 55, 232, 234
Trewman, H.F., Second Lieutenant 48, 65, 101, 232, 236
Tribe, W., Private 138, 230
Tridgett, Arthur Albert, Private 224
Tridgett, W., Private 226
Tripp, A., Private 229
Trussell, A., Sergeant 160
Trussell, H., Sergeant 163
Tuck, Frederick George, Private 224
Tucker, H., Lance Corporal 162
Tucker, Harold Frederick, Private 233

INDEX OF PERSONAL NAMES

Turner, G.A., Private 234
Turner, G.J., Private 138
Turner, Herbert Walter, Corporal 228
Turner, John Wright, Captain (RAMC) 72, 73, 138, 140
Turner, W., Corporal 161
Turney, Arthur, Private 141
Turney, H., Lance Corporal 162
Turnham, Private (6th Northamptonshires) 150
Turvey, Arthur E., Private 138, 229
Turvey, Ernest, Lance Corporal 161
Turville, Albert Lance Sergeant 140, 232
Tutton, A.P., Private 230
Tyler, B., Private 152
Tyler, R., Sergeant 226
Tysoe, W., Second Lieutenant 100, 101, 103
Underwood, Walter, Private 138, 227
Uren, E., Private 138
Vaulkhard, John Vincent, Second Lieutenant (2nd Bedfords) 116
Vernon, A., Private 233
Vickery, William, Private 225
Vlasto, J.A., Captain (RAMC) 85, 154, 235
Waddy, A.H., Second Lieutenant 58, 61, 122, 125, 126, 232
Wagstaff, H., Private 230
Walby, Sidney, Sergeant 102
Walden, Private (6th Northamptonshires) 150
Waldock, G., Private 152
Waldron, H.E., Private 226
Wale, Oscar George, Corporal 161
Walker, A., Private 231
Walker, F.A., Second Lieutenant 58
Walker, J., Private 153
Wall, William, Private 140
Walter, H.W., Captain 104
Walton, Harry, Private 226
Ward, Walter, Private 141
Warley (Buffs) 108
Warner, Harry, Lance Corporal 228
Warwick, B., Private 226
Waters, L.W., Private 226
Waterton, Sidney, Private 16, 228
Watson, A., Private 230
Watson, E.C., Private 230
Watson, James, Sergeant 225
Watts, E.J., Lance Corporal 162
Watts, Sir Herbert Edward, Lieutenant General (XIX Corps) 101
Watts, John, Private 226
Waugh, H., Private 230
Webb, A.J., Corporal 161–163
Webb, J., Private 234
Webb, John George, Private 231
Weeks, Reginald Charles, Corporal 153, 161
Welch, Edwin Herbert, Lance Corporal 162
West, B.J., Private 234
West, Frank, Private 227
West, J.H., Private 234
Westlake, Thomas Richard, Private 224

Weston, Sergeant 147
Weston, L., Lance Corporal 162, 234
Wheeler, F., Private 227
Whelan, R., Private 226
Wheton, J., Private 234
White, Sydney Charles, Private 225
White, W.C., Private 229
White, W.S., Private 138
Whiting, Private (6th Northamptonshires) 150
Whiting, J., Sergeant 160
Whittaker, Charles Jesse, Lance Corporal 231
Wightman (RE) 125
Wilkinson, C.H., Private 234
Wilkinson, William Thomas, Private 224
Wilbury, H., Private 226
Wilde, E., Private 226
Willacy, Robert, Private 140, 233
Williams, Private (6th Northamptonshires) 150
Williams, A., Private 227
Williams, Albert, Lance Sergeant 160
Williams, John Henry, Private 228
Williams, T.F., Private 226
Wilsher, Charles, Private 44
Wilsher, J., Lance Corporal 162
Wilson, A., Private 230
Wilson, Augustus Edwin, Sergeant 230
Wilson, J., Private 226
Wilson, Theodore Percival (or Thomas Percy), Second Lieutenant xxvii, 48, 199, 228
Winch, S.J., Private 227
Winfield, Lance Corporal 228
Winmill, Westropp Orbell Peyton, Lieutenant 98
Winterbourne, John James, Private 140
Wolsey, J.K., Private 226
Wood, Gilbert Henry, Private 234
Woodcock, F., Private 229
Woods, A.E., Private 234
Woods, E.A., Private 234
Woods, W., 234
Woodyer, H.M., Second Lieutenant 58, 61, 232
Wooley, Lance Corporal (6th Northamptonshires) 149
Wootton, F., Sergeant 227
Worby, Walter, Private 138
Wordley, W., Private 153
Worley, W., Private 227
Worrell, Sergeant 153
Worsley. Lionel Ralph, Private 224
Wright, H.E., Lance Corporal 162
Wright, Percy Harry, Private 228
Wright, S.W., Private 230
Wyatt, Alfred W., Sergeant 119, 140, 230
Wynne 124–125
Wynne, R.O., Lieutenant Colonel 103
Yearley, R.W., Private 229
York, C., Private 226
York, W.G., Private 230, 234
Young, F., Private 227, 234
Zimmerman, Graf von 63

Index of Place Names

Note map references and points have been excluded but trench numbers/names included with a rough guide to their position

18th Division Memorial near Hooge 222
45 (British trench near Carnoy) 133
46 (British trench near Carnoy) 133
47 (British trench near Carnoy) 133
48 (British trench near Carnoy) 38
49 (British trench near Carnoy) 133
50 (British trench near Carnoy) 38
51 (British trench near Carnoy) 133
52 (British trench near Carnoy) 133
53 (British trench near Carnoy) 133
54 (British trench near Carnoy) 133
65 (British trench near Fricourt) 17
71 (British trench near Fricourt) 33
73 (British trench near Fricourt) 14
75 (British trench near Fricourt) 32
76 (British trench near Fricourt) 24, 27
77 (British trench near Fricourt) 23, 24, 26, 32, 35, 36
78 (British trench near Fricourt) 24–26, 32
79 (British trench near Fricourt) 31, 34, 35
81 (British trench near Fricourt) 25, 34
82 (British trench near Fricourt) 23–25, 35
83 (British trench near Fricourt) 21, 22, 26, 31–33, 35
84 (British trench near Fricourt) 9, 17, 20–22, 34, 35
85 (British trench near Fricourt) 9, 12, 16, 20, 21
86 (British trench near Fricourt) 9, 19, 20, 22
87 (British trench near Fricourt) 7, 8, 11, 12, 14, 20
88 (British trench near Fricourt) 7–12, 14–17
89 (British trench near Fricourt) 9, 12
90 (British trench near Fricourt) 7, 12
91 (British trench near Fricourt) 7, 10, 11, 15, 18, 19, 22
92 (British trench near Fricourt) 7, 9, 10, 12
93 (British trench near Fricourt) 7, 8, 11, 22
94 (British trench near Fricourt) 7, 8, 15, 22, 27
107 (British trench near Fricourt) 23
Abancourt 105, 132
Abancourt Camp 105
Abbeville 103, 104, 108, 123, 124, 126
Abeele 77, 130
Ablainzevelle 216
Accrington xiv
Acheux-en-Amienois 55, 57
Achiet Line (German trenches near Achiet-le-Grand) 69

Achiet-le-Grand 63, 70, 71, 130, 199, 200, 216, 217, 232, 239
Achiet-le-Grand Communal Cemetery 200
Achiet-le-Petit 69, 70, 216
Aden House, near Boezinge 94
Aeroplane Sap (German trench near Fricourt) 9
Aeroplane Trench (German trench near Fricourt) 7, 10–14, 17, 31, 32, 35
Agenvillers 61, 123, 129
Aisne, River 63
Ajax House, near Boezinge 151
Albert 13, 32, 38, 59, 60, 93, 122, 123, 129, 196
Aldershot 2, 77
Alwalton 113
Amiens 5, 37, 44, 92, 101, 109, 110, 112, 116
Ancre, River 30, 118, 120, 121, 124, 170, 173, 199, 215
Armentieres 50, 116, 117, 129
Arneke 83–85, 130
Arques 49
Arqueves 55
Arras 63, 64, 74, 93, 127, 130, 196
Arras Memorial to the Missing 127
Aspley Guise xxii
Atlantic Ocean 63
ATN Track, near Hooge 191
Aubercourt 195
Australia 237
Austrian Junction (German trench near Montauban-de-Picardie) 178, 203
Austrian Support Trench (German trench near Montauban-de-Picardie) 170, 181
Austrian Trench (German trench near Montauban-de-Picardie) 46, 114, 129, 170, 179–181, 203
Autreville 157
Authuille 55, 56, 129, 198, 209, 212
Aveluy 124, 125, 143, 144
Aveluy Wood 125
Avesnes-Chaussoy 101, 131
Baboeuf xiii, 98, 131
Baboon Camp, near Boezinge 87–89, 94, 131, 150, 151
Bailleul 49–52, 116, 118, 129
Bailleul-les-Pernes 74, 130
Baizieux 102, 131
Bapaume 123
Barnes 113
Battersea 237

252 INDEX OF PLACE NAMES

Bay Point, near Montauban-de-Picardie 178, 179, 203
Bazentin Ridge 30
Bazentin Wood (Bois de Bazentin) 207
Bazentin-le-Grand 8
Bazentin-le-Petit 8, 47
Beaudricourt 54, 104, 131
Beaumont-Hamel 123, 199, 215
Beauval 59, 123, 129
Bécordel 6, 11, 14, 36, 128
Bedford 2, 121, 199, 237
Bedfordshire xiii, 237
Beetle Alley (German trench near Montauban-de-Picardie) 46, 114, 129, 165, 168, 180, 181, 184, 197, 203
Beetle Trench (German trench near Montauban-de-Picardie) 182
Béhen 104, 132
Béhencourt 102, 103, 131
Bellevue Farm, near Albert 36
Bellewaarde Amusement Park 196, 201
Berkshire 237
Bermondsey 237
Bernaville 122, 123
Bertangles 71, 130
Berwick Avenue (British trench near Carnoy) 133
Béthancourt 96, 131
Bihucourt 69, 71, 216
Bihucourt Line (German trenches near Bihucourt) 70, 71, 130, 200, 216
Bihucourt Trench (German trench near Bihucourt) 70
Billon Farm, near Carnoy 167
Billon Wood, near Carnoy 41, 128, 135
Black Alley (German trench near Montauban-de-Picardie), 164, 181, 203
Black House Bridge, near Authuille 55, 139
Boezinge 87–89, 94, 95, 131, 150
Bohemia 237
Bois Allemand (near Fricourt) 13, 16, 17, 19, 24, 27
Bois de Bazentin 207
Bois de Forneau 48
Bois de Mametz (or Mamatz Wood) 14, 30, 115, 207
Bois de Nieppe, near Armentieres 51, 117, 126, 129
Bois de Vieville 157
Bois des Herombus, near la Thieuloye 52
Bois des Montagnes (Caterpillar Wood), near Montauban-de-Picardie 207
Bois des Tailles (Somme) 47, 48, 115, 116, 129, 136
Bois des Vaches, near La Motte 51, 52
Bois Francais (near Fricourt) 6, 13, 15, 16, 18, 20
Bois Ronde (near Fricourt) 22
Bonfire Farm, near Bray-sur-Somme 111
Bonté Redoubt (near Fricourt) 6, 9, 19
Boom Ravine, near Miraumont 67, 126, 239
Borden 119
Borre 49
Boulogne Eastern Cemetery 119

Boulogne-sur-Mer 3, 107, 116, 124, 127, 128
Bours 74
Boutillerie 100, 131
Bouzincourt 55, 59, 122, 129, 139
Bovelles 71, 76, 130
Boves 99, 100, 131
Box Camp, near Ondank 87, 88, 131
Bray Military Cemetery 111
Bray-sur-Somme 23, 36, 38–47, 108, 110, 112, 113, 128, 134–137
Brick Alley (British trench near Carnoy) 166
Bristol 237
Bronfay Farm, near Carnoy 39, 40, 41, 47, 111, 115, 128, 129, 132, 135, 166, 167
Bronfay Farm Military Cemetery 111
Broodeseinde 3, 64
Buckinghamshire 237
Buigny-Saint-Maclou 126
Buire 49
Bullecourt 64
Bund Support Trench (German trench near Montauban-de-Picardie) 115, 203
Bund Trench (German trench near Montauban-de-Picardie) 114, 164, 165, 168, 170, 179, 181, 182, 203
Butte de Warlencourt 30
Buysscheure 83, 84, 130
Cable Trench (German trench near Fontaine-les-Croisilles) 76
Cachy xiii, xxiii, 92, 100, 101, 131, 240
Café Meraut, Froissy 109
Caftet Wood, near Carnoy 46, 129, 165, 167
Caillouel 95, 96, 98, 131, 159
Calais 116
Cambrai 64
Cambridgeshire 237
Canal Bank, near Ypres 86–89, 131
Candas 57, 65, 105, 121, 124, 129, 132
Cane Trench (British trench near Ypres) 87, 131
Canterbury Avenue (British trench near Fricourt) 31, 35
Cappy 41
Carnoy 38, 40, 45, 46, 108, 109, 113, 114, 128, 129, 133, 166, 167, 192, 197, 203, 204
Carnoy Alley (British trench near Carnoy) 166
Carnoy Avenue (British trench near Carnoy) 133, 167
Carnoy Military Cemetery 113
Carnoy Wood 46
Casino Point, near Montauban-de-Picardie 197, 203, 204
Caterpillar Alley (German trench near Montauban-de-Picardie) 182
Caterpillar Trench (German trench near Montauban-de-Picardie) 46, 47, 129
Caterpillar Valley, near Montauban-de-Picardie 114, 165
Caterpillar Wood (Bois des Montagnes), near Montauban-de-Picardie 207
Champagne 3, 63
Chateau Segard, near Hooge 79, 82, 130, 190
Chauny 157
Chépy-Valines 103, 132

INDEX OF PLACE NAMES 253

Chérisy xii, xiii, 64, 74, 75, 127, 130, 173, 174, 196, 200, 201, 218–220, 234, 239
Cherry Wood, near Chérisy 218
Cheshire 237
Cissy 110
Citerne 48, 49, 116, 129
Clapham Junction, near Hooge 81, 201, 202, 221, 222
Clapham Park xi
Clarges Street, near Boezinge 151
Clastres 157
Claude Chappe Camp, near Roesbrugge-Haringe 90, 91, 93, 131
Cloth Hall Museum, Ypres 196
Codford St.Mary 3, 128
Coigneux 77
Colchester 2, 109, 113, 118
Colombo House, near Boezinge 151
Compiegne 99
Conchy 124
Concrete Trench (British trench near Fontaine-les-Croisilles) 76, 77, 130
Connaught Camp, near Wippenhoek 78, 79, 130
Connaught Military Cemetery, Thiepval xxi, xxii, 119, 197–199, 212
Contalmaison 7, 19
Contay 101, 102, 130
Cooper Street (British trench near Montauban-de-Picardie) 166
Copse Trench (British trench near Contay) 101, 102, 131
Corbie 37–39, 42, 44, 112, 128, 136, 137
Courcelette 30, 59, 129
Courcelette Trench (German trench near Courcelette) 171
Courcelles-le-Comte 216
Crab Crawl (British trench near Hooge) 82, 130
Crécy 123
Crepigny Line 98
Croisilles 71
Crozat Canal 97, 131
Crucifix Corner, near Aveluy 143
Curtain Trench (British trench near Fontaine-les-Croisilles) 77
Cutcliff Place, Bedford 121
Dampcourt 157
Dantzig Alley British Cemetery, Mametz 197, 204
Daours 4, 5
Darling Support (British trench near Contay) 101, 102, 131
Delville 30
Delville Wood 48, 115, 193
Derbyshire 237
Dernancourt 20, 49
Desire Trench (German trench near Miraumont) 123, 124
Devon 237
Dieppe 104, 105
Dikkebus New Camp 82, 130
Dikkebus Railhead 83, 130
Dirty Bucks Camp, near Ypres 87, 131
Domqueur 123, 124

Domvast 61, 62, 65, 124, 129
Dormy House, near Hooge 79
Doullens 77, 104, 123, 130
Dovercourt 107
Dublin Camp, near Ypres 94
Dunkirk 83, 93
Durham 237
Ealing 113
East Miraumont Road 68, 171, 173
Ecluse Mericourt 41
École des Garcons, Rainchavel 54
Edgehill Station, near Dernancourt 49
Egypt 1
Egypt House, near Boezinge 150
Elverdinge 95, 131
Elverdinge Chateau 153
Emden Trench (German trench near Montauban-de-Picardie) 46, 129, 164, 165, 170, 179–181, 183, 184, 203
English Channel 93
Eperlecques 84
Ergnies 104, 132
Erquinghem 50–52, 116, 129
Ervillers 71, 130
Essex 237
Estaminets, near Fricourt 12
Estrée-Wamin 54
Étaples 5, 107
Eu 103
Fabian Trench, near Miraumont 126
Faidherbe Road, near Ypres 88
Faillouel 97, 98, 131, 157
Farback Trench (former German trench near Thiepval) 67, 130
Festubert 3
Fiennes Street (German trench near Thiepval) 211, 212, 215
Flers 30
Flesselles 4, 128
Flixecourt 104
Folkestone 3, 107
Fontaine Trench (German trench near Fontaine-les-Croisilles) 75, 201, 218, 219, 220
Fontaine Wood, near Fontaine-les-Croisilles 218
Fontaine-les-Croisilles 75, 76, 130, 201, 219, 220
Forest Hill xxv
Fort (near Fricourt) 33, 35
Fort Crater (near Fricourt) 35
Fort Gap (near Fricourt) 34
Friere-Faillouel 157
Frezenberg 3
Fricourt 7–17, 19, 20, 22, 23, 30, 109, 128
Fritz Trench (German trench near Montauban-de-Picardie) 182
Froissy 41, 42, 109, 110, 128
Fulham 111
Gallipoli 1, 116
Gare Centrale, Boulogne-sur-Mer 3
Gentelles 99, 131, 239
Ginchy 30, 48
Glasgow xx

INDEX OF PLACE NAMES

Glencorse Wood, near Hooge 81, 82, 93, 130, 176, 189, 190, 196, 201, 221–223, 239
Gloucester Huts, near Martinsart 68, 130
Gloucestershire 237
Godewaersvelde 77, 78, 130
Gorges 58, 59, 121, 129
Grandcourt 68, 198, 209, 212
Grandcourt Trench (German trench near Grandcourt) 126, 171–173
Grandru 98
Gravel Pits, near Aveluy 143
Gravenstafel 3
Grévillers 199, 216
Grovetown Camp (Somme) 45, 47, 113, 128
Guemappe 218, 219
Guillemont 30, 48, 115, 116
Guivry 98
Gulley, near Miraumont 67, 130
Halloy 54
Hamel 198, 199, 209, 212
Hampshire 237
Hangard 99, 131
Harpenden 119
Haute Tombelle Wood, near Caillouel 97
Hazebrouck 49, 116, 126
Headquarters Camp, near Krombeke 95
Hédauville 55, 125
Heilly 113
Hemel Hempstead 237
Henencourt Wood 103
Héninel 64, 75, 127, 175
Hénu 77, 130
Herefordshire 237
Hertford 127, 237
Hertfordshire xiii, 237
Hertingfordbury 121
Hessian Trench (British trench near Miraumont) 170
"High Street", Méaulte 36
High Wood (Somme) 30
Hill 130, near Achiet-le-Grand 69–71, 130
Hill 60, Ypres 3, 201
Hill Row (British trench near Contay) 101, 102, 131
Hindenburg Line 63, 126, 127, 199
Hindenburg Support (British trench near Fontaine-les-Croisilles) 76, 77, 130
Hitchin 237
Hooge 130
Hooge Tunnel 79–81, 130
Horseshoe Post (British post near Fontaine-les-Croisilles) 76
Houthulst Forest 88, 89, 94, 95, 131
Houvin-Houvigneul 54
Hulluch 3
Huntingdonshire xiii, 237
Hupoutre 85
Hurst Park, near Ypres 86
International Corner, near Ypres 87, 89, 93–95, 131
Inverness Copse, near Hooge 81–83, 176, 190, 202, 221, 222
Ireland 1, 237

Irish Farm, near Ypres 86, 131
Irles 171, 199
Isle of Wight 237
Ivergny 54, 104, 105, 129, 132
J Camp, near Ypres 89, 90, 93–95, 131
Jargon Trench (German trench near Hooge) 177, 190, 196, 201, 221–223
Jussy 157
Kempston Barracks xi, 1
Kempston xi, 1, 237
Kent xiii, 237
King Street (British trench near Montauban-de-Picardie) 166
King's Langley 200
Kokuit Dump, near Boezinge 94
Krombeke 95, 131
la Boisselle 12, 14, 30
la Chapelle d'Armentieres xxv
la Grande Ferme, Thiepval 198, 210, 212, 213
la Guerre Wood, near Carnoy 133
la Houssoye 5, 36, 37, 128
la Montagne Bridge, over Crozat Canal 97, 131
la Motte 51, 52, 129
la Neuville 4, 5, 42, 128
la Pierriere 74, 130
la Thieuloye 52–54, 118, 129
la Vicogne 4
Lady's Leg (German trench near Hooge) 190
Lambeth 237
Lancashire 237
Langemarck 3, 64
Larry Camp, near Elverdinge 95, 131
Laviéville 6, 101, 102, 131
le Carcaillot 36
le Cateau 2
le Souich 104, 131
le Touquet 107
le Treport 104
Léalvillers 55
Ledringhem 85
Leicester 237
Leicestershire 237
Leith Walk (British trench near Armentieres) 51
Liévin 64
Liez 157
Lille 50
Lillers 127
Lincolnshire 237
Little Missenden 119
Liverpool Street (British trench near Montauban-de-Picardie) 165
London xiii, 124, 127, 237
Longpré-les-Corps-Saints 49, 116
Longueval 47, 193
Loop (German trench near Montauban-de-Picardie) 46, 47, 129, 203
Loop Trench (German trench near Montauban-de-Picardie) 182, 183, 203
Loos 3, 109,
Loupart Line (German trench near Achiet-le-Grand) 69–71, 130
Loupart Wood 69

INDEX OF PLACE NAMES 255

Lower Baboon Camp, near Boezinge 95
Luton 198, 199, 237
Lydd xviii
Maidstone Avenue (British trench near Fricourt) 23, 167
Maillet Wood 57, 58, 129
Mailly-Maillet 57, 121, 129
Mametz 7, 16, 22, 28, 32, 165, 197, 203, 204, 207
Mametz Wood (or Bois de Mametz) 14, 30, 115, 207
Manicamp 157
Maple Redoubt (near Fricourt) 33
Maple Trench (German trench near Montauban-de-Picardie) 164, 165, 180, 181, 184, 203
Mardyck 85
Maricourt 47, 48, 109, 115, 116, 129
Maricourt l'Abbé 112
Maricourt Wood 48
Marieux 54
Market Trench (German trench near Thiepval) 187, 199, 212
Marlborough Huts, near Achiet-le-Grand 71, 130
Marne, River 2, 127
Marquay 54
Martin's Lane (German trench near Thiepval) 186, 208
Martinsart 55, 68, 125, 126, 129, 130, 139
Martinsart Wood 66, 129
Matterhorn Gap (near Fricourt) 31, 33
Matterhorn Trench (German trench near Fricourt) 32–34
Maxwell Trench (German trench near Thiepval) 211
Méaulte 11, 12, 16, 17, 19, 23, 25, 28, 33, 36, 37, 128
Mennessis 157
Menin 202, 222
Menin Gate, Ypres 196, 201
Menin Road 64, 79, 80, 189, 191, 201, 202, 221, 222
Mericourt 108, 137
Mesnil 98, 99, 131
Messines Ridge 64
Middlesex 237
Mill Road Camp, near Thiepval 68
Mill Road Cemetery, Thiepval xxvii, 121, 197–199, 210, 212, 213
Millencourt 61, 123, 129
Mine Trench (German trench near Montauban-de-Picardie) 203
Miraumont 60, 68, 122–126, 171, 172
Miraumont Trench (German trench near Miraumont) 171, 172
Molliens-au-Bois 4
Monchéaux 54, 103, 104, 132
Monchy-au-Bois 77, 130
Monchy-Breton 123
Mons 2, 93
Mont de Grandru 98
Montauban Alley (German trench near Montauban-de-Picardie) 180–183, 197, 203

Montauban Avenue (German trench near Montauban-de-Picardie) 184
Montauban-de-Picardie 38, 46, 48, 129, 165, 182, 197, 203, 204, 207
Montescourt 157
Montescourt Switch (British trench near Caillouel) 97, 131
Moolenaeker 49
Morlancourt 11, 23, 26, 28
Morval 30
Mount Pleasant, Aspley Guise xxii
Mouquet Farm (near Thiepval) 30, 67, 68, 126, 130
Mullingar 1
Musée des Abris, Albert 196
Nab Road, near Aveluy 125
Nab Valley, near Ovillers 143
Nampzel 98, 99
Naours 4
Neuve Chapelle 3
Neuville-Vitasse 74–76, 127, 130
New Canal Reserve Camp, near Ypres 79, 130
New Cut (British trench near Montauban-de-Picardie) 165
Newcastle-upon-Tyne 127
Newfoundland Memorial Park 196
New Southgate xxiii
New Trench (German trench near Montauban-de-Picardie) 46, 129, 182, 184
Nonne Bosschen Wood, near Hooge 81, 177, 190, 201, 221, 222
Norfolk 237
Northampton 237
Northamptonshire xiii, 237
North Bluff, near Authuille 55, 56, 129, 139, 185, 186
"North Road", Méaulte 36
Northumberland 237
Nottinghamshire 237
Noureuil 96, 97, 131, 159
Noyon 95, 98, 131, 155
Occoches 104, 132
Oise, River 98, 194
Oissy 41
Old Kent Road (British trench near Fricourt) 33
Ondank 87, 131
Ondank Siding 88, 150
Orlencourt 54
Ostronove Rest Camp 3, 128
Ouderdom 78, 79, 130
Ovillers 30, 60, 129, 143
Oxford Copse, near Bray-sur-Somme 111
Oxfordshire 237
Paddington 237
Paisley Avenue (British trench near Thiepval) 56, 129
Paisley Dump, near Thiepval 69
Palace Camp, near Ouderdom 78, 79, 130
Palestine 1
Paris 90
Paris-Plage, le Touquet 107
Park Lane (British trench near Fricourt) 34

256 INDEX OF PLACE NAMES

Passchendaele xiii, 64, 65, 93, 196
Pernes 127
Peronne Avenue (German trench near Montauban-de-Picardie) 169
Peronne Road, near Montauban-de-Picardie 168
Petit Miraumont 67, 68, 170, 173
Piccadilly (British trench near Montauban-de-Picardie) 46, 129, 166, 168
Picquigny 29, 44, 45, 112, 113, 128, 137–139, 183
Pierremande 157
Pilckem 3, 65
Pioneer Avenue (British trench near Carnoy) 167
Poelcapelle 65
Polygon Wood (Ypres) 64, 190
Pommiers Lane (German trench near Montauban-de-Picardie) 165, 182, 203
Pommiers Redoubt, near Montauban-de-Picardie 46, 49, 93, 109, 112, 114, 129, 164, 165, 168–170, 178–184, 193, 196, 197, 203–206, 224, 238
Pommiers Trench (German trench near Montauban-de-Picardie) 46, 47, 129, 164, 165, 168, 169, 179–183, 197, 203, 204
Pont Noyelles 5
Poperinghe 85
Poppof Lane (German trench near Montauban-de-Picardie) 178, 179, 197, 203, 204
Poulainville 103
Pozieres 122, 123, 129, 143, 198, 208, 209, 211, 212
Pozieres Memorial to the Missing xxiii
Pozieres Ridge 30
Pradelles 49
Pretoria 1
Price Street (German trench near Thiepval), 199, 211, 212
Prouville 65, 129
Proven 87, 95, 155, 156
Proven Station 155, 156
Putney Camp, near Ypres 87, 131
Quarry, near Fricourt 35
Quarry Gap (near Fricourt) 35, 36
Querrieu 4, 48
Quierzy 157
Railway Avenue (British trench near Fricourt) 18, 21
Railway Cutting, near Fricourt 13
Railway Dugouts, near Hooge 79, 82, 130
Raincheval 54, 55, 118, 129
Ration Farm Military Cemetery, la Chapelle d'Armentieres xxv
Regent Street, London 117
Regina Trench (British trench near Miraumont) 59, 60, 67, 121, 123, 125, 129, 130, 170, 171
Remigny 96, 131
Reninghelst 78
Reninghelst New Cemetery 78
Resurrection Trench (British Trench near Miraumont) 68
Ribemont 5, 6, 35, 128

Rifle Dump, near Martinsart 125
Ripley Trench (German trench near Thiepval) 211, 212
Ritz Trenches (British trenches near Hooge) 79, 80, 130, 189, 191
Roberts Heights, Pretoria 1
Roesbrugge-Haringe 90, 91, 131
Rogeant 103, 132
Romescamps 105
Rondall Avenue (British trench near Fricourt) 7
Rookery (British trench near Fontaine-les-Croisilles) 76, 77, 130
Rouez 96
Rouez Camp 96–98, 131, 157–160
Round Pond (near Fricourt) 35
Rubempré 65, 124, 129
Rue Albert (British trench near Fricourt) 23, 25, 26, 32–35
Rue Faidherbe, Bray-sur-Somme 43
Rue Gambetta, Bray-sur-Somme 41, 43
Rue Marle, near Armentieres 51, 52, 129
Rue Phillipe Auguste, Bray-sur-Somme 43
Saint Albans 237
Saint-Aubin 99, 131
Saint-Julien 3
Saint-Just 99
Saint-Léger 71
Saint-Omer 49, 116
Saint-Pierre-Divion 68, 69, 121, 126, 130, 187, 199, 208, 209, 211
Saint-Pierre Cemetery, Amiens 113
Saint-Pol-sur-Ternoise 52, 118, 129
Saint-Riquier 60, 129
Saisseval 137
Salency 95, 131
Salieux 71, 130
Salisbury Plain 2
Sanctuary Road, near Ypres 88
Sanctuary Wood, near Hooge 80
Sandy 237
Sawtry 200
Schwaben Redoubt, near Thiepval 30, 56, 57, 85, 120, 129, 185, 187, 188, 198, 199, 210–215, 227, 238, 239
Scotland 237
Senlis 71
Sergueux 105, 132
Serre 196
Shaft Trench (British trench near Fontaine-les-Croisilles) 76, 77, 130
Shooting Lodge, near la Houssoye 37
Shrapnel Corner, near Hooge 79, 130
Shropshire 237
Signal Farm, near Boezinge 150
Singapore 93
Sint-Jan-ter-Biezen 85, 86, 130, 131
Soissons 63
Somerset 237
Somme, River xiii, xiv, 29–31, 62–64, 93, 109, 110, 112, 116, 122, 193, 196 197, 199
South Africa 1
South Avenue (British trench near Fricourt) 6, 12, 16, 23

INDEX OF PLACE NAMES 257

South Miraumont Trench (German trench near Miraumont) 67, 69, 173
Staffordshire xiii, 237
Stazeele 49
Steenbecque 71–74, 126
Steenbecque-le-Bas 71, 130
Steenvoorde 78, 79, 130
Stirling Castle (British trenches near Hooge) 82, 83, 130, 190, 221, 222
Stuff Redoubt, near Thiepval 66, 129
Sucrerie, near Ribemont 5
Suffolk 237
Suicide Corner, near Carnoy 46, 129
Surbiton Villas (British trenches near Hooge) 80, 130, 189, 196, 201, 221, 222
Surrey 237
Sussex xiii, 91, 237
Suzanne 47, 111, 112
Talmas 4, 128
Tambour (near Fricourt) 10, 14, 15, 18–20, 22, 25, 34
Tara Hill, near Ovillers-la Boisselle 60, 129
Ternas 54, 129
Thiepval xxi, xxii, xxiv, xxvii, 30, 54, 55, 66, 85, 93, 118–121, 129, 185, 193, 197, 198, 208–213, 227, 238, 239
Thiepval Chateau 118, 119, 185, 186
Thiepval Memorial to the Missing 119, 121, 196–198, 209, 212
Thiepval Wood 55–57, 118, 129, 185, 186
Thievres 54
Tilbury xx
Tincques 156
Transloy Ridge 30
Triangle (German trenches near Montauban-de-Picardie) 114, 165, 166, 168–170, 182, 197, 203, 204
Trigger Wood (Somme) 47, 129
Trones Wood (Somme) 30, 47, 48, 115, 193, 238
Trowbridge 111
Tunnelling Camp, near Sint-Jan-ter-Biezen 85–87, 130, 131
Tyne Cot Cemetery, Passchendaele 196, 201
Ulster Tower Memorial, Thiepval 197–199
United States of America 63
Vacquerie 58, 59, 129
Vadencourt Wood 59, 129
Val-des-Maisons 4
Vallée de Carnoy 196, 197, 204
Vancouver Trench (British trench near Miraumont) 125, 129, 170
Varennes 55, 118, 129, 185
Varesnes 98
Verdun 29, 196
Verlorenhoek 3

Villa Reserve (British trench near Contay) 101, 102, 131
Villequier-Aumont 98, 131, 157, 159
Villequier-Aumont Chateau 159
Villers-Bocage 4
Ville-sur-Ancre 11
Vimy 3
Vimy Ridge 64
Vis-en-Artois 75, 218, 219
Volkeringhove 85
Vouel 97
Waldorf Hotel, London 117
Wallon-Cappel 49, 116, 129
Ware 237
Warloy-Baillon 101, 102
Warlus 101, 102
Warwick Huts, near Thiepval 66–69, 125, 129, 130
Warwickshire 237
Waterlot Farm, near Guillemont 115
Watford xxi 237
Watling Street (British trench near Fricourt) 32, 33
Werrieux 4
Westhoek 3, 176
West Miraumont Road 122, 171, 173
White City, near Auchonvillers 215
White Crater (near Fricourt) 31
White New Trench (German trench near Montauban-de-Picardie), 182
White Trench (German trench near Montauban-de-Picardie) 180, 181, 197, 203, 207
Willow Avenue (British trench near Fricourt) 10
Willow Bed (near Fricourt) 8
Willow Ravine (British trench near Fricourt) 36
Wiltshire 237
Wippenhoek 78, 79, 130
Wiry 49
Wolverhampton 237
Wonder Work (former German trenches near Thiepval) 66
Wood Trench (German trench near Fontaine-les-Croisilles) 75, 76, 201, 218–220
Worcestershire 237
Yorkshire 237
Ypres 2, 3, 64, 79, 93, 130, 131, 196, 201, 222, 223, 235
Yzengremer 104, 132
Zillebeke 78
Zillebeke Lake 78
Zollern Redoubt (former German position near Thiepval) 143
Zollern Trench (former German trench near Thiepval) 67, 129, 130
Zonnebeke 3

Organisation Names Index

Bedfordshire & Luton Archives & Records Service xi, xii, xv
Church of England xv, 77
Commonwealth War Graves Commission xxii
Ministry of Munitions 94
Royal Flying Corps xvii, 45
Royal Navy 92
War Office xi, 2

American Army

Brigades
89th Infantry 104
90th Infantry 104
160th Infantry 104
197th Infantry 104

Divisions
27th 104
30th 104
33rd 103
66th 104
80th 104

Regiments
107th Infantry 104
129th Infantry 103, 104
320th Infantry 104

British Army

Armies
2nd 50, 64, 194
3rd 4, 92, 127
4th 43, 192
5th (Reserve) 53, 54, 62, 64, 84, 92, 155, 194

Brigades
7th Infantry 176
8th Artillery 194
20th Infantry 36
21st Infantry 41
53rd Infantry 38, 39, 43–45, 48, 58, 59, 68, 74, 75, 82, 83, 112, 164, 166, 178, 179, 182, 183, 186, 238
54th Infantry 3, 4, 6, 14, 16, 20, 25, 36–38, 40–50, 52–59, 61, 62, 65–69, 71, 73–76, 82, 83, 88, 90, 92, 94, 96, 97, 101, 102, 112, 114, 115, 122, 124–126, 137, 140, 143, 147, 149, 152, 156–158, 164, 166, 167, 172, 174–176, 178, 182, 185, 188, 189, 191, 192, 194, 195, 238–240
55th Infantry 27, 39, 47, 66, 68, 74–76, 94, 122, 123, 176, 238
83rd Artillery 194
90th Infantry 136, 193
91st Infantry 182
154th Infantry 5
290th RFA 97

Corps
II 193
IV 3
X 23
XIII 37, 43, 62, 124, 172, 174, 192, 193
XIX 101, 156, 158, 195
Indian 3

Divisions
6th 2
7th 30, 71
14th (Light) 75
17th (Northern) 89
18th (Eastern) xiii, xv, 2, 11, 13, 29, 30, 32, 37, 38, 42–44, 53, 54, 59, 73, 74, 77, 83, 84, 90, 92, 93, 97, 102, 120, 123, 126, 136, 164, 165, 172, 176, 192–195, 222
21st 136
24th 2
25th 176
30th 29, 38, 41, 136, 193
32nd 95
35th (Bantam) 48, 107
37th 2
48th (South Midland) 36
50th (Northumbrian) 77
58th (London) 99
63rd (Royal Naval) 1, 123

Regiments
Accrington Pals (11th East Lancashire Regiment) xiv
Argyll & Sutherland Highlanders xv
Argyll & Sutherland Highlanders, 2nd Battalion 104
Argyll & Sutherland Highlanders, 8th (Argyllshire) Battalion 5
Bedfordshire & Hertfordshire Regiment xi, xiii
Bedfordshire Regiment xi, xiii, xv, 1, 2
Bedfordshire Regiment, 1st Battalion 1, 55
Bedfordshire Regiment, 2nd Battalion 1, 93, 103, 116

ORGANISATION NAMES INDEX 259

Bedfordshire Regiment, 3rd Battalion 1
Bedfordshire Regiment, 4th Battalion xi, 1, 104, 123, 125
Bedfordshire Regiment, 1st/5th Battalion 1
Bedfordshire Regiment, 2nd/5th Battalion 1
Bedfordshire Regiment, 3rd/5th Battalion 1
Bedfordshire Regiment, 6th Battalion xi, 2, 107, 118
Bedfordshire Regiment, 8th Battalion 2, 95, 107
Bedfordshire Regiment, 9th Battalion 55
Bedfordshire Regiment, 10th Battalion 107, 108, 111, 112, 116, 118
Bedfordshire Yeomanry 115
Birmingham, 3rd (16th Royal Warwickshire Regiment) 28, 33
Border Regiment, 11th (Lonsdale) Battalion 104
Buffs, The (East Kent Regiment) xv, 108
Cheshire Regiment xv
Cheshire Regiment, 1st Battalion 26, 27, 31
Durham Light Infantry 107
Durham Light Infantry, 1st/5th Battalion 77
East Kent Regiment (The Buffs) xv, 108
East Kent Regiment (The Buffs), 7th Battalion 43, 94, 102, 238
East Lancashire Regiment, 11th Battalion (Accrington Pals) xiv
East Surrey Regiment, 8th Battalion 122, 238
Entrenching Battalion, 2nd 44
Entrenching Battalion, 5th 43
Entrenching Battalion, 6th 40
Essex Regiment xi
Essex Regiment, 10th Battalion 44, 82, 102, 182, 186, 238
Hertfordshire Regiment xiii
Indian Cavalry Regiments 115
King's (Liverpool) Regiment xvi
King's (Liverpool) Regiment, 14th Battalion 47
King's (Liverpool) Regiment, 17th (1st City) Battalion 74
King's (Liverpool) Regiment, 18th (2nd City) Battalion 41, 109
King's (Liverpool) Regiment, 20th (4th City) Battalion 74
Lancashire Fusiliers 188
Lancashire Fusiliers, 16th (2nd Salford) Battalion 95
Leicestershire Regiment, 9th Battalion 75, 173
London Regiment, 2nd Battalion 87
London Regiment, 1st/21st (1st Surrey Rifles) Battalion 101
London Regiment, 22nd (Queen's) Battalion 102
Lonsdale Battalion (11th Border Regiment) 104
Loyal North Lancashire Regiment, 8th Battalion 177
King's Own (Lancaster) Regiment 9
Machine Gun Corps xvi, 118
Manchester Regiment xvi, 43, 111
Manchester Regiment, 19th (4th City) Battalion 40

Manchester Regiment, 21st (6th City) Battalion 38
Manchester Regiment, 22nd (7th City) Battalion 38
Middlesex Regiment xvi, 108
Middlesex Battalion, 10th Battalion 104
Middlesex Regiment, 12th Battalion 4, 6, 11, 12, 14, 16, 19, 20, 25, 26, 28, 33, 36, 37, 38, 39, 40, 44, 46, 47, 48, 56, 66, 67, 68, 80, 83, 84, 86, 92, 115, 118, 125, 136, 137, 150, 153, 155, 171, 173, 185, 238, 239
Norfolk Regiment xvi
Norfolk Regiment, 1st Battalion 27, 28
Norfolk Regiment, 8th Battalion 23, 66, 82, 203, 238
Northamptonshire Regiment xvi
Northamptonshire Regiment, 6th Battalion 9, 11, 21, 23, 30, 33, 38–40, 44, 46–48, 51, 56, 67, 68, 70, 71, 74, 76, 90, 97, 99, 104, 114, 115, 118, 122, 125, 133–137, 149, 150, 159, 168, 170, 176, 183, 185, 195, 203, 238–240
North Staffordshire Regiment xiii, 83
Northumberland Fusiliers 2
Oxfordshire & Buckinghamshire Light Infantry xvi, 12
Queen's (Royal West Surrey Regiment) xvii
Queen's (1st/22nd London Regiment) 102
Salford, 2nd (16th Lancashire Fusiliers) 95
Rifle Brigade 83
Royal Anglian Regiment, 3rd Battalion xi
Royal Berkshire Regiment xvii
Royal Berkshire Regiment, 6th Battalion 68, 69, 82, 83, 87–89, 179, 182, 190, 191, 201, 203, 238
Royal Engineers xvii, xx, 36, 38, 45, 66, 146, 156
Royal Field Artillery xvii
Royal Fusiliers xvi, xvii, 2
Royal Fusiliers, 11th Battalion xvi, 6, 26, 30, 31, 33, 38–41, 46–48, 56, 66–68, 70, 81, 82, 84–89, 91, 94, 95, 97, 99, 118, 125, 144, 145, 149–151, 157, 164, 173, 174, 176, 177, 181, 182, 190, 201, 203, 238–240
Royal Garrison Artillery, 119th Heavy Battery 185, 186
Royal Scots 104
Royal Sussex Regiment xvii
Royal Sussex Regiment, 8th Battalion 34, 75, 76
Royal Warwickshire Regiment xvii
Royal Warwickshire Regiment, 2nd/6th Battalion 65, 124, 143
Royal Warwickshire Regiment, 16th (3rd Birmingham) Battalion 28, 33
Royal West Kent Regiment xvii
Royal West Kent Regiment, 7th Battalion 30, 100, 115, 187, 193, 238
Royal West Surrey (Queen's) Regiment xvii
Royal West Surrey (Queen's) Regiment, 7th Battalion 36, 74, 76, 81, 86, 89, 121, 126, 187, 238
St.Helens Pioneers (11th South Lancashire Regiment) 104

260 ORGANISATION NAMES INDEX

Seaforth Highlanders 1st/5th Battalion 5
South Lancashire Regiment, 11th (St. Helens Pioneers) Battalion 104
South Staffordshire Regiment xiii, 42
Suffolk Regiment xvii
Suffolk Regiment, 8th Battalion 60, 68, 69, 76, 238
Surrey Rifles, 1st (1st/21st London Regiment) 101
Tank Corps 96
West Yorkshire Regiment, 1st/5th Battalion 186–188
Wiltshire Regiment xvii
Wiltshire Regiment, 2nd Battalion 41
Yorkshire Dragoons 71
Yorkshire Regiment, 2nd Battalion 38
Yorkshire Regiment, 1st/5th Battalion 57

Units:
Field Ambulance, 55th 73, 166, 167
Hood Battalion 123
Machine Gun Company, 54th 73, 101, 133, 144, 165, 171, 174, 175
Nelson Battalion 123
Officer Training Corps 107
Royal Army Medical Corps xvii, 85, 102, 167
Royal Army Service Corps 115
Royal Engineers, 80th Field Company 73, 85
Royal Military Police 115
Trench Mortar Battery, 54th 55, 145, 147, 149, 150, 165, 171, 174, 175

Schools:
2nd Army Bomb School 50
4th Army School 43
18th Divisional School 42, 110, 126
54th Brigade Bombing School 65, 125
54th Brigade School of Instruction for Specialists 41, 43, 61

Canadian Army

Brigades
11th 60, 171, 173

Divisions
1st 3

French Army

Divisions
1st Dismounted Cavalry 194

Regiments
43rd 88

German Army

Regiments
62nd 40
156th 50
459th 76

New Zealand Army

Brigades
1st 50

Regiments
Wellington Regiment, 1st Battalion 50